Creativity in Word Formation and Word Interpretation

There are many ways in which we, as speakers, are creative in how we form and interpret new words. Working across the interfaces of psychology, linguistics, psycholinguistics, and sociolinguistics, this book presents cutting-edge interdisciplinary research, showing how we manipulate the range of linguistic tools at our disposal to create an infinite range of words and meanings. It provides both a theoretical account of creativity in word formation and word interpretation, and an experimental framework with the corresponding results obtained from more than 600 participants. Data drawn from this vast range of speakers show how creativity varies across gender and age, and demonstrate the complexity of relationships between the examined variables. Pioneering in its scope, this volume will pave the way for a brand new area of research in the formation and interpretation of complex words.

Lívia Körtvélyessy is a professor in the Department of British and American Studies, Pavol Jozef Šafárik University in Košice, Slovakia. Her research has focused on the typology of word formation and evaluative morphology. Recent publications include *Derivational Networks across Languages* (co-authored with Štekauer and Bagasheva).

Pavol Štekauer is a professor in the Department of British and American Studies, Pavol Jozef Šafárik University in Košice, Slovakia. Recent publications include *Derivational Networks across Languages* (co-authored with Körtvélyessy and Bagasheva).

Pavol Kačmár is a research assistant in the Department of Psychology, Pavol Jozef Šafárik University in Košice, Slovakia. His research interests include psychology of time, goal-directed behaviour, self-regulation, social priming, and meta-research. Recent publications include "To Which World Regions Does the Valence–Dominance Model of Social Perception Apply?" (2021).

Creativity in Word Formation and Word Interpretation

Creative Potential and Creative Performance

Lívia Körtvélyessy
Pavol Jozef Šafárik University in Košice

Pavol Štekauer
Pavol Jozef Šafárik University in Košice

Pavol Kačmár
Pavol Jozef Šafárik University in Košice

Shaftesbury Road, Cambridge CB2 8EA, United Kingdom

One Liberty Plaza, 20th Floor, New York, NY 10006, USA

477 Williamstown Road, Port Melbourne, VIC 3207, Australia

314–321, 3rd Floor, Plot 3, Splendor Forum, Jasola District Centre, New Delhi – 110025, India

103 Penang Road, #05–06/07, Visioncrest Commercial, Singapore 238467

Cambridge University Press is part of Cambridge University Press & Assessment, a department of the University of Cambridge.

We share the University's mission to contribute to society through the pursuit of education, learning and research at the highest international levels of excellence.

www.cambridge.org
Information on this title: www.cambridge.org/9781009054423

DOI: 10.1017/9781009053556

First published 2022
First paperback edition 2024

A catalogue record for this publication is available from the British Library

Library of Congress Cataloging-in-Publication data
Names: Körtvélyessy, Lívia, author. | Štekauer, Pavol, author. | Kačmár, Pavol, author.
Title: Creativity in word formation and word interpretation : creative potential and creative performance / Lívia Körtvélyessy, Pavol Štekauer, Pavol Kačmár.
Description: Cambridge, UK ; New York : Cambridge University Press, 2021. | Includes bibliographical references and index.
Identifiers: LCCN 2021030244 (print) | LCCN 2021030245 (ebook) | ISBN 9781316511695 (hardback) | ISBN 9781009054423 (paperback) | ISBN 9781009053556 (epub)
Subjects: LCSH: Grammar, Comparative and general–Word formation. | Creativity (Linguistics)
Classification: LCC P245.K63 2021 (print) | LCC P245 (ebook) | DDC 415/.92–dc23
LC record available at https://lccn.loc.gov/2021030244
LC ebook record available at https://lccn.loc.gov/2021030245

ISBN 978-1-316-51169-5 Hardback
ISBN 978-1-009-05442-3 Paperback

Contents

Figures

Tables

Acknowledgements

There are many to thank for their invaluable help with this project. First and foremost, we are indebted to Milana Kovaničová for her expertise, supervision, and overall contribution to the Torrance Test of Creative Thinking (TTCT) evaluation.

We are especially grateful to Ivana Antoniová and all the teachers who were involved in the organization of the process of testing at the secondary comprehensive schools of Milana Rastislava Štefánika, Park Mládeže 5, Poštová 9, Trebišovská 12, and Opatovská cesta 7, and to Vesna Kalafus Antoniová, Bernadett Bodnárová, Lýdia Desiatniková, Zuzana Eperiesiová, Lukáš Lukačín, Dominika Mohňanská, Veronika Nogolová, Zuzana Solejová, and Alena Tomková, who helped us with testing the undergraduates at Pavol Jozef Šafárik University and the Technical University in Košice as well as with the evaluation of the tests.

It should be stressed that this book would not come into existence without the participation of the students of the aforementioned secondary schools and of the two universities in Košice who kindly agreed to take part in three tests.

Special thanks go to Anthony Wright for his excellent and careful proofreading job.

We also owe a great deal to Helen Barton and Isabel Collins for their encouragement and support throughout the whole reviewing and publishing process, and to all anonymous referees whose comments helped us improve the original manuscript.

1 Introduction

> Rather than complain about the variable character of the meanings of words, we should recognize the existence of an extraordinary ability of human beings to apply words to the world in a creative way.
>
> William Labov

This book presents interdisciplinary research that lies on the crossroads of psychology, linguistics, psycholinguistics, and sociolinguistics. It is anchored in psychology through the concepts of creativity, creative potential, and creative performance; it is anchored in linguistics through the examination of the influence of creative potential upon creative performance in word formation and word interpretation; it is anchored in psycholinguistics through the examination of language user's preferences for particular naming and interpreting strategies; and it is anchored in sociolinguistics through the examination of the age-based and gender-based differences in the formation and interpretation of new complex words. These interrelated areas indicate the complexity of the present research and the complexity of relations between the examined variables. This intricate complexity, however, is hoped to be productive rather than destructive, because this book provides both a theoretical account of the word formation and word interpretation creativity and an empirical framework with the corresponding results obtained from more than 600 participants.

Although research into creativity has been abundant in the last two decades and the theoretical and empirical endeavour to uncover 'big' questions related to creativity has proliferated (Kaufman & Sternberg 2019; Ward & Kennedy 2017), comprehensive interdisciplinary research interrelating psychology (creative potential), (psycho)linguistics (word formation and word interpretation), and sociolinguistics (the role of age and gender) is still absent. In the present research, in addition to creativity, a few other crucial concepts are at play, notably competition, economy of expression, semantic transparency, and meaning

This research has been implemented with financial support from the APVV-16-0035 research grant.

predictability, all of them examined against the theoretical background of an integrated onomasiological theory of complex words. In sum, the influence of the creative potential upon the formation and interpretation of new complex words in two different age groups and with regard to potential gender differences is studied on the principles of an onomasiological theory of complex words (Štekauer 1998, 2005a, 2005b).

Research into word formation and word interpretation has a long tradition, even though exploration of these two areas has (surprisingly) always been separated from and independent of each other. Since the early 1960s when the fundamental works by Marchand (1960) and Dokulil (1962) set the scene in the semasiological and onomasiological directions, respectively, there has been a dynamic development in the field, manifested in various theoretical frameworks.[1] In spite of the comprehensiveness of this area of research and a large number of publications, there is still an unexplored area that has not yet been studied at all by any morphological or psycholinguistic school. It concerns an interdisciplinary account of creative behaviour of language users as complex word coiners and interpreters. In particular, the present research interrelates

(a) psychology, specifically, its concept of the creative potential represented by six creativity scores, viz. Originality, Fluency, Flexibility, Elaboration, Creative Strengths, and Composite Score, and the concept of creative performance;
(b) linguistics, specifically, word formation focused on the dynamic aspect of the formation of new complex words in terms of an onomasiological theory;
(c) psycholinguistics, represented by a theory of the meaning predictability of potential/new complex words; and
(d) sociolinguistics, in particular, the role of age and gender in the formation and interpretation of complex words.

These areas of research are interrelated through (i) the examination of the potential effects of the psychological concept of creative potential upon the creative performance manifested in the way language users form and interpret new complex words in response to the naming needs of a language community, by taking into account the age and gender of a sample of respondents and through (ii) a proposal of an integrated onomasiological model of complex words that interrelates their linguistic and psycholinguistic aspects of complex words.

[1] For an overview of various theoretical approaches to word formation, see Štekauer and Lieber (2005), Lieber and Štekauer (2009, 2014), and Müller et al. (2015/2016).

The scope of the present research thus establishes a network of relations that makes it possible to examine (i) the extent of the influence of the creative potential on the formation and interpretation of new words; (ii) the extent of the influence of a selected word formation strategy upon word interpretation; (iii) the extent to which word formation and word interpretation strategies are affected by the age and the gender of language users; and (iv) all this in relation to the individual creativity indicators.

Abraham maintains that "[c]reativity refers to the singularly complex human capacity to produce novel ideas, generate new solutions, and express oneself in a unique manner" (2016: 609). Accordingly, in terms of word formation, our approach is based on the postulate that the general creative potential of all language speakers affects word formation creativity as a concrete manifestation (performance) of this creative capacity. We understand word formation creativity as the ability of any and all language speakers to form a new complex word in response to the specific need of a speech community to give a name to a new object of extralinguistic reality or a new name to an already named object. Since giving names to objects is not an automatic process, it is assumed that every act of naming is a creative act that employs a language speaker's cognitive abilities in order to select and employ one of a number of possible naming strategies. The creativity of word formation in this sense is manifested at each level of the naming process, that is, at the conceptual level, the onomasiological level, and the onomatological (morphematic) level.

When dealing with creativity, various hierarchical levels of analysis come into consideration (Jauk 2019). The deepest level of analysis covers neurobiological systems, such as the executive control system and the default mode network. This layer is the basis for various psychological constructs, namely personality dispositions and cognitive abilities. Here, the cognitive creative potential in terms of divergent thinking is crucial and will be the main topic of the present analysis because it can be characterized, according to Runco and Acar (2019: 244), as a "measure of ideation that fuels creative thinking" and consequent creative performance.

In word formation, the main criterion for the evaluation of the creative performance in terms of the individual indicators and subscores is the preferred *naming strategy*, that is, the preference for *formally economical* versus *semantically transparent* coinages. The *competition* between these two contradictory tendencies that are present in every language and manifested at every level of linguistic description is evaluated by means of a set of onomasiological types, each of which represents a different degree of economy and transparency, depending on the naming strategy employed. While a system of onomasiological types that underlies the evaluation of the transparency versus economy tendencies in the examined age-based and gender-based groups of our respondents is described in detail in Section 3.1.1, Example (1) illustrates the very essence of this aspect of our research:

(1) (a) spider-explore-er
(b) spider-man
(c) explor-er
(d) Explore

Example (1) illustrates four different strategies in the formation of new words. (1a) is semantically the most transparent representation of the concept of 'a person exploring spiders'. At the same time, it is least economical. (1b) misses the expression of what is performed with spiders by a person. There are a high number of options. Hence, while more economical, this complex word is less transparent than (1a). (1c) is as economical as (1b), but it is even less transparent because there are an infinite number of objects that can be explored. Finally, the converted agent noun in (1d) as a potential word is the most economical solution. Example (1) thus illustrates the method for the evaluation of creative performance of our respondents in forming new complex words.

The test used to evaluate word formation creativity includes three sets of tasks. Each of them examines, in a different way, the naming strategy of the respondents in giving a name to a person who performs a particular activity, namely, (i) by multiple choice, (ii) by coining a complex word on the basis of a verbal description, and (iii) by coining a complex word on the basis of the drawing of a situation.

Creative performance in interpreting new/potential complex words is conceived as a manifestation of a speaker's creative potential reflected in the speaker's ability to identify a potential reading or several potential readings for a new/potential complex word, that is, for a complex word encountered by the speaker for the first time. The degree of interpretation creativity is determined by the number of readings and by the originality of the readings a language speaker is able to propose for a given complex word.

The major part of the psycholinguistic research into complex words has been concentrated on the interpretation of Noun + Noun compounds. This is because their interpretation poses problems due to the absence of a morpheme that represents the semantic relation between the two nouns (modifier and head). Consequently, there are ample possibilities for the interpretation of new/potential complex words of this type due to the numerous possible relations between two nominal constituents of a compound. This has also been confirmed in our experimental research: for none of the experimental words and in no cohort the number of proposed original readings of the test words dropped under ten. Example (2) illustrates some of the proposed readings for *flower hat* as one of the words used in our experiment:

(2) *a hat with a flower in it*
a hat made of flowers
a hat with a flower pattern
a hat with a flower shape
a hat full of flowers
a hat for gardening
top of a flower
a person wearing a flower hat
a hat placed on flowers
a pretty hat
a colourful hat
a haircut

This stream of research has, therefore, been aimed at the evaluation of the respective roles of the head and the modifier, the ways of identifying possible semantic relations, the role of word families, the role of the semantic transparency of the compound constituents, etc. Like with word formation, no previous research has examined the influence of the creative potential of language speakers on the interpretation of new complex words.

The main criteria for the evaluation of interpretation creativity and the differences between the two cohorts in terms of the individual creativity indicators and subscores are (i) Predictability Rate, (ii) Objectified Predictability Rate, both in accordance with Štekauer (2005a), (iii) the average number of proposed readings by a cohort member, and (iv) hapax legomena (readings occurring only once in a given cohort).

The interpretation test covers two types of new/potential complex words: Noun + Noun compounds and converted words. These two types of complex words lend themselves very well to the examination of creativity because both of them offer a large number of potential readings due to the incomplete morphemic realization of the prototypically ternary onomasiological structure.

Since general creativity in the sense of creative potential is highly individual, this is necessarily projected onto the formation as well as interpretation of new complex words. Our research, therefore, evaluates the general creative potential using the *Torrance Test of Creative Thinking* (TTCT) (Torrance 1966, 1974, 1987, 1990, 1998) in its most recent locally adapted version (Jurčová & Szobiová 2008). The TTCT has been translated into more than thirty languages and, with its rich research history, is considered as the most widely referenced and used test related to creativity (Kim 2006). The test focuses on divergent thinking abilities that are necessary for situations in which more than one correct answer exists (Runco & Acar 2012, 2019). The TTCT test is based on Guilford's *Structure of Intellect* theory (Guilford 1956, 1986) and enables the measurement of various scores, namely Originality, Elaboration, Fluency, and Flexibility. Originality captures the uniqueness of answers; Elaboration reflects the number of details provided; Fluency captures the number of answers; and Flexibility covers the diversity among answers. In addition, a Composite Score and a score capturing Creative Strengths can be derived. These scores can be understood as indicators of creative potential and have previously been empirically demonstrated to be predictors of various creativity-related outcomes (see e.g. Cramond et al. 2005; Runco et al. 2010).

By reflecting the essence of TTCT, it is possible to divide respondents into two basic groups: a group of respondents with high scores in the TTCT (H(igh)-cohort) and a group with low scores (L(ow)-cohort). This division makes it possible to evaluate the achievements of the two cohorts in the word formation test and the word interpretation test in relation to the main individual creativity indicators (Originality, Elaboration, Flexibility, and Fluency) and the additional subscores (Creative Strengths and Composite Score) of the TTCT and to assess whether and to what degree the general creative potential is reflected in the word formation creativity and word interpretation creativity of language speakers. The division into two extreme cohorts pursues two objectives: (i) it may be postulated that a comparison of a cohort with the highest TTCT scores with a cohort featuring the lowest TTCT scores for the individual creativity indicators and subscores aptly reflects the influence of creative potential upon creative performance in word formation and word interpretation; (ii) this methodological procedure is necessitated by the nature of the interpretation test's evaluation, which relies on the theory of meaning predictability (Štekauer 2005a). For the sake of, first, the uniformity of the data evaluation across the book and, second, the comparability of the word formation creativity and the interpretation creativity results, we decided to stick to a dichotomized solution in evaluating all parameters.

Certainly, the division of the respondents into an L-cohort and an H-cohort involves certain risks, such as the loss of a considerable amount of information with the consequence of a potentially diminished statistical power. To assess the role of the potential disadvantages of the employed procedure with dichotomized data, in selected cases, we provide a specific form of a sensitivity analysis where several ways of analyzing the data are conducted, and the robustness of the results across the methods of statistical analysis is corroborated. Therefore, instead of dichotomizing the data into an L-cohort and an H-cohort, data are used in a continuous form, a non-parametric correlation analysis is calculated, and the results are compared to the dichotomized solution. Furthermore, in addition to the classical null hypothesis significance testing, the effect size is reported and the Bayesian approach is incorporated in our statistical evaluation. The motivation for including the Bayes factor is to provide a more nuanced interpretation and to distinguish between "evidence for H0 rather than H1, evidence for H1 rather than H0, or not much evidence either way" (Dienes and McLatchie 2018: 215). This issue is elaborated in Section 4.4.4.

The individual criteria employed in word formation and word interpretation are used to compare two *age groups* of respondents, 323 secondary school students (age group of 16–17) and 309 university undergraduates (age group of 21–22), and two *gender groups* (381 females and 251 males).

Our research pursues the objective of corroboration of the fundamental hypothesis postulating that the TTCT-based differences between the high and low cohorts in the individual creativity indicators (i.e. the differences in the creative potential of language users) will be reflected in the differences in their achievements in the word formation test and the interpretation test (i.e. in their creative performance). It is hypothesized that these differences are manifested differently for the individual creativity indicators and subscores, and that better achievements in the creative performance of the H-cohort compared to the L-cohort will be most striking for those creativity indicators that are directly related to the creative performance tasks specified in the word formation and the interpretation tests. Furthermore, it is hypothesized that the age-based groups and the relevant cohorts differ in their preferences for semantic transparency versus economy of expression. Given the different nature of the formation of new words and their interpretation (different micro-domains within the domain of complex words), it may be expected that the results in word formation creativity will not coincide with the results in the interpretation creativity. A detailed formulation of our hypotheses is provided in Section 4.5.

Following this introduction, Chapter 2 of this book discusses various aspects of creativity as a potential and as a performance. It overviews the latest psychological approaches to this issue, such as the bio-psychological basis of creativity and various methods of creativity examination (Section 2.1). The creative performance is related to the core topics of our research: word formation creativity and interpretation creativity (Section 2.2). An important point in this respect concerns the influence of word formation creativity, projected onto the selected word formation strategy, on interpretation creativity, which gives further support to the assumption of a close relation between word interpretation and word formation (Štekauer 2016). This is reflected in their comprehension as parts of a more general field of complex words and in the conception of creativity in the field of complex words.

Chapter 3 introduces the theoretical foundations of our quasi-experimental research. It starts with a theory of complex word formation (Section 3.1) by introducing a system of onomasiological types (Section 3.1.1). They reflect different word formation strategies in respect to the scalar opposition between the economy of expression and the semantic transparency (Section 3.1.2) of new/potential complex words. Section 3.2 deals with the theoretical foundations of our research into complex word interpretation. It starts with a brief summary of the basic principles of the theory of meaning predictability (Section 3.2.1) that is a point of departure for our treatment of interpretation creativity. Individual evaluation parameters are presented in Section 3.2.2, in particular, Predictability Rate (Section 3.2.2.1), Objectified Predictability Rate (Section 3.2.2.2), average number of readings proposed by a cohort member (Section 3.2.2.3), and the criterion of hapax legomena (Section 3.2.2.4).

Chapter 4 explains and justifies the principles of the Torrance Test of Creative Thinking (Section 4.1), the word formation test (Section 4.2), and the word interpretation test (Section 4.3). Section 4.4 describes our sample of respondents and the method of data collection (Section 4.4.1), explains the reasons for working with two age-based groups (Section 4.4.2), discusses the relevance of data obtained from non-native speakers (Section 4.4.3), and accounts for the division of the sample of respondents into two cohorts for each of the creativity indicators/subscores (Section 4.4.4). Finally, Section 4.5 presents our hypotheses that are examined and verified in the experimental research.

Chapter 5 is focused on our research, and analyzes and evaluates the data obtained by testing the age-based and gender-based groups of respondents. Section 5.1 discusses the results concerning word formation creativity for the group of secondary school students (Section 5.1.1) and the group of university undergraduates (Section 5.1.2). Their results are compared in Section 5.1.3. Section 5.2 provides an analysis of the results related to interpretation creativity for the group of secondary school students (Section 5.2.1) and the group of university undergraduates (Section 5.2.2). Section 5.2.3 compares the results of both groups. Section 5.3 focuses on creativity in word formation and word interpretation from the perspective of gender. A theoretical introduction to this topic (Section 5.3.1) is followed by an analysis of gender differences in terms of word formation creativity (Section 5.3.2) and interpretation creativity (Section 5.3.3) in both groups.

Finally, Chapter 6 evaluates the creative performance of the individual groups of respondents by relating the data on word formation and word interpretation and by evaluating the results in terms of the individual hypotheses specified in Section 4.5.

2 On the Notion of Creativity

Creativity has been in the foreground of scientific research in various areas of human activity (see Section 2.1) for quite a long time now. Our research directs its focus on two closely interrelated areas of linguistic activities, word formation and word interpretation, areas which represent an untilled field in this respect. It primarily pursues an answer to the following fundamental question: What is the influence of the general *creative potential* upon the *creative performance* in these two specific areas of language, manifested in coining and interpreting new complex words? For obvious reasons, the comprehension of creative performance in linguistics or any other area of research is preconditioned by the comprehension of the fundamental views, theories, and principles of the concept of creativity. A broader introduction to more general questions is important not only because there has been a growing interest in linguistic creativity recently (for example, Bergs 2019; Carter 2015b; Jones 2015a, 2015b; Sampson 2016; Vásquez 2019) but also, and especially, because the relation between creative potential and creative performance has not yet been studied in the fields of word formation and word interpretation at all.

For this reason, and because there are various approaches to the concept of creativity and because creative potential has been studied and evaluated by various psychological methods, we start with a general overview of various aspects of creativity from the psychological point of view (Section 2.1). Following a general introduction (Section 2.1.1), we account for gradual developments and modifications of views of creativity over time (Section 2.1.2) and proceed to the bio-psychological basis of creativity (Section 2.1.3). Since our research relies on the evaluation of the creative potential of the respondents, relevant attention is devoted to various methods used for the study and evaluation of creativity (Section 2.1.4). Here, the Torrance Test of Creative Thinking (TTCT), crucial to our research, is introduced. Section 2.1 thus sets the scene, a theoretical background, for a discussion of linguistic creativity in Section 2.2. This section illustrates two contradictory, or extreme, positions on the concept of linguistic creativity as well as one which understands creativity as a graded phenomenon. The position assumed in our approach to word formation and word interpretation creativity is presented in Section 2.2.2. It will be shown that our approach relies on (i) an onomasiological theory of word formation (see chiefly Körtvélyessy & Štekauer 2014; Körtvélyessy, Štekauer, & Zimmermann 2015; Štekauer 1998, 2005b, 2016; Štekauer et al. 2005), (ii) an onomasiological theory of meaning predictability (Štekauer 2005a), and (iii) a theory of competition in word formation and word interpretation (Štekauer 2017).

2.1 Creativity from the Psychological Point of View

A quick Google search for the term ‘creativity’ reveals more than 400 million hits. If the Web of Science is used instead and search criteria are specified to include creativity as a specific research topic, more than 46,000 scientific resources can be identified from the last two decades alone. These are just two brief illustrations of the vast interest in the topic of creativity. When considering the social importance of the topic, creativity could be, as instantiated by Florida (2006) and Kaufman and Beghetto (2009), described as the “most important economic resource in the twenty-first century” (Kaufman & Beghetto 2009: 1). In line with this statement, at least according to some authors, creativity represents “one of the key competencies for the twenty-first century” (Ritter & Mostert 2017: 243). No wonder, therefore, that scientific research reflects this social demand and pursues a broadening of our understanding of creativity in various contexts.

In fact, the number of research topics is abundant, ranging from the role of creativity in the everyday life of individuals (Cotter, Christensen, & Silvia 2019) to a broader socially relevant context, such as organizational (Reiter-Palmon, Mitchell, & Royston 2019), educational (Beghetto 2019; Gajda, Karwowski, & Beghetto 2017), or sociocultural areas (Gabora 2019; Lubart et al. 2019; Simonton 2019c). When mapping specific areas of research, a wide range of themes can be identified, ranging from the corroboration of the relationship between creativity and mood (Baas 2019; Baas, de Dreu, & Nijstad 2008), and intelligence and wisdom (Karwowski et al. 2016; Kim 2005; Silvia 2015; Sternberg, Kaufman, & Roberts 2019), to the role of creativity in well-being, mental health, and psychopathology (Fink et al. 2014; Forgeard 2019; Simonton 2019b). Much attention is paid to the neural basis of creativity (Abraham 2019a, 2019b; Kleinmintz, Ivancovsky, & Shamay-Tsoory 2019; Takeuchi & Kawashima 2019; Vartanian 2019) and related areas such as genetics (Barbot & Eff 2019; Ren, Yang, & Qiu 2019).

In this book, we aim to broaden the understanding of the topic further, especially the psycholinguistic point of view, by focusing on a previously highly neglected topic: the role of creative potential in word formation and word interpretation. However, to accomplish this goal, we need to start more broadly by means of an overview of various approaches to the concept of creativity in mainstream research in psychology and related fields.

2.1.1 General Discussion

At first glance, there is no need to explicitly define creativity, at least according to folk wisdom, as everybody intuitively knows what creativity is. This is, however, not only a problematic approach but, unfortunately, also one that is not uncommon even in the scientific literature. For instance, Plucker, Beghetto, and Dow (2004) selected ninety articles with the term 'creativity' in their title. They found that only 38 per cent of them provided an explicit definition of creativity. If creativity was explicitly defined, then the most common definitions included two crucial aspects – uniqueness and usefulness. In accordance with this finding, Kampylis and Valtanen (2010) extensively reviewed forty-two explicit definitions of creativity and found that the majority of them understood creativity as the ability of an individual to generate products that are based on an intentional activity, occur in a specific context, and are both novel and appropriate.

Thus, when focusing on the first aspect, uniqueness, the product of an individual (e.g. invention) could be considered as creative if it is novel enough, original, or unique, or different from other products that already exist. However, for creativity to occur, novelty is a crucial but not sufficient condition. Creativity must also be effective, useful, or appropriate (Runco & Jaeger 2012). If the invention no longer serves the purpose, it is not considered to be creative. For example, while an individual in an acute phase of psychosis can produce thoughts that could be considered novel and unique according to some standards, these thoughts are not appropriate and should not be considered as creative according to this definition.

In fact, according to what is considered as a standard definition, "creativity requires both originality and effectiveness" (Runco 2008; Runco & Jaeger 2012). Such an understanding of creativity is not new and can be traced back to the 1950s (Runco & Jaeger 2012). According to Runco and Jaeger, it was Stein (1953: 311) who first highlighted the role of both aspects, stating that "[t]he creative work is a novel work that is accepted as tenable or useful or satisfying by a group in some point in time." This emphasis is still widely echoed across the literature, while additional aspects are being further emphasized. For instance, according to Plucker, Beghetto, and Dow (2004: 90), creativity can be understood as "the interaction among aptitude, process, and the environment by which an individual or group produces a perceptible product that is both novel and useful as defined within a social context."

When considering the concept of creativity in this specific context, many eminent figures from science (e.g. Newton or Einstein) and the arts (e.g.

Beethoven, Picasso, or Shakespeare) can be mentioned as epitomes who passed the aforementioned criteria. These "creative geniuses" (Simonton 2019a) are, though, only the tip of the iceberg, and various forms of creativity can be identified in the everyday lives of more ordinary people. To reflect upon such a distinction, two important terms have been proposed and consequently corroborated – the 'Big-C' Creativity and the 'Little-c' creativity (Kaufman & Beghetto 2009).

The term 'Big-C' Creativity is reserved for prominent experts with a high level of expertise in the field. These people influence the field and, many times, the whole of society. Moreover, they are highly revered for their achievements. For example, as summarized by Kaufman and Beghetto (2009), people with entries longer than 100 sentences in the *Encyclopaedia Britannica* or winners of the Pulitzer Prize could be encompassed in this 'Big-C' category.

In contrast to 'Big-C' Creativity, the term 'Little-c' creativity is reserved for the more mundane activities of ordinary people. This type of creativity can be traced to such daily activities as non-professional home cooking. For instance, if different styles of cooking are combined in a new but still meaningful way, the final product could be considered creative in the 'Little-c' way. Similarly, imagine a poem that could be considered as creative even though it is not written by a publicly renowned poet.

The 'Little-c' category is crucial as many empirical findings and theories cover this type of creativity. We will focus mainly on this type of creativity. However, it is important to note that instead of two strictly dichotomized categories – the 'Little-c' versus the 'Big-C' – creativity can rather be understood as two poles on a continuum (Kaufman & Beghetto 2009; Runco 2014). For example, Kaufman and Beghetto (2009) extend the twofold classification with the addition of more c's. 'Pro-c' creativity, for instance, can be conceptually situated between 'Big-C' and 'Little-c' creativity. It is reserved for professionals in a specific domain who did not attain the 'Big-C' level of expertise but are more professional than the 'Little-c' level covers. As instantiated by Kaufman and Beghetto (2009), imagine, for instance, a professional chef who did not revolutionize his profession (at least, not for now), even though he is creative in his work, and this is widely acknowledged by his diners. Similarly, imagine a writer who has not obtained the Pulitzer Prize, but his/her writings are widely considered as highly original.

Why is it important to consider all these issues? It can help us understand research into creativity in its breadth and realize its various nuances. However, it is not enough. To understand the topic further, it is necessary to consider a broader historical context and gradual changes in the comprehension of creativity. For this purpose, Section 2.1.2 briefly discusses the history of the concept of creativity in general and research into creativity specifically.

2.1.2 The Concept of Creativity from a Historical Perspective

As noted in Section 2.1.1, in our society, novel and useful products are valued, and "creative thinking can be considered as one of the key competencies" (Ritter & Mostert 2017). Similar statements are echoed across the media and literature and are considered as universally true. Approaches to creativity, however, radically vary across cultures and have evolved significantly over the centuries.

For instance, when considering cultural differences, Batey (2012) distinguishes two broad traditions: the Western and Eastern traditions. According to the Eastern tradition, creativity can be understood mainly as personal growth. In contrast, the Western tradition is related to the understanding of creativity in terms of the novelty and originality of the product, as depicted earlier. Since the Western tradition is dominant in the scientific literature, our review stems from this tradition. However, even when analyzing the Western tradition, a heterogeneity of approaches can be identified within it. For instance, Kampylis and Valtanen (2010) distinguish three periods of the development of the concept of creativity.

For example, Glăveanu and Kaufman (2019) and Weiner (2000) maintain that if one focuses on the inception of creativity in human history, it is possible to trace creativity back to prehistoric times when various inventions crucial for our civilization, such as the alphabet, emerged. In this period, however, creativity was understood mainly as a divine act. The same is true of antiquity and the Middle Ages when creativity was mainly understood as a creation *ex nihilo* and through divine inspiration (Glăveanu & Kaufman 2019; Weiner 2000). These periods are considered as a metaphysical period of the development of the creativity concept (Kampylis & Valtanen 2010).

According to Glăveanu and Kaufman (2019), this pattern of thinking started to change slowly during the Renaissance, when various explorations, social changes (e.g. the Reformation), and crucial inventions related to the spreading of ideas (e.g. the printing press) occurred. In this era, an individual's work was appreciated more than before; nevertheless, creativity was still perceived as something suspicious at best. The notion of 'genius' was emerged in this period (Glăveanu & Kaufman 2019; Weiner 2000). According to Kampylis and Valtanen, this era could be called aristocratic as a few charismatic genii were "considered to be able to create from something" in comparison to the previous era when only a few "chosen" people were "considered to be able to create from nothing ('ex nihilo') through divine (or other) inspiration" (2010: 209).

In the following period, due to deepening social changes during the Enlightenment, such as the emphasis on the belief in progress and human reason, creativity started to be seen in a slightly different light. This era is especially important for the present understanding of scientific creativity with its accent on effectivity, reason, and order, as well as for later scientific explorations of creativity (Glăveanu & Kaufman 2019; Weiner 2000). However, for the modern understanding of creativity and especially for the understanding of creativity related to the arts, the next period – the period of Romanticism – was crucial with its emphasis on imagination and fantasy.

Finally, as stressed by Glăveanu and Kaufman (2019), in the more recent epoch, far less emphasis is laid on the uniqueness of the creative genius. Creativity is rather distributed collectively, and this has been bolstered especially by the dawn of the Internet. Statements such as 'everyone can be creative' and 'everyone can have his fifteen minutes of fame' are widely accepted and crucial for the present understanding of creativity. In addition, the concept of creativity started to be related to various parts of everyday life and became 'democratized'. The main emphasis is put on blending various cultural aspects and innovations and on the relation with economic interests (Glăveanu & Kaufman 2019; Weiner 2000).

According to Kampylis and Valtanen, this last phase could be labelled as the democratic period of the development of the concept. Creativity is not only possible for everybody but "anyone is considered able to create from anything" (2010: 209). This position is important because the present research is built upon this kind of paradigm.

When the perspective is shifted to the scientific understanding of creativity, three broad paradigms can be delineated (Glăveanu 2010). While an overlap with the previous approach is obvious, the emphasis is put elsewhere – on the scientific corroboration of the topic.

The first, *He-paradigm*, was symptomatic for the time preceding the mainstream scientific research into creativity. It attempted to understand a creative person in terms of genius and hereditary aspects. This paradigm reflects a shift in the understanding of creativity from a divine act to more natural causes during the Renaissance and afterwards; however, from a scientific perspective, the focus on heredity and biological nature, as studied, for instance, by Francis Galton (1869), is especially important. Galton focused on how and to what extent a genius is of hereditary nature, and his approach influenced later research into creativity.

The second, *I-paradigm*, was characterized by the emergence of psychological research into the topic. Creativity was understood as reserved not only for some extraordinary individuals but for everyone (Glăveanu 2010). In line with this shift, creativity started to be considered by many as something that is not only expected but also demanded – for instance, by teachers or employees – and even regarded as a sign of well-being and health (Simonton 2000). While many figures indirectly interested in the topic can be mentioned, such as Carl Rogers, Wolfgang Köhler, and Herbert Simon, Joy Paul Guilford (1950) is considered to be the most prominent of that period as he encouraged further elaboration of the topic during a meeting of the American Psychological Association. This was a crucial but, of course, not the only catalyst for future research. Some other social incentives played an important role as well. For instance, as noted by Kaufman and Beghetto (2009), social demands for talent identification, which emphasized creativity and ability in the USA, were radically increased after the launch of Sputnik by the Soviet Union. These issues are, however, beyond the scope of our present research.

In the third paradigm, the *We-paradigm*, a shift from the individual to the broader social aspects is emphasized. For example, Csikszentmihalyi (1999) emphasizes the role of a broader social environment because of its crucial role. No creative product can exist without other people because there is nobody to recognize it (see also Glăveanu 2010; Kaufman & Beghetto 2009).

Why is all this important to reflect upon? From Galton's (1869) attempts to ascertain the heredity of genius up to Guilford's (1950) seminal speech which instigated research into creativity and beyond, the broad conceptualization of creativity as well as scientific discussions of the topic were deeply rooted in the sociocultural milieu of that time, and this is not different in the present day (Glăveanu & Kaufman 2019; Weiner 2000). Given this background, we move to the state of the art in various conceptualizations of creativity. In Section 2.1.3, we cover one of the major current research topics related to creativity research – the bio-psychological basis of creativity and beyond.

2.1.3 Bio-psychological Basis of Creativity

Although some limitations to the recent neuroimaging research can be identified (e.g. the usage of a non-equivalent control task or high degrees of freedom, combined with small statistical power; see Abraham 2013; Takeuchi & Kawashima 2019), recent decades have brought an abundance of research findings and a remarkable deepening of our understanding of the biological foundations of creativity.

To present a succinct but integrative overview of the state of the art and to provide a broad conceptual background for the present research, we follow two interpretational lines attempting to integrate the existing body of evidence. In the first part, we present a bio-psycho-behavioural model of creativity (Benedek & Jauk 2019; Jauk 2019) that provides a broad framework for the integration of diverse lines of research across various scientific disciplines dedicated to creativity research. Crucially, we identify a key aspect – the creative potential captured by the term of divergent thinking. Subsequently, we will shift our perspective and continue with a more process-oriented framework accenting neurobiological systems behind creativity (Kleinmintz, Ivancovsky, & Shamay-Tsoory 2019).

Starting with a broader integrative framework, according to the bio-psycho-behavioural model (Benedek & Jauk 2019; Jauk 2019), three hierarchical levels of analysis can be delineated. At the top level, real-life creative behaviour is situated. This level of analysis encompasses both 'Big-C' creative achievements as well as 'Little-c' everyday creative activities. More specifically, everyday creative activities are a behavioural prerequisite of creative achievement, and although creative achievements are an intriguing topic per se, we will focus mainly on the 'Little-c' level as this level is more related to creativity in word formation and word interpretation, and it has been studied more extensively.

As a higher level that is built upon a lower level, a deeper level behind creative behaviour is represented by psychological constructs related to individual differences. For instance, when considering psychological constructs related to *personality* from the perspective of the Big Five-Factor Model of personality traits, openness to experience could be mentioned. In particular, people characterized by openness are curious, imaginative, and open-minded. Openness seems to play a role in creativity because it seems both to diminish the threshold for everyday creative activity engagement and to encourage the accumulation of knowledge and experience crucial for later creative products (Kaufman et al. 2016).[1]

Although personality is an important factor for the emergence of creativity at the behavioural level in general, in the present context, it is too broad and vague. When considering word formation and word interpretation, we will rather focus on a more established factor that plays its role in creativity more directly: the concept of cognitive abilities.

When considering cognitive abilities, cognitive potential in terms of divergent thinking ability and intelligence could be highlighted (Jauk 2019). Accordingly, *intelligence* can be understood as the ability to adapt oneself to one's environment, to learn, and to think. Various psychological theories explore the relationship between creativity and intelligence (for a review, see e.g. Silvia 2015; Sternberg, Kaufman, & Roberts 2019). However, as indicated by recent empirical evidence, the pattern of results related to this relationship is rather ambiguous and potentially moderated by many factors (Kim 2005; Runco 2008). Kim (2005), for example, conducted a meta-analysis of 21 studies with more than 45,000 participants. Across these studies, she found a relationship between intelligence and creativity. This relationship was, however, rather modest ($r = 0.17$) and was moderated by other factors such as age and the type of creativity test. The unequal role played by various creativity

[1] Note, however, that various facets of openness to experience can be identified (Christensen, Cotter, & Silvia 2019), and their engagement could differ based on the area of creative achievement (Kaufman et al. 2016).

tests could be explained by differences in the setting of the administration and the cognitive processes involved.

As the role of intelligence in creativity is rather complex[2] and mediated by various cognitive processes, we will focus on a more direct predictor of creativity that has been considered as a cornerstone or even as a synonym of creativity – cognitive abilities.

Cognitive abilities can be conceptualized as creative potential in the form of divergent thinking. More specifically, as a "measure of ideation that fuels creative thinking" (Runco & Acar 2019: 244), divergent thinking represents a specific mode of thinking that is necessary when more than one solution exists. This is crucial as both word formation and word interpretation could be considered as this kind of task. For instance, word formation creativity can be conceived as the ability of any speaker of a language to approach the naming act in a creative way by selecting one out of a number of possible ways of semiotically representing an object to be named (Štekauer et al. 2005).

According to Guilford's theory of divergent thinking (1956, 1986), four main dimensions of divergent thinking can be delineated as indicators of the creative potential that can lead to various creative outcomes (Cramond et al. 2005; Runco et al. 2010). These dimensions are Originality, Elaboration, Fluency, and Flexibility. Since these dimensions are crucial for the present work and need to be presented in a broader context of measurement, we will focus on them more deeply in Section 2.1.4, which is dedicated to measurement methods.

According to the bio-psycho-behavioural model (Jauk 2019), the middle psychological level is built upon deeper neurobiological systems, such as the default mode network and the executive control system (Jauk 2019). How do these systems operate to create creative products? According to the more linear approach, Kleinmintz, Ivancovsky, and Shamay-Tsoory (2019) identify two phases operating in a cyclical manner. In the first phase, the *generation phase*, which stresses novelty, new ideas are created via a combination of associations in semantic networks. For this purpose, the default mode network, including midline anterior and posterior regions and a temporoparietal junction, is employed (Kleinmintz, Ivancovsky, & Shamay-Tsoory 2019).

[2] One of the most influential hypotheses that considers the relationship between creativity and intelligence is the necessary condition hypothesis. According to this hypothesis, a minimal level of intelligence is a necessary but not sufficient condition for creativity to emerge (Karwowski et al. 2016). Karwowski et al. (2016) looked for support for this hypothesis across 8 studies with more than 12,000 participants, various operationalizations of creativity and intelligence, and a more recent statistical approach. This is important as, in the light of various recent neuroimaging studies, it is reasonable to expect a common cognitive basis where executive functions represented by an executive network play a prominent role (Benedek et al. 2014; Silvia 2015).

Crucially, these brain regions seem to be related to the first aspect of the definition of creativity – novelty. Various dimensions of divergent thinking abilities (Wu et al. 2015), such as originality/novelty and ideation fluency, could play a prominent role there. Especially these dimensions could underlie some aspects of word formation and word interpretation as hypothesized and further elaborated.

In the second phase, the *evaluation phase*, which is responsible for appropriateness, the ideas are evaluated and consequently further elaborated or rejected. For this purpose, the executive control network, including the ventrolateral prefrontal cortex (inhibition), dorsolateral prefrontal cortex (working memory), temporoparietal junction (updating), medial prefrontal cortex (error detection), and frontoparietal regions (switching), is involved (Kleinmintz, Ivancovsky, & Shamay-Tsoory 2019). Moreover, it should be noted that, beyond executive functions, the evaluation phase could also be related to a 'hotter' component and motivational and emotional aspects and, therefore, structures like the amygdala (Kleinmintz, Ivancovsky, & Shamay-Tsoory 2019).

Crucially, these regions seem to be related to the second aspect of the definition of creativity – appropriateness. From the perspective of divergent thinking abilities, let us mention elaboration because the creative product created in the first phase is further elaborated upon in this phase. As in the previous case, this could also relate to word formation and word interpretation as discussed later.

Such a distinction is in line not only with the ample body of empirical evidence (see e.g. Beaty et al. 2016; Benedek & Jauk 2019) and the definition of creativity depicted earlier but also with other theoretical approaches. For example, Jung and Chohan (2019) proposed that when speaking about individual differences in general, not only creativity but also personality and intellect unfold upon two major axes related to adaptive behaviour. These two axes are *exploratory* and *restraining actions*. They represent "flexibility, novelty, and rapid problem solving," on the one hand, and "consistency, utility, and accuracy" on the other (Jung & Chohan 2019: 186). Moreover, these processes seem to operate in a very similar manner even when considering other phenomena that are proposed to be related to creative cognition, such as daily mind wandering (Fox & Beaty 2019).[3]

[3] However, it is important to note that biological underpinnings of creativity seem to be more complex than previously assumed. For instance, connectivity and shifting the balance between the two neural systems responsible for novelty and appropriateness have been shown to be related to broader environmental factors, such as enculturation (Ivancovsky et al. 2018). In addition, let us mention much deeper dimensions, such as neuropsychopharmacological regulation. More specifically, the dopaminergic and noradrenergic systems have been shown to play an important role (Beversdorf 2019; Boot et al. 2017). This is, however, beyond the scope of the present discussion.

Why is this important to reflect upon? The present broad bio-psychological theories could help organize the existing body of evidence and provide potentially important candidates underpinning creativity on both the psychological level, such as divergent thinking abilities, and on a deeper level of neurobiological systems in the form of two systems. However, as the level of neurobiological systems is beyond the scope of the present discussion, we will focus on the psychological level. To accomplish this, in Section 2.1.4, we will discuss the methods that are used in creativity research.

2.1.4 *Methods for Studying Creativity*

Is it even possible to measure creativity? According to folk wisdom, creativity is hard or even impossible to measure. As stressed by Plucker, Makel, and Qian (2019), this common belief is related to broader definitional issues depicted earlier (e.g. the lack of an explicit definition of creativity). However, as noted, creativity can be defined and, consequently, operationalized. But how?

To provide an introductory conceptual framework for this section, Rhodes' conception of the four *p*'s will be used (Rhodes 1961). Despite being proposed many decades ago, it is still a highly recognized and useful approach, employed in many contexts (see e.g. Runco & Kim 2013). Rhodes analyzed various definitions of creativity and imagination. While attempting to integrate them, he realized that some overlaps could be identified between these definitions and, based on this, he delineated four levels of analysis. They are person, process, press, and product. According to this approach, (a) a *creative product* could be considered as the outcome of the interaction between (b) a *person* with specific abilities, traits, and personality, (c) a *process* that produces the product, and (d) the *press* encompassing the relationship with the environment. More recently, Glăveanu (2013) extended Rhodes' proposal with the *five a*'s approach.

Both of these approaches emphasize that every attempt to measure creativity covers some but not necessarily all levels, and an informed decision should be made regarding which level will be covered. For instance, as noted by Glăveanu (2013), the self-reports of an individual cannot capture the distinction between inner psychological factors and outer behavioural dynamics of creation and, for this purpose, another measurement approach should be used.

When considering various methods employed for research into creativity, one can encounter various approaches for their integration (see e.g. Batey 2012; Cropley 2000; Hocevar 1981; Plucker & Makel 2010; Plucker, Makel, & Qian 2019). For example, Hocevar (1981) identified ten broad categories of creativity assessment, namely (i) tests of divergent thinking; (ii) judgements of products, (iii) eminence ratings; (iv) self-reported creative activities and achievements; (v) teacher nominations; (vi) peer nominations; (vii) supervisor/peer/teacher ratings; (viii) personality inventories; (ix) biographical inventories; and (x) interest and attitude inventories. While this kind of classification is important, it lacks a deeper integrative structure.

In an attempt to integrate the list of various measures, Eysenck (1994) proposed a broad distinction between traits that follow a normal distribution (e.g. focus on intelligence or personality) and creative achievements that are not normally distributed. While this could be considered as a step in the right direction, two broad categories do not appear to be sufficient for capturing all the nuances across measurements. Batey (2012) therefore proposed an extensive integrative heuristic framework in the form of a three-dimensional conceptual cube ($4 \times 4 \times 3$ matrix) that we will stick to.

According to this heuristic framework, three axes (x, y, and z) capture various aspects of the measurements (Batey 2012). For example, in line with Rhodes (1961) and Glăveanu (2013), the x-axis represents various facets capturing which level is analyzed. The related question is – is it a trait, process, press,[4] or product? The y-axis represents the measurement approach capturing how creativity is assessed. The related question is – is it an objective rating, a self-rating, or a rating of others? Finally, the z-axis represents the focal point of an analysis – is it an individual, team, or organization, or is the analysis based on a broader cultural level?

Since the z- and y-axes are more obvious, in the following, we will pay attention to the x-axis and corroborate the types of investigations proposed by Plucker, Makel, and Qian (2019): creative products, attributes of creativity-fostering environments, personality and behavioural correlates of creativity, and creative processes.

First, according to Plucker, Makel, and Qian (2019), the category of a *creative product* is important as it encompasses real objects that are to be evaluated. Here, the Consensual Assessment Technique (CAT) can be used as an example. In CAT, expert evaluations play a prominent role. While this approach has some merits, such an evaluation is rather subjective and not suitable for the purposes of the present research.

Second, when considering another aspect, *creative environments*, many situational factors influencing creativity could be emphasized. Hunter, Bedell, and Mumford (2007), for instance, conducted a meta-analysis of forty-two prior studies. They found out that factors such as organizational structure, leadership, and interactions play a role in creative performance. How can such environmental factors be assessed? Plucker, Makel, and Qian (2019)

[4] This term is used by Batey (2012) in reference to a social environment in which creativity is examined (for example, does the organizational climate in a workplace support creative performance?).

used an example of such an approach as is applied by Forbes and Domm (2004), who used a survey where the importance of factors related to the completion of the project was assessed. This leads to the identification of environmental factors, such as constraints related to time and resources. However, as in the previous case, the broader milieu is not a suitable level of analysis for the present research.

Third, when considering the category of assessment related to the *creative person*, personality scales, an activity checklist, and attitude measures can be mentioned (Plucker, Makel, & Qian 2019). For instance, regarding the personality scales, one can mention the *Big Five Inventory* assessing five general personality traits. For the purpose of the present analysis, this approach seems to be more suitable; however, a more process-oriented framework would be beneficial due to the focus on the cognitive level of analysis.

Finally, the creative process should be mentioned. When dealing with the creative process, various 'creativity tests' such as psychometric measures of creative potential could be suggested (Plucker, Makel, & Qian 2019). These tests are based on divergent thinking as a "measure of ideation that fuels creative thinking" (Runco & Acar 2019: 244). In comparison to convergent thinking, which is required in tests where only one possible solution exists (e.g. intelligence tests), divergent thinking captures what is necessary for situations where more than one correct answer exists. This can be traced to an influential psychometric approach and Guilford's theory (1956, 1986) of divergent thinking (Cramond et al. 2005; Plucker, Makel, & Qian 2019; Runco et al. 2010). Based on this theory, the TTCT was created and consequently revised numerous times (Torrance 1966, 1974, 1987, 1990, 1998). As this level of analysis is most suitable for the present research, we will stick to it (see Section 4.1).

As noted by authors like Kim (2006) and Sternberg (2006), the TTCT represents the most widely used and referenced test of creative potential. Runco et al. (2010: 362) maintain that Torrance aimed to create "a reliable and valid test of creative thinking abilities that could be administered to individuals from kindergarten through adulthood" and that could be easily used for both practical and research purposes. The purpose of the TTCT is threefold. First, to assess; second, to understand; and third, to nurture the capacity for creativity in individuals (Kim 2006; Runco et al. 2010).

In the TTCT, four main indicators can be derived according to the classical distinction, namely Originality, Fluency, Flexibility, and Elaboration. Originality reflects uniqueness; Fluency captures the number of relevant answers; Flexibility reflects the presence of qualitatively different categories; and finally, Elaboration captures the number of details (these categories are described and instantiated more thoroughly in Section 4.1). Based on Guilford's theory (1956, 1986), these indicators can be understood as indicators of creative potential that can lead to various creative outcomes (Cramond et al. 2005; Runco et al. 2010). For instance, in their longitudinal study, Runco et al. (2010) examined if creative achievements can be predicted by TTCT tests measured in the 1950s. It was found out that the Composite Score, as a summarizing score derived from all scores, as well as separate TTCT scores, namely Fluency and Elaboration, were related to personal achievements many years later. Based on this and similar evidence, we predict that divergent thinking is a "measure of ideation that fuels creative thinking" (Runco & Acar 2019: 244) measured by TTCT that relates not only to the level of creative achievements ('Big-C' and 'Pro-c' creativity) but also to everyday linguistic creativity, as further elaborated.

2.2 Linguistic Creativity

2.2.1 Creativity versus Productivity

Linguistic creativity has become a field of rapid growth and is of growing interest to linguists, psychologists as well as philosophers. Carter (2015a: x) in his Foreword to *The Routledge Handbook of Language and Creativity* points out "the remarkable extent and variety of current research into the domain of language and creativity." Its scope ranges (to mention at least some of the relevant areas) from the philosophy of language (e.g. Fischer 2000) through language teaching/learning (e.g. Deshors, Götz, & Laporte 2018; Tin 2015; Vizmuller-Zocco 1985, 1987), translation studies (e.g. Kenny 2001; Prinzl 2017; Robinson 2015), discourse (e.g. Jones 2015a; Semino 2008), and literary studies and poetry (e.g. Hall 2015; Miall 2015; Toolan 2015) to applied linguistics as well as theoretical linguistics (e.g. Bergs 2019; Chomsky 1964, 1965, 1966, 1974, 1976, 1980; Zawada 2005).

As pointed out by Carter, and in accordance with the "Little-c" creativity approach depicted earlier, "creativity is not the exclusive preserve of the individual genius" (2015b: 11). Carter emphasizes that "linguistic creativity is not simply a property of exceptional people, but an exceptional property of *all people*" (2015b: 13, our emphasis). This view is also reflected in the cognitive approach to language because "grammar is considered the product of the creativity of its speakers" (Hamawand 2011: 21). No doubt, this idea is the cornerstone of any consideration of linguistic creativity. As manifested in Section 2.2.2, this principle also underlies our approach to word formation creativity and word interpretation creativity.

While mapping various approaches to linguistic creativity, we encounter a variety of views of its nature and scope (see e.g. Carter 2015b; Swann, Pope, & Carter 2011). In general, however, there is an agreement that the fundamental feature of linguistic creativity is "the ability to transcend traditional ideas, rules, patterns, relationships, or the like, and to create meaningful new ideas, forms, methods, interpretations, etc." (Zhu, Xu, & Khot 2009: 87). This implies unexpectedness, a difference from the existing, goal orientation (Gervás 2010: 23), unconventionality, interestingness, and imagination (Kuznetsova, Chen, & Choi 2013: 1247).

In principle, there are two extreme positions with regard to linguistic creativity. One of them relates creativity to productivity, and the other puts creativity in strict contrast to productivity and restricts creativity to cases of deviation from the rules of grammar.

The first approach is represented by Chomsky, who distinguishes between true human creativity and creativity in linguistic behaviour (1966: 27). He calls the latter normal creativity (1974: 152) or Cartesian creativity in reference to Descartes and his emphasis on logical analysis and mathematical methods. While novelty is a characteristic feature of both of these types of creativity, they also require a system of rules that are partly determined by intrinsic human capacities (Chomsky 1976: 133). Therefore, the 'creative aspect of language use' for him is primarily a rule-governed feature of language, that is, creativity based on productive rules of syntax, and it is therefore defined as the language speaker's ability to produce and understand an infinite number of entirely new sentences. However, he is sceptical about our ability to understand the nature of linguistic creativity and maintains that "the creative use of language is a mystery that eludes our intellectual grasp" (Chomsky 1980: 222). The abundance of literature mapping and extensive research into creativity in a diversity of areas of human activity (cf. Section 2.1) have not proven the correctness of this postulate.

The criticism of Chomsky's understanding of creativity, as presented in linguistic literature, can be summarized in three main points. First, it identifies creativity with the productivity of a language. For this reason, some linguists label the use of the expression 'linguistic creativity' in this sense a misnomer, because "this term ascribes properties to the system and this meaning is . . . best dubbed productivity – the potential of the system" (Bagasheva & Stamenov 2013: 76) and also because "rule-governed creativity is a mechanical function of the language system" (Onsman 1982: 72). Second, it is restricted to a single level (syntax) of the language system. In fact, linguistic creativity is characteristic of all language levels, including the semantic, morphological, syntactic, and pragmatic levels; or, from a different perspective, of textuality, contextuality, and critique (see e.g. Benczes 2005, 2006; Cook 2000; Kecskes 2016, 2019; Maybin & Swan 2007; Onsman 1982). Third, according to Lamb (1999), Chomsky's approach does not concern creativity but the ability that is common in our everyday life, in any type of activity that requires the ordering of items into sequences. Lamb compares the generation of new sentences to going through a cafeteria line – both activities are of sequential nature and display our *ability*, not creativity. Real creativity, in his view, is at work

> when we invent new lexemes for new or old concepts; when we build a new concept, especially one which integrates ideas in our conceptual systems that have not previously been connected; when we devise new metaphors in our attempts to understand some combination of complex experiences; when we invent a story or a tune or a machine; when we visualize and then draw plans for a new structure, perhaps a new landscape or building; when we invent a new way of saying something that does not fit the standard syntax. (1999: 205)

A similar sort of criticism comes from Sampson (2016), who distinguishes between F-creative (F stands for 'fixed') and E-creative activities (E stands for 'extending'). The former corresponds with Chomsky's conception because F-creative activities "characteristically produce examples drawn from a fixed and known (even if infinitely large) range" (Sampson 2016: 19). E-creative activities, on the other hand, are "activities which characteristically produce examples that enlarge our understanding of the range of possible products of the activity" (Sampson 2016). As noted by Bergs (2019: 175), "generating even the most complex sentence out of a finite set of rules can only be F-creative."

Bergs' view brings us to the opposite extreme. He suggests that the only genuine type of linguistic creativity is an *aberration*: "It signifies certain uses that apparently do not conform to any (obvious) linguistic rule and that are not subject to any (obvious) constraints. In other words, these new structures appear to be absolutely unpredictable" (2019: 180), even if, as he admits, such cases are extremely rare. A similar view is taken by Lyons, according to whom creativity is the language user's ability to extend the system by means of motivated, but unpredictable, principles of abstraction and comparison (1977: 549). Not so radical a view, even if emphasizing the deviation from the expected patterns and expected uses, is connected with authors working on lexical creativity (see, mainly, the papers in Munat 2007 and Arndt-Lappe et al. 2018). In their opinion, creativity refers to the coinages and usages of existing words that serve primarily as attention-seeking devices by means of humour, playfulness, ludicity, puns, wordplay, etc., and are, therefore, as pointed out by Dal and Namer (2018), mostly shifted to the area of performance and pragmatics. Examples in (3) are taken from Munat (2007: 171–172):[5]

(3) (a) blends + clippings: *relpol* (religio-political),
(b) combining forms + free morph: *autoshovels*, *psych-chemist*
(c) compounds: *instruction-well* (of the cab), *homeostatic beams*
(d) (pseudo) derivations – *confessionator*, *hallucinosis*

[5] The examples were selected by Munat from Philip Dick's science-fiction novel *The Simulacra.*

(e) neosemes – *jalopy* (a one-man-driven space ship), *simulacrum* (a clone or reproduction of a human being that is taken for the real thing)
(f) analogical creations – *unmarsed* (by anology with *unearthed*)
(g) metaphor and metonymy – *wheel* (a vehicle)

It is important to stress that there are linguists who believe that linguistic creativity is "a graded phenomenon ranging from the more conventional and predictable to the less conventional and unpredictable" (Kecskes 2016: 3). This comprehension of creativity as a graded phenomenon will clearly follow from our discussion about word formation and word interpretation creativity in Section 2.2.2.

2.2.2 *The Nature of Creativity in word formation and word interpretation*

Two crucial general observations underlie our conception of both word formation creativity and word interpretation creativity.

First, it is generally acknowledged that creativity is a universal feature of all human beings and that not only is creativity possible for everybody but also anyone is considered able to create from anything (Kampylis & Valtanen 2010). This assumption reflects the most recent comprehension of creativity as the ability of an individual to generate products that are novel (original), appropriate (relevant), effective, based on an intentional activity, and that occur in a specific context (e.g. Kampylis & Valtanen 2010; Kim, Cramond, & Vantassel-Baska 2010; Runco 2008). Creativity is thus viewed as the creative potential of each human being. In everyday life, this creative potential can be implemented through creative performance (e.g. Runco, Cramond, & Pagnani 2010: 343). And, as stressed by Vizmuller-Zocco (1985: 305), "speakers have the ability not only to generate sentences never before heard, but also to create and understand derived words never before heard."

Second, the theoretical framework for our understanding of word formation creativity and word interpretation creativity is built on the theory of *domains of creativity* (see e.g. Csikszentmihalyi 1990) and, more specifically, on the idea of *task specificity*:

> This task specific (or microdomain specific) view of creativity argues that the skills that lead to creativity on one task in a broadly defined domain of knowledge, such as writing, are not the same (and show little overlap with) the skills that lead to creativity in another task within the same writing domain. Thus, for example, poetry-writing and story-writing creativity may not rely on the same set of cognitive skills, and creativity in writing plays might call on yet a third distinct set of creativity-relevant writing skills. (Baer 2020: 377)

The fundamental principles of this theory are formulated in a hierarchical four-level Amusement Park Theoretical (APT) Model of Creativity (Baer & Kaufman 2005). This model postulates varying degrees of domain specificity and generality, ranging from the most general – such as general intelligence,[6] motivation, and suitable environments – down to microdomains or specific tasks. Creativity as a domain-general ability "which has no single brain region or brain network specializing in creative cognition" (Abraham 2019b: 527) can be employed in various areas. Two such areas where it can obviously be 'activated' are word formation and word interpretation, that is, the areas explored in this research.

From this perspective, the kinds of creativity required for the formation and interpretation of new/potential complex words represent a hierarchical system. The tasks of the word formation test and the tasks of the word interpretation test represent two different microdomains of the more general domain of word formation/interpretation creativity, which falls within the even more general domain represented by the integrated model of complex words that operates within the domain of language. All these domains represent areas of creative performance, and their creative potential is implemented in a different way by each language user.

2.2.2.1 General Framework of word formation Creativity

Vizmuller-Zocco (1985) maintained that word formation had not been granted relevant attention in psycholinguistics, and the situation thirty-five years later does not seem to be much different. This is especially true of psycholinguistic research into word formation creativity, not to mention exploration of the influence of the creative potential of language speakers upon their creative performance in word formation and word interpretation creativity. In fact, both of these areas are still a tabula rasa.[7]

Nevertheless, a more prolific discussion has been devoted to the definition of the nature of creativity in word formation. There are views that put creativity and productivity in this area of the linguistic system in strict opposition as well as positions preferring to view the relation between word formation productivity and creativity as a graded phenomenon (see our discussion on the various approaches to linguistic creativity in Section 2.2.1). For example, Lieber

[6] It should be noted, however, that some authors assume "a negligible relationship between IQ and creativity, which indicates that even without high IQs, individuals may be highly creative" (Kim 2017: 318).

[7] It should be pointed out, however, that some aspects of research into creative performance in word formation and word interpretation that are employed in the present research have been studied before, for example, preference for semantic transparency or economy of expression with regard to age, profession, occupation, bilingual versus monolingual speakers, native versus non-native speakers, and with regard to different semantic categories (see Hrubovčák 2016; Klembárová 2012; Körtvélyessy 2010; Körtvélyessy, Štekauer, & Zimmermann 2015; Štekauer et al. 2005).

(2010) and Schultink (1961) define creativity in contrast to productivity, that is, as the ability to consciously (intentionally) coin a new word on an unproductive pattern. In Schultink's view, truly productive word formation processes are unintentional and can give rise to potentially unlimited numbers of new words. Morphological creativity, in contrast, will give rise to a fixed, countable, and presumably small number of new forms. The terms 'creativity' and 'productivity' are thus understood as mutually excluding principles in coining new words. Lieber, in accordance with Schultink, maintains that morphological creativity is a process based on consciously coining a new word in contrast to productivity and competence which refer to the formation of words by applying automated word formation rules. Morphological creativity is, in her view, the domain of unproductive or marginal processes consciously employed by speakers to form new words. Thus, while productivity is said to be rule governed, creativity is conceived of as any deviation from the productive rules. This approach to creativity in word formation basically corresponds with the conception of 'extra-grammatical morphology' (Dressler 2005; Dressler & Merlini Barbaresi 1994; Mattiello 2013) that "applies to a set of heterogeneous formations ... which do not belong to morphological grammar, in that the processes through which they are obtained are not clearly identifiable and their input does not allow a prediction of a regular output" (Mattiello 2013: 1). In fact, extra-grammatical morphological formations comprise fairly heterogeneous phenomena such as blends, acronyms, initialisms, clippings, hypocoristics, reduplicatives, back-formations, and expletive infixes (Mattiello 2013). However, as pointed out by Dressler (2005: 268) "[w]hat unites extragrammatical morphology are various violations of universal properties."

Bauer (1983: 63), too, defines creativity as "the native speaker's ability to extend the language system in a motivated, but unpredictable (non-rule-governed) way," in contrast to productivity, which is defined as a "rule-governed innovation." Later he claims that creativity is a non-productive innovation that represents three basic areas of linguistic creativity, that is, the formation of simple words (complex words are, in his view, the matter of productivity), the figurative extension of existing words, and formations produced by isolated individuals or by the extension of non-productive patterns (Bauer 2001). Let us also mention Ronneberger-Sibold (2012: 116), according to whom creative word formation encompasses "not only the coining of entirely new words not based on any previously existing linguistic elements but includes all operations for the production of new lexemes which are not covered by regular word formation" (Ronneberger-Sibold 2008: 201).[8] Instances of the former are extremely rare; they belong to 'word-manufacture'

[8] For a comprehensive analysis of the relation between productivity and creativity in word formation, see Fernandez-Dominguez (2009).

as its 'purest cases' in which a new word "is created *ex nihilo*" Bauer (1983: 239). A few examples from the same reference are given in (4):

(4) *Kodak*
grok 'to communicate sympthetically' (from R. Heinlein's novel *Stranger in a Strange Land*)
wampeter, foma and *granfalloon* (occurring in the title of K. Vonnegut's novel)
quark (from J. Joyce novel Finnegan's Wake)

These views clearly contradict Chomsky's aforementioned comprehension of creativity as a rule-governed feature of syntax.

Bauer (2001), nevertheless, maintains that it is not always possible to draw a sharp line between productivity and creativity. His fuzzy boundary position has gained considerable support recently among linguists who prefer to speak of a cline or a scale whose two opposite poles are represented, respectively, by productivity and creativity (see e.g. Hohenhaus 2007; Ladányi 2000; Mattiello 2018; Munat 2007). For example, Hohenhaus (2007: 16) points out that the opposition between creativity and productivity can be formulated in terms of a cline, "reflected in different degrees of 'noteworthiness' of the formations in question: the outputs of rules at the more productive end of the scale tend to pass without much notice, while the more creative 'coinages' tend to be more foregrounded." Creativity in the works of these authors is mostly illustrated with the 'products' of creativity, such as acronyms, clippings, blends, back-formations, splinters, combining forms, and secreted affixes, but also with an unconventional function of productive affixes, metaphorical and metonymical compounds, converted words, tmesis, etc.

This brief overview suggests that linguists tend to impose limits on word formation creativity by applying this term only to a part of new complex words. Our approach differs from them through the scope of the term 'word formation creativity' because it covers all new complex words as a manifestation of a universal human endowment to form new complex words, thanks to their creative potential.

2.2.2.2 *Fundamental Principles of word formation Creativity*

As a point of departure for defining the fundamental characteristics of word formation creativity, it is useful to look at more general psychological and neuroscientific perspectives of the problem that define the basic characteristics of creativity in general. Abraham (2019b) labels them as *originality* (uniqueness and novelty) and *effectiveness* (relevance); Sternberg and Kaufman (2010) as *novelty* and *quality*; Weiner (2000) emphasizes novelty; Kim, Cramond, and Vantassel-Baska (2010: 400) stress *novelty* (i.e. originality, unexpectedness) and *appropriateness* (i.e. adaptivity concerning task constraints); Simonton (2012: 173) defines creativity as *originality* times *appropriateness* – "So, ideas need to be both new (original) and appropriate in a given situation to be truly 'creative'" – and van Dijk et al. (2018) highlight *originality* and *usefulness*.

Our approach to creativity in word formation is built on all these pillars: the formation of *new* words (novelty, originality) that are *appropriate* signs of a class of objects to be named (relevance, appropriateness) as a result of the *deliberate creativity* (cognitive activity) of language users; these signs are *useful* and *effective* because they serve the communication purposes of a speech community; and since word formation creativity manifests the universal, biologically preconditioned feature of human beings (see e.g. D'Agostino 1984), any and all speakers of a language can produce a new word. Moreover, if we accept the view that the product of creativity has to be something "different, new, or innovative" (Kaufman and Sternberg 2019: xiii), each new complex word meets these criteria because each such *new* coinage is *different* from the existing actual words, that means, from the institutionalized vocabulary of a language and, by definition, it is *innovative* with regard to the naming needs of a speech community. The criterion of *quality* is guaranteed by the acceptance (institutionalization) of a new complex word by a speech community for the designation of an object of extra-linguistic reality and its use for communication purposes.

From this point of view, each new word results from the creative activity (creative performance) of a speaker of a language. Unlike the aforementioned approaches that mostly emphasize the product, that means, the result of creative processes, our conception of word formation creativity lays emphasis precisely on the creative process that underlies each new complex word, that is, on the act of naming. This complies with the recent trend in psychology that is more focused on the creative process (Ratul 2019). This creative process, in accordance with an onomasiological theory of word formation (Körtvélyessy & Štekauer 2014; Körtvélyessy, Štekauer, & Zimmermann 2015; Štekauer 1998, 2005b, 2016, 2017; Štekauer et al. 2005), includes:

(a) A *deliberate* (conscious) identification of a *new* class of objects that has no semiotic representation in a given language and is thus needed by a speech community and is, therefore, *relevant* to the extension of the vocabulary of a given speech community by an original linguistic sign.
(b) An *appropriate* conceptual analysis of this *new* class of objects to be represented by an *original* linguistic sign, including the cognitive processes of abstraction and generalization.
(c) An *appropriate* representation of the conceptual analysis through the identification/selection of an onomasiological structure determined creatively by a *relevant* combination of semantic categories in accordance with the preferred naming strategies by a language user (coiner) that

creatively resolve the coiner's preference for either semantic transparency or for economy of expression.

(d) An *appropriate* representation of the individual semantic categories of the onomasiological structure by a creative selection of appropriate morphemes out of a usually large number of options, thus producing an original combination of linguistic units.

From this, it follows that the most characteristic features of word formation creativity consist of cognitive processes connected with the formation of a concept and with the selection from a number of options within individual steps of the process of forming new complex words. These processes are, obviously, affected by a number of factors, such as general knowledge and experiences, linguistic knowledge and experiences, the intellectual capacity of a coiner, and – importantly – from the perspective of our research, one's creative potential.

The extensive space available for word formation creativity in this sense of the term is discussed in Section 3.2.1, which presents the theoretical basis of an onomasiological theory of word formation, that is, the system of onomasiological types.

2.2.2.3 General Framework of word interpretation Creativity

As far as the interpretation aspect of complex words is concerned, there has been a lot of morphological and, especially, psycholinguistic research into the role of the head, the modifier, and the relations between them in the process of interpretation, and a number of related issues, such as interpretation models, the processing of compounds, semantic transparency, the role of morphological families, competition, etc. Since comprehensive overviews of this direction of research can be found in Štekauer (2005a), Gagné and Spalding (2014), Libben (2015), and Gagné (2017), this section concentrates on our conception of the fundamental concepts underlying our conception of word interpretation creativity. These comprise competition, semantic transparency, the classification of semantic relations, and the evaluation of interpretation tests.

Competition[9]

Our approach to competition in the field of complex word interpretation is defined within the theory of meaning predictability (Štekauer 2005a). This theory lays emphasis on the interconnection between the field of word formation and the field of word interpretation in the sense that competition

[9] For a discussion of various aspects of competition in natural languages, see MacWhinney, Malchukov, and Moravscik (2014) and Santana-Lario and Valera (2017).

between the tendency towards economy and the tendency towards semantic transparency in the process of word formation directly affects both the way a new complex word is interpreted and the degree of competition between all potential readings of such a new complex word. In other words, the competition in word formation is projected onto the competition in word interpretation. Furthermore, it is assumed that the predictability of individual potential readings can be computed by means of the Predictability Rate, the Objectified Predictability Rate, and the Predictability Rate Gap. These terms are explained in Section 3.2.2. Importantly, in both word formation and word interpretation, there are a number of factors that affect competition between semantic transparency and economy, on the one hand, and its consequences for the predictability of competing readings of a potential word in the process of interpretation (age, education, profession, bilingual setting, generic knowledge and experiences, etc.), on the other. For illustration, Janovcová (2015) examined the influence of cognitive abilities upon meaning predictability. Her data suggest that there are differences between high-ability participants (high verbal and high non-verbal) and low-ability participants (low verbal and low non-verbal).

Semantic Transparency

Semantic transparency, as one of the key concepts of our research, plays a central role in our evaluation of both word formation creativity and word interpretation creativity. In general, semantic transparency is of vital importance in psycholinguistic theories exploring the interpretation of compound words (primarily noun + noun compounds).

Schäfer (2018: 1) defines semantic transparency as "a measure of the degree to which the meaning of a multimorphemic combination can be synchronically related to the meaning of its constituents and the typical way of combining the constituent meanings." In the same vein, Pollatsek and Hyönä (2005: 261) maintain that "[a] compound word is usually defined as transparent when the meaning of the compound word is consistent with the meanings of the constituents (e.g., *carwash*). In contrast, a compound word is defined as semantically opaque, when its meaning cannot be constructed by directly combining the meanings of the individual constituents (e.g., *pineapple*)."

For Zwitserlood (1994), it means that at the semantic level, opaque compounds behave as monomorphemic words: an opaque compound has a single semantic representation that is not linked with the semantic representations of its constituents. On the other hand, transparent compounds have their own semantic representations that are related to the semantic representations of their constituents. She illustrates this assumption with *blueberry* and *strawberry*. While both *blue* and *berry* are related to *blueberry* at the conceptual level, *straw* in *strawberry* is not.

This kind of consideration inspired Borgwaldt and Lüttenberg (2010) to define semantic transparency as the strength of the relationship between the meaning of the whole compound and the meaning of its constituents.

These views, in fact, reflect the prevailing understanding of semantic transparency in psycholinguistic literature, and according to El-Bialy, Gagné, and Spalding (2013), they represent the so-called *conjunctive activation approach*, that is, it is only semantically transparent constituents that facilitate compound processing; opaque constituents have no influence. On the other hand, the *meaning computation approach* (Gagné & Spalding 2009; Ji, Gagné, & Spalding 2011) postulates the involvement of both transparent and opaque constituents in meaning interpretation: while the former facilitates it, the latter hinders it.

The view of semantic transparency that emphasizes a synchronic relation between a compound and its constituents and a scalar nature of semantic transparency can be found in the majority of psycholinguistic works. Discussions mostly concentrate on the (unequal) contribution of the individual compound constituents, that is, the respective roles of modifier and head (the so-called asymmetric models), and on the role of the semantic relations between the head and the modifier in interpreting the meaning of a compound.

For illustration, Gagné, Spalding, and Nisbet (2016: 17) suggest that the two constituents (of a bi-morphemic compound) do not equally contribute to determining the transparency of the entire compound. Their data suggest that semantic transparency is not a direct reflection of the semantic overlap between a constituent and the whole word and that the semantic transparencies of the constituents are not independent of each other. This is also reflected in El-Bialy, Gagné, and Spalding (2013) who maintain that the ease of processing a compound is also influenced by whether the compound constituents have a similar semantic transparency, that is, the transparency of the first and the second constituents matches (when both are transparent or when both are opaque) but not when the transparency of the constituents differs.

Similarly, Bell and Schäfer (2016: 157) maintain that "although compound transparency is a function of the transparencies of the constituents, the two constituents differ in the nature of their contribution." When identifying the factors which influence the transparency of compounds, they assume that "compounds are perceived as more transparent when the first noun is more frequent, hence more expected, in the language generally; when the compound semantic relation is more frequent, hence more expected, in association with the first noun; and when the second noun is more productive, hence more expected, as the second element of a noun-noun compound" (Bell & Schäfer 2016: 157).

Our approach to semantic transparency differs from the mainstream psycholinguistic comprehension. It follows from our integrated onomasiological model of complex words and from our theory of meaning predictability. Both of these fundamental principles are explained in Section 3.2.1, so it suffices to say here that the main differences between our theory and mainstream psycholinguistic research consist in

(a) our emphasis on the dependence of complex word interpretation upon complex word formation;
(b) the same fundamental principles upon which both of these areas are examined, that is, the onomasiological theory and its basic principles comprising the theory of onomasiological types, the competition between semantic transparency and economy of expression, and the principle of creativity within and beyond productivity constraints;
(c) the classification of interpreted readings; and
(d) the theory of meaning predictability that makes it possible to compute the meaning predictability of individual readings.

Classification of Semantic Relations

There have been several attempts at proposing a classification of semantic relations. The best known – and, at the same time, extensively criticized[10] – are those of Lees (1960, 1970) and Levi (1978). The most serious problem which these and similar classifications face has been aptly identified by Downing and Plag. Downing points out the futility of the former's attempts to reduce the possible meanings of primary compounds to several broadly defined semantic classes and aptly assumes that a number of interpretations of novel compounds "are at best REDUCIBLE to underlying relationships . . . but only with the loss of much of the semantic material considered by the subjects to be relevant or essential to the definitions" (1977: 826). Plag (2003: 148) also emphasizes the uselessness of such semantically based taxonomies because of the arbitrariness with which they arise. More promising, Plag argues, "is to ask what kinds of interpretations are in principle possible, given a certain compound" (2003: 149).

This is precisely reflected in our approach to the classification of readings of potential words. The main reason for taking up the approach mentioned by Plag is the fact that one and the same general predicate can subsume a number of readings of the same new/potential word with similar but still different

[10] See, for example, Marchand (mainly 1965a, 1965b, 1974), Rohrer (1966), Motsch (1970), Carroll and Tanenhaus (1975), Bauer (1983), Scalise (1984), and Lieber (1992) with regard to Lees, as well as Downing (1977), Finin (1980), van Lint (1982), and Murphy (1988), to mention just a few. The limitations of these systems made some authors modify them (for example, Shoben 1991 and Gagné and Shoben 1997 added three more thematic relations to Levi's system) or come up with a different classification, some of them including several dozen categories (for example, Arnaud (2003), Bourque (2014), or Pepper and Arnaud (2020)).

semantics, thus necessarily disregarding the subtle meaning differences which are central to the discussion of word interpretation creativity. In other words, the concept of meaning predictability as one of the fundamental principles for the evaluation of interpretation creativity is far from being exhausted by any general thematic relation/recoverably deletable predicate (RDP) for the simple reason that one such RDP can subsume several specific meanings of unequal degrees of predictability.[11]

Furthermore, the existing classifications are restricted to compounds and are not applicable to converted words (which are also employed in the present research), unlike our conception of meaning predictability, which is applicable to all new/potential words irrespective of the underlying word formation process.

Methods of Evaluating Interpretation Tests

Ji, Gagné, and Spalding (2011: 36) conclude that three methods have been used in various experiments in compound interpretation research: (a) evaluation of constituent occurrence in definitions of compounds – for example, Sandra (1990) and Zwitserlood (1994); (b) Likert scale ratings to evaluate the transparency of a compound as a whole, the transparency of its modifier and head, the predictability of compounds from their constituents, and/or the contribution of the compound constituents to the overall meaning of a compound – for example, Zwitserlood (1994), Libben et al. (2003), Marelli and Luzzatti (2012), Juhasz (2007), Pollatsek and Hyönä (2005), Frisson, Niswander-Klement and Pollatsek (2008), Ji, Gagné, and Spalding (2011), Wong and Rotello (2010), Pham and Baayen (2013), Reddy, McCarthy, and Manandhar (2011); and (c) mixed and other methods. The rating method seems to be the most common one in this field of research.

While our research pursues objectives different from the aforementioned works, we also rely on Likert scale ratings in the judgements of our respondents, who were asked to propose as many readings for each of the experimental words as they could think of and to rate the probability of occurrence of the individual proposed readings in the actual language. Seven points assigned in our research indicate the highest probability of the actualization of a proposed reading and therefore suggest that such a reading is the most predictable one. One point means a minimum chance for a proposed reading to become actualized in a language. These judgements were then used for the computation of the crucial variables employed for the evaluation of the interpretation creativity, in particular, the Predictability Rate, the Predictability Rate Gap,

[11] For a discussion of this issue, see Štekauer (2005a).

and the Objectified Predictability Rate. Large samples of both secondary school and university respondents guarantee the representativeness of the subjective ratings obtained.

It should be stressed that the judgements of the respondents necessarily depend on several factors, such as one's general knowledge and experiences and also, as postulated in our hypotheses at the beginning of this monograph, on the creative potential of language users which, according to our hypotheses given in Section 4.5, may differ by both age and gender.

2.2.2.4 Fundamental Principles of word interpretation Creativity

If we now return to the basic characteristics of creativity proposed in psychological literature, they can equally be applied to interpretation creativity: the interpretation of *new* words by proposing their potential reading(s) (novelty, originality) that is (are) *appropriate* and *relevant* for a class of objects represented by a morpheme/morphemes of a language (relevance, appropriateness) as a result of the *deliberate creativity* (cognitive activity) of language users. These readings are *useful* and *effective* because they serve the communication purposes of a speech community, and since complex word interpretation creativity as an inherent part of linguistic creativity in general manifests the universal, biologically preconditioned feature of human beings (see, for example, D'Agostino 1984), *any and all speakers* of a language can interpret a *new* word. Moreover, if we accept the view that the product of creativity has to be something "different, new, or innovative" (Kaufman and Sternberg 2010: xiii), each reading proposed for a new complex word encountered for the first time by a language speaker meets these criteria because each such reading is *different* from what was encountered by a language speaker before, that means, from the institutionalized vocabulary of a language and, by definition, it is *innovative* with regard to the naming needs of a speech community. The criterion of *quality* is guaranteed by the potential of each such reading to be accepted by a speech community as the meaning of an actual word.

2.2.2.5 Creativity in the Field of Complex Words

By taking into consideration the complexity of creative potential and the previously outlined comprehension of word formation creativity and word interpretation creativity, it is possible to provide a definition of creativity that covers both of these areas, that is, a unified definition of creativity in the field of complex words that reflects the multiplicity of factors that play an important role in the creative performance of language users. Thus, creativity in the field of complex words is defined as the cognitively founded creative performance of language speakers in the formation and/or interpretation of complex words that are variously predetermined by individual aspects of their creative potential (i.e. Originality, Fluency, Flexibility, Elaboration, Creative Strengths, and Composite Score) and that are characterized by originality, usefulness, appropriateness, relevance, and effectiveness. It is postulated that creativity in the field of complex words is also affected by factors such as general knowledge and experiences, linguistic knowledge, age, gender, and education.

3 Theoretical Foundations of Our Research

This chapter presents the fundamental theoretical principles underlying our research. Section 3.1 concentrates on the theoretical foundations of examining word formation creativity, in particular, the system of onomasiological types (Section 3.1.1) and the conception of the competition between two contradictory tendencies that can be identified (not only) in the field of word formation, namely, semantic transparency and economy of expression (Section 3.1.2). Section 3.2 discusses the theoretical foundations underlying our research into interpretation creativity, that is, a theory of meaning predictability (Section 3.2.1) reflected in an integrated onomasiological model of complex words. Section 3.2.2 accounts for the parameters that are used for the evaluation of interpretation creativity. They include Predictability Rate (Section 3.2.2.1), Objectified Predictability Rate (Section 3.2.2.2), the average number of readings proposed by a cohort member (Section 3.2.2.3), and hapax legomena (Section 3.2.2.4).

3.1 Complex Word Formation

3.1.1 System of Onomasiological Types

A theoretical basis for our research is an onomasiological theory of word formation (Štekauer 1998, 2005b). One of its core components is the concept of the onomasiological type, which replaces the traditional division of word formation processes into compounding, prefixation, suffixation, conversion, blending, reduplication, etc. by treating all of them in a unified fashion. Each word formation act is understood as a creative act of a language speaker who reflects the need of a speech community to give a name to a new specific class of objects. With the language speaker in the central position of the onomasiological theory, the emphasis is, logically, laid on the cognitive processes underlying the resulting new complex word.

Each onomasiological type is constituted by an onomasiological (conceptual) structure and an onomatological (morphemic) structure.[1] The former results from the cognitive processes of abstraction and generalization, employed in producing a concept of a class of objects to be named by a new word. This step results in a combination of semantic categories, such as Action, Process, State, Agent, Patient, Logical Object, Instrument, Time of Action, Location of Action, Manner of Action, Result of Action, etc., which establish an onomasiological structure. The onomasiological structure prototypically includes three semantic categories – this ternary structure[2] contrasts with the binary structure of complex expressions in the generative tradition:

(5)	Determining constituent of the mark	Determined constituent of the mark	Onomasiological base

The onomasiological base identifies a whole class of objects to be represented by a new complex word. The determining constituent of the onomasiological mark narrows down the object to be named with regard to all the other members of the class. The determined constituent of the onomasiological mark generally stands for the concept of ACTION in its three different manifestations (Process, Action, and State). The determined mark thus expresses the relation between the polar members of the onomasiological structure. We adhere here to the terminology introduced in the 'classical' onomasiological theory of word formation developed by Dokulil (1962), although the label 'determined constituent of the mark' used for this constituent of the onomasiological structure may be misleading because it does not reflect the crucial role of the conceptual category of ACTION for both word formation and word interpretation.

While in the traditional generative binary analysis of complex words it is the head that is considered to be the most important constituent, in the onomasiological theory of word formation and word interpretation the core element of the onomasiological structure is the determined constituent of the mark prototypically represented by the conceptual category of ACTION. Similar to the verb which, with its valency, is at the core of sentence semantics, the crucial role of the semantic category ACTION in complex words stems from its

[1] The distinction between the terms 'onomasiology' and 'onomatology' draws on Horecký's onomasiological model of word formation (Horecký 1983; Horecký et al. 1989). This distinction refers to two different levels in the process of coining a new linguistic sign. Onomasiology establishes the cognitive basis for the naming act by identifying the semantic categories and the relations between them. Onomatology 'cares' for the representation of these semantic categories by morphemes of a language by means of the Morpheme-to-Seme-Assignment Principle and thus determines the form of a new complex word.

[2] Note that the onomasiological structure is ternary in prototypical cases. Nevertheless, there are also onomasiological types (OT7 and OT8) that are characterized by a binary structure.

capacity to semantically relate the other two constituents of the onomasiological structure. Any of the three semantic categories constituting the onomasiological structure can, but does not have to, be represented at the onomatological level by a morpheme of a language. The onomasiological and the onomatological structures constitute an onomasiological type. Individual onomasiological types reflect the relations between the two structures in terms of the manner of representation of the onomasiological structure by morphemes at the onomatological level. Given this theoretical framework, four basic criteria can be proposed for the classification of the individual onomasiological types in terms of semantic transparency and economy of expression:

(i) ternary versus binary onomasiological structure;
(ii) the number of constituents of the onomasiological structure represented by morphemes in the onomatological structure;
(iii) constituents of the onomasiological structure that are/are not represented by a morpheme:
- base
- determining mark
- determined mark

(iv) shared representation of two constituents of an onomasiological structure by one common morpheme.

In the following, we introduce individual onomasiological types by defining their basic features and illustrate them with examples taken from our experimental research. The examples also refer to the word formation test item (the first numeral indicates the task and the numeral after a full stop indicates the subtask).

In Onomasiological Type 1, all three onomasiological structure constituents, that is, the base and the determining and determined constituents of the mark, are linguistically expressed at the onomatological level by being assigned morphemes with the corresponding meaning.

(6)	OT1	DingM –	DedM –	Base	
		R	*R*	*R*	
	Example:	Object–	Action –	Agent	
		miracle	*believe*	*er*	1.3
		bird	*hunt*	*er*	3.2
		car	*hold*	*er*	3.1

Only two constituents are represented by morphemes in (7) and (8). In Onomasiological Type 2, the determining constituent of the onomasiological mark is left unexpressed:

(7)	OT2	DingM –	DedM –	Base
		Ø	*R*	*R*

Example: Object– Action – Agent

Ø	*interrupt*	*er*	1.2
Ø	*welcome*	*er*	2.2
Ø	*smiling*	*guy*	1.1

In Onomasiological Type 3, the determined constituent of the onomasiological mark is left unexpressed:

(8) OT3 DingM – DedM – Base

Example: Result– Action – Agent

miracle	Ø	*man*	1.3

Stative – State – Patient

baby	Ø	*clone*	2.3
clone	Ø	*ie*	2.3

Onomasiological Type 4 ranks among the most economical of all onomasiological types because a ternary structure is represented by a single morpheme standing for both the base and the determined constituent of the mark. It is based on the ACTION-TO-SUBSTANCE recategorization or, in traditional terminology, on the conversion of a verb to a noun:

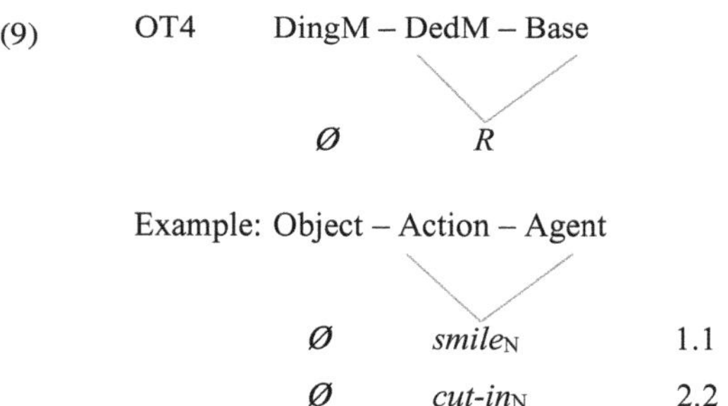

Onomasiological Type 5 employs the same feature as OT4, that is, a joint representation of the base and the ACTION category. However, unlike OT4, the determining constituent of the onomasiological structure is represented by a morpheme. For illustration, this type is exemplified with complex words proposed, respectively, for Task 1.1 – giving a name to 'a person whose smiling face is used for billboard advertisements' – and Task 2.1 – coining a name for 'someone who researches spiders' webs' – in (10).

(10) OT5 DingM – DedM – Base

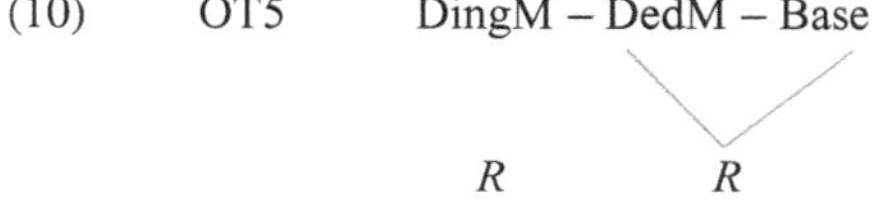

R *R*

Example: Location – Action – Agent

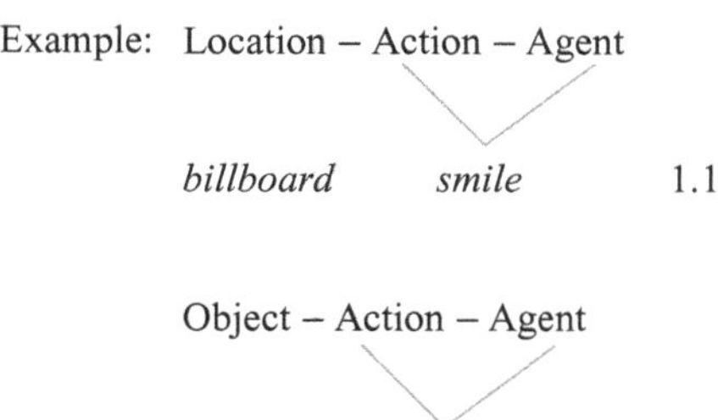

billboard *smile* 1.1

Object – Action – Agent

spider *search* 2.1

Onomasiological Type 6 is another extremely economical onomasiological type. Neither the base nor the determined mark is expressed, as is the case with exocentric compounds like *spiderweb*, that is, 'someone who researches spiders' webs'. The absence of the base and the determined constituent of the mark at the morphemic level can only be explained by the effort of a coiner to achieve the maximum possible economy of expression. By implication, the semantic transparency of this onomasiological type is poor: anything/anyone and any action can be related to 'spiderweb'.

(11) OT6 DingM – DedM – Base
R *Ø* *Ø*

Example: Object – Action – Agent
spiderweb *Ø* *Ø* 2.1

In Onomasiological Type 7, the mark cannot be structured into the determining and determined parts, which yields a binary onomasiological structure, including a mark and a base. Both base and mark are morphemically represented.

(12) OT7[3] Mark – Base
R *R*

Example: Negation – Quality
un *happy*

[3] OT7 and OT8 did not occur in the research. Hence, they cannot be illustrated with research-based examples.

In Onomasiological Type 8, the mark of a binary onomasiological structure is not expressed. This can be illustrated with an example of a SUBSTANCE-TO-ACTION conversion such as 'to bridge (something)'.

(13)	OT8	Mark – Base
		Ø *R*
	Examples:	Object – Action
		Ø *bridge*
		Manner – Action
		Ø *laze*

In Onomasiological Type 9, both mark constituents are expressed with the meaning 'a person whose face is smiling on a billboard'. This type develops OT6, which is restricted to the expression of the determining mark. Moreover, it differs from OT5 in which the base and the determining mark are represented by a common morpheme. In the following example, the two mark constituents swap their positions:

(14)	OT9	DingM – DedM – Base	
		R *R* *Ø*	
	Example:	State – Location – Patient	
		smile *face*	1.1

It follows from this outline that the differences between the extent of the morphemic representation of a ternary or binary onomasiological structure reflect the competition between the tendency towards economy of expression and the tendency towards semantic transparency. The system of onomasiological types thus makes it possible to determine the word formation strategy preferred by various groups of speakers distinguished by age, profession, education, the psychological concept of creativity, etc.

Our original approach to word formation creativity, presented in Štekauer (1998) and Štekauer et al. (2005), is labelled as *Creativity within Productivity Constraints* and, as such, it is in accordance with the so-called *Limit Thesis* (see e.g. D'Agostino 1984: 89), according to which, while creativity is biologically preconditioned, there are limits set on it. Creativity is, therefore, limited by constraints and rules. This principle is roughly reflected by Hamawand (2011: 21–22), in whose view "[word formation] creativity is the ability of language users to coin a novel expression from a conventional expression or construe the same situation in alternate ways using different linguistic expressions. The use of a novel expression involves creativity because the speaker has to find an already existing expression or pattern in the language on the basis of which the new expression can be produced."

What is defined by Hamawand is the rule-governed sphere of coining new words. The reality of word formation, however, teaches us that this claim imposes a rather narrow space upon word formation creativity as there are cases of new words that violate the limits imposed by word formation rules (disregarding the degree of their productivity). Therefore, the original principle is extended in the present research to the principle of *Creativity within and beyond Productivity Constraints* to encompass all potential results of the act of naming. This is in accordance with Langlotz, who maintains that creativity is a "fundamental human capacity to create regular, but new, linguistic patterns, such as new words, sentences, or texts" and can also be associated with "unconventional communicative products that are creatively produced through language" (2015: 41).

Given the previously outlined principles, our conception of word formation creativity lays emphasis on an active role of a language user in coining new complex words by reflecting the fact that, in each act of naming, there is considerable space for a coiner's individual creativity manifested in their selection from usually numerous naming options. The language user's selection of a naming strategy reflects his/her unequal linguistic knowledge and experiences, general knowledge and experiences, intellectual capacity, imagination, education, age, professional interests, and, last but not least, general creativity. Furthermore, the aforementioned principle lays emphasis on the *competition* between two contradictory tendencies that are present in every language and manifested at every level of linguistic description: the tendency towards *economy of expression* and the tendency towards *semantic transparency* (Štekauer 2016, 2017). It is precisely this type of *competition-based word formation creativity* that interests us in the present research and that is examined in relation to the individual indicators/subscores of the psychological concept of creativity.

3.1.2 Evaluation Parameter: Competition between Economy of Expression and Semantic Transparency

The competition between economy of expression and semantic transparency is not only a matter of word formation and, consequently, word interpretation. It pertains to all levels of language and appears to be an inherent and universal feature of natural languages. This is emphasized, for example, by MacWhinney (2012), Aronoff (2013), and Lindsay and Aronoff (2013), who draw an analogy with biological evolution by pointing out that language forms compete to fulfil the fundamental function of language: the communicative function. Consequently, "nothing in language makes sense except in the light of competition ... because we use language as the basic glue for our social lives, these competing motivations are as diverse as the many facets of human life and thought" (MacWhinney 2014: 386). The biological competition between species captured in the well-known Darwinian assumption (1859) that in the struggle for survival, the fittest win out at the expense of their rivals because they succeed in adapting themselves best to their environment translates in word formation, inter alia, as a competition between synonymous affixes and synonymous words (see e.g. Aronoff 1976, 2020; Bauer 2001, 2009; Lindsay 2011; Lindsay & Aronoff 2013; Plag 1999; Rainer 1988; van Marle 1986).

A special type of linguistic competition is the competition between the preferences of speakers/writers and the preferences of listeners/readers. While the former aim to communicate as much as possible within a given period of time, the latter aim to receive a comprehensible message that can be easily decoded. Linguists have been aware of these contradictory tendencies for a long time now. So, for example, Georg von der Gabelentz (1901: 181–185) uses in this connection the terms *Bequemlichkeit*, preferred by the speaker, and *Deutlichkeit*, preferred by the listener.[4] And Leopold (1930: 102) points out that "[l]inguistic development follows not one tendency, but two opposing ones: towards distinctness and towards the economy. Either of these poles prevails, but both are present and alternately preponderant. At the basis of this polarity is the fundamental dualism speaker-hearer."

In an onomasiological theory of word formation, this kind of competition is reflected in the competition between various onomasiological types available for the act of naming. As illustrated in Section 3.1.1, they differ in both economy and transparency. These differences can be captured by means of a cline, as represented in Figure 3.1.

The reasoning that underlies Figure 3.1 builds on the crucial role of the morphemic representation of the cognitive category ACTION:

- The transparency of OT1 is maximum possible because each semantic constituent of the ternary structure is morphemically represented.
- OT2 is more transparent than OT3, thanks to the morphemic representation of the cognitive category of ACTION. The same is true of OT4.
- OT5 is more transparent than OT4 because, apart from the base and the ACTION being merged, it is also represented by a morpheme standing for the determining mark.
- OT2 is more transparent than OT4 because both the base and the ACTION are represented by morphemes.
- OT5 is more transparent than OT2. Although its ACTION and base are represented by a common morpheme, in contrast to OT2, the determining mark is also represented by a morpheme.

[4] For similar views see also, among others, Marty (1908), Martinet (1955), Vicentini (2003), Moravcsik (2014), and Haspelmath (2014).

From the perspective of transparency:

Maximum						**Minimum**
OT1	OT5	OT2	OT4	OT9	OT3	OT6

From the perspective of economy:

Maximum		**Minimum**
OT4	OT2	OT1
OT6	OT3	
	OT5	
	OT9	

Figure 3.1 Scales of transparency and economy (OTs that occurred in our research)

- OT9 is more transparent than OT3 because while it lacks a morpheme for the base, the ACTION and the determined mark are expressed.
- OT9 is less transparent than OT4, which contains morphemes for the ACTION as well as for the base.
- OT6 is the least transparent because it only contains the determining element of the mark.

This overview manifests (i) the influence of the onomasiological type, selected in the process of word formation, upon the difficulty/ease of the interpretation of novel/potential complex words and (ii) the relevance of the integrated onomasiological model of complex words.

3.2 Complex Word Interpretation

3.2.1 A Theory of Meaning Predictability

Our research into the influence of the creative potential of language speakers on the interpretation of new/potential words rests on the theory of meaning predictability (Štekauer 2005a) and the observation that the interpretation of complex words depends on the way they are formed. Semantically more transparent onomasiological types, that is, mainly the type with the morphemic representation of all the three constituents of the onomasiological structure as well as those types with 'incomplete' representation at the onomatological level that represent the Actional constituent, establish better conditions for the interpretation of new/potential words than economical onomasiological types, that is, the types with the morphemic representation of a single constituent of the onomasiological structure, especially the types

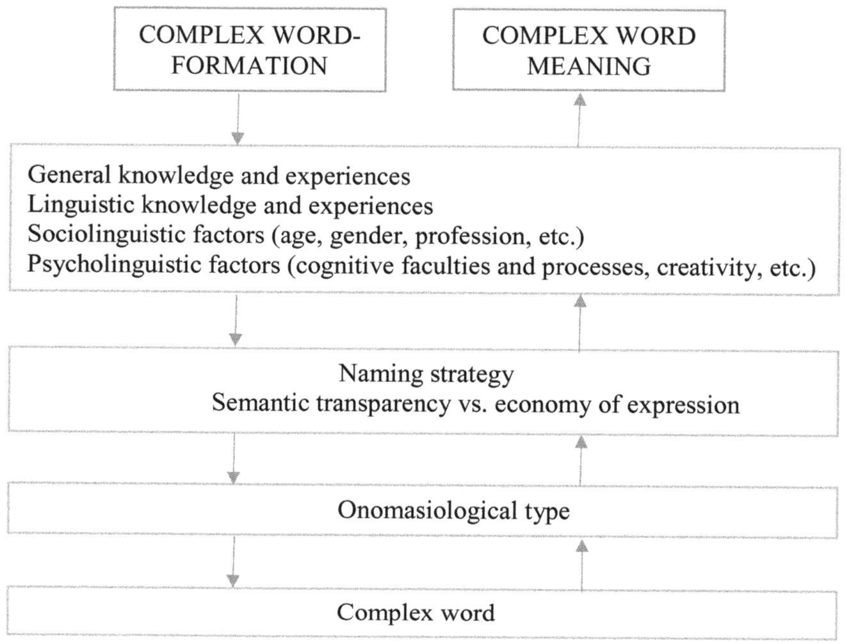

Figure 3.2 An integrated onomasiological model of complex words

without the representation of the Actional constituent. These instances offer the greatest space for speakers' creative imagination in interpreting new/potential words because the number of possible readings abounds. The influence of word formation on word interpretation is captured in an *integrated onomasiological model of complex words*.

The model in Figure 3.2 represents the relation between the act of complex word formation and the act of complex word interpretation or, more precisely, the dependence of the latter on the former. The arrows show the succession of steps in the formation/interpretation of complex words. It is manifested that the preference for a particular naming strategy affects the choice of a specific onomasiological type underlying the resulting complex word. From the perspective of interpretation, the underlying onomasiological type determines, for the speaker, the degree of transparency/economy and, therefore, the ease/difficulty with which the word can be interpreted. In other words, the act of word formation predetermines the meaning predictability of the coined word: the higher the semantic transparency of an onomasiological type, the better its general meaning predictability.

Referring to Štekauer (2005a), a language speaker first encounters the phonological form of a complex word and identifies individual morphemes. This enables him/her to recognize the onomatological (morphematic) structure of the word (that is, a productive word formation rule in traditional terminology). The identification of the individual morphological constituents is indicative of the possible range of general semantic relations between the constituents of the novel complex word. In principle, this step is based on an attempt to *reconstruct* the relation between the onomasiological and the onomatological levels, established by the application of the Morpheme-to-Seme-Assignment Principle (MSAP) in the process of word formation. The identification of a potential onomasiological structure is the first step in the meaning prediction process. This step relies on one's linguistic competence (knowledge of productive word formation rules, knowledge of the meaning of words and affixes, awareness of the existence of language families, etc.) and, certainly, general knowledge and experiences.

The process of interpretation and meaning prediction outlined earlier indicates that the interpretation process, especially in its first, general word formation-meaning-identification step, crucially benefits from a language user's linguistic knowledge of productive word formation rules (types) and that this knowledge functions as a filter through which only those possible readings of a novel word pass that comply with productive word formation rules. Next, a fine-grained filter employs a language user's extra-linguistic knowledge and experiences. The two filters make it possible to determine the predictability of individual potential readings.

While this is a typical scenario captured by the concept of *Creativity within Productivity Constraints*, the addition of the attribute 'beyond' to this principle, that is, *Creativity within and beyond Productivity Constraints*, suggests that another line of meaning predictability is possible too in which the first filter is inapplicable, and the language speaker relies exclusively on his/her general knowledge and experiences.

3.2.2 Evaluation Parameters

This part of our research is aimed at the evaluation of whether – and if so, to what degree – the psychological factor of creativity (creative potential) affects the creative performance in interpreting new/potential complex words. Like in the word formation part of our research, the respondents were divided into two cohorts for each of the creativity indicator/subscore, based on their scores (high/low) achieved in the Torrance Test of Creative Thinking (TTCT).

The evaluation process is primarily based on Štekauer's theory of meaning predictability (2005a), according to which it is possible to predict the most acceptable, that is, the most predictable, readings of novel complex words out of a relatively large number of potential readings proposed by speakers of a language. This principle applies not only to novel compound words but also to words resulting from other word formation processes, such as affixation and conversion.

To determine the most predictable reading, the meaning predictability theory works with three basic variables: the Predictability Rate, the Predictability Rate Gap, and the Objectified Predictability Rate. These were introduced on the basis of the postulate that the meaning predictability of novel complex words is a scalar indicator that can be computed. This approach, in principle, differs from the majority of research works within the psycholinguistic framework. As noted by Costello and Keane (1996), "[m]ost previous research on concept combination has concentrated on the production of a single best interpretation for a novel conceptual combination . . . This research has tended to underplay the creativity of the combination process." In contrast to this, our approach, as indicated earlier, takes into account all readings proposed by the respondents and evaluates the degree of their predictability.

In addition to these two evaluation criteria, we will assess the influence of the creative potential on interpretation creativity by means of two other criteria: the average number of readings proposed per cohort member and the hapax legomenon, that is, a reading proposed by a single member of a cohort. All these evaluation criteria are introduced in the following sections.

3.2.2.1 Predictability Rate

As pointed out by Štekauer (2005a), the predictability of new/potential words correlates with the acceptability of their meanings to listeners/readers. It is assumed that a language user, when facing a word never heard before, prefers the interpretation which, in their view, is most acceptable. The most acceptable reading is therefore considered to be the most predictable of all those readings that come to a speaker's mind. By implication, the degree of acceptability of the individual possible readings may be used as an indicator of the Predictability Rate of the individual readings of a new word. This conception is, in principle, in accordance with Zimmer, where the notion of an *appropriately classificatory* (AC) relationship, applied to endocentric non-idiomatic N+N compounds, is defined as follows (1972: 4):

(15) Noun A has an AC relationship with noun B if this relationship is regarded by a speaker as significant for his classification – rather than description – of B.

This means to us that the reading proposed by a language speaker for a new/potential word can be acceptable and, hence, predictable according to the degree to which the relation between the objects of extra-linguistic reality, represented by the two constituents of a compound word, is significant. In the theory of meaning predictability, this postulate equally applies to all the other word formation processes.

The Predictability Rate's calculation is based on the following postulates:

1. The predictability of individual readings of complex words correlates with (i) the number of language users who consider a particular reading acceptable and (ii) the degree of acceptability of that particular meaning to language users.
2. Since there is no clear-cut boundary between acceptable and unacceptable meanings, the predictability of the meanings of naming units is a cline.

Then, the Predictability Rate (PR) of a particular reading of a novel, context-free complex word can be calculated as its frequency of occurrence weighted for the scores is assigned:

(16) $$PR = \frac{r}{R_{max}} \times \frac{p}{P_{max}}$$

where r is the number of respondents identifying a particular reading as acceptable
R_{max} is the total number of respondents
p is the sum total of the points assigned to a given meaning by all respondents (on a scale from 1 to 7, where 7 stands for the highest acceptability of the reading)
P_{max} is the maximum possible number of points assignable by all respondents

For example, the reading 'a book for babies (fairy tales, rhymes, pictures, drawings)' of the naming unit *baby book* was proposed by 31 out of 76 respondents in the L-cohort of the university undergraduate group within the Fluency parameter, that is, the frequency of occurrence of this reading is 31/76 = 0.41. The score assigned to this reading is 96 points out of a total of 532 assignable points, which is 0.18. The resulting PR of this particular reading is therefore 0.41 × 0.18 = 0.074. This is much lower than the PR of, for example, the reading 'a book for a baby' the PR of which in the same cohort is 0.612.

By implication, this method of calculating the PR makes it possible to evaluate the strength of various readings proposed for a novel, context-free word, and thus to determine the degree of their predictability.

3.2.2.2 *Objectified Predictability Rate*

As it follows from the preceding section, the PRs calculated for the individual predictable readings take into consideration two variables: first, the number of respondents who adduce a particular complex word reading, which indicates that the reading is acceptable to them; second, the assigned/assignable scores proportion for the individual readings, determined by the respondents' rating activity. The PR is therefore directly proportional to the number of respondents who identify the reading and the points assigned to this reading.

Štekauer (2005, 2017) and Körtvélyessy, Štekauer, and Zimmermann (2015) point out that the potential readings of a novel complex word compete with one another. This fact is reflected in the notion of the *Objectified Predictability Rate* (OPR). An important indicator of the strength of a particular potential reading relative to the other potential readings of that complex word is expressed by the so-called *Predictability Rate Gap* (PRG) between the PR of the most predictable reading of a complex word and the next lowest PRs of the same complex word. In other words, the greater the PRG, the stronger the position of the most predictable reading. By implication, the OPR is directly proportional to the value of the PRG.

For illustration, let us recall Štekauer's example (2005a: 96). Let us suppose that there are two complex words: X and Y. Their three most predictable readings are X_1, X_2, and X_3 and Y_1, Y_2, and Y_3, respectively. Let us further suppose that X_1 and Y_1 are the top PR readings of their respective complex words and happen to have identical PRs of, let us say, 0.486. Furthermore, let us suppose that the PR of X_2 is 0.194 and that the PR of Y_2 is 0.362. Finally, let us assume that the third-rank readings of PRs are identical, for example, X_3 and Y_3 are both 0.088. This situation is given in (17):

(17)	Potential word X		Potential word Y	
	PR		PR	
	X_1	0.486	Y_1	0.486
	X_2	0.194	Y_2	0.362
	X_3	0.088	Y_3	0.088

Since the competition of predictable readings in the case of complex word Y is much tougher than in the case of X, intuitively, the actual (objectified) predictability of X_1 is higher than that of Y_1. This fact is captured by the proposed OPR.

This type of relation may be advantageously calculated by Luce's (1959) choice rule that makes it possible to weigh the strength (PR) of the most predictable reading against the strength (PRs) of any number of other competing readings. As stressed by Pleskac (2015: 895), "Luce's choice axiom (LCA) is a theory of individual choice behavior that has proven to be a powerful tool in the behavioral sciences for over 50 years." This method was applied, for example, by Gagné and Shoben (1997) for the calculation of the strength of the thematic relation that is the best candidate for the interpretation of a particular complex word.

The formula adopted for the calculation of the OPR (adding the fourth reading in the ranking to the original version), is as follows:

(18) $$OPR = \frac{PR^{top}}{PR^{top} + PR^{top-1} + PR^{top-2} + PR^{top-3}}$$

If formula (18) is now applied to (17), we get $OPR_X = 0.633$ and $OPR_Y = 0.519$. By implication, with the other values being identical, it is the higher PRG_{X1-X2} value compared to the PRG_{Y1-Y2} value that is responsible for the higher OPR of X_1. This result confirms our intuition, according to which reading Y_1 faces much 'tougher competition' on the part of reading Y_2 than X_1 on the part of X_2. Consequently, the predictability of X_1 is much better than that of Y_1 despite these two having identical PR values.

From this, it follows that a high absolute PR does not guarantee a high OPR: a complex word reading of a lower PR may be comparably more predictable than a reading of another complex word with a higher PR if the former can take advantage of a considerable PRG.

The PR and OPR are, however, not the only variables used for the evaluation of our data. To obtain a comprehensive picture of the interrelation between the various aspects of creativity and the interpretation of novel complex words, we also take into consideration two other variables, namely the number of readings per respondent and the number of single-occurrence readings in individual TTCT-based cohorts of respondents.

The data are evaluated and compared for each of the four experimental words separately, for all four complex words as a whole, for each indicator and subscore of creativity in terms of the 'high' and 'low' cohorts, and separately for secondary school students (SS) and university undergraduates (UU), and, eventually, the data for these two large groups of respondents are compared for each of the previously mentioned parameters.

3.2.2.3 Average Number of Readings Proposed by a Cohort Member

If interpretation creativity is defined as the ability to interpret a new complex word by selecting a reading out of a number of possible readings of that word, the degree of interpretation creativity of a speaker is determined by the number of readings proposed by a cohort member in relation to the number of the readings proposed by the cohort as a whole. From this point of view, the average number of readings proposed by a cohort member is an indicator that lends itself very well to comparing the H-cohort's and L-cohort's performances in interpreting new complex words.

3.2.2.4 Hapax Legomena

We introduce the term 'hapax legomena' to the interpretation of new words, even if it was primarily used in Baayen's theory of morphological productivity

(Baayen & Lieber 1991; see also a series of Baayen's subsequent papers, e.g. 1992, 1993, 1994a, 1994b, 2001) on the basis of a large corpus. The term denotes the derivatives that occur only once in a corpus. A single occurrence of a complex word in a multimillion word corpus indicates, according to Baayen, its novelty and, by implication, the synchronic productivity of the underlying word formation rule.

We employ this term to identify those readings that were proposed by a single respondent of a cohort. This is in accordance with the view that

> [a] creative response or product is one that is determined to be both original and relevant. [...] The level of originality of a given response is defined in terms of its novelty, uniqueness or statistical rarity, whereas relevance is assessed in terms of the functionality, usefulness or fit of the response to a particular end or within a specific context. (Abraham 2016: 610)

Hapax legomena meet all these characteristics: They are original because they provide a new and unique, single-occurrence interpretation in a particular cohort of language users, and they are functional and useful because they respond relevantly to the task of interpreting a novel combination of word formation constituents. Nevertheless, this concept may mean two contradictory things. First, since the reading occurs only once, it may indicate the creativity of a member of the respective cohort. However, it may also, contrary to this, indicate a lack of creativity of the whole cohort provided that the reading in question occurs more than once in the other cohort. In that case, the creativity is on the side of the cohort with the larger number of occurrences of such a 'peripheral' reading, that is, a reading with a very low predictability rate. If, now, we hypothesize that high creativity in any of its indicators/subscores is directly proportional to creativity in meaning interpretation, we may expect that a hapax legomenon in the L-cohort will correspond to several occurrences of that reading in the H-cohort.

4 Methodological Principles

Since the objective of our research is to examine the influence of the creative potential of language speakers on their creative performance in the formation and interpretation of new/potential complex words, there are several fundamental methodological principles that have to be taken into consideration. First of all is the method of measuring the creative potential of language speakers and the methods of testing their creative performance in forming and interpreting new complex words. Therefore, Section 4.1 introduces the Torrance Test of Creative Thinking (TTCT), accounts for the basic characteristics of creativity indicators and subscores, and justifies its relevance to our research. Section 4.2 presents a word formation test employed in our research and accounts for its objectives and principles of evaluation. It includes three tasks, each of which consists of three subtasks. Section 4.3 explains the nature and the principles of evaluation of the word interpretation test. This is followed by introducing the sample of respondents (Section 4.4.1), justifying the decision to rely on an age-based comparison between a group of secondary school students and a group of university students (Section 4.4.2), justifying the decision to rely on a sample of non-native speakers (Section 4.4.3), and, finally, explaining the reasons for data evaluation on the basis of a comparison of two cohorts: one that achieved the highest scores in the TTCT and one with the lowest scores in this test (Section 4.4.4). Section 4.5 formulates the hypotheses underlying our research.

4.1 Torrance Test of Creative Thinking

Of the most widely cited and used tests of creativity, the most prominent place belongs to the *TTCT* (Kim 2006; Sternberg 2006). To illustrate the prominence of the test, one could mention that the first version of the test (Torrance 1966) has been cited more than 850 times, according to the Web of Science, and the test itself has been translated into more than thirty languages (Kim 2006).

The TTCT was created by Torrance with the aim of providing "a reliable and valid test of creative thinking abilities that could be administered to individuals from kindergarten through adulthood" (Runco et al. 2010: 362) and with a goal to understand and nurture the capacity for creativity in individuals (Kim 2006; Runco et al. 2010). The author of the test, Ellis Paul Torrance, understood creativity as "the process of becoming sensitive to problems, deficiencies, gaps in knowledge, missing elements, disharmonies, and so on; identifying the difficulty; searching for solutions, making guesses, or formulating hypotheses about the deficiencies; testing and retesting these hypotheses and possibly modifying and retesting them" (1966: 664).

The TTCT measures the creative potential of an individual that can lead to various creativity-related outcomes in real life (Cramond et al. 2005; Runco et al. 2010). More specifically, the test assesses divergent thinking abilities as inspired by Guilford's *Structure of Intellect* theory in which he clearly distinguished between convergent and divergent thinking (1956, 1986). According to Runco and Acar, divergent thinking can be understood as the "measure of ideation that fuels creative thinking" (2019: 244). Divergent thinking is necessary for situations where more than one correct answer exists, as opposed to convergent thinking. According to the *integrative bio-psycho-behavioural model* of creativity (Jauk 2019), based on deeper neurobiological systems, divergent thinking, as the cognitive creative potential of an individual, is one of the major psychological constructs related to everyday creative activities and creative achievements. In fact, in the past, divergent thinking was even considered as a synonym for creativity (Glăveanu & Kaufman 2019; Jauk 2019; Runco & Acar 2019; Runco et al. 2010).

At present, various versions of the TTCT (Torrance 1966, 1974, 1987, 1990, 1998) and two distinct forms (figural vs. verbal form) can be found in the literature. Crucially, the test and its manual were adapted by Jurčová and Szobiová (2008) to the local context in a figural form. When pondering the difference between the figural and the verbal forms, it is important to stress that, according to Kim (2017), the figural form could be considered as a more "comprehensive, reliable and valid measure of creativity" in comparison to the verbal form. Moreover, as the present linguistic tasks are language based, the usage of the verbal form of the TTCT could introduce complications to the interpretation of the results. Thus, the figural form is deemed to be more suitable in the present research context.

Although drawing as a process is inherent in the figural form, Jurčová and Szobiová (2008) point out that the test instructions emphasize the fact that drawing skills are not necessary for its completion and that this is not a task where drawing skills are crucial but rather a task where participants should come up with an object or a picture that no one else would propose. Furthermore, according to the test manual, a playful atmosphere during testing should be ensured to facilitate a creative process. Thus, this should not inhibit or disadvantage even participants who do not think that they have drawing skills.

The TTCT consists of three tasks that encourage participants to create something that can be considered special or unique. For every task, a time limit of ten minutes is provided.

The first task is called *Picture construction*. In this task, a blank sheet of paper and an orange sticker in the shape of a jelly bean are provided. As illustrated in Figure 4.1, the goal is to stick the sticker to the paper and create a picture where the sticker is an integral part of the product.

The instructions for the first task are as follows: *In front of you, there is a piece of a rounded coloured paper. Think of a picture of an object that you can draw when you use this piece as a part of the overall drawing. Then, draw lines to create the intended image. Try to think of a picture that you assume no one else would invent. Add elements to your sketch so that the image you create expresses a most interesting phenomenon. When you finish drawing, think of a name for your image and write it at the bottom of the page. Think of the most accurate and unusual name to help explain your drawing. The task is conceptually illustrated later.*

The second task is named *Picture completion*. In this task, ten incomplete figures are provided to the participants. Its illustration is provided in Figure 4.2 The goal is to complete them.

The instructions for the second task are as follows: *By adding lines to the incomplete figure on the next page, you can turn the sketched shapes into interesting objects or pictures. Again, try to think of an object or picture that no one else would invent. Complete and expand your first idea and try to add lines to create the most complete and interesting image. Think of an interesting title for your drawing and write it at the bottom of the frame next to the image number. The task is conceptually illustrated later.*

The third task is called *Circles*. In this task, two pieces of paper with thirty-six circles are provided to the participants. The goal is to complete the circles. The stimulus material is illustrated in Figure 4.3.

The instructions for the third task are as follows: *In the next ten minutes, you will see how many objects and pictures you can create from the circles on this and the next page. Circles should be the main part of everything you create. Draw a line to the circles to create an image. Try to figure out things that no one else could come up with. You can draw between, inside, and outside the circles. Create as many different pictures as you can and put as many ideas into each as possible. Let them show the most interesting scene. Write names under the pictures. The task is conceptually illustrated later.*

Across the aforementioned tasks, four main areas can be identified for scoring purposes, namely, Originality, Fluency, Flexibility, and Elaboration. Moreover, additional scores can be derived as illustrated in the following.

The first main score, *Originality*, reflects the uniqueness of the product based on the existing population norms. Norms are provided in the test manual

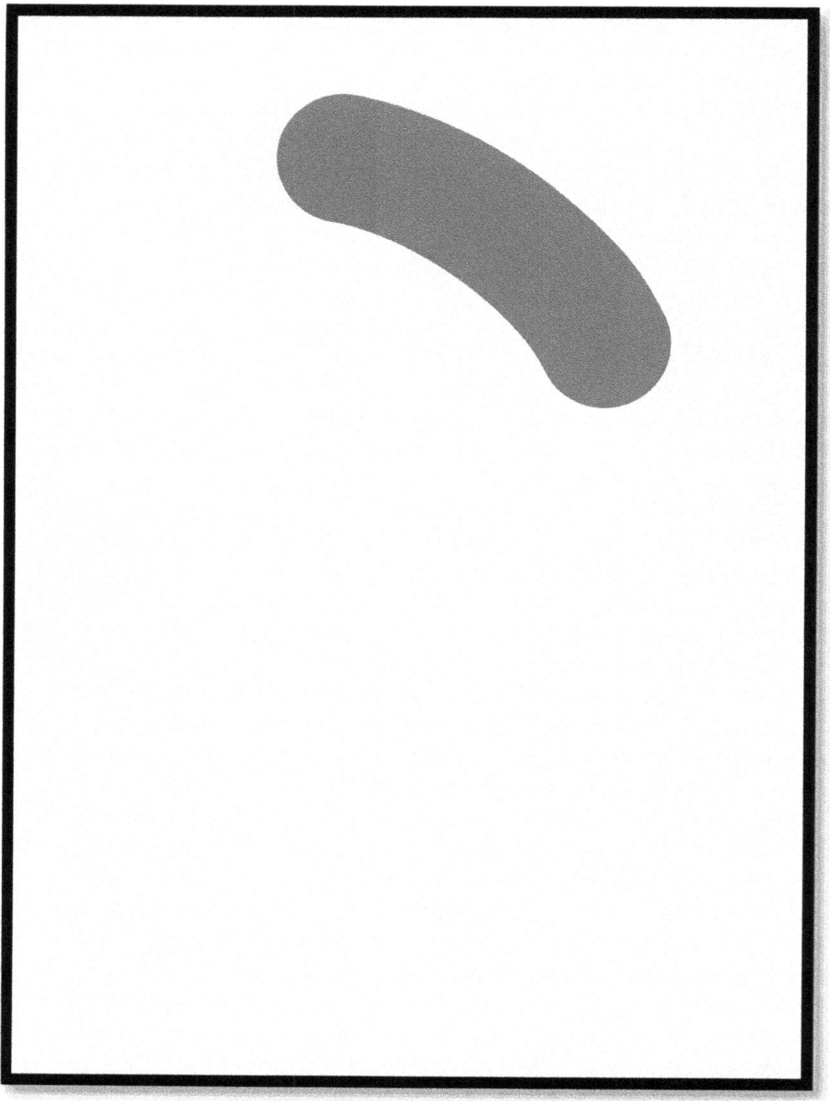

Figure 4.1 A sheet of paper with a sticker as an illustration of a stimulus material for the first task

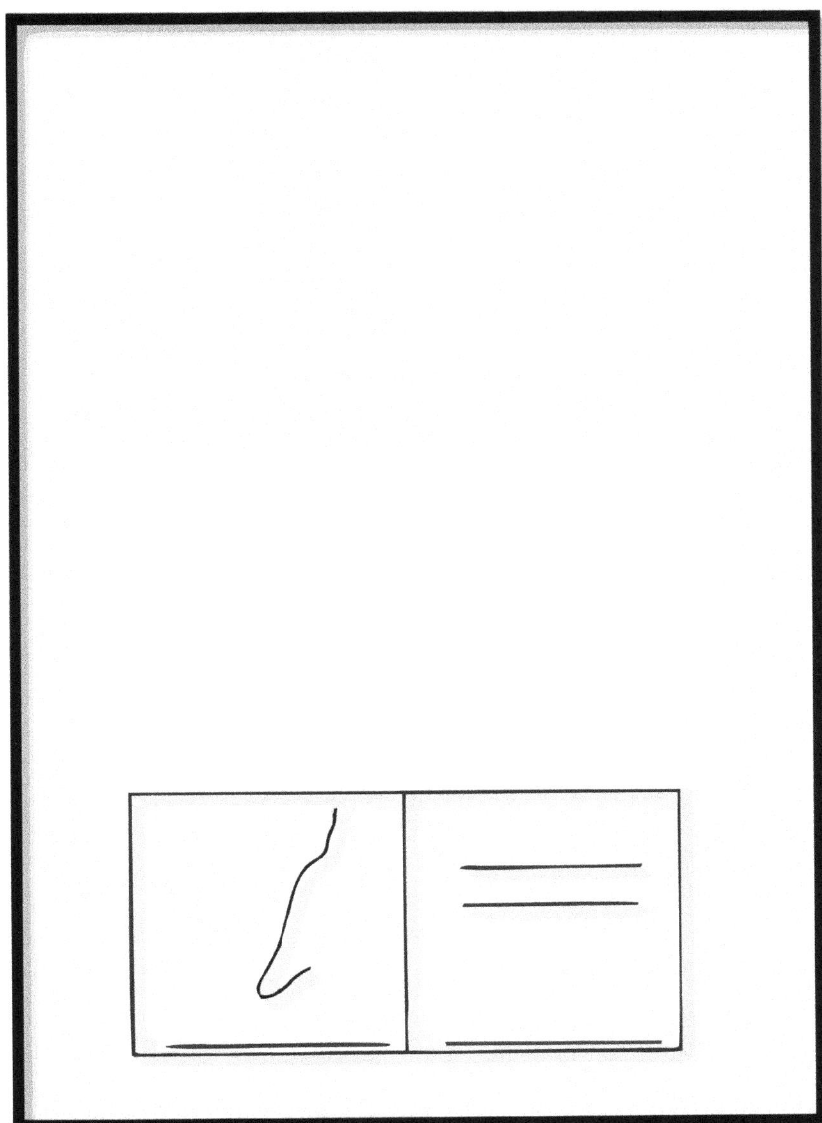

Figure 4.2 A sheet of paper with incomplete figures as an illustration of a stimulus material for the second task

Figure 4.3 A sheet of paper with circles as an illustration of a stimulus material for the third task

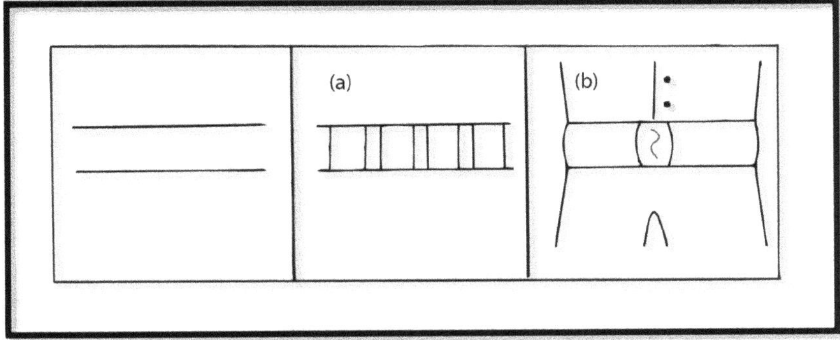

Figure 4.4 Illustration of (a) a less versus (b) a more creative drawing

with illustrations, categories, frequency of occurrence in a normative sample, and points that should be assigned in scoring for a given category. In particular, the less frequent the answer in the normative sample, the higher the score for Originality. For instance, considering the prevalence of the answer in the normative sample, if the creative product in the first task (Picture construction) is rare (an occurrence of less than 1 per cent in the normative sample), three points are given to a participant. Two points are given if the prevalence is less unique (1–3 per cent of participants responded similarly). One point is given if the prevalence of the answer is at the level of 3–5 per cent, and no points are given when the prevalence is more than 5 per cent – that is, if the answer is common (Jurčová & Szobiová 2008).

For instance, in the fourth drawing of the second task (Picture completion), as illustrated in Figure 4.4, two horizontal lines (on the left-hand side of the picture) can be hypothetically completed as both (a) 'a ladder' (the middle part of Figure 4.4) and (b) 'a belt of a soldier' (the right-hand side drawing). Since 'belt' is a less frequent answer according to the standards (less than 1 per cent in the normative sample in comparison to 3–5 per cent for the ladder), this answer is considered as more original and, therefore, the originality score is higher (three points) in comparison to 'a ladder'. Note, however, that an even more common answer can be found. For instance, as it is common to draw a brick or a road (more than 5 per cent of people in the normative sample), these answers will be scored with zero points. In the event of ambiguity, first, the test manual was consulted and, second, all ambiguous cases were resolved under supervision.

The second score, *Fluency*, reflects the number of relevant answers. The more pictures are meaningfully completed, the higher the score for Fluency (Jurčová & Szobiová 2008). For instance, Figure 4.5 illustrates two situations

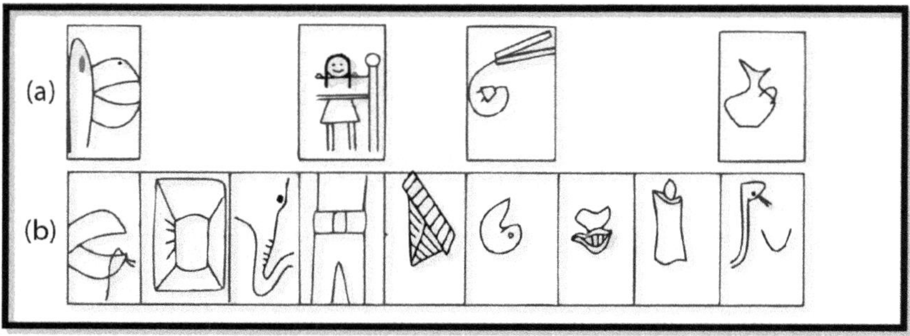

Figure 4.5 An illustration of (a) less versus (b) more fluent answers

that can hypothetically occur in the second task (Picture completion). In the upper (a) line, (only) four legitimate answers are provided. Therefore, the score for Fluency is 4. In comparison, in the lower line (b), all ten pictures are completed, which results in a score of 10 with regard to Fluency.

While Fluency reflects the number of relevant answers, these answers can be considered as more or less similar depending on the content of the drawing. This is an important aspect of creativity evaluation and is captured by the third score, Flexibility. Flexibility thus captures the presence of qualitatively different categories in a drawing. The higher the content diversity in drawings, the higher the Flexibility score. More specifically, one point is gained for every new category that is presented in a drawing (Jurčová & Szobiová 2008). This can be illustrated with two hypothetical scenarios in one part of the third task (Circles). As illustrated in the upper line (a) of Figure 4.6, the circles can be completed in such a way that every circle is from the same category. As all pictures in this example capture an emoticon, no points for Flexibility will be provided to a participant. On the other hand, in the lower line (b) below, all three drawings differ regarding their content because both the football and the seven-spotted ladybird represent categories different from the yin-yang symbol. Since the category was shifted twice, two points will be given to the participant.

The fourth score is Elaboration. Elaboration captures the number of details provided in a drawing. The more details are provided beyond what is necessary to capture the idea, the more points are given to the participant. An exact scoring procedure with examples is provided in the test manual (Jurčová & Szobiová 2008). To illustrate this score, let us refer to the third picture of the second task (Picture completion) where the initial line should be completed (the left-hand side drawing). Two hypothetical scenarios are illustrated in Figure 4.7. In (b) (the right-hand side drawing), a lot of additional details

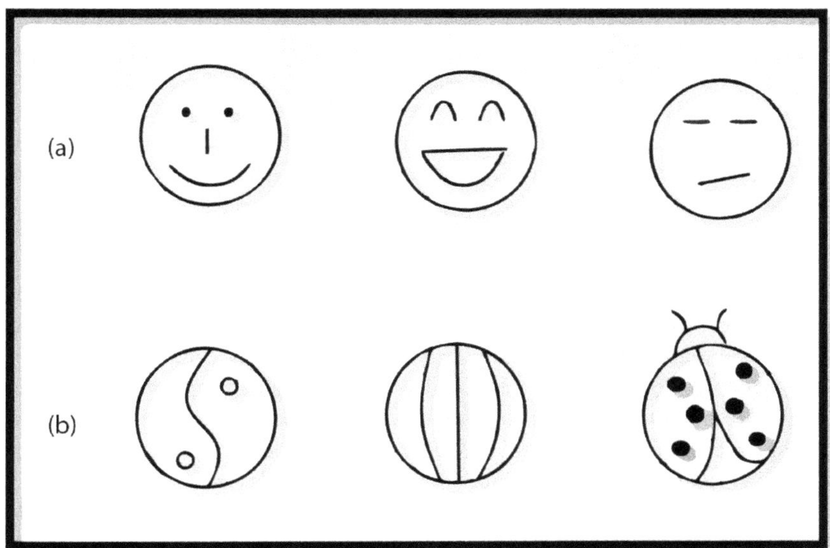

Figure 4.6 An illustration of (a) lower versus (b) higher flexibility

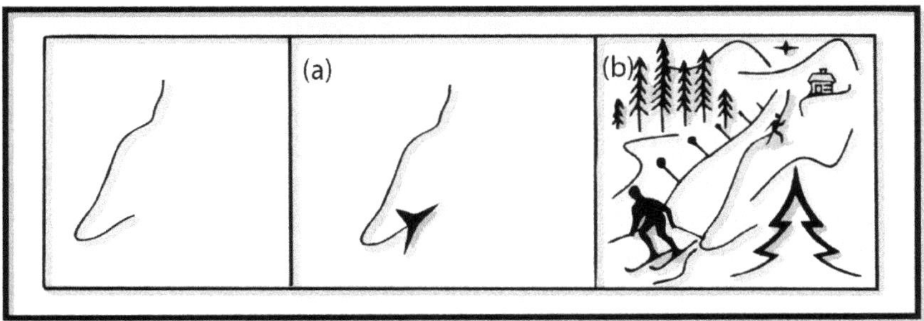

Figure 4.7 An illustration of (a) lower versus (b) higher elaboration

can be found (a ski slope with trees, people, and so on). For every clearly distinguishable detail beyond what is necessary to capture the idea, one point is provided. In contrast to the first situation (a) (the middle drawing), the picture of a needle and a thread lacks any additional details, and, therefore, no points for Elaboration are given to the participant for this picture completion.

In addition to the four main scores, a score for *Creative Strengths* can be assigned. Creative Strengths consist of thirteen categories: (1) fantasy;

(2) expression of feelings and emotions; (3) storytelling; (4) movement and action; (5) expressiveness of titles; (6) combination of two or more figures; (7) synthesis of circles; (8) unusual visual perspective; (9) extension of boundaries; (10) humour; (11) internal visual perspective; (12) richness of imagery; and (13) colourfulness of imagery. The more categories that can be found, the more points are obtained for Creative Strengths (Jurčová & Szobiová 2008).

Finally, a score capturing the general creative energy can be computed in the form of the Composite Score (Runco et al. 2010). However useful this may be, this score should not replace the more nuanced individual scores described earlier. According to Runco et al. (2010), in order to calculate the Composite Score, the scores for Originality, Elaboration, Fluency, and Flexibility are converted into *z*-scores and then added into a single composite score. This procedure makes it possible to obtain a common scale across all scores. The *z*-score is calculated as the specific score of an individual for a category minus the mean score in a sample divided by the standard deviation.

Based on the scores obtained in the TTCT, the participants were divided into two cohorts for the purposes of the consequent analysis. Two cohorts (high and low cohorts) were created by identifying the respondents with the lowest score (lowest 25 per cent – L-cohort) and the highest score (highest 25 per cent – H-cohort) within every score via a quartile split procedure. Further information is provided in Section 4.4.4.

4.2 Word Formation Test

The word formation test employed in the present research draws on the version introduced in Štekauer et al. (2005), which was successfully re-applied in our subsequent research projects for the sake of comparability of results. Our decision to make use of this test was further motivated by the fact that the individual tasks of the test in their complementarity have proved relevant, reliable, and justified in assessing word formation strategies in an onomasiological framework. The use of established tests for various objectives is quite common in general. A nice example is the TTCT, employed in the present work, that has been used in a diversity of research projects.

The basic task of the respondents was to give names to 'objects' for which there did not exist any actual (institutionalized) word at the time of the experiment. All the objects to be named in the individual test tasks were either Agents or Patients. Our decision to concentrate on these two semantic categories stemmed from the fact that there are numerous ways for their word formation realization in English (among other languages). To avoid distorted results and to observe the principles of microdomains (task specificity) of creativity (see Section 2.2.2), the test consisted of three sets of tasks, each of which included three specific tasks. The first set was based on selection. The respondents were offered a number of options for naming a person described by a text, ranging across various onomasiological types and thus representing various word formation strategies. The last option indirectly prompted them to come up with a non-rule-governed solution by offering a 'free choice'. The second set of tasks differed from set 1 by offering no options. The respondents were asked to propose their own new complex word based on a brief specification of the object to be named. Finally, the third set of three tasks replaced the wording with a drawing of a situation in which an object performed an unusual activity.

Since the test was aimed at the formation of new words, the respondents were expressly asked not to use existing words in a shifted meaning or descriptive phrases. In spite of this warning, there was a fairly high number of what we labelled 'failed answers'. By 'failed answers' we do not mean 'incorrect' complex words. Rather, these included (a) no answers to the particular subtask and (b) answers that did not comply with the instructions mentioned earlier, that is, if a respondent proposed an existing simple or complex word or a phrasal description instead of using a new coinage, or if he/she proposed an existing (actual) word in a shifted meaning. Examples of cases under (b) are given in (19):

(19)

Example	**Subtask**
researcher	2.1
Nerd	2.1
scientist	2.1
overgrown kid	2.1
smart guy	2.2
representative of human race	2.2
child of clones	2.3
stuntman	3.1
daredevil	3.1
maniac	3.1
killer of birds	3.2
madman	3.2
worker	3.3
stupid man	3.3
acrobat	3.3

In the following, the whole word formation test is presented, including the respective instructions.

Word Formation Test

Task 1 Choose the word that you think is the most suitable for the person described in the task.

Task 1.1 A person whose smiling face is used for billboard advertisements:

a. smiler
b. smilist
c. smileman
d. smile
e. smile-person
f. smile-face
g. billboard smile-face
h. [free choice]

Task 1.2 A person who frequently interrupts other people when they are talking:

a. interrupter
b. cutter-in
c. cutter-inner
d. interrupt
e. talk-interrupter
f. talk-interrupt
g. interrupt-man
h. [free choice]

Task 1.3 A person who believes in miracles:

a. miraclist
b. miracler
c. miracle-man
d. miracle-believer
e. miracle-hoper
f. miracle-hope
g. [free choice]

Task 2 Each question describes a person in an unusual situation. If you had to come up with a name or title for the person, what would it be? You may make up a word or choose a word that already exists in English.

1. What would you call someone who researches spiders' webs?
2. Suppose that aliens were about to land on Earth for the first time. What would you call a person who was supposed to meet them as a representative of the human race?
3. Suppose that a woman has a clone made of herself. Then suppose that a man has a clone made of himself. Now suppose that the two clones marry each other and have a child. What would you call the child?

Task 3 Each drawing below shows a person performing an unusual action. If you had to come up with a name or title for the person in each drawing, what would it be? You may invent a word or choose a word that already exists in English.

Figure 4.8 A drawing for Task 3.1

4.3 Word Interpretation Test

According to van Dijk et al. (2018: 179), "creative thinking is conceived as a person's ability to generate new ideas or products, which consists of (multiple cycles of) divergent and convergent thinking." Divergent thinking is defined as "the process that allows people to generate as many responses as possible to a particular trigger or problem" (van Dijk et al. 2018) and lays emphasis on "the generation of varied, original, or unusual ideas in response to an open-ended question or task" (Baer 2020: 377). Convergent thinking is defined as "a constraining process, which aims at finding a single, best outcome given a particular problem" (van Dijk et al. 2018: 179).

Our interpretation creativity test draws on that employed by Štekauer (2005a) because it enabled us to meet the pursued objectives. It takes into consideration both of the aforementioned aspects of creative thinking. On the one hand, it tests the level of divergent thinking by asking the respondents to propose as many readings for each of our four experimental words as they can think of. On the other hand, it tests their convergent thinking by asking them to assess the proposed readings by determining their degree of acceptability by

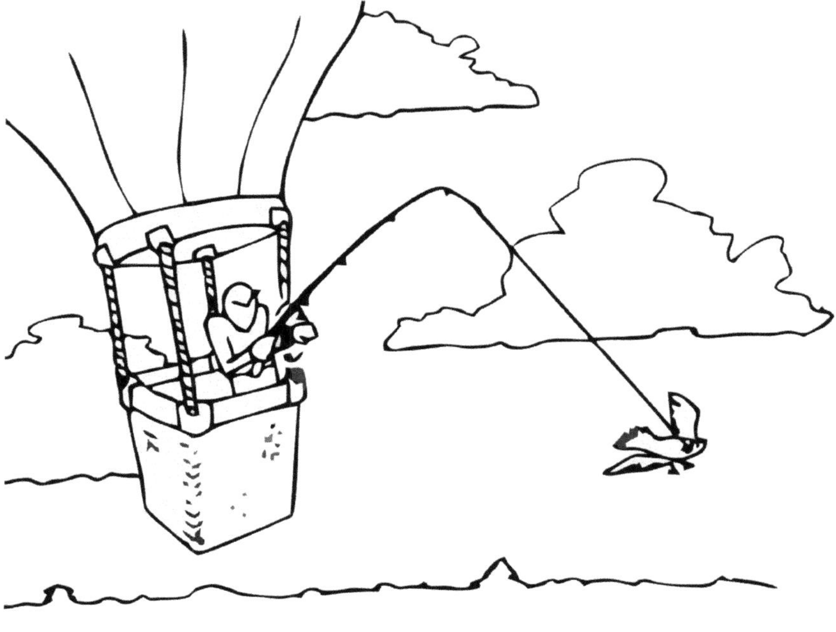

Figure 4.9 A drawing for Task 3.2

means of selecting a value on a scale from 7 (highly acceptable reading) to 1 (a reading with very low acceptability). In this way, they identified the 'best outcome' of the interpretation problem.

The experimental research (Štekauer 2005a) that covered thirty experimental words has unambiguously shown for both compounds and converted words that, out of a large number of potential readings for each such potential word, there is usually only one, rarely two readings that clearly dominate all the other readings in the meaning predictability value. This finding was confirmed by the data obtained for the compound and converted words used in the present research. This important generalization enabled us to restrict the number of experimental words in the present interpretation test and concentrate on obtaining the largest possible sample of respondents. Namely, this universal meaning predictability scenario means that the results are not affected by the increasing number of experimental words.[1]

[1] This observation was crucial for obtaining reliable data and for drawing undistorted conclusions on their basis, especially with regard to the limited time available for performing our word formation and word interpretation creativity tests (one 45-minute school hour).

Figure 4.10 A drawing for Task 3.3

Two of the words were potential compounds of the Noun + Noun (N+N) type: *baby book* and *flower hat*; the other two words were potential converted words of the Noun > Verb type: *to boy* and *to tulip*. Given our onomasiological theory of word formation and the integrated onomasiological model of complex words, it is obvious that the most semantically transparent and, therefore, the most predictable words are those in which all semantic categories of the ternary onomasiological structure are explicitly represented by morphemes at the onomatological level. If this is not the case, the demands on interpretation increase, especially in words like those selected for our experimental research. The absence of a morpheme that would represent the ACTION category in our N+N compounds substantially increases the number of potential readings, some of them being more acceptable and others less acceptable for speakers of a language. This scale of acceptability is captured by the previously defined measure of the Predictability Rate. The same is true of the two potential conversions in the event there is only one morpheme corresponding to the ternary onomasiological structure, a morpheme that represents both the onomasiological base and the determined constituent of the onomasiological mark. As a result, the number of potential readings available for *to boy* and *to tulip* is fairly high.

Before performing the test, the respondents were explicitly instructed that their task was

(i) to propose as many readings as they could think of rather than to concentrate on a single reading that seemed to be the most acceptable to them. This enabled us, in the process of data processing, to evaluate the mutual influence of the individual competing readings that come to one's mind when processing a novel, context-free complex word;
(ii) based on their subjective assessment, to determine the degree of acceptability of the individual readings they proposed by rating them on a scale from 7 (most acceptable) to 1 (least acceptable). Points (i) and (ii) enabled us to quantify the competition among the readings by means of the Objectified Predictability Rate;
(iii) based on the explicit instruction that there was no 'correct' or 'incorrect' interpretation, and therefore each interpretation that is somehow related to the meaning of the nominal constituents of the compounds and the nominal basis of the converted words is acceptable.

In the process of evaluating the data, two fundamental principles were adhered to the classification of various readings:

(i) the semantic identity of readings – readings expressing the same or similar meaning in different words; that means, if they were semantically cognate, they were grouped as a single reading. For example, the readings 'to act as a boy' and 'to behave as boys do' were grouped together;
(ii) the classification of readings pursued the objective of roughly the same degree of generalization of various readings. For example, 'to behave like a boy' and 'to speak like a boy' were classified as two different readings.

The classification was performed by two experts in meaning predictability theory (two of the co-authors of this text); first independently of each other; and subsequently, their classifications were compared and unified in the event of different views.

4.4 Sample of Respondents and Data Collection

4.4.1 *Sampling and the Structure of Respondents*

Our experimental research initially covered 748 participants from secondary schools and universities. The respondents from secondary grammar schools were from six institutions in Košice, Slovakia. All of them were attending their second year of secondary education, which means that they were about 16–17 years old. The level of English skills of this group of students is about B1, according to the Common European Framework of Reference for Languages.

The other group of respondents came from two universities in Košice. One part of them studied at the Faculty of Arts, Pavol Jozef Šafárik University. These students were selected from two study programs: British and American Studies and Translation and Interpretation. The other part was drawn from three faculties of the Technical University in Košice: the Faculty of Civil Engineering, the Faculty of Economics, and the Faculty of Fine Arts and Design.

The group of university undergraduates was homogeneous with respect to their age (21–22 years old) and their level of English (B2/C1, according to the Common European Framework of Reference for Languages).

The total of 748 respondents consisted of 391 secondary grammar school students and 357 university undergraduates. This number included 447 female and 301 male respondents. As for their structure, there were 240 secondary school females and 151 males, and 207 university females and 150 males. Their participation was voluntary and was implemented in class settings. The participants were allowed to end their participation at any time. No financial benefits were provided as compensation. As compensation, information about the TTCT testing as well as its results was offered to the students. Testing was conducted in accordance with the APA's ethical standards for research.

The testing was implemented in two rounds. In the first round, the respondents were tested on creative potential by means of the TTCT. In the second round, which took place about two months after the first, they were tested on word formation and word interpretation creativity. The time-gap between the TTCT and the other two tests had practical reasons. First, although further research is necessary for assessing the role of causality, the temporal order of tasks allows some preliminary reasoning regarding the hypothesized causal scheme (creative potential measured at one time point predicts creativity in word formation and word interpretation). Moreover, this time gap eliminates simultaneous measurement errors due to, for example, fatigue resulting from time-consuming testing. This strengthens the validity of the interpretation of test results. The other two reasons are of a pragmatic nature. It was necessary to evaluate the TTCT scores of each respondent as part of an agreement with the secondary schools and university undergraduates because the respondents wished to know their results before the second round of tests. Second, secondary school teachers could not afford to 'lose' two classes in succession.

In the second round of tests, the word formation and word interpretation creativity tests were held on the same day within one school hour (forty-five minutes) at each school. The time reserved for the two tests themselves was thirty minutes. Due to the time gap between the two tests, the number of respondents in the second round dropped to 632 for various reasons. Obviously, only those respondents who undertook all three tests were taken into consideration in our research. This means that our evaluation is based on 632 respondents, comprising 323 secondary grammar school students and 309 university undergraduates. This number is made up of 381 female and 251 male respondents. In terms of their structure, there were 198 secondary school females and 125 males, and 183 university females and 126 males.

4.4.2 Relevance of the Age-Based Groups

Research dedicated to the corroborating the role of age in creativity in general (and divergent thinking as cognitive creative potential in particular) is present and evolving (for overviews, see e.g. González Restrepo, Arias-Castro, & López-Fernández 2019; Kleibeuker et al. 2013; Runco 2014; Runco & Acar 2019). This line of research, however, mainly focuses on comparisons of the performances of young people and old adults, examining the decline in divergent thinking performance in older age (Palmiero, Di Giacomo, & Passafiume 2012; Ruth & Birren 1985) or, with the aim of comparing performances across the age spectrum of younger students, examining potential trends in early development (e.g. Chang et al. 2017). So, for example, a positive relation between creativity and age has been observed by Smith and Carlsson (1983), who found out that children become more creative as they grow older.

Unfortunately, studies that focus on the comparison of adults and adolescents are scarce, although the difference between adolescence and young adulthood could be crucial, considering both theoretical assumptions and emerging empirical evidence.

For instance, Kleibeuker et al. (2013) have found differences between adults (25–30 years) and adolescents (12–15 years) with regard to Originality in verbal divergent thinking. When the figural visuospatial task was used, differences were found regarding Fluency, but only between 15/16 year olds and 12/13 year olds. In contrast, Wu et al. (2005) found out that when university students and younger students were compared, the two groups did not differ in verbal tasks, but differences in figural and real-world problem creativity tasks were found among the two groups.

This is in line with what could be expected from the developmental point of view. As noted by Chang et al., from the point of view of the development of cognitive abilities, adolescence could be considered as "a key period" (2017: 113). For instance, when considering such factors as brain maturation and impulse control, in particular, the period of adolescence is related to differences in the limbic reward system and top–down control associated with the prefrontal cortex (Casey, Getz, & Galvan 2008). As summarized by Kleibeuker, de Dreu, and Crone (2016), associations between the prefrontal cortex and creative performance can be found across the empirical literature, and the developmental trajectory seems to be present but not linear in all cases. For instance, the study of Kleibeuker et al. (2013) indicated enhanced activation of the prefrontal cortex in adolescence, related to their exploration.

Considering the (a) scarcity of research examining the differences between adolescence and young adulthood and (b) potential differences concerning divergent thinking abilities in these two age groups, the present research is aimed at an exploration of this issue in relation to two samples – a group of secondary school students and a group of university undergraduates.

4.4.3 Relevance of Non-native Speakers

It follows from the outline of the theoretical principles of an onomasiological theory of complex word formation and complex word interpretation (meaning predictability) that both of these processes are, at their core, cognitive processes. As suggested in the integrated model of complex words (Figure 3.2), in word formation, they enable language speakers to produce a concept of a class of objects of extra-linguistic reality to be labelled by a linguistic sign and to determine an onomasiological structure that reflects the analysis of the class of objects at the conceptual level. Linguistic knowledge and experiences identify the final 'surface' form of a new complex word by means of the Morpheme-to-Seme-Assignment Principle (MSAP). In word interpretation, the 'surface' form of a new complex word is an input for cognitive processes that result in predicting potential meaning(s) of that word. In accordance with Štekauer (2005a) and (2009), it may be assumed that, given the role of the conceptual level analysis, extra-linguistic knowledge and experiences, and the onomasiological level as the conceptual basis for the naming process and the meaning-prediction process, there is no principled difference between native speakers and non-native speakers in their ability to form new complex words and interpret/predict the meaning of novel/potential complex words provided that (a) a non-native speaker has a standard command of a particular language (which implies that he/she 'knows' the basic rules and principles of word formation and understands the meanings of the morphemes constituting a particular complex word) and that (b) his/her world knowledge and experiences are comparable to those of a common native speaker. In the countries of Western civilization at least, the latter condition is met. What can make the difference is knowledge of the rules of word formation if we are referring to rule-governed creativity. The B1, B2, and C1 levels of our respondents appear to be sufficient levels of language skills that guarantee appropriate naming and interpreting results on a par with native speakers. Therefore, it is postulated that experimental results for native speakers should not considerably differ from those for non-native speakers. In this respect, our position differs from the view of Vizmuller-Zocco. While she admits that "no essential differences exist between native and non-native speakers regarding their ability to utilize this competence" in word formation (1985: 305), she maintains that differences are apparent at the level of production. As indicated earlier, these differences are predetermined by the language skills of non-native speakers. Our assumption has been confirmed in two experiments reported by Štekauer (2005a) and Körtvélyessy, Štekauer, and Zimmermann (2015).

The former experiment was focused on meaning prediction and brought similar findings: The differences in the PR values between the native and the non-native groups of respondents were negligible and confirmed the assumption of an equal meaning-prediction capacity of native and non-native speakers. This was borne out by the remarkable agreement between the native and non-native speakers in their ranking of the individual readings and by the mostly small differences in the respective PR values of the most predictable readings.

In the latter experiment, the authors examined the influence of a mother language on the process of forming new complex words in English. The experiment covered three typologically different mother languages: Slovak – inflectional, Bulgarian – in its nominal system more inflectional than English and less inflectional (fusional) than Slovak, and Hungarian – agglutinative. Like in the present experiment, forty respondents for each language were asked to propose Agent names in English within word formation tasks similar to the present ones. It was postulated that if the word formation system of the speaker's mother tongue affects the naming process, the results should be different. If it is the word formation system of the target language (English, in this case) that determines the formation of new complex words without any strong influence of the word formation system of one's mother tongue, the results are expected to be roughly the same.

The evaluation of the data showed that (i) the influence of the mother tongue upon the target language (the language in which complex words are coined) approaches zero, which means that the naming strategies are crucially determined by the word formation system of the target language and (ii) the native speakers of English did not differ in their naming strategies from the non-native respondents.

In addition, as found out by Gleitman and Gleitman (1970) in their experiment on interpretations of ternary structure compounds, there are considerable differences between language users of different levels of education. By implication, a proficient non-native speaker may be more 'skilful' in this respect than a native speaker of low language proficiency. This seems to be another reason supporting the assumption that if non-native speakers master a foreign language at a relatively high proficiency level (no matter how it may be defined), they are not disadvantaged in their capacity to form and/or interpret new complex words in their non-native language.

4.4.4 *High Cohort and Low Cohort*

For the sake of the evaluation, the respondents were divided into two contrasting quasi-experimental groups – the H-cohort and the L-cohort – on the basis of their TTCT results. More specifically, the continuous TTCT subscores were dichotomized into two groups by identifying the respondents with the lowest 25 per cent values and the highest 25 per cent values within every creativity indicator and subscore. This was done via the quartile split procedure.

As a first step, the answers of all participants were rated according to the official test manual (Jurčová & Szobiová 2008). Subsequently, scores for Originality, Elaboration, Fluency, Flexibility, and Creative Strengths were computed across all three tasks. This was also done according to the manual. One additional score, the Composite Score, was computed according to Runco et al. (2010). This score is calculated by converting all subscores into *z*-scores and then adding them up into a single composite index. The *z*-score, also known as the standard score, represents the number of standard deviations a data point is away from the mean. The *z*-score is calculated as a score minus the mean score in a sample divided by the standard deviation. The reason behind this standardization is to provide a common scale across all scores and to enable us to sum them into one summary score.

Next, as some respondents were more original, fluent, flexible, or elaborative than others, the identification of extreme/contrasting groups was possible. To summarize a specific variable, the mean and the standard deviations can be identified at a more general sample level. At the individual level of analysis, an individual score for every participant is available. Based on this information, cumulative percentages could be used to divide the participants into two extreme groups – the low and high cohorts. More specifically, for the sake of the identification of the two cohorts for all indicators and subscores, the individual values of participants were ordered from lowest to highest, and the cumulative percentage for each respondent was identified. Then, based on the cumulative percentage, four quartiles were identified so that in every subgroup, approximately 25 per cent of participants could be found. Specifically, approximately 25 per cent of respondents were placed in a group with the lowest scores; 25 per cent in a group with relatively low scores (under 50 per cent) but higher than the first group; 25 per cent in a group with scores over 50 per cent but still lower than best 25 per cent; and, finally, 25 per cent in a group with the highest scores. The less extreme quartiles (the second and the third) were omitted from the subsequent analysis, and the most extreme quartiles (the first and the fourth) were preserved, thus establishing the contrasting high and low cohorts. Accordingly, the L-cohort and the H-cohort were created for every TTCT indicator – Originality, Elaboration, Fluency, and

Flexibility – as well as for the additional subscores – Creative Strengths and Composite Score.

Note that dichotomizing the data into two extreme groups was a necessary approach for the computation of some types of analysis dedicated to linguistic creativity in word formation and word interpretation (e.g. Predictability Rate and the Objectified Predictability Rate; see Sections 3.2.2.1 and 3.2.2.2 for further information). Thus, due to the attempt to provide a uniform approach across the whole book, this solution was deemed to be preferable. However, as the dichotomizing approach inherently brings potential limitations, such as lower statistical power, we decided to provide a sensitivity analysis wherever it was appropriate to assess the robustness of the results and interpretations. In the sensitivity analysis, instead of dividing participants into two contrasting groups and omitting participants without extreme scores, all participants were used and all TTCT scores were analyzed in their continuous form. In particular, instead of analyzing differences among the L-cohort and the H-cohort, the pattern of relations across the variables was examined and compared with the results where the extreme group approach was used.

4.5 Research Hypotheses

Our research concentrates on the examination of the following hypotheses.

General Hypothesis

In general, owing to the higher creative potential in the TTCT test, the H-cohort will be able to comply with the word formation and word interpretation tasks better than the L-cohort. This should comply with the data obtained in the sensitivity analysis.

Hypothesis 1

Referring to Körtvélyessy (2010), it is hypothesized that while university undergraduates will prefer to form new complex words with higher semantic transparency, the tendency towards economy of expression will be stronger in the younger group of respondents. This hypothesis will be evaluated in relation to

(i) the two age-based groups of respondents;
(ii) the H-cohort and the L-cohort specified for each creativity indicator and subscore in both age groups; and
(iii) male and female respondents.

A general version of this hypothesis suggests that word formation strategies change with increasing age (see also, for example, Berko-Gleason 1958; Štekauer et al. 2005).

Hypothesis 2

The percentage of failed/zero answers in the word formation test will be lower in the H-cohort than in the L-cohort owing to the much higher scores of the H-cohort in the TTCT test. By implication, word formation creativity is higher in the H-cohort.

Hypothesis 3

The values of the Objectified Predictability Rate (OPR) in the individual creativity indicators/subscores in the L-cohort should be higher than those in the H-cohort. This hypothesis is based on the idea that language speakers with a lower creative potential (as determined by the TTCT) prefer more common interpretations (primarily, the most acceptable, most predictable reading) while the H-cohort members are also able to come up with (thanks to their higher creative potential) less predictable, more peripheral, and more 'creative' interpretations. This difference is projected onto tougher competition between the predictability rates of the readings proposed by the H-cohort which, consequently, is reflected in the lower OPR values of the H-cohort (Štekauer 2005a).

Hypothesis 4

The average number of readings proposed by the H-cohort members will be higher than that proposed by the L-cohort members owing to the higher creativity potential identified by the TTCT. This hypothesis has two parts:

Hypothesis 4A is primarily relevant to the creativity indicators Fluency and Elaboration, according to which the H-cohort, identified within the TTCT, is characterized by a higher number of relevant answers (Fluency) or higher number of details (Elaboration) than the L-cohort. A substantial difference in the TTCT scores between the two cohorts should be projected onto a substantial difference in the interpretation creativity test between the two cohorts.

Hypothesis 4B postulates that the H-cohort achieves better results in all the other creativity indicators/subscores in the interpretation test than the L-cohort, even if the differences between the two cohorts can vary owing to unequal creativity features represented by the individual creativity indicators.

Hypothesis 5

This hypothesis derives from the use of the concept of hapax legomena as used in computing productivity in word formation (see Section 3.2.2.4), according to which

(*cont.*)

a hapax legomenon in a large corpus is the evidence for the productive use of a particular word formation rule since novelty indicates creativity, and this concept is also relevant to the interpretation of new/potential complex words. A reading proposed by a single member of a cohort may indicate creativity when opposed to the readings proposed by a large number of a cohort's members. Nevertheless, the single occurrence of a particular reading can reflect two different situations, and therefore, Hypothesis 5 has two parts:

Hypothesis 5A postulates that a reading proposed by a single member of the L-cohort (hapax legomenon) is proposed by more than a single member of the H-cohort. This hypothesis is based on the postulate that a hapax legomenon of the L-cohort is proposed by more than one member of the H-cohort owing to their higher creative potential.

Hypothesis 5B postulates that the H-cohort proposes more hapax legomena readings that correspond to zero occurrences of those readings in the L-cohort than vice versa. This hypothesis is based on the postulate that a cohort with a higher creative potential is able to propose more 'peripheral' readings of low meaning predictability that will not appear in the L-cohort.

Both Hypotheses 5A and 5B are primarily relevant to the creativity indicator Originality, which concerns the uniqueness of answers. In other words, less frequent answers are valued more in terms of the creativity indicator Originality. Since the H-cohort achieved much higher scores in this creativity indicator in the TTCT than the L-cohort, it is hypothesized that this result will be projected onto the hapax legomenon results in the interpretation creativity test. This postulate is in accordance with the assumption that creativity is related to uniqueness or statistical rarity (Abraham 2016: 610).

Hypothesis 6

The results of the H-cohort and the L-cohort in word formation creativity will not coincide with their results in interpretation creativity. This hypothesis is based on the conception of microdomains and task specificity (Baer 2020; Baer & Kaufman 2005), the implications of which for our research mean that the tasks of the word formation test and the word interpretation test represent two different microdomains, two different specific tasks.

No hypothesis is proposed for two sociolinguistic aspects of our research – the age-based and the gender-based differences. The age-based hypothesis is precluded by (i) the non-existence of any research results in the field under investigation in this monograph and (ii) a number of factors that influence age-based creativity, such as knowledge and experience, thinking styles, language ability, and motivation (Wu et al. 2005: 325). The available data are rather ambiguous. For instance, as pointed out by Runco (1996), experiences may hinder creativity, because experienced individuals may act on the basis of automated and therefore rigid skills, this being an obstacle to creativity. For illustration, Wu et al. (2005) compared the creativity of 12-year-old pupils and university undergraduates by means of three different tasks. One of the tasks, the verbal task, required the participants to name as many unusual uses for a common object as possible. As assumed by the authors of that experiment, the knowledge and experience of the university students were not expected to enhance creative solutions to this task. On the contrary, it was expected that they would provide less unusual uses of a common object because they were more familiar with the normal functions of objects (Wu et al. 2005: 323).

This view contradicts the assumption of Weisberg (1999), who maintains that knowledge is related to creativity, and Albert, who notes that "an individual's knowledge of self and particular aspects of his or her world is the ultimate medium of creative behavior, for knowledge determines decisions as much as opportunities" (1990: 19).

All this contributes to uncertainty in approaching the question of the influence of age upon creative performance in word formation and word interpretation and prevents us from formulating a sound hypothesis.

There is no hypothesis for gender differences in word formation creativity or interpretation creativity either because "there is a consistent lack of gender differences both in creativity test scores and in the creative accomplishments of boys and girls" (Baer & Kaufman 2008: 75) and because "[d]espite the intuitive appeal of the idea that females are more creative at verbal and artistic domains whereas males are more creative at mechanical and scientific domains, there is little empirical evidence to support such notions of domain-general advantages as a function of gender" (Abraham 2016: 611).

5 Research

This chapter analyzes the data obtained in the word formation and word interpretation tests in relation to the results of the Torrance Test of Creative Thinking (TTCT). The analysis covers several levels:

(i) word formation creativity and word interpretation creativity;
(ii) two age-based groups of respondents, that is, secondary school students and university undergraduates;
(iii) separate evaluations with regard to the individual creativity indicators and subscores in order to find out whether they boost word formation and word interpretation creativity and, if so, which of them does so; this question is examined with regard to
  (a) the low cohort (L-cohort) and the high cohort (H-cohort) that are identified separately for each creativity indicator/subscore by the TTCT as well as with regard to all respondents wherever applicable;
  (b) the individual evaluation parameters, that is, the naming strategies, reflected in the preference for economy of expression or semantic transparency, and the number of failed answers in the word formation test; the Predictability Rate (PR), the Objectified Predictability Rate (OPR); the average number of readings proposed by a cohort member; and hapax legomena in the interpretation test; and
  (c) the individual experimental words.
(iv) the two age groups of respondents in terms of each of the aforementioned criteria; and
(v) the male and the female groups of respondents for each of the aforementioned criteria.

5.1 Creativity and Word Formation

This section first summarizes the data in the form of tables, and then the data are analyzed and commented on with regard to the two age groups covered in this experiment and with regard to the individual creativity indicators/ subscores, each of which is examined by comparing the two creativity cohorts as well as all respondents wherever applicable. The analysis is based on the parameters of semantic transparency and economy of expression; specifically, on the scales of transparency and economy presented in Section 3.1.2 and on the percentage of failed answers as an indicator of low creative performance. We start with secondary school students (Section 5.1.1) and then proceed to university undergraduates (Section 5.1.2).

5.1.1 Secondary School Students

5.1.1.1 Data Analysis

The data will be analyzed in terms of two criteria. The first concerns Hypothesis 2, according to which the percentage of failed answers (see Section 4.2 for their delimitation) in the word formation test in the H-cohort should be lower than that in the L-cohort. It is based on the postulate that each word formation act is a creative act. By implication, it may be expected that those language users who have a higher creative potential, expressed by high values of the individual TTCT indicators/subscores, can cope with the naming tasks better than language users with low TTCT scores. This should be reflected in a lower percentage of failures of the H-cohort in the individual word formation tasks.

The second evaluation criterion concerns the expected differences between the H-cohort and the L-cohort in preferring semantic transparency and economy of expression in forming new complex words. This criterion is not captured by any hypothesis because it is difficult to predict the tendency in one or other direction. The two criteria will be evaluated for each indicator/subscore by comparing the results of both cohorts. We start with the presentation of the experimental data in the form of tables by individual creativity indicators/subscores and by cohort (Tables 5.1 and 5.2). This will be followed by a discussion and summary of our findings.

Failed Answer Criterion

Originality The data show that the percentage of respondents who failed to answer the experimental tasks is almost identical in the two cohorts (19% vs. 20%), with a slightly higher percentage of failures in the L-cohort in the cognitively most demanding Task 3 that is based on drawings, that is, on the highest number of features that might motivate the formation of a new word. Task 1, which is based on making a selection from a number of options, and Task 2, which relies on verbal descriptions, favour (surprisingly) the L-cohort.

The Originality indicator does not show any substantial differences in the preferences for semantic transparency or economy between the two cohorts, and, therefore, it does not seem to influence the formation of new words.

Table 5.1. *Low Originality (data are given in %; 76 respondents)*

Task/transparency scale	7	6	5	4	3	2	1	Fail answers (F) (no.)	F (%)
Task 1									
1	3	0	41	3	52	1	0	1	
2	57	0	43	0	0	0	0	4	
3	76	1	6	0	0	17	0	5	
∑ 1	**45**	**0**	**30**	**1**	**18**	**6**	**0**	**10**	**4**
Task 2									
1	50	1	0	0	0	49	0	2	
2	42	2	17	2	0	33	4	28	
3	6	0	2	0	0	90	2	27	
∑ 2	**35**	**1**	**5**	**1**	**0**	**56**	**2**	**57**	**33**
Task 3									
1	67	0	13	0	0	20	0	30	
2	65	0	10	0	0	25	0	13	
3	67	0	9	0	0	24	0	22	
∑ 3	**66**	**0**	**11**	**0**	**0**	**23**	**0**	**65**	**29**
∑ 1–3	**48**	**1**	**16**	**1**	**7**	**26**	**1**	**132**	**19**

Table 5.2. *High Originality (data are given in %; 79 respondents)*

Task/transparency scale	7	6	5	4	3	2	1	F (no.)	F (%)
Task 1									
1	9	3	42	0	41	5	0	3	
2	44	0	54	0	0	2	0	9	
3	74	1	13	0	0	11	1	7	
∑ 1	**42**	**2**	**36**	**0**	**14**	**6**	**0**	**19**	**8**
Task 2									
1	38	0	3	0	0	59	0	5	
2	52	2	8	0	0	38	0	31	
3	8	2	2	0	0	88	0	28	
∑ 2	**33**	**1**	**4**	**0**	**0**	**62**	**0**	**64**	**27**
Task 3									
1	56	0	12	2	0	30	0	22	
2	63	0	4	0	0	33	0	15	
3	68	0	5	2	2	23	0	23	
∑ 3	**62**	**0**	**7**	**1**	**1**	**29**	**0**	**60**	**25**
∑ 1–3	**45**	**1**	**18**	**0**	**6**	**30**	**0**	143	**20**

Table 5.3. *Low Elaboration (data are given in %; 84 respondents)*

Task/transparency scale	7	6	5	4	3	2	1	F (no.)	F (%)
Task 1									
1	6	0	41	1	47	5	0	1	
2	49	3	48	0	0	0	0	7	
3	75	1	4	0	0	19	1	6	
∑ 1	**43**	**1**	**32**	**0**	**16**	**8**	**0**	**14**	**6**
Task 2									
1	40	0	2	0	0	58	0	6	
2	41	6	20	0	0	30	3	30	
3	0	2	2	0	0	94	2	33	
∑ 2	**29**	**2**	**7**	**0**	**0**	**60**	**2**	**69**	**27**
Task 3									
1	53	2	19	0	0	26	0	26	
2	68	0	8	0	0	22	2	12	
3	57	2	14	3	0	22	2	26	
∑ 3	**60**	**1**	**13**	**1**	**0**	**24**	**1**	**64**	**25**
∑ 1–3	**44**	**2**	**19**	**0**	**6**	**28**	**1**	**147**	**19**

The H-cohort shows a slightly higher preference for a more economical naming strategy, which follows from the lower percentage of transparency degree 7 (Onomasiological Type 1 (OT1)) (partly compensated by a higher percentage of transparency degree 5 (OT2)) and a higher share of the economical OT3 (transparency degree 2). This result can be observed in all three tasks.

Elaboration As in the case of Originality, the Elaboration indicator manifests similar total percentages of failures (19% vs. 18%) in the L-cohort and the H-cohort (Tables 5.3 and 5.4). This time, the percentage of failed answers in the H-cohort is lower in Task 2 as well as in Task 3; however, the differences are not substantial (5% for Task 2 and 2% for Task 3).

The results of the two cohorts in terms of semantic transparency are very similar, too. The figure of 3% in favour of the H-cohort in the case of OT1 (transparency degree 7) is partly compensated by the same difference in favour of the L-cohort in the case of OT2 (transparency degree 5). The percentages of OT3 (transparency degree 2) are almost identical.

Flexibility The data on failed answers are slightly in favour of the H-cohort, thanks to Tasks 2 and 3. In each of them, their percentage is lower in the H-cohort by 2% (Tables 5.5 and 5.6).

Table 5.4. *High Elaboration (data are given in %; 77 respondents)*

Task/transparency scale	7	6	5	4	3	2	1	F (no.)	F (%)
Task 1									
1	5	2	37	0	53	3	0	4	
2	42	1.5	55	1.5	0	0	0	6	
3	78	1	9	0	0	12	0	9	
∑ 1	**41**	**1**	**34**	**1**	**18**	**5**	**0**	**19**	**8**
Task 2									
1	42	0	1	0	0	57	0	5	
2	57	8	8	1	0	25	1	24	
3	7	3	5	0	0	85	0	22	
∑ 2	**36**	**3**	**4**	**0.5**	**0**	**56**	**0.5**	**51**	**22**
Task 3									
1	60	2	9	2	0	27	0	24	
2	65	1	3	0	0	31	0	12	
3	71	2	7	2	0	18	0	18	
∑ 3	**66**	**2**	**6**	**1**	**0**	**25**	**0**	**54**	**23**
∑ 1–3	**47**	**2**	**16**	**1**	**7**	**27**	**0**	**124**	**18**

Table 5.5. *Low Flexibility (data are given in %; 73 respondents)*

Task/transparency scale	7	6	5	4	3	2	1	F (no.)	F (%)
Task 1									
1	3	0	35	4	54	4	0	1	
2	41	1	58	0	0	0	0	7	
3	77	3	10	0	0	10	0	12	
∑ 1	**38**	**1**	**35**	**1**	**20**	**5**	**0**	**20**	**9**
Task 2									
1	43	3	3	0	0	51	0	6	
2	45	4	24	4	0	22	1	22	
3	4	0	4	0	0	90	2	24	
∑ 2	**32**	**2**	**10**	**1**	**0**	**54**	**1**	**52**	**24**
Task 3									
1	46	2	13	2	0	37	0	27	
2	61	0	8	0	0	31	0	19	
3	58	0	13	4	0	23	2	21	
∑ 3	**55**	**1**	**11**	**2**	**0**	**30**	**1**	**67**	**31**
∑ 1–3	**41**	**1.5**	**20**	**1.5**	**8**	**28**	**0**	**139**	**21**

Table 5.6. *High Flexibility (data are given in %; 72 respondents)*

Task/transparency scale	7	6	5	4	3	2	1	F (no.)	F (%)
Task 1									
1	8	3	48	1.5	38	1.5	0	1	
2	50	0	50	0	0	0	0	6	
3	71	1	5	0	0	23	0	6	
∑ 1	**42**	**2**	**34**	**1**	**13**	**8**	**0**	**13**	**6**
Task 2									
1	29	0	2	0	0	69	0	4	
2	44	3	13	2	0	38	0	24	
3	4	0	6	0	2	88	0	20	
∑ 2	**26**	**1**	**6**	**0.5**	**0.5**	**66**	**0**	**48**	**22**
Task 3									
1	46	2	16	2	0	34	0	22	
2	51	3	11	0	0	35	0	15	
3	61	0	9	0	2	28	0	26	
∑ 3	**52**	**2**	**12**	**0.5**	**0.5**	**33**	**0**	**63**	**29**
∑ 1–3	**40**	**1**	**19**	**0**	**6**	**34**	**0**	124	**19**

The share of the most transparent OTs is almost identical. The only more substantial difference between the two cohorts concerns the use of OT3 (transparency degree 2), which suggests the H-cohort's tendency towards the use of a more economical word formation strategy in comparison to the L-cohort as far as the Flexibility indicator is concerned. This is especially manifested in Task 2 (the share of OT3 in Task 2 in the H-cohort is higher by as much as 12% than in the L-cohort). On the other hand, the same Task 2 shows a much higher preference of the L-cohort for OT1 (by 6%) as well as for OT2 (by 4%).

Fluency The data on the failures in the Fluency indicator run against Hypothesis 2 because the percentage of failed answers is higher in the H-cohort, especially in Task 2, where the difference is 8% (Tables 5.7 and 5.8). The transparency criterion provides us with almost identical results, with slightly higher total percentages for the more transparent OTs (OT1 and OT2) in Tasks 2 and 3.

Creative Strengths Creative Strengths also features a slightly higher percentage of failed answers in the H-cohort (by 2%), mainly due to Task 2 (a 6% difference) (Tables 5.9 and 5.10).

Table 5.7. *Low Fluency (data are given in %; 79 respondents)*

Task/transparency scale	7	6	5	4	3	2	1	F (no.)	F (%)
Task 1									
1	3	1	36	4	53	3	0	2	
2	48	1.5	49	0	0	1.5	0	8	
3	85	2	4	0	0	9	0	12	
∑ 1	**43**	**1.5**	**31**	**1.5**	**19**	**4**	**0**	22	**9**
Task 2									
1	42	3	0	0	0	55	0	5	
2	42	5	22	4	0	25	2	24	
3	4	4	4	0	0	87	1	25	
∑ 2	**31**	**4**	**8**	**0.5**	**0**	**56**	**0.5**	54	**23**
Task 3									
1	47	2	14	2	0	35	0	28	
2	67	0	10	0	0	21	2	18	
3	61	0	14	2	0	21	2	22	
∑ 3	**59**	**1**	**13**	**1**	**0**	**25**	**1**	68	**29**
∑ 1–3	**44**	**2**	**18**	**1**	**7**	**27**	**1**	144	**20**

Table 5.8. *High Fluency (data are given in %; 83 respondents)*

Task/transparency scale	7	6	5	4	3	2	1	F (no.)	F (%)
Task 1									
1	6	3	45	1	40	5	0	3	
2	46	0	53	1	0	0	0	13	
3	72	1	13	0	0	11	3	11	
∑ 1	**40**	**1**	**37**	**1**	**14**	**6**	**1**	**27**	**11**
Task 2									
1	38	0	3	0	0	59	0	9	
2	51	0	16	0	0	33	0	32	
3	6	0	2	0	2	90	0	35	
∑ 2	**33**	**0**	**6**	**0**	**1**	**60**	**0**	**76**	**31**
Task 3									
1	55	0	13	2	0	30	0	27	
2	61	3	10	0	0	26	0	21	
3	70	2	5	0	2	21	0	26	
∑ 3	**62**	**2**	**9**	**0.5**	**0.5**	**26**	**0**	74	**30**
∑ 1–3	**45**	**1**	**19**	**1**	**6**	**28**	**0**	**177**	**24**

Table 5.9. *Low Creative Strengths (data are given in %; 70 respondents)*

Task/transparency scale	7	6	5	4	3	2	1	F (no.)	F (%)
Task 1									
1	1.5	1.5	38	0	59	0	0	2	
2	44	3	53	0	0	0	0	4	
3	72	2	6	0	0	20	0	5	
∑ 1	**39**	**1**	**33**	**0**	**20**	**7**	**0**	**11**	**5**
Task 2									
1	36	0	3	0	0	61	0	3	
2	44	6	15	0	0	33	2	22	
3	2	0	5	0	0	91	2	25	
∑ 2	**29**	**2**	**7**	**0**	**0**	**61**	**1**	**50**	**24**
Task 3									
1	42	2	28	0	0	28	0	27	
2	53	0	14	0	0	32	1	13	
3	60	0	13	0	0	26	1	23	
∑ 3	**52**	**1**	**18**	**0**	**0**	**28**	**1**	**63**	**30**
∑ 1–3	**39**	**2**	**20**	**0**	**8**	**30**	**1**	124	**20**

Table 5.10. *High Creative Strengths (data are given in %; 84 respondents)*

Task/transparency scale	7	6	5	4	3	2	1	F (no.)	F (%)
Task 1									
1	3	0	48	1	42	6	0	4	
2	41	0	56	1.5	0	1.5	0	9	
3	74	0	12	0	0	13	1	7	
∑ 1	**39**	**0**	**38**	**1**	**15**	**7**	**0**	**20**	**8**
Task 2									
1	41	0	3	0	0	56	0	6	
2	52	3	12	0	0	33	0	42	
3	7	2	5	0	2	84	0	28	
∑ 2	**33**	**1**	**6**	**0**	**0**	**60**	**0**	**76**	**30**
Task 3									
1	59	0	19	2	0	20	0	30	
2	65	0	7	0	0	28	0	16	
3	72	1.5	7	1.5	0	18	0	23	
∑ 3	**66**	**1**	**10**	**1**	**0**	**22**	**0**	**69**	**27**
∑ 1–3	**45**	**1**	**20**	**1**	**6**	**27**	**0**	**165**	**22**

Table 5.11. *Low Composite Score (data are given in %; 80 respondents)*

Task/transparency scale	7	6	5	4	3	2	1	F (no.)	F (%)
Task 1									
1	4	1	35	4	53	3	0	1	
2	52	1	47	0	0	0	0	5	
3	75	3	4	0	0	18	0	8	
∑ 1	**42**	**2**	**29**	**1**	**19**	**7**	**0**	**14**	**6**
Task 2									
1	41	3	0	0	0	56	0	5	
2	44	3	21	3	0	26	3	22	
3	2	0	2	0	0	94	2	24	
∑ 2	**30**	**2**	**7**	**1**	**0**	**58**	**2**	**51**	**21**
Task 3									
1	46	0	19	0	0	35	0	28	
2	64	0	9	0	0	25	2	16	
3	59	0	14	1.5	0	24	1.5	22	
∑ 3	**57**	**0**	**14**	**1**	**0**	**27**	**1**	**66**	**28**
∑ 1–3	**43**	**2**	**17**	**1**	**7**	**29**	**1**	**131**	**18**

In this subscore, however, the percentage of the most transparent OT is higher in the H-cohort by 6%. This results primarily from Task 3, where the difference between the two cohorts is as high as 14%. On the other hand, the percentage of the economical OT3 is lower in this cohort by 3%, also mainly due to Task 3 (a 6% difference).

Composite Score The results for the Composite Score do not deviate from the preceding creativity indicators. A slightly higher percentage of failed answers in the H-cohort (by 3%) is primarily due to Task 2; whereas in Task 3 (a 7% difference), it is the H-cohort that has a better result (Tables 5.11 and 5.12).

With almost all the other data being very similar or identical, the H-cohort shows a higher percentage of the most transparent OT1 (a 3% difference), mainly thanks to a 7% difference in Task 3.

Discussion

The data for the secondary school students provide ambiguous results in view of Hypothesis 2. This is evident from Table 5.13.

The data in Table 5.13 point out two factors that affect the failed answer percentages. The first is the nature of the word formation task, that is, task specificity, and the second is the creativity indicator/subscore.

Table 5.12. *High Composite Score (data are given in %; 81 respondents)*

Task/transparency scale	7	6	5	4	3	2	1	F (no.)	F (%)
Task 1									
1	7	2	43	1	41	3	3	2	
2	49	0	50	1	0	0	0	9	
3	73	1	9	0	0	16	1	11	
∑ 1	**42**	**1**	**34**	**1**	**15**	**6**	**1**	**22**	**9**
Task 2									
1	38	0	3	0	0	59	0	7	
2	55	4	8	2	0	31	0	32	
3	6	0	6	0	1	87	0	29	
∑ 2	**33**	**1**	**5**	**1**	**1**	**59**	**0**	**68**	**28**
Task 3									
1	55	0	12	2	0	31	0	23	
2	69	3	5	0	1	22	0	17	
3	69	0	5	0	2	24	0	23	
∑ 3	**64**	**1**	**7**	**1**	**1**	**26**	**0**	**63**	**26**
∑ 1–3	**46**	**1**	**17**	**1**	**6**	**29**	**0**	**153**	**21**

If we go by tasks, contrary to our expectations specified in Hypothesis 2, the number of failed answers in Tasks 1 and 2, taken as a whole, is smaller in the L-cohort than in the H-cohort. Task 3 apparently suited the H-cohort better.

Taking the data by creativity indicators/subscores, *Flexibility* is the only indicator that shows a smaller percentage of failed answers in Task 1 in the H-cohort. The achievements of the L-cohort are better in Task 2 in four out of the six indicators. In this case, the differences are large, especially for Fluency, Creative Strengths, and Composite Score. *Elaboration* is the only indicator that gives strong support to Hypothesis 2 in Task 2. The H-cohort achieved better results in Task 3 in five out of the six indicators/subscores, the only exception being Flexibility, that is, the indicator that gives support to Hypothesis 2 in Task 1. While the differences between the two cohorts are not big in Task 3, the strongest support to Hypothesis 2 comes from *Originality*.

Given the evaluation criterion, that is, the number of failed answers, the basic creativity indicator should be Fluency as it takes into consideration the number of relevant answers in the TTCT. The data for this creativity indicator evidently run counter to Hypothesis 2 in all three tasks, most evidently in Task 2. While the percentage of the H-cohort is lower in Task 3, the difference of a mere 1% cannot be considered meaningful.

The differences in the achievements of the two cohorts in individual tasks may, intuitively, be explained by the different natures of these tasks that

Table 5.13. *Comparison of the total percentages of failed answers (lower percentage values are given in bold)*

	Task 1		Task 2		Task 3		Total (Tasks 1–3)	
	L-cohort	H-cohort	L-cohort	H-cohort	L-cohort	H-cohort	L-cohort	H-cohort
Originality	**4**	8	**25**	27	29	**25**	**19**	20
Elaboration	**6**	8	27	**22**	25	**23**	19	**18**
Flexibility	9	**6**	24	**22**	31	**29**	21	**19**
Fluency	**9**	11	**23**	31	**29**	30	**20**	24
Creative Strengths	**5**	8	**24**	30	30	**27**	**20**	22
Composite Score	**6**	9	**21**	28	28	**26**	**18**	21

impose different demands on the creative thinking of language users. As noted earlier, Task 1 does not impose high demands on word formation creativity because a respondent chooses from a limited list of options. This fact could obliterate the differences in the creative potential of the respondents in two different creativity cohorts. The verbal description in Task 2 restricts the motivation for a new complex word to what is expressly and explicitly verbalized and, as such, it, in a way, guides the coiner in the naming act. Contrary to this, the number of motivating details in drawings in Task 3 is much higher. The drawing-based Task 3 offers a larger number of motivating elements underlying the naming act and, therefore, requires a much deeper and more subtle analysis of the named situation by a language user. This is where word formation creativity can be manifested most clearly and where the lack of creativity may function as a limiting factor in word formation. On the other hand, these differences may be partly relativized by the fact that the respondents were offered the option 'other' in Task 1 and could employ their visual imagination in Task 2 as well.

To sum up, if we take the criterion of failed answers as an indicator of word formation creativity in general, the naming tasks that, according to the previous considerations, impose lower demands on word formation creativity seem to favour the L-cohort more, while Task 3, which is most demanding in terms of word formation creativity, slightly favours language speakers with higher TTCT scores, that is, the H-cohort (even if the differences in percentages are small).

The conclusion that can be drawn from the previous discussion is that *the creative potential of the secondary school respondents does not seem to affect their word formation creativity. This finding runs against Hypothesis 2.*

Semantic Transparency versus Economy of Expression

What are the results with regard to the other criterion – the competition between semantic transparency and economy of expression?

First and foremost, each naming task is dominated by (a maximum of) two onomasiological types, with all the other types playing a peripheral role or even no role at all. Very rarely, there is a balanced share of two major onomasiological types. One of them is usually evidently more frequent. Interestingly, they are usually on the opposite sides of the transparency scale, thus evidently manifesting the competition between transparency and economy. In the vast majority of cases, it is the competition between the 'non-economical', most transparent OT1 (transparency degree 7) and the more economical OT3 (transparency degree 2). A less conspicuous role is played in some tasks by OT2 (transparency degree 5).

In general, OT1 is the most frequently employed type in both cohorts. As can be seen from Table 5.14, its use is found with slightly higher frequency in the L-cohort.

Table 5.14. *Comparison of the L-cohort and the H-cohort with regard to the use of OT1 (transparency degree 7) (the higher percentage values are given in bold)*

	Task 1		Task 2		Task 3		Total (Tasks 1–3)	
	L-cohort	H-cohort	L-cohort	H-cohort	L-cohort	H-cohort	L-cohort	H-cohort
Originality	**45**	42	**35**	33	**66**	62	**48**	45
Elaboration	**43**	41	29	**36**	60	**66**	44	**47**
Flexibility	38	**42**	**32**	26	**55**	52	**41**	40
Fluency	**43**	40	31	**33**	59	**62**	44	**45**
Creative Strengths	39	39	29	**33**	52	**66**	39	**45**
Composite Score	42	42	30	**33**	57	**64**	43	**46**

As in the case of failed answers, the results are, no doubt, affected by the nature of the naming task and vary by individual creativity indicators/subscores. While in general the differences in the use of OT1 in the two cohorts are rather small, the data for Task 1 show a slight preference of the L-cohort to use a more transparent onomasiological type; in the other two tasks, it is the H-cohort that tends to use OT1 more frequently. The same is true of the total percentages for all three tasks.

The role of creativity indicators/subscores varies by task. In Task 1, *Flexibility* is the only indicator that supports the higher semantic transparency of coinages in the H-cohort. In Tasks 2 and 3, the same indicator evidently supports semantic transparency in the L-cohort.

There are three indicators that evidently support the employment of a more transparent naming strategy of the H-cohort in Tasks 2 and 3. They are *Elaboration*, *Creative Strengths*, and *Composite Score*. These could be completed by Fluency, but the differences in this indicator are rather small. The other two indicators, Originality and Flexibility, deviate from this kind of effect. The cumulative data are parallel to those for Tasks 2 and 3. The most evident tendency towards the higher semantic transparency of coinages produced by the H-cohort can be observed for the *Creative Strengths* subscore.

Table 5.14 can be related to Table 5.15, which shows the data on the employment of a more economical OT3.

There are no big differences between the two cohorts in the use of the more economical OT3 either, and, with one exception, the maximum difference does not exceed 6%. In both Tasks 2 and 3, the use of OT3 is supported by four creativity indicators, even though they are not completely identical. In any case, the most striking difference in favour of the H-cohort is manifested in Flexibility (12%) and Originality (6%) for Task 2 and Originality (6%) for Task 3. The opposite effect (with a 6% difference) can be identified for Creative Strengths in Task 3. In sum, taking into consideration the total percentages for all three tasks, it may be concluded that the creativity indicators *Flexibility* and *Originality* appear to support the use of the economical OT3 more in the H-cohort than in the L-cohort. This is in accordance with the data in Table 5.13, where these two indicators seem to support higher semantic transparency in the L-cohort. The data also correspond with those on *Creative Strengths*, however, in an opposite sense: while this indicator tends to support the higher semantic transparency of new coinages in the H-cohort, it, at the same time, features a higher share of a more economical OT3 in the L-cohort.

While it was pointed out that almost every naming task is dominated by two onomasiological types on opposite sides of the semantic transparency scale and that these two types are, in the majority of cases, OT1 and OT3, Task 2.3 is an exception owing to the almost exclusive use of OT3 – its share of all

Table 5.15. *Comparison of the percentages of OT3 (transparency degree 2)*

	Task 1		Task 2		Task 3		Total (Tasks 1–3)	
	L-cohort	H-cohort	L-cohort	H-cohort	L-cohort	H-cohort	L-cohort	H-cohort
Originality	6	6	56	**62**	23	**29**	26	**30**
Elaboration	**8**	5	**60**	56	24	**25**	**28**	27
Flexibility	5	**8**	54	**66**	30	**33**	28	**34**
Fluency	4	**6**	56	**60**	25	**26**	27	**28**
Creative Strengths	7	7	**61**	60	**28**	22	**30**	27
Composite Score	**7**	6	58	**59**	**27**	26	29	29

complex words produced in this task is around 90%. The explanation may be sought for in the fact that the object to be named is not an Agent. Instead, the respondents were asked to give a name to a Patient. Let us recall Task 2.3: "Suppose that a woman has a clone made of herself. Then suppose that a man has a clone made of himself. Now suppose that the two clones marry each other and have a child. What would you call the child?"

Rather than being on an action performed by a person, the emphasis is on the feature of the named object. Therefore, the determined mark of the onomasiological structure does not necessarily have to be represented by a morpheme. This is a completely different situation from Tasks 2.1 and 2.2, which are aimed at Agents. In these two tasks, the share of OT1 is much higher than in Task 2.3. This is especially true of Task 2.2: "Suppose that aliens were about to land on Earth for the first time. What would you call a person who was supposed to meet them as a representative of the human race?" Here, the emphasis on the act of representing the human race calls for an explicit expression of the Actional constituent of the onomasiological structure (although not absolutely, which follows from around 30% share of OT3 across the individual creativity indicators/subscores in both cohorts). Contrary to Task 2.2 in which OT1 dominates in all cases, Task 2.1 shows an opposite proportion of OT1 and OT3 with roughly similar percentage differences. This task – "What would you call someone who does research about spiders' webs?" – is a nice example of a competition between two different naming strategies: while about 40% of the respondents across the creativity indicators/subscores in both cohorts concentrated on the action of the expert, more than 50% of them focused on the object of the expert's activity, thus taking the activity 'for granted'.

Tasks 3.1–3.3 were based on a drawing and apparently motivated the majority of respondents to concentrate on the activity of a person in the drawing. This is reflected in universally higher percentages of OT1 compared to OT3.

If we pointed out that the majority of tasks manifested competition between OT1 and OT3, the situation in Task 1.1 is different. Here, we face a competition between OT2 and OT9, that is, two onomasiological types of roughly the same degree of economy and closer to mid-transparency on the scale. This task required the respondents to give a name to "a person whose smiling face is used for billboard advertisements." This task is another typical example of competition between two different naming strategies, one of which employs a metonymical representation of a person by a part of the person, that is, face. This strategy produced a fairly high number of coinages that are known as exocentric compounds, that is, compounds whose head constituent (in our terminology – the onomasiological base) is not morphemically represented. The use of this strategy is different in the two cohorts. While in the L-cohort, the percentage of OT9 is higher than that of OT2 in all indicators/subscores; in the H-cohort, it is lower in all but one indicator (Elaboration). This finding indicates that the *H-cohort prefers more transparent naming strategies*. At the same time, this is the only task in which OT9 is employed.

Another case which deviates from the prevailing competition between OT1 and OT3 is Task 1.2: "Give a name to a person who frequently interrupts other people when they are talking." Here, the emphasis on the activity of a person makes it difficult to avoid expressing the Actional constituent of the onomasiological structure. This is reflected in the absolute prevalence of OT1 and OT2 and the totally peripheral or even zero role of OT3. Task 1.2 is the only task in which the percentage of OT2 is in many instances higher than that of OT1. This is especially true of the H-cohort. In the L-cohort, there are three exceptions: in Originality, Creative Strengths, and, by a narrow margin, Elaboration.

Based on this section, in Section 5.1.1.2, we provide additional statistical evidence concerning the general tendency to form words transparently/ economically.

5.1.1.2 Statistical Evaluation of the Differences between the L-Cohort and the H-Cohort

This section examines the tendency towards economy of expression or semantic transparency mainly with respect to null hypothesis significance testing, which tells us whether the differences between the L-cohort and the H-cohort are statistically significant and whether H0 can be rejected or not. For this purpose, the non-parametric Mann–Whitney U test will be employed. While the interpretational framework will be primarily based on the null hypothesis significance testing, the effect size, the confidence intervals, and the Bayes factor will be reported and interpreted as well. The motivation for including the Bayes factor is to provide a more nuanced interpretation and to distinguish between "evidence for H0 rather than H1, evidence for H1 rather than H0, or not much evidence either way" (Dienes and McLatchie 2018: 215). The motivation for including the effect size and confidence interval is to further examine the magnitude of the effect. Next, a sensitivity analysis will be provided with the aim of corroborating the robustness of the results.

Elaboration and Semantic Transparency

Concerning Elaboration and semantic transparency, the differences between the H-cohort and the L-cohort are not statistically significant.

More specifically, as shown in Table 5.16 and Figure 5.1, there are no statistically significant differences between the L-cohort (M = 10.70, Med = 10, SD = 3.19) and the H-cohort (M = 10.55, Med = 10, SD = 3.4) in the general transparency index (U = 3171, p = 0.826, Cohen's d = 0.05, BF_{10} = 0.186, BF_{01} = 5.367); between the L-cohort (M = 10.98, Med = 10, SD = 2.71)

Table 5.16. *Mann–Whitney U test for Elaboration and semantic transparency*

	BF_{10}	U	p	95% confidence interval Lower	Upper	Cohen's d
General transparency	0.19	3171.00	0.826	−4.35e−5	3.81e−5	0.05
Transparency Task 1	0.20	3072.50	0.652	−6.37e−5	1.46e−5	0.05
Transparency Task 2	0.23	2862.50	0.407	−1.79e−5	7.21e−5	−0.15
Transparency Task 3	0.48	2514.50	0.233	−1.37e−5	5.19e−5	−0.17

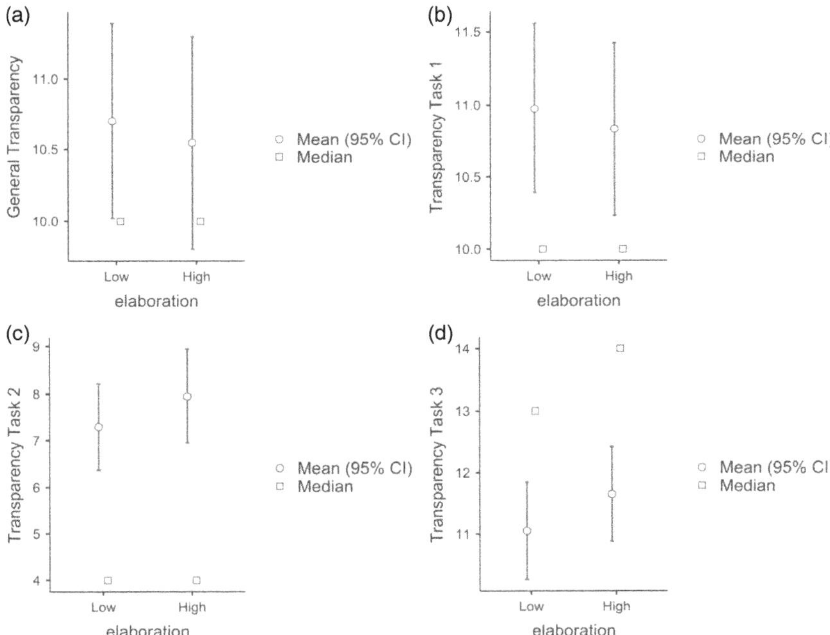

Figure 5.1 Descriptive plots for Elaboration and semantic transparency

and the H-cohort (M = 10.83, Med = 10, SD = 2.66) in the first word formation task (U = 3073, p = 0.652, Cohen's d = 0.05, BF_{10} = 0.199, BF_{01} = 5.023); between the L-cohort (M = 7.30, Med = 4, SD = 4.24) and the H-cohort (M = 7.95, Med = 4, SD = 4.44) in the second word formation task (U = 2863, p = 0.407, Cohen's d = −0.15, BF_{10} = 0.234, BF_{01} = 4.275); or between the L-cohort (M = 11.05, Med = 13.00, SD = 3.60) and the H-cohort (M = 11.65,

Table 5.17. *Mann–Whitney U test for Elaboration and economy of expression*

	BF_{10}	U	p	95% confidence interval Lower	Upper	Cohen's d
General economy	0.21	3175.00	0.824	−3.44e−6	5.71e−5	−0.03
Economy Task 1	0.23	3104.00	0.713	−2.06e−5	3.84e−6	−0.06
Economy Task 2	0.26	2873.00	0.403	−2.52e−5	2.22e−5	0.13
Economy Task 3	0.64	2431.00	0.121	−3.85e−5	4.51e−5	0.25

Med = 14, SD = 3.31) in the third word formation task (U = 2515, p = 0.233, Cohen's d = −0.17, BF_{10} = 0.484, BF_{01} = 2.065).

Elaboration and Economy of Expression

Concerning Elaboration and economy of expression, the differences between the H-cohort and the L-cohort are not statistically significant.

More specifically, as depicted in Table 5.17 and Figure 5.2, there are no statistically significant differences between the L-cohort (M = 3.15, Med = 4, SD = 0.94) and the H-cohort (M = 3.18, Med = 4, SD = 0.96) regarding the general economy index (U = 3175, p = 0.824, Cohen's d = −0.03, BF_{10} = 0.212, BF_{01} = 4.717); between the L-cohort (M = 3.27, Med = 4, SD = 0.98) and the H-cohort (M = 3.32, Med = 4, SD = 0.94) in the first word formation task (U = 3104, p = 0.713, Cohen's d = −0.06, BF_{10} = 0.225, BF_{01} = 4.444); between the L-cohort (M = 3.43, Med = 4, SD = 0.85) and the H-cohort (M = 3.32, Med = 4, SD = 0.91) in the second word formation task (U = 2873, p = 0.403, Cohen's d = 0.13, BF_{10} = 0.262, BF_{01} = 3.821); or between the L-cohort (M = 2.81, Med = 3, SD = 0.91) and the H-cohort (M = 2.59, Med = 2, SD = 0.82) in the third word formation task (U = 2431, p = 0.121, Cohen's d = 0.25, BF_{10} = 0.640, BF_{01} = 1.563).

Fluency and Semantic Transparency

Concerning Fluency and semantic transparency, the differences between the H-cohort and the L-cohort are not statistically significant.

More specifically, as depicted in Table 5.18 and Figure 5.3, there are no statistically significant differences between the L-cohort (M = 10.49, Med = 10, SD = 3.0) and the H-cohort (M = 10.41, Med = 10, SD = 3.49) in semantic transparency in general (U = 3200, p = 0.893, Cohen's d = 0.02, BF_{10} = 0.181, BF_{01} = 5.527); between the L-cohort (M = 11.22, Med = 10, SD = 2.43) and the H-cohort (M = 10.67, Med = 10, SD = 2.71) in the first word formation task (U = 2820, p = 0.200, Cohen's d = 0.21, BF_{10} = 0.434, BF_{01} = 2.305); between the L-cohort (M = 7.58, Med = 4, SD = 4.27) and the H-cohort (M = 7.58, Med = 4, SD = 4.39) in the second word formation task (U = 2977,

Table 5.18. *Mann–Whitney U test for Fluency and semantic transparency*

	BF_{10}	U	p	95% confidence interval Lower	Upper	Cohen's d
General transparency	0.18	3200.00	0.893	−3.12e−5	3.03e−5	0.02
Transparency Task 1	0.43	2819.50	0.200	−7.50e−5	2.99e−5	0.21
Transparency Task 2	0.19	2976.50	0.921	−3.33e−5	4.30e−5	7.69e−4
Transparency Task 3	0.25	2522.50	0.766	−1.56e−5	6.46e−5	−0.10

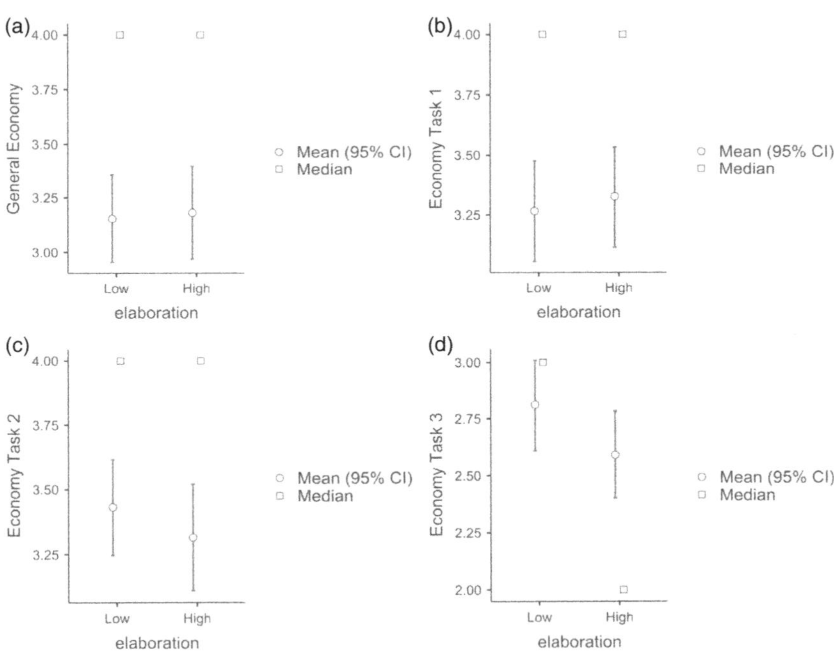

Figure 5.2 Descriptive plots for Elaboration and economy of expression

$p = 0.921$, Cohen's d = 7.69e−4, $BF_{10} = 0.188$, $BF_{01} = 5.305$); or between the L-cohort (M = 10.79, Med = 14, SD = 3.96) and the H-cohort (M = 11.18, Med = 14, SD = 3.53) in the third word formation task (U = 2523, $p = 0.766$, Cohen's d = −0.10, $BF_{10} = 0.245$, $BF_{01} = 4.075$).

Fluency and Economy of Expression

Concerning Fluency and economy of expression, the differences between the H-cohort and the L-cohort are not statistically significant.

Table 5.19. *Mann–Whitney U test for Fluency and economy of expression*

	BF_{10}	U	p	95% confidence interval Lower	Upper	Cohen's d
General economy	0.26	3005.50	0.373	−8.86e−5	6.38e−5	0.11
Economy Task 1	0.54	2836.50	0.195	−1.47e−5	8.05e−5	−0.20
Economy Task 2	0.23	2888.00	0.633	−4.70e−5	4.14e−5	0.07
Economy Task 3	0.31	2438.00	0.499	−1.36e−5	1.57e−6	0.15

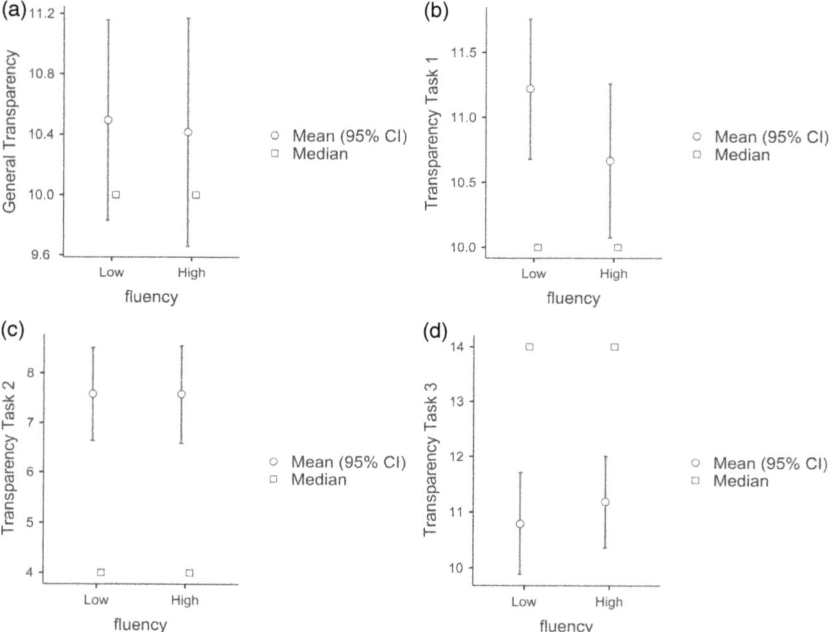

Figure 5.3 Descriptive plots for Fluency and semantic transparency

More specifically, as depicted in Table 5.19 and Figure 5.4, there are no statistically significant differences between the L-cohort (M = 3.30, Med = 4, SD = 0.92) and the H-cohort (M = 3.2, Med = 4, SD = 0.97) in economy of expression in general (U = 3006, p = 0.373, Cohen's d = 0.11, BF_{10} = 0.257, BF_{01} = 3.867); between the L-cohort (M = 3.23, Med = 4, SD = 0.94) and the H-cohort (M = 3.42, Med = 4, SD = 0.97) in the first word formation task (U = 2837, p = 0.195, Cohen's d = −0.20, BF_{10} = 0.543, BF_{01} = 1.842); between

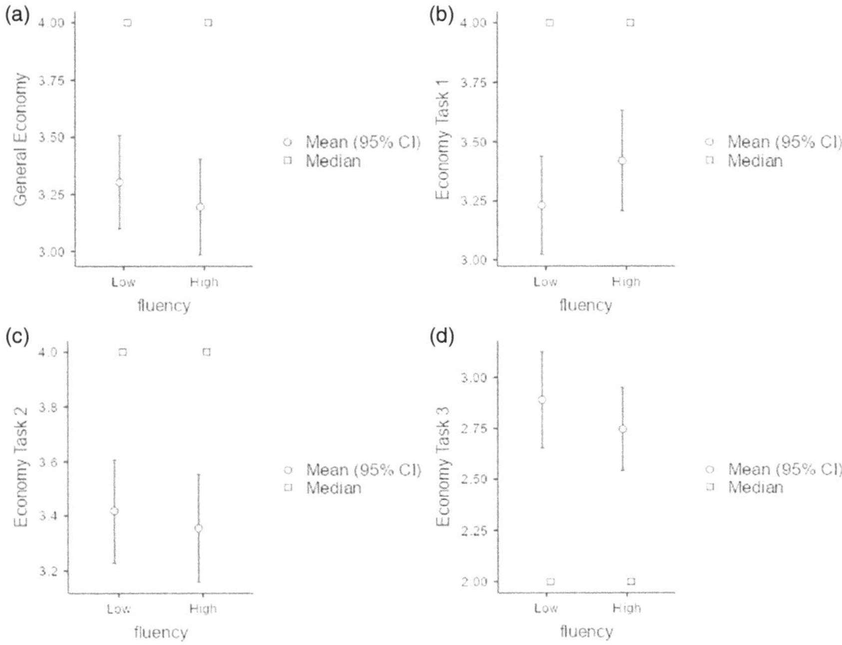

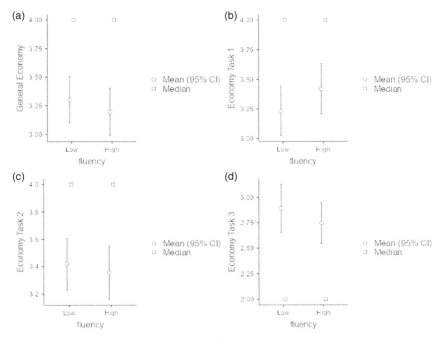

Figure 5.4 Descriptive plots for Fluency and economy of expression

the L-cohort (M = 3.42, Med = 4, SD = 0.86) and the H-cohort (M = 3.36, Med = 4, SD = 0.87) in the second word formation task (U = 2888, p = 0.633, Cohen's d = 0.07, BF_{10} = 0.233, BF_{01} = 4.296); or between the L-cohort (M = 2.89, Med = 2, SD = 1.02) and the H-cohort (M = 2.75, Med = 2, SD = 0.87) in the third word formation task (U = 2438, p = 0.499, Cohen's d = 0.15, BF_{10} = 0.308, BF_{01} = 3.248).

Flexibility and Semantic Transparency

Concerning Flexibility and semantic transparency, the differences between the H-cohort and the L-cohort are not statistically significant.

More specifically, as depicted in Table 5.20 and Figure 5.5, there are no statistically significant differences between the L-cohort (M = 10.15, Med = 10, SD = 2.980) and the H-cohort (M = 9.60, Med = 10, SD = 3.61) in semantic transparency in general (U = 2407, p = 0.368, Cohen's d = 0.17, BF_{10} = 0.313, BF_{01} = 3.192); between the L-cohort (M = 10.93, Med = 10, SD = 2.32) and the H-cohort (M = 10.83, Med = 10, SD = 2.53) in the first word formation task (U = 2567, p = 0.913, Cohen's d = 0.04, BF_{10} = 0.215,

Table 5.20. *Mann–Whitney U test for Flexibility and semantic transparency*

	BF_{10}	U	p	95% confidence interval Lower	Upper	Cohen's d
General transparency	0.30	2407.00	0.368	−2.84e−5	2.00	0.17
Transparency Task 1	0.21	2566.50	0.913	−4.67e−5	4.25e−5	0.04
Transparency Task 2	0.47	2188.00	0.131	−4.16e−5	1.77e−5	0.21
Transparency Task 3	0.22	2039.50	0.723	−7.49e−6	2.76e−5	−0.07

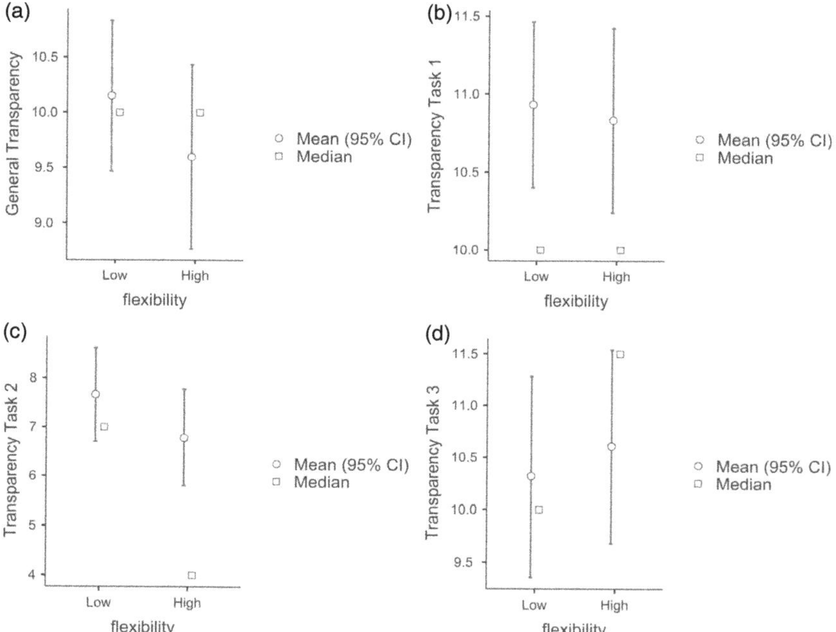

Figure 5.5 Descriptive plots for Flexibility and semantic transparency

BF_{01} = 4.659); between the L-cohort (M = 7.67, Med = 7, SD = 4.14) and the H-cohort (M = 6.7, Med = 4, SD = 4.20) in the second word formation task (U = 2188, p = 0.131, Cohen's d = 0.21, BF_{10} = 0.478, BF_{01} = 2.124); or between the L-cohort (M = 10.32, Med = 10, SD = 3.98) and the H-cohort (M = 10.61, Med = 11.50, SD = 3.79) in the third word formation task (U = 2040, p = 0.723, Cohen's d = −0.07, BF_{10} = 0.218, BF_{01} = 4.593).

Table 5.21. *Mann–Whitney U test for Flexibility and economy of expression*

	BF_{10}	U	p	95% confidence interval Lower	Upper	Cohen's d
General economy	0.26	2514.00	0.584	−9.62e−6	6.79e−5	0.09
Economy Task 1	0.21	2578.50	0.952	−1.42e−5	5.17e−6	0.00
Economy Task 2	0.29	2353.00	0.410	−2.83e−5	1.32e−5	−0.11
Economy Task 3	0.24	2024.50	0.660	−2.45e−5	5.11e−5	0.10

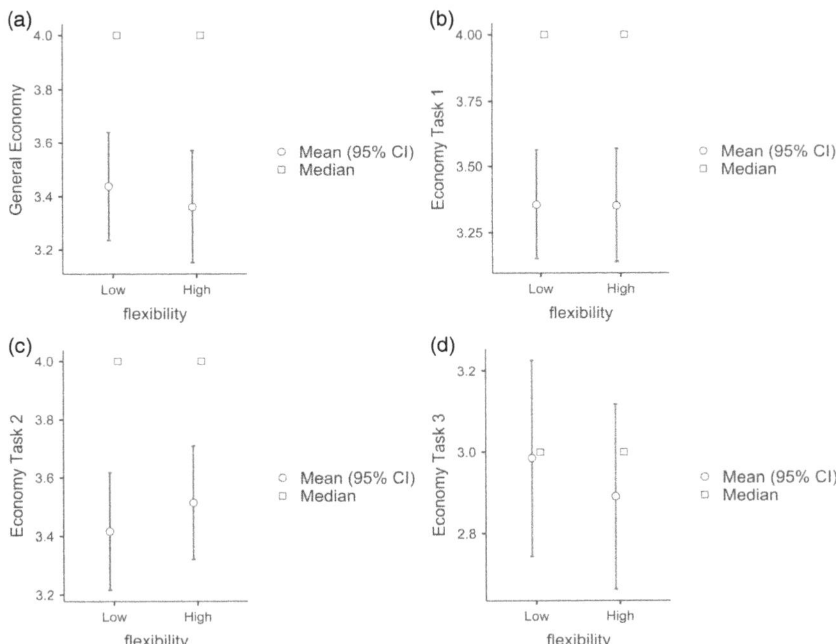

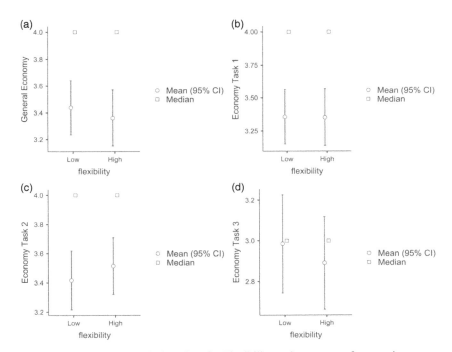

Figure 5.6 Descriptive plots for Flexibility and economy of expression

Flexibility and Economy of Expression

Concerning Flexibility and economy of expression, the differences between the H-cohort and the L-cohort are not statistically significant.

More specifically, as depicted in Table 5.21 and Figure 5.6, there are no statistically significant differences between the L-cohort (M = 3.44, Med = 4, SD = 0.88) and the H-cohort (M = 3.36, Med = 4, SD = 0.91) in economy of

Table 5.22. *Mann–Whitney U test for Originality and semantic transparency*

	BF_{10}	U	p	95% confidence interval Lower	95% confidence interval Upper	Cohen's d
General transparency	0.24	2721.00	0.360	−4.15e−5	1.00	0.14
Transparency Task 1	1.34	2467.00	0.051	−1.70e−5	2.26e−5	0.34
Transparency Task 2	0.20	2787.50	0.685	−1.14e−5	1.52e−5	0.09
Transparency Task 3	0.19	2382.00	0.752	−2.77e−6	2.43e−5	0.05

expression in general (U = 2514, p = 0.584, Cohen's d = 0.09, BF_{10} = 0.256, BF_{01} = 3.902); between the L-cohort (M = 3.36, Med = 4, SD = 0.90) and the H-cohort (M = 3.35, Med = 4, SD = 0.93) in the first word formation task (U = 2579, p = 0.952, Cohen's d = 0.00, BF_{10} = 0.206, BF_{01} = 4.849); between the L-cohort (M = 3.42, Med = 4, SD = 0.87) and the H-cohort (M = 3.51, Med = 4, SD = 0.83) in the second word formation task (U = 2353, p = 0.410, Cohen's d = −0.11, BF_{10} = 0.295, BF_{01} = 3.390); or between the L-cohort (M = 2.98, Med = 3, SD = 1) and the H-cohort (M = 2.89, Med = 3, SD = 0.93) in the third word formation task (U = 2025, p = 0.660, Cohen's d = 0.10, BF_{10} = 0.242, BF_{01} = 4.140).

Originality and Semantic Transparency

Concerning Originality and semantic transparency, the differences between the H-cohort and the L-cohort are not statistically significant.

More specifically, as depicted in Table 5.22 and Figure 5.7, there are no statistically significant differences between the L-cohort (M = 10.88, Med = 10, SD = 3.31) and the H-cohort (M = 10.42, Med = 10, SD = 3.46) in general (U = 2721, p = 0.360, Cohen's d = 0.14, BF_{10} = 0.240, BF_{01} = 4.160); between the L-cohort (M = 11.58, Med = 10, SD = 2.49) and the H-cohort (M = 10.67, Med = 10, SD = 2.48) in the first word formation task (U = 2467, p = 0.051, Cohen's d = 0.34, BF_{10} = 1.340, BF_{01} = 0.746); between the L-cohort (M = 7.83, Med = 4, SD = 4.50) and the H-cohort (M = 7.45, Med = 4, SD = 4.19) in the second word formation task (U = 2788, p = 0.685, Cohen's d = 0.09, BF_{10} = 0.200, BF_{01} = 5.004); or between the L-cohort (M = 11.57, Med = 14, SD = 3.64) and the H-cohort (M = 11.37, Med = 14, SD = 3.66) in the third word formation task (U = 2382, p = 0.752, Cohen's d = 0.05, BF_{10} = 0.190, BF_{01} = 5.258).

Originality and Economy of Expression

Concerning Originality and economy of expression, the differences between the H-cohort and the L-cohort are not statistically significant.

Table 5.23. *Mann–Whitney U test for Originality and economy of expression*

	BF_{10}	U	p	95% confidence interval Lower	Upper	Cohen's d
General economy	0.21	2818.50	0.558	−6.32e−5	1.62e−6	−0.11
Economy Task 1	0.85	2523.00	0.063	−4.01e−5	2.50e−5	−0.30
Economy Task 2	0.24	2725.50	0.493	−1.63e−5	3.96e−6	−0.13
Economy Task 3	0.19	2397.50	0.806	−1.32e−5	1.22e−5	−0.04

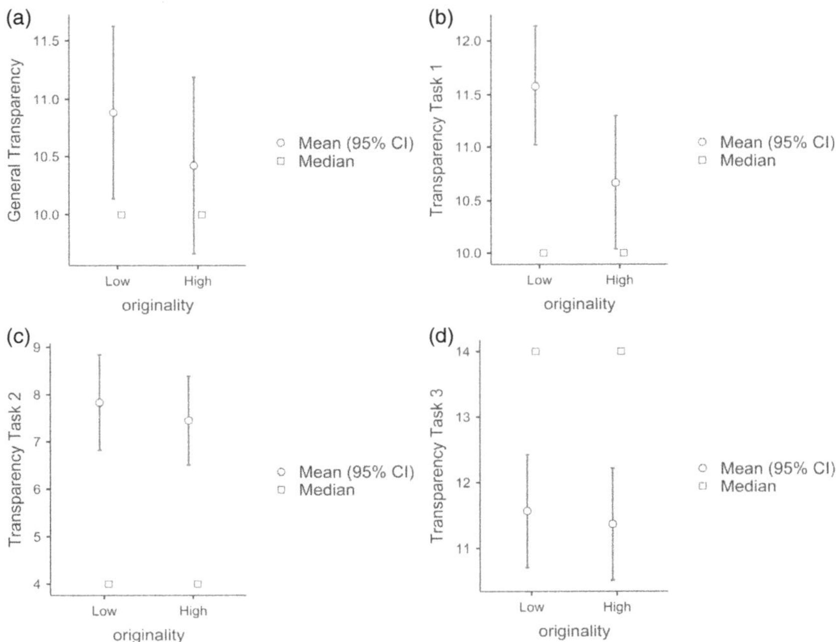

Figure 5.7 Descriptive plots for Originality and semantic transparency

More specifically, as depicted in Table 5.23 and Figure 5.8, there are no statistically significant differences between the L-cohort (M = 3.07, Med = 4, SD = 0.98) and the H-cohort (M = 3.17, Med = 4, SD = 0.92) in economy of expression in general (U = 2819, p = 0.558, Cohen's d = −0.11, BF_{10} = 0.212, BF_{01} = 4.718); between the L-cohort (M = 3.07, Med = 4, SD = 1) and the H-cohort (M = 3.36, Med = 4, SD = 0.98) in the first word formation task

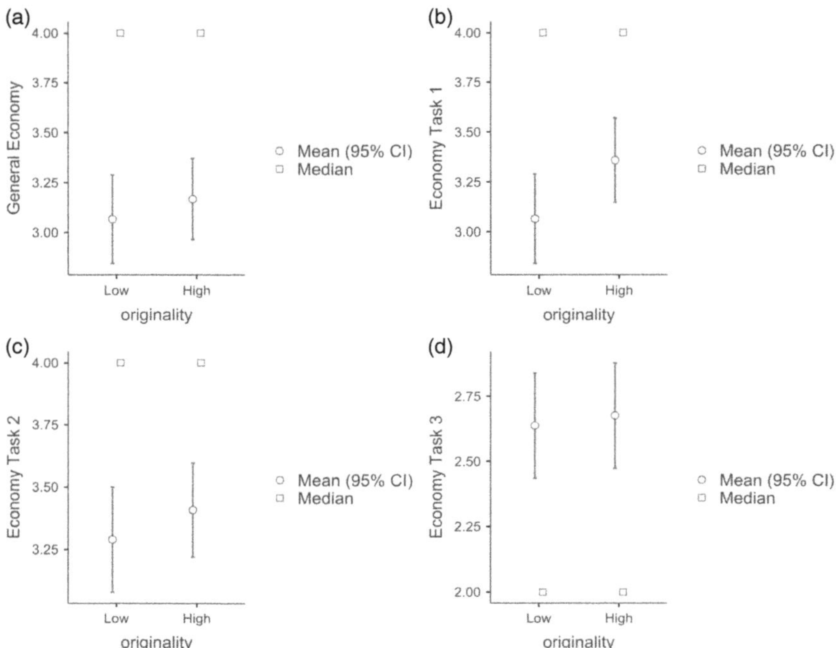

Figure 5.8 Descriptive plots for Originality and economy of expression

(U = 2523, p = 0.063, Cohen's d = −0.03, BF_{10} = 0.853, BF_{01} = 1.173); between the L-cohort (M = 3.29, Med = 4, SD = 94) and the H-cohort (M = 3.41, Med = 4, SD = 0.84) in the second word formation task (U = 2726, p = 0.493, Cohen's d = −0.13, BF_{10} = 0.239, BF_{01} = 4.193); or between the L-cohort (M = 2.64, Med = 2, SD = 0.86) and the H-cohort (M = 2.68, Med = 2, SD = 0.87) in the third word formation task (U = 2398, p = 0.806, Cohen's d = −0.04, BF_{10} = 0.187, BF_{01} = 5.343).

Creative Strengths and Semantic Transparency

Concerning Creative Strengths and semantic transparency, the differences between the H-cohort and the L-cohort are not statistically significant except in the third task.

More specifically, as depicted in Table 5.24 and Figure 5.9, there are no statistically significant differences between the L-cohort (M = 9.81, Med = 10, SD = 3.25) and the H-cohort (M = 10.73, Med = 10, SD = 3.28) in semantic transparency in general (U = 2347, p = 0.076, Cohen's d = −0.28, BF_{10} = 0.655, BF_{01} = 1.527); between the L-cohort (M = 11.06, Med = 10, SD = 2.35)

Table 5.24. *Mann–Whitney U test for Creative Strengths and semantic transparency*

		U	p	95% confidence interval		Cohen's d
				Lower	Upper	
General transparency	0.65	2437.00	0.076	−2.00	1.36e−5	−0.28
Transparency Task 1	0.28	2674.00	0.348	−7.04e−5	6.66e−5	0.16
Transparency Task 2	0.28	2617.00	0.448	−2.86e−5	1.34e−5	−0.11
Transparency Task 3	2.56	1972.50	0.027*	−2.00	−3.56e−5	−0.39

Note. *p < 0.05

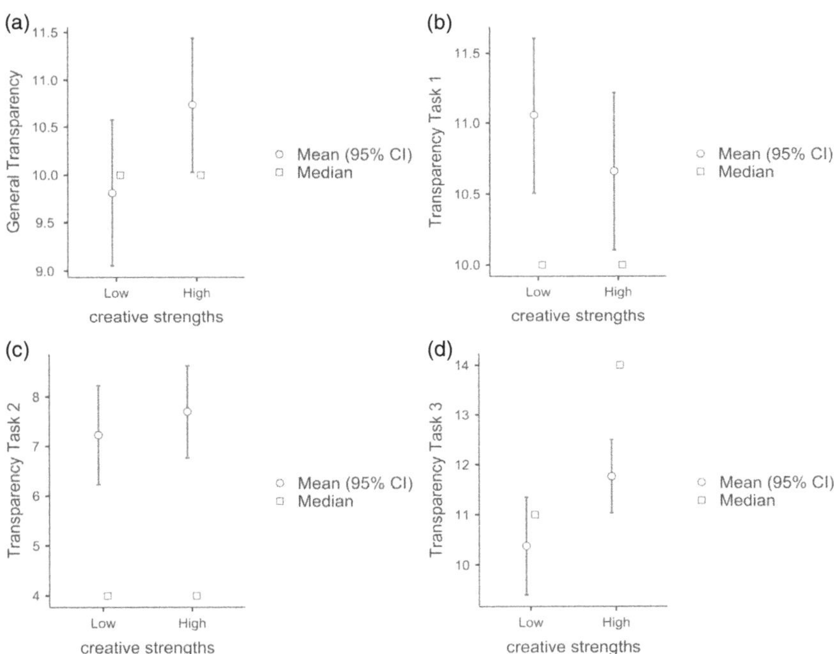

Figure 5.9 Descriptive plots for Creative Strengths and semantic transparency

and the H-cohort (M = 10.66, Med = 10, SD = 2.60) in the first word formation task (U = 2674, p = 0.348, Cohen's d = 0.16, BF_{10} = 0.283, BF_{01} = 3.531); or between the L-cohort (M = 7.28, Med = 4, SD = 4.27) and the H-cohort (M = 7.70, Med = 4, SD = 4.25) in the second word formation task (U = 2617, p = 0.448, Cohen's d = −0.11, BF_{10} = 0.279, BF_{01} = 3.582).

Table 5.25. *Mann–Whitney U test for Creative Strengths and economy of expression*

	BF_{10v}	U	p	95% confidence interval		Cohen's d
				Lower	Upper	
General economy	0.57	2512.50	0.100	−4.66e−5	8.78e−5	0.25
Economy Task 1	0.21	2872.50	0.887	−1.61e−5	5.44e−5	−0.04
Economy Task 2	0.23	2686.00	0.619	−2.17e−5	1.60e−5	0.06
Economy Task 3	3.19	1933.50	0.016*	2.27e−5	1.00	0.43

Note. *$p < 0.05$

However, there is a statistically significant difference between the L-cohort (M = 10.38, Med = 11, SD = 3.97) and the H-cohort (M = 11.77, Med = 14, SD = 3.28) in semantic transparency in the third word formation task (U = 1972, p = 0.027, Cohen's d = −0.39, BF_{10} = 2.560, BF_{01} = 0.391).

Creative Strengths and Economy of Expression

Concerning Creative Strengths and economy of expression, the differences between the H-cohort and the L-cohort are not statistically significant except in the third task.

More specifically, as depicted in Table 5.25 and Figure 5.10, there are no statistically significant differences between the L-cohort (M = 3.41, Med = 4, SD = 0.88) and the H-cohort (M = 3.18, Med = 4, SD = 0.99) in economy of expression in general (U = 2513, p = 0.100, Cohen's d = 0.25, BF_{10} = 0.570, BF_{01} = 1.755); between the L-cohort (M = 3.34, Med = 4, SD = 0.95) and the H-cohort (M = 3.39, Med = 4, SD = 0.96) in the first word formation task (U = 2873, p = 0.887, Cohen's d = −0.04, BF_{10} = 0.212, BF_{01} = 4.717); or between the L-cohort (M = 3.43, Med = 4, SD = 0.88) and the H-cohort (M = 3.38, Med = 4, SD = 0.85) in the second word formation task (U = 2686, p = 0.619, Cohen's d = 0.06, BF_{10} = 0.227, BF_{01} = 4.399). However, there is a statistically significant difference between the L-cohort (M = 3.02, Med = 3, SD = 0.98) and the H-cohort (M = 2.62, Med = 2, SD = 0.84) in economy of expression in the third word formation task (U = 1934, p = 0.016, Cohen's d = 0.43, BF_{10} = 3.187, BF_{01} = 0.314).

Composite Score and Semantic Transparency

As far as the Composite Score and semantic transparency are concerned, the H-cohort formed slightly more transparent words in the majority of cases; however, the differences between the H-cohort and the L-cohort are not statistically significant.

Table 5.26. *Mann–Whitney U test for Composite Score and economy of expression*

	BF_{10}	U	p	95% confidence interval		Cohen's d
				Lower	Upper	
General transparency	0.18	2839.50	0.745	−7.53e−6	2.85e−5	−0.02
Transparency Task 1	0.30	2634.50	0.308	−2.43e−5	4.75e−5	0.17
Transparency Task 2	0.19	2691.50	0.853	−3.80e−5	4.84e−5	−0.05
Transparency Task 3	0.26	2299.00	0.498	−3.65e−5	4.52e−5	−0.14

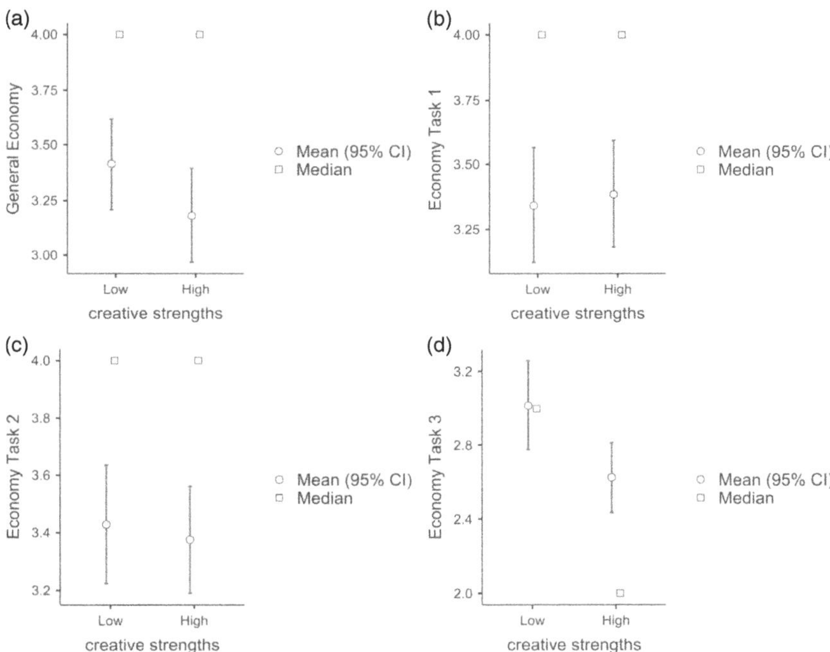

Figure 5.10 Descriptive plots for Creative Strengths and economy of expression

More specifically, as depicted in Table 5.26 and Figure 5.11, there are no statistically significant differences between the L-cohort (M = 10.29, Med = 10, SD = 3.10) and the H-cohort (M = 10.36, Med = 10, SD = 3.48) in semantic transparency in general (U = 2840, p = 0.745, Cohen's d = −0.02, BF_{10} = 0.177, BF_{01} = 5.66); between the L-cohort (M = 11.40, Med = 10,

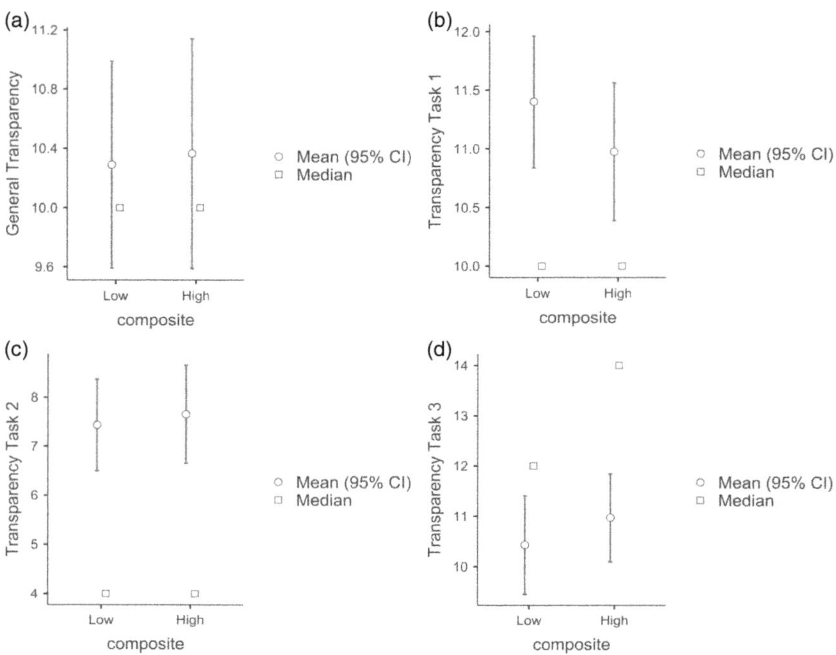

Figure 5.11 Descriptive plots for Composite Score and semantic transparency

SD = 2.49) and the H-cohort (M = 10.29, Med = 10, SD = 2.63) in the first word formation task (U = 2635, p = 0.308, Cohen's d = 0.17, BF_{10} = 0.302, BF_{01} = 3.314); between the L-cohort (M = 7.43, Med = 4, SD = 4.16) and the H-cohort (M = 7.65, Med = 4, SD = 4.34) in the second word formation task (U = 2692, p = 0.853, Cohen's d = −0.05, BF_{10} = 0.190, BF_{01} = 5.259); or between the L-cohort (M = 10.43, Med = 12, SD = 4.16) and the H-cohort (M = 10.97, Med = 14, SD = 3.74) in the third word formation task (U = 2299, p = 0.498, Cohen's d = −0.14, BF_{10} = 0.257, BF_{01} = 3.899).

Composite Score and Economy of Expression

Concerning Composite Score and economy of expression, the H-cohort formed words in a less economical way; however, these differences are not statistically significant.

More specifically, as shown in Table 5.27 and Figure 5.12, there are no statistically significant differences between the L-cohort (M = 3.34, Med = 4, SD = 0.92) and the H-cohort (M = 3.22, Med = 4, SD = 0.98) in economy of expression in general (U = 2698, p = 0.341, Cohen's d = 0.13, BF_{10} = 0.280,

Table 5.27. *Mann–Whitney U test for Composite Score and economy of expression*

	BF_{10}	U	p	95% confidence interval Lower	Upper	Cohen's d
General economy	0.28	2698.00	0.341	−9.44e−5	7.11e−5	0.13
Economy Task 1	0.32	2677.50	0.372	−5.06e−5	9.59e−6	−0.15
Economy Task 2	0.26	2642.00	0.672	−3.29e−6	1.56e−5	0.07
Economy Task 3	0.31	2263.00	0.391	−3.43e−5	1.29e−5	0.17

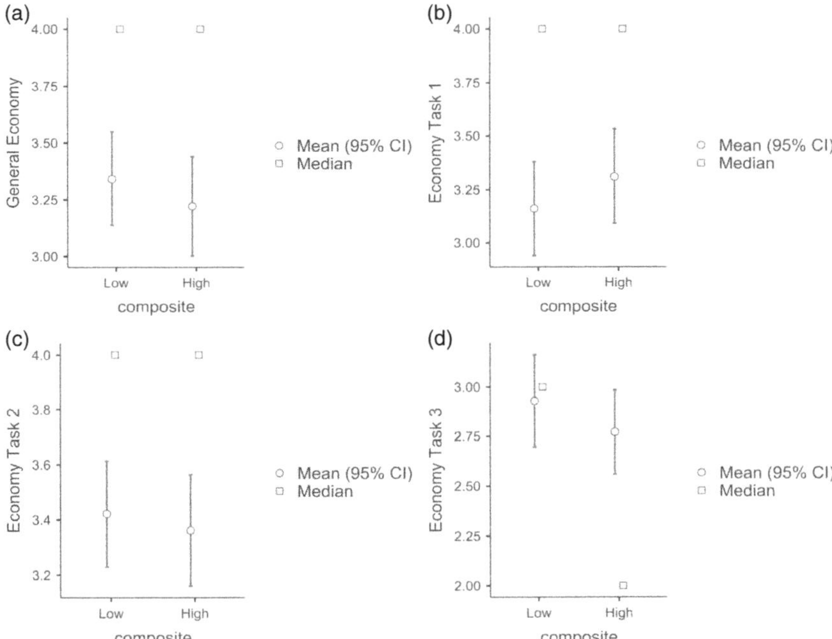

Figure 5.12 Descriptive plots for Composite Score and economy of expression

BF_{01} = 3.565); between the L-cohort (M = 3.16, Med = 4, SD = 0.97) and the H-cohort (M = 3.31, Med = 4, SD = 0.99) in the first word formation task (U = 2678, p = 0.372, Cohen's d = −0.15, BF_{10} = 0.321, BF_{01} = 3.113); between the L-cohort (M = 3.42, Med = 4, SD = 0.85) and the H-cohort (M = 3.36, Med = 4, SD = 0.88) in the second word formation task (U = 2642, p = 0.672, Cohen's d = 0.07, BF_{10} = 0.261, BF_{01} = 3.833); or between the L-cohort (M = 2.93, Med = 3, SD = 1) and the H-cohort (M = 2.77, Med = 2, SD = 0.90) in the third word formation task (U = 2263, p = 0.391, Cohen's d = 0.17, BF_{10} = 0.313, BF_{01} = 3.194).

Further Issues and Summary

Owing to the potential type I error increase (rejection of the true null hypothesis) due to multiple comparisons, we employ two procedures for controlling a false positive finding. When controlling the family-wise error rate with the more stringent Bonferroni (1936) correction across 46 comparisons, only p values lower than 0.001 should be considered as statistically significant. If we apply this more conservative criterion, none of the differences will be considered as statistically significant. In this case, however, the type II error (non-rejection of a false null hypothesis, also known as false negative findings) could be exaggerated due to the diminished statistical power, thus masking potential findings. Therefore, we prefer to control the false discovery rate through Benjamini and Hochberg's (1995) procedure. Accordingly, from all the results that are below 0.05, one result could be considered statistically significant even after the adjustment (p values for FDR < 0.01).

Furthermore, the effect size is reported to provide a magnitude of the effect. If we summarize the magnitude of the effect size according to the classical benchmarks of Cohen (1977, 1988),[1] (a) none of the results can be viewed as large in magnitude; (b) a medium effect size was found for differences between the L-cohort and the H-cohort regarding Creative Strengths and word formation Task 3 for both the transparency and economy indices; however, (c) a small effect size was found for some differences between the L-cohort and the H-cohort (e.g. regarding Elaboration and transparency and economy in word formation Tasks 2 and 3; Fluency and both transparency and economy in Tasks 1 and 3; Flexibility and both transparency and economy in Tasks 2 and 3; and Originality and both transparency and economy in Task 3).

In addition, from the Bayesian perspective (and the verbal interpretational scheme provided by Wagenmakers et al. 2017), there is anecdotal to moderate evidence for the alternative hypothesis relative to H0 for the differences between the L-cohort and the H-cohort in Creative Strengths and Task 3 for both the transparency and the economy indices. More decisive evidence for the alternative hypothesis has not been found. When considering the evidence for the null hypothesis, there was moderate evidence for the null hypothesis in the majority of comparisons.

[1] Although we are aware that the universal application of such benchmarks could be debatable, due to the lack of previous studies on the topic, we will list it for illustrational and summary purposes.

Summary of Inferential Statistics and Sensitivity Analysis

In a nutshell, although some differences are visible, only the differences between the L-cohort and the H-cohort in Creative Strengths in the third task for both transparency and economy indices are statistically significant with some evidence for the alternative hypothesis (according to the Bayes factor and moderate effect sizes).

Since it can be argued that dichotomizing the data into the L-cohort and the H-cohort by a quartile split procedure can lead to the loss of statistical power and other undesirable consequences, we aimed to corroborate the robustness of the previous analysis by means of a sensitivity analysis in which all variables are used in a non-dichotomized form, unlike the previous analysis. For this purpose, Kendall's τ correlation coefficient was used to find out whether there is a relationship between the number of readings in the three word formation tasks and the TTCT subscores.

As can be seen in Table 5.28, which represents a correlation matrix among the variables, small but statistically significant correlations are found between Creative Strengths and the transparency and economy indices in the third task, and this pattern of results is in line with the previous analysis.

In order to provide additional evidence, the Bayes factor, indicating the amount of evidence in support of the alternative hypothesis relative to H0, as well as the lower and upper 95% credible intervals (interpretable in such a way, given the observed data, that the effect has a 95% probability of falling within the range) is computed (Table 5.29). For the results that have been shown to be statistically significant, there is anecdotal to moderate evidence for the alternative hypothesis over the null hypothesis in the data.

5.1.1.3 Summary I

(i) The data for secondary school students show that Hypothesis 2 has not found much support. The percentage of failed answers varies according to the nature of tasks. Three different word formation tasks seem to impose different demands on creative performance. In addition, the creative potential represented by the six creativity indicators/subscores of language speakers appears to affect word formation creativity in different ways, which is reflected in the unequal results of the two cohorts. While Hypothesis 2 has been violated in almost all creativity indicators/subscores, this is especially due to Task 2. This means that the L-cohort achieved better results in the majority of creativity indicators in the verbal description task while the H-cohort did so in the drawing-based Task 3. The only creativity indicator in which the H-cohort achieved much better results than the L-cohort in Task 1 is Flexibility; in Task 2, it is Elaboration; and in Task 3, it is Originality.

Table 5.28. *Correlation matrix among all variables*

	Composite	Fluency	Flexibility	Originality	Elaboration	Creative Strengths
General transparency	0.01	0.00	−0.05	−0.03	−0.00	0.06
Transparency Task 1	−0.05	−0.03	−0.02	−0.07	−0.02	−0.06
Transparency Task 2	0.00	−0.02	−0.05	−0.03	0.05	0.04
Transparency Task 3	0.04	0.00	0.01	0.01	0.04	0.10*
General economy	−0.03	−0.04	0.00	−0.00	−0.00	−0.06
Economy Task 1	0.04	0.04	0.02	0.07	0.01	0.04
Economy Task 2	−0.00	−0.01	0.02	0.04	−0.04	−0.02
Economy Task 3	−0.04	−0.02	−0.01	−0.01	−0.04	−0.11*

Note. $^*p < 0.05$

Table 5.29. *Correlation matrix among all variables*

		Composite	Fluency	Flexibility	Elaboration	Originality	Creative Strengths
General transparency	Kendall's τ	0.01	5.17e−4	−0.05	−0.00	−0.03	0.06
	BF_{10}	0.07	0.07	0.17	0.07	0.10	0.31
	Upper 95% CI	0.08	0.07	0.02	0.07	0.04	0.14
	Lower 95% CI	−0.07	−0.07	−0.12	−0.08	−0.10	−0.01
Transparency Task 1	Kendall's τ	−0.05	−0.03	−0.02	−0.02	−0.07	−0.06
	BF_{10}	0.15	0.11	0.08	0.08	0.43	0.32
	Upper 95% CI	0.03	0.04	0.05	0.06	0.00	0.01
	Lower 95% CI	−0.12	−0.11	−0.09	−0.09	−0.14	−0.14
Transparency Task 2	Kendall's τ	0.00	−0.02	−0.05	0.05	−0.03	0.04
	BF_{10}	0.07	0.08	0.18	0.18	0.10	0.12
	Upper 95% CI	0.08	0.06	0.02	0.12	0.04	0.11
	Lower 95% CI	−0.07	−0.09	−0.12	−0.03	−0.10	−0.04
Transparency Task 3	Kendall's τ	0.04	0.00	0.01	0.04	0.01	0.10
	BF_{10}	0.12	0.08	0.08	0.12	0.08	1.78
	Upper 95% CI	0.11	0.08	0.08	0.11	0.08	0.17
	Lower 95% CI	−0.04	−0.08	−0.07	−0.04	−0.07	0.02
General economy	Kendall's τ	−0.03	−0.04	0.00	−0.00	−3.91e−4	−0.06
	BF_{10}	0.11	0.13	0.07	0.07	0.07	0.32
	Upper 95% CI	0.04	0.03	0.07	0.07	0.07	0.01
	Lower 95% CI	−0.11	−0.11	−0.07	−0.08	−0.07	−0.14
Economy Task 1	Kendall's τ	0.04	0.04	0.02	0.01	0.07	0.04
	BF_{10}	0.12	0.13	0.08	0.08	0.35	0.12
	Upper 95% CI	0.11	0.11	0.09	0.08	0.14	0.11
	Lower 95% CI	−0.04	−0.03	−0.06	−0.06	−0.01	−0.04
Economy Task 2	Kendall's τ	−0.00	−0.01	0.02	−0.04	0.04	−0.02
	BF_{10}	0.07	0.07	0.08	0.12	0.14	0.09
	Upper 95% CI	0.07	0.07	0.09	0.03	0.11	0.05
	Lower 95% CI	−0.08	−0.08	−0.06	−0.11	−0.03	−0.10
Economy Task 3	Kendall's τ	−0.04	−0.02	−0.01	−0.04	−0.01	−0.11
	BF_{10}	0.14	0.09	0.08	0.13	0.08	3.93
	Upper 95% CI	0.03	0.06	0.07	0.04	0.06	−0.03
	Lower 95% CI	−0.12	−0.10	−0.08	−0.12	−0.09	−0.19

(ii) The choice of a naming strategy seems to be partly determined by the nature of the naming task. This is evident from the different naming strategies in individual tasks and subtasks. In the majority of cases, we witness competition between two naming strategies that represents an opposition between semantically transparent and economically onomasiological types, that is, OT1 and OT3.

(iii) Considerable differences can also be found in individual subtasks, which suggests that the specific features of an object to be named may exert their influence upon the selection of a naming strategy. This is especially evident in the key role of transparency degree 3 (OT9) in Task 1.1. In the other experimental subtasks, its role approaches zero.

(iv) The data show a minimum or peripheral role (in giving names to Agents/Patients) of three onomasiological types, which represent various degrees of economy of expression: OT4 (transparency degree 4) and OT6 (transparency degree 1) represent the highest economy of expression. To them, one can add OT5 (transparency degree 6; medium economy).

(v) From the perspective of null hypothesis significance testing, the differences between the L-cohort and the H-cohort are not statistically significant. Furthermore, there is more evidence in favour of H0 relative to H1 according to the Bayes factor in the majority of cases. There is a tendency for the H-cohort to employ the most transparent onomasiological type more frequently than the L-cohort. *Elaboration*, *Fluency*, *Creative Strengths*, and *Composite Score* support the selection of OT1 in the H-cohort in comparison to the L-cohort. Contrary to this, Flexibility and Originality seem to support more economical solutions in the form of OT3 in this cohort. However, it is only *Creative Strengths* that shows substantial differences between the H-cohort and the L-cohort in terms of their preference for semantic transparency and for economy of expression, respectively, in Task 3.

(vi) Since Fluency is the creativity indicator that reflects the number of relevant answers, its data with regard to the failed answer criterion should be indicative of the influence of creative potential upon creative performance in word formation. Surprisingly, this is not the case. The percentages of failed answers in each of the three word formation tasks as well as cumulatively are higher in the H-cohort. From this, it follows that, in the group of secondary school students, this factor does not have the expected effect.

(vii) The different results in individual word formation tasks can be accounted for by the domain of creativity theory and, more specifically, by the idea of task specificity, according to which "the skills, traits, or knowledge that underlie creative performance in different microdomains within the same more general domain are different and largely unrelated" (Baer 2020: 1)

> and, importantly, by the finding that "creativity in performing one kind of task within a broad cognitive domain may be unrelated to creativity in performing other tasks within the same domain." Certainly, this microdomain creativity perspective should be viewed from a broader perspective as proposed, for example, in the hierarchical four-level Amusement Park Theoretical (APT) model of creativity (Baer and Kaufman 2005). This model postulates varying degrees of domain specificity and generality, ranging from the most general, such as general intelligence, motivation, and suitable environments, down to microdomains or task specificity. Similarly, the componential model identifies three factors, comprising general creativity skills and knowledge, domain-specific skills and knowledge, and task motivation (Amabile 1996).

From this perspective, the kinds of creativity required for the formation of new/potential complex words represent a hierarchical system. The three different tasks of the word formation test – multiple choice, verbal motivation, and drawing-based motivation of the naming act – represent three microdomains of the more general domain of word formation creativity, which falls within an even more general domain represented by the integrated model of complex words. This assumption is consistent with the research of Palmiero et al. (2010: 369), who conclude that "visual creativity is largely domain- and task-specific, whereas verbal creativity, even though mostly domain-specific, may, to some extent, be sensitive to processes in the visual domain as well."

5.1.2 University Undergraduates

5.1.2.1 Data Analysis

As with the data on secondary school students, we start with a presentation of the experimental data in the form of tables by individual creativity indicators/subscores (Tables 5.30 and 5.31).

Originality

The data show that the number of respondents who failed to answer the experimental tasks is much higher in the L-cohort than in the H-cohort (21% vs. 14%). This difference is substantial in Tasks 2 and 3 (13% and 12% difference, respectively) in which the respondents could not select from a certain number of options. Instead, they had to come up with their own naming solutions. This means that a more demanding task in terms of word formation creativity favours language users with higher creative potential, represented by the Originality indicator.

As for the naming strategy, the H-cohort, more than the L-cohort, favours OT1, that is, the type with the maximum degree of semantic transparency (degree 7) and the minimum degree of economy. The difference of 10%

Table 5.30. *Low Originality (data are given in %; 72 respondents)*

Task/transparency scale	7	6	5	4	3	2	1	F (no.)	F (%)
Task 1									
1	4	0	48	2	46	0	0	1	
2	35	0	65	0	0	0	0	1	
3	59	0	7	0	0	32	2	4	
∑ 1	**32**	**0**	**40**	**1**	**16**	**10**	**1**	6	**3**
Task 2									
1	48	0	0	0	0	52	0	8	
2	58	2	13	2	0	25	0	32	
3	0	7	2	0	0	91	0	28	
∑ 2	**36**	**3**	**4**	**1**	**0**	**56**	**0**	68	**31**
Task 3									
1	46	0	12	2	0	40	0	22	
2	61	1	16	0	0	22	0	21	
3	63	2	6	0	0	29	0	21	
∑ 3	**57**	**1**	**11**	**1**	**0**	**30**	**0**	64	**30**
∑ 1–3	**41**	**1**	**21**	**1**	**6**	**30**	**0**	138	**21**

Table 5.31. *High Originality (data are given in %; 70 respondents)*

Task/transparency scale	7	6	5	4	3	2	1	F (no.)	F (%)
Task 1									
1	9	1	38	1	47	3	1	1	
2	47	0	49	2	0	2	0	3	
3	75	2	6	0	2	15	0	4	
∑ 1	**44**	**1.5**	**31**	**1.5**	**16**	**6**	**0**	8	**4**
Task 2									
1	60	0	2	0	0	38	0	5	
2	44	2	13	4	0	37	0	16	
3	2	0	6	2	0	90	0	20	
∑ 2	**38**	**1**	**6**	**2**	**0**	**53**	**0**	41	**20**
Task 3									
1	78	0	6	0	0	16	0	15	
2	64	0	3	0	0	33	0	9	
3	73	0	9	0	0	18	0	14	
∑ 3	**72**	**0**	**5**	**0**	**0**	**23**	**0**	38	**18**
∑ 1–3	**51**	**1**	**15**	**1**	**6**	**26**	**0**	87	**14**

Table 5.32. *Low Elaboration (data are given in %; 76 respondents)*

Task/transparency scale	7	6	5	4	3	2	1	F (no.)	F (%)
Task 1									
1	3	0	40	3	53	0	1	1	
2	39	0	61	0	0	0	0	0	
3	64	0	0	0	0	34	2	6	
∑ 1	**35**	**0**	**34**	**1**	**18**	**11**	**1**	7	**3**
Task 2									
1	43	2	2	0	0	53	0	12	
2	38	6	18	2	0	34	2	26	
3	4	14	4	2	0	76	0	26	
∑ 2	**30**	**7**	**7**	**1**	**0**	**54**	**1**	64	**28**
Task 3									
1	55	2	13	0	0	30	0	23	
2	60	0	13	0	0	27	0	14	
3	64	4	7	0	0	25	0	23	
∑ 3	**60**	**2**	**11**	**0**	**0**	**27**	**0**	60	**26**
∑ 1–3	**41**	**2**	**19**	**1**	**7**	**29**	**1**	131	**19**

primarily stems from Task 3 (15% difference) that requires naming on the basis of drawings, and also from Task 1 (12% difference). This is compensated by higher percentages of transparency degrees 2 and 5 in the L-cohort. These transparency degrees feature medium economy. The results of the two cohorts in Task 2 are similar.

Elaboration

Like with the Originality indicator, the total number of failures is higher in the L-cohort than in the H-cohort (19% vs. 15%) (Tables 5.32 and 5.33). In this case as well, the difference stems from Tasks 2 and 3 (8% and 6% difference, respectively). Even if the difference in failed answers is considerable, it is smaller than for the Originality indicator. This correlates with a smaller difference between the two cohorts in using the most transparent onomasiological type.

The most frequent onomasiological type is the most transparent one (OT1), which competes with OT3 in the majority of the subtasks. An exception is subtask 1.1 in which OT9 and OT2, which correspond with transparency degrees 3 and 5, are mostly implemented. While in the L-cohort it is transparency degree 3 that has the highest frequency in this subtask, in the H-cohort it is OT2, that is, an OT with a much higher transparency degree (even though the differences are not high). OT3 is more frequent than OT1 in Task 2 thanks

Table 5.33. *High Elaboration (data are given in %; 69 respondents)*

Task/transparency scale	7	6	5	4	3	2	1	F (no.)	F (%)
Task 1									
1	4	3	45	2	42	4	0	2	
2	47	0	52	0	0	1	0	3	
3	73	0	5	0	1	21	0	7	
∑ 1	**41**	**0.5**	**34**	**0.5**	**15**	**9**	**0**	12	**6**
Task 2									
1	50	0	0	0	0	50	0	3	
2	44	0	6	2	0	48	0	21	
3	6	0	6	0	0	88	0	18	
∑ 2	**35**	**0**	**3**	**1**	**0**	**61**	**0**	42	**20**
Task 3									
1	73	0	5	0	0	22	0	18	
2	70	0	5	0	0	25	0	9	
3	72	2	7	0	0	19	0	15	
∑ 3	**71**	**1**	**6**	**0**	**0**	**22**	**0**	**42**	**20**
∑ 1–3	**48**	**1**	**16**	**1**	**5**	**29**	**0**	96	**15**

to subtask 2.3 especially; OT1 is more frequent in all subtasks of Task 3. All in all, the data show a tendency for the H-cohort to choose OT1 more often than the L-cohort. This is evident in all three tasks as well as in the cumulative data, with the difference being highest in Task 3 (11%).

Flexibility

While Hypothesis 2 was unambiguously corroborated for the *Originality* and *Elaboration* indicators, it does not work so clearly for Flexibility (Tables 5.34 and 5.35). While the percentages of failed answers in Task 2 and in Tasks 1–3 as a whole are in favour of the H-cohort, the differences are very small.

The tendency for the H-cohort to prefer the most transparent OT1 more frequently than the L-cohort which emerged for the previous two creativity indicators is confirmed for OT1 and OT3 (6% and 7% difference, respectively), but it has not been confirmed here for Task 2 in which the L-cohort's percentage of the use of OT1 is higher by 8%. The cumulative figures are similar for both cohorts.

Fluency

What has been said about the failed answers in the Flexibility indicator applies to Fluency, too (Tables 5.36 and 5.37), even though the difference in Task 2 in favour of the H-cohort is as much as 6%.

Table 5.34. *Low Flexibility (data are given in %; 70 respondents)*

Task/transparency scale	7	6	5	4	3	2	1	F (no.)	F (%)
Task 1									
1	7	0	42	1.5	48	0	1.5	1	
2	31	0	69	0	0	0	0	2	
3	71	0	2	0	0	27	0	4	
∑ 1	**36**	**0**	**38**	**0.5**	**16**	**9**	**0.5**	7	**3**
Task 2									
1	58	1.5	1.5	0	0	39	0	6	
2	46	7	9	3	0	35	0	27	
3	0	9	3	0	0	88	0	27	
∑ 2	**38**	**5**	**4**	**1**	**0**	**52**	**0**	60	**29**
Task 3									
1	51	0	14	2	0	33	0	15	
2	69	0	13	0	0	18	0	15	
3	59	2	2	0	0	37	0	21	
∑ 3	**60**	**0.5**	**10**	**0.5**	**0**	**29**	**0**	51	**24**
∑ 1–3	**44**	**2**	**19**	**1**	**6**	**28**	**0**	118	**19**

Table 5.35. *High Flexibility (data are given in %; 76 respondents)*

Task/transparency scale	7	6	5	4	3	2	1	F (no.)	F (%)
Task 1									
1	4	1	41	0	52	1	1	2	
2	40	1	58	1	0	0	0	3	
3	82	2	0	0	0	15	1	3	
∑ 1	**42**	**2**	**33**	**0**	**17**	**5**	**1**	8	**4**
Task 2									
1	40	1	0	0	0	59	0	8	
2	43	4	8	0	0	45	0	27	
3	4	4	2	0	0	90	0	24	
∑ 2	**30**	**3**	**3**	**0**	**0**	**64**	**0**	59	**26**
Task 3									
1	63	2	7	0	0	28	0	19	
2	57	2	5	2	0	34	0	15	
3	82	2	11	0	0	5	0	20	
∑ 3	**67**	**2**	**7**	**1**	**0**	**23**	**0**	54	**24**
∑ 1–3	**46**	**2**	**16**	**0**	**7**	**29**	**0**	119	**17**

Table 5.36. *Low Fluency (data are given in %; 59 respondents)*

Task/transparency scale	7	6	5	4	3	2	1	F (no.)	F (%)
Task 1									
1	3	0	46	0	47	2	2	0	
2	39	0	61	0	0	0	0	0	
3	74	0	2	0	0	24	0	5	
∑ 1	**38**	**0**	**37**	**0**	**16**	**8**	**1**	5	**3**
Task 2									
1	63	0	2	0	0	35	0	5	
2	59	0	6	3	0	29	3	25	
3	3	11	9	0	0	77	0	24	
∑ 2	**45**	**3**	**4**	**1**	**0**	**46**	**1**	54	**31**
Task 3									
1	41	0	13	2	0	44	0	14	
2	61	0	20	0	0	19	0	13	
3	60	2	2	0	0	36	0	17	
∑ 3	**53**	**1**	**12**	**1**	**0**	**33**	**0**	44	**25**
∑ 1–3	**45**	**1**	**20**	**0.5**	**6**	**27**	**0.5**	103	**19**

Table 5.37. *High Fluency (data are given in %; 75 respondents)*

Task/transparency scale	7	6	5	4	3	2	1	F (no.)	F (%)
Task 1									
1	7	1	37	1	53	1	0	1	
2	37	1	59	3	0	0	0	2	
3	71	1	6	0	0	21	1	3	
∑ 1	**38**	**1**	**34**	**1**	**8**	**7**	**1**	7	**3**
Task 2									
1	50	0	0	0	0	50	0	9	
2	48	4	10	0	0	38	0	25	
3	8	1	1	0	0	90	0	22	
∑ 2	**36**	**2**	**4**	**0**	**0**	**58**	**0**	56	**25**
Task 3									
1	70	2	7	0	0	21	0	19	
2	59	1.5	5	1.5	0	33	0	14	
3	82	0	11	0	0	7	0	20	
∑ 3	**70**	**1**	**7**	**1**	**0**	**21**	**0**	53	**24**
∑ 1–3	**47**	**1**	**17**	**1**	**7**	**27**	**0**	115	**17**

Table 5.38. *Low Creative Strengths (data are given in %; 54 respondents)*

Task/transparency scale	7	6	5	4	3	2	1	F (no.)	F (%)
Task 1									
1	3	0	41	3	51	0	0	1	
2	39	0	59	0	0	0	2	0	
3	61	0	4	0	0	35	0	3	
∑ 1	**34**	**0**	**36**	**1**	**17**	**11**	**1**	4	**2**
Task 2									
1	47	0	0	0	0	53	0	9	
2	43	7	23	4	0	23	0	24	
3	3	11	0	0	0	86	0	19	
∑ 2	**32**	**5**	**6**	**2**	**0**	**55**	**0**	52	**32**
Task 3									
1	50	3	14	0	0	33	0	18	
2	62	0	20	0	0	18	0	9	
3	62	3	9	0	0	26	0	20	
∑ 3	**57**	**4**	**14**	**0**	**0**	**25**	**0**	47	**29**
∑ 1–3	**41**	**2**	**21**	**1**	**7**	**28**	**0**	103	**21**

The percentages of the most transparent OT1 are almost identical, even if they are not distributed in the same way across the individual tasks. While in Task 1 the percentages of OT1 are identical, the H-score's share of this OT is much higher in the drawing-based Task 3 (70% vs. 53%), the proportion in Task 2 is the opposite, that is, in favour of the L-cohort (36% vs. 45%). The second most frequent OT3 (transparency degree 2) shows in total an identical share of the overall percentage, with the opposite preferences in Task 2 and Task 3, that is, a higher share of the H-cohort in Task 2 (58% vs. 46%) and a lower share in Task 3 (21% vs. 33%).

Creative Strengths

The Creative Strengths subscore gives (Tables 5.38 and 5.39) strong support to Hypothesis 2. The cumulative percentage of failures is much higher in the L-cohort (21% vs. 12%), and this is related to Task 2 (15% difference) and Task 3 (12% difference).

The H-cohort's cumulative share of the most transparent OT is higher than that of the L-cohort (50% vs. 41%). The share of the second most frequent transparency degree (degree 2), that is, OT3, is identical. The lower OT1 share is compensated in the L-cohort by a higher percentage of transparency degree 5 (OT2) compared to the H-cohort. If we look at the individual tasks, the percentage of OT1 is higher in the H-cohort in all three tasks. The biggest difference occurs in the drawing-based Task 3 (73% vs. 57%). Accordingly,

Table 5.39. *High Creative Strengths (data are given in %; 69 respondents)*

Task/transparency scale	7	6	5	4	3	2	1	F (no.)	F (%)
Task 1									
1	6	1	32	0	54	6	1	0	
2	45	0	54	0	0	1	0	2	
3	78	1	5	0	1	15	0	2	
∑ 1	**41**	**1**	**30**	**0**	**19**	**7**	**1**	4	**2**
Task 2									
1	57	0	1	0	0	42	0	2	
2	47	0	10	0	0	45	0	18	
3	0	2	7	0	0	91	0	15	
∑ 2	**35**	**1**	**6**	**0**	**0**	**58**	**0**	35	**17**
Task 3									
1	71	0	5	0	0	24	0	14	
2	69	0	3	0	0	28	0	8	
3	79	0	7	0	0	14	0	13	
∑ 3	**73**	**0**	**5**	**0**	**0**	**22**	**0**	35	**17**
∑ 1–3	**50**	**1**	**15**	**0**	**7**	**27**	**0**	74	**12**

the difference in the frequency of OT3 in favour of the L-cohort is most striking in Task 3 (5% vs. 14%).

Composite Score

The results for the Composite Score (Table 5.40 and 5.41) map those for Creative Strengths in all transparency degrees. In the case of the failure criterion, the differences between the two cohorts are also similar both in the individual tasks (14% difference in Task 2 and 7% difference in Task 3) and in the total percentages (22% vs. 15%).

Discussion

Failed Answer Criterion Let us recall that Hypothesis 2 expects a lower percentage of failed answers in the H-cohort due to its higher creative potential evaluated by means of the TTCT. The data show that the general comments on the failed answer criterion, as evaluated for the secondary school students, also apply to the results obtained from the group of university undergraduates. In particular, the type of task and the object of naming affect the general word formation strategy, irrespective of the creativity potential represented by the creativity indicators/subscores. The data also confirm the observation that the influence of these indicators/subscores varies. This conclusion applies to both the L-cohort and the H-cohort. More specific findings follow from Table 5.42.

Table 5.40. *Low Composite Score (data are given in %; 70 respondents)*

Task/transparency scale	7	6	5	4	3	2	1	F (no.)	F (%)
Task 1									
1	3	0	51	1	45	0	0	1	
2	33	0	67	0	0	0	0	1	
3	62	0	5	0	0	33	0	7	
∑ 1	**32**	**0**	**42**	**1**	**15**	**10**	**0**	9	**4**
Task 2									
1	54	0	0	0	0	46	0	11	
2	45	8	16	3	0	26	2	32	
3	0	19	2	0	0	79	0	28	
∑ 2	**35**	**8**	**5**	**1**	**0**	**50**	**1**	71	**34**
Task 3									
1	40	0	13	1	0	46	0	22	
2	68	0	16	0	0	16	0	15	
3	65	2	4	0	0	29	0	21	
∑ 3	**58**	**0.5**	**11**	**0.5**	**0**	**30**	**0**	58	**28**
∑ 1–3	**41**	**2**	**22**	**1**	**6**	**28**	**0**	138	**22**

Table 5.41. *High Composite Score (data are given in %; 71 respondents)*

Task/transparency scale	7	6	5	4	3	2	1	F (no.)	F (%)
Task 1									
1	4	4	37	0	51	4	0	1	
2	45	2	49	2	0	2	0	2	
3	74	1	3	0	1	21	0	3	
∑ 1	**41**	**2**	**30**	**0**	**18**	**9**	**0**	6	**3**
Task 2									
1	51	0	0	0	0	49	0	4	
2	45	4	9	2	0	40	0	18	
3	2	2	6	0	0	90	0	21	
∑ 2	**35**	**2**	**5**	**0**	**0**	**58**	**0**	43	**20**
Task 3									
1	74	0	7	0	0	19	0	17	
2	64	0	2	2	0	32	0	10	
3	80	2	9	0	0	9	0	17	
∑ 3	**72**	**0.5**	**6**	**0.5**	**0**	**21**	**0**	44	**21**
∑ 1–3	**49**	**1**	**15**	**0**	**7**	**28**	**0**	93	**15**

Table 5.42. *Comparison of the total percentage of failed answers (the lower percentage values are given in bold)*

	Task 1		Task 2		Task 3		Total (Tasks 1–3)	
	L-cohort	H-cohort	L-cohort	H-cohort	L-cohort	H-cohort	L-cohort	H-cohort
Originality	**3**	4	31	**20**	30	**18**	21	**14**
Elaboration	**3**	6	28	**20**	25	**20**	19	**15**
Flexibility	**3**	4	29	**26**	24	24	19	**17**
Fluency	3	3	31	**25**	25	**24**	19	**17**
Creative Strengths	2	2	32	**17**	29	**17**	21	**12**
Composite Score	4	**3**	34	**20**	28	**21**	22	**15**

As could be expected, the biggest problems for solving the test tasks – as evidenced by the percentage of failures – were posed by Tasks 2 and 3, that is, the tasks in which the respondents could not select from among several optional coinages. Instead, they had to rely on a verbal description (Task 2) and a drawing (Task 3) of an object to be named. These kinds of tasks obviously increased the demands on their word formation creativity. Based on the data in Table 5.42, it can be assumed that a verbal description (Task 2) appears to be slightly more difficult for language speakers from the word formation point of view, especially in the L-cohort, where the share of failed answers was as high as around 30% of all answers (34% for Composite Score, 32% for Creative Strengths, 31% for Originality and Fluency, 29% for Flexibility, and 28% for Elaboration). Exceptions to the higher percentage of failed answers in Task 2 compared to Task 3 include Elaboration and Creative Strengths in the H-cohort, where the failure values are identical, and the H-cohort's Composite Score with its 1% higher share of failed answers in Task 3.

Table 5.42 shows that the most striking differences between the two cohorts occurred in Task 2. Hypothesis 2 has been given the strongest support from Task 2 and also (to a slightly lesser degree) from Task 3. In both cases, the strongest evidence comes from *Creative Strengths*, *Originality*, and *Composite Score* and also, if not so strikingly, from *Elaboration*. Fluency seems to play a certain role in Task 2, but not in Task 3. Flexibility does not support the hypothesis. The results in Task 1 do not support the hypothesis as the differences between the two cohorts are very small.

The conclusion that can be drawn from the previous data is that *the creative potential of university undergraduates seems to affect their word formation creativity primarily through Creative Strengths, Originality, and Composite Score. This finding confirms Hypothesis 2 to a restricted extent.*

Semantic Transparency versus Economy of Expression

With regard to this criterion, it is possible to reiterate what was stated concerning the results for the secondary school respondents, that is, each naming task is dominated by (a maximum of) two onomasiological types, with all the other types playing a peripheral or even zero role. Very rarely, there is a balanced share of two major onomasiological types. One of them is usually evidently more frequent. Interestingly, they are usually on the opposite sides of the transparency scale, thus evidently manifesting the competition between transparency and economy. In the vast majority of cases it is the competition between the 'non-economical', most transparent OT1 (transparency degree 7) and the more economical OT3 (transparency degree 2). A less conspicuous role is played in some tasks by OT2 (transparency degree 5).

The data show an unambiguous tendency for the H-cohort to prefer the most semantically transparent OT1 more than the L-cohort. This tendency is most evident in relation to the drawing-based Task 3. The biggest differences between the two cohorts in using OT1 in Task 3 are found in *Fluency* (17%), *Creative Strengths* (16%), *Originality* (15%), and *Composite Score* (14%). However, the difference in the other two indicators does not fall under 7%. This finding is paralleled in the cumulative data, even if the differences are smaller. For Flexibility and Fluency, they are very low (2%). The smaller cumulative data differences are primarily due to Task 2 where the previously noticed tendency does not hold, with Flexibility and Fluency showing a higher proportion of OT1 in the L-cohort. The other indicators/subscores show small differences between the two cohorts. Finally, Task 1 gives unambiguous support to the observed tendency, except for Fluency. This is especially true of *Originality* (12% difference) and *Composite Score* (9% difference).

The proportion of the use of OT1 in coining new words is very consistent in all three tasks across all creativity indicators in both the L-cohort and the H-cohort and, by implication, in the cumulative data as well.

Let us relate Tables 5.43 to 5.44, which shows the data on the use of the more economical OT3.

Given the higher use of OT1 by the H-cohort in Tasks 1 and 3, it may be expected that the L-cohort manifests higher percentages in these tasks. This expectation is confirmed by the data for Task 1, where the percentages of the L-cohort in all six indicators/subscores are slightly higher, as well as for Task 3, where the differences between the two cohorts are more striking for all six indicators/subscores. Task 2, as with the use of OT1, provided the opposite results, with the exception of Originality. This mainly applies to Fluency (12% difference), Composite Score (8%), and Elaboration (7%). This result could be expected for Flexibility, Fluency, and Composite Score because of the L-cohort's higher/equal use of OT1 than the H-cohort; the Elaboration indicator shows the higher use of both OT1 and OT3 by the H-cohort. This is due to the higher use of OT2 and OT5 (transparency degrees 5 and 6, respectively) by the L-cohort.

If we go by subtasks, we find three that deviate from the prevailing competition between OT1 and OT3, namely subtasks 1.1, 1.2, and 2.3. In these tasks, the situation is similar to that in the secondary school group. The reasons for this situation are identical, and therefore they are not reiterated here (for details, see Section 5.1.1.1). For this reason, we restrict our comments in this section to a comparison of the two cohorts in each of these tasks.

In Task 1.1, we face the competition between OT2 and OT9 (transparency degrees 5 and 3) of roughly the same economy. The data for the two cohorts differ. While the use of OT9 is substantially higher than the use of OT2 in the H-cohort for all indicators/subscores (with the exception of Elaboration), with differences as high as 22% for Creative Strengths, 16% for Fluency, and 14% for Composite Score, in the L-cohort, the preference for OT9 is present only for Elaboration (in contrast to the H-cohort), Creative Strengths, and

Table 5.43. *Comparison of the L-cohort and the H-cohort with regard to the use of OT1 (transparency degree 7) (the higher percentage values are given in bold)*

	Task 1		Task 2		Task 3		Total (Tasks 1–3)	
	L-cohort	H-cohort	L-cohort	H-cohort	L-cohort	H-cohort	L-cohort	H-cohort
Originality	32	**44**	36	**38**	57	**72**	41	**51**
Elaboration	35	**41**	30	**35**	60	**71**	41	**48**
Flexibility	36	**42**	**38**	30	60	**67**	44	**46**
Fluency	38	38	**45**	36	53	**70**	45	**47**
Creative Strengths	34	**41**	32	**35**	57	**73**	41	**50**
Composite Score	32	**41**	35	35	58	**72**	41	**49**

Table 5.44. *Comparison of the L-cohort and the H-cohort with regard to the use of OT3 (transparency degree 2) (the higher percentage values are given in bold)*

	Task 1		Task 2		Task 3		Total (Tasks 1–3)	
	L-cohort	H-cohort	L-cohort	H-cohort	L-cohort	H-cohort	L-cohort	H-cohort
Originality	**10**	6	**56**	53	**30**	23	**30**	26
Elaboration	**11**	9	54	**61**	**27**	22	29	29
Flexibility	**9**	5	52	**64**	**29**	23	28	**29**
Fluency	**8**	7	46	**58**	**33**	21	27	27
Creative Strengths	**11**	7	55	**58**	**25**	22	**28**	27
Composite Score	**10**	9	50	**58**	**30**	21	28	28

Flexibility. *This observation runs counter to the tendency for the H-cohort to prefer more transparent coinages.* On the other hand, the use of exocentric compounds can be considered a manifestation of higher word formation creativity. As pointed out by Benczes (2006: 184),

> "the main difference between endocentric compounds such as *apple tree* and exocentric compounds such as *hammerhead* is not transparency of meaning, but creativity: the latter represent a type of nominal construction that has been coined by a more imaginative, associative and creative word formation process, based on conceptual metaphor and metonymy."

It should be noted that Task 1.1 is the only task in which OT9 plays a more important role. In all the other tasks, its use approaches zero. On the other hand, the cumulative frequency of the use of OT2 in both cohorts is between 15% and 22%.

Task 1.2 ("Give a name to a person who frequently interrupts other people when they are talking.") presents a notable competition between two highly transparent strategies, represented by OT1 and OT2. The two cohorts behave differently in solving this task, too. The L-cohort evidently prefers the more economical and less transparent OT2 in each of the indicators/subscores. The differences range from 18% (Flexibility) to 30% (Originality). Contrary to this, *the H-cohort's preference for OT2 is not so striking, with the exceptions of Fluency (22% difference) and Flexibility (18%). This situation thus confirms the general tendency that is observed earlier.*

Finally, in Task 2.3 ("Suppose that a woman has a clone made of herself. Then suppose that a man has a clone made of himself. Now suppose that the two clones marry each other and have a child. What would you call the child?"), the most demanding naming task from the perspective of the number of failed answers in the H-cohort and the second most demanding task according to this criterion in the L-cohort, the prevailing OT1 versus OT3 competition is replaced with a unique dominance of OT3 in both cohorts which, in some creative indicators/subscores, reached as much as about a 90% share of all proposed coinages. In the L-cohort, this is true of Originality (91%), Flexibility (88%), and Creative Strengths (86%); in the H-cohort, it applies to all indicators/subscores: Creative Strengths (91%), Composite Score (90%), Originality (90%), Flexibility (90%), Fluency (90%), and Elaboration (88%). From this, it follows that the use of OT3 for this subtask is slightly higher in the H-cohort than in the L-cohort. The biggest differences between the two cohorts in this respect concern Fluency (13%) and Elaboration (12%). In any case, subtask 2.3 is a typical example of the influence of the object to be named upon the selection of a word formation strategy, as accounted for in Section 5.1.1.1.

While subtask 1.3 shows the clear dominance of OT1 over OT3 in both cohorts, this dominance is much stronger in the H-cohort.

In subtasks 2.1 ("What would you call someone who does research about spiders' webs?") and 2.2 ("Suppose that aliens were about to land on Earth for the first time. What would you call a person who was supposed to meet them as a representative of the human race?"), the preference for OT1 is not of a universal nature; the word formation strategies used by the respondents vary by creative indicator/subscore. The L-cohort's preference for OT1 compared to OT3 is much higher in Fluency, Flexibility, and Composite Score, that is, the indicators in which the H-cohort prefers OT3 (except for Composite Score). Originality and Creative Strengths, on the other hand, show the opposite tendency, that is, an evident prevalence of OT1 in the H-cohort and a slight prevalence of OT3 in the L-cohort. From the point of view of these two subtasks, it is mainly *Originality* and *Creative Strengths* that support more transparent coinages while *Fluency* and *Flexibility* seem to have the opposite effect. Moreover, as the data show, while there is a strong tendency for the H-cohort to prefer more transparent onomasiological types, the L-cohort appears to incline to more economical word formation strategies.

All subtasks of Task 3, that is, the tasks based on drawings, *show a remarkable preference for the most transparent, that is, the least economical, OT1*, which can be explained by the effort of the respondents to capture in a coinage as many motivating features of a drawing as possible. However, we can observe a very strong tendency for the H-cohort to show a much higher preference for OT1 in comparison to the L-cohort. There are three exceptions, all of them occurring in subtask 3.2 (where the drawing represents a man performing bodybuilding exercises on a crane). They come to bear on Originality, Fluency and, surprisingly, also Composite Score.

Based on this section, in Section 5.1.2.2, we will provide additional statistical evidence concerning the general tendency to form new words transparently/economically.

5.1.2.2 Statistical Evaluation of the Differences between the L-Cohort and the H-Cohort

As was done for secondary school students (Section 5.1.1.2), this section examines the tendency towards economy of expression or semantic transparency, mainly with respect to the null hypothesis significance testing that provides us with information concerning whether the differences between the L-cohort and the H-cohort are statistically significant and if H0 could be rejected or not. As was done previously in Section 5.1.1.2, a non-parametric Mann–Whitney U test is employed and supplemented with the Bayes factor and effect size.

Originality and Semantic Transparency

Concerning Originality and semantic transparency, the differences between the H-cohort and the L-cohort are not statistically significant except for the general transparency index

Table 5.45. *Mann–Whitney U test for Originality and semantic transparency*

	BF_{10}	U	p	95% confidence interval Lower	Upper	Cohen's d
General transparency	1.72	2228.50	0.040*	−2.00	−6.53e−6	−0.30
Transparency Task 1	0.63	2300.00	0.111	−1.98e−5	2.39e−5	−0.26
Transparency Task 2	0.18	2492.50	0.902	−7.42e−6	6.59e−5	0.02
Transparency Task 3	1.14	1988.50	0.087	−1.82e−5	2.92e−5	−0.28

Note. $^*p < 0.05$

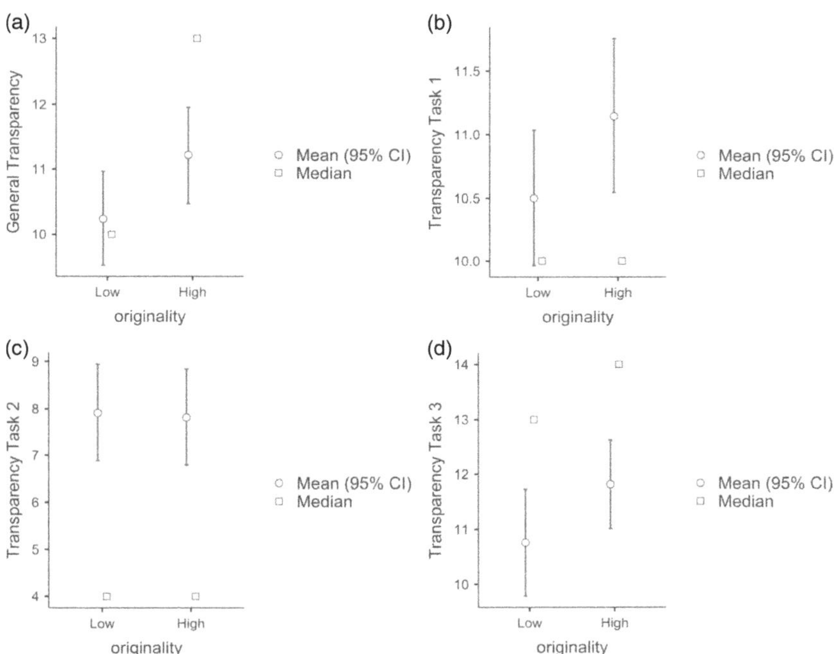

Figure 5.13 Descriptive plots for Originality and semantic transparency

More specifically, as depicted in Table 5.45 and Figure 5.13, there are statistically significant differences between the L-cohort (M = 10.24, Med = 10, SD = 3.17) and the H-cohort (M = 11.22, Med = 13, SD = 3.26) in general semantic transparency across the three word formation tasks (U = 2229, p = 0.040, Cohen's d = −0.30, BF_{10} = 1.718, BF_{01} = 0.582).

However, there are no statistically significant differences between the L-cohort (M = 10.50, Med = 10, SD = 2.32) and the H-cohort (M = 11.50,

Table 5.46. *Mann–Whitney U test for Originality and economy of expression*

	BF_{10}	U	p	95% confidence interval Lower	Upper	Cohen's d
General economy	3.85	2159.00	0.011*	1.66e−5	1.69e−5	0.43
Economy Task 1	2.40	2207.50	0.030*	−1.85e−5	1.52e−5	0.37
Economy Task 2	0.31	2332.00	0.375	−7.65e−6	7.08e−5	−0.14
Economy Task 3	1.98	1903.50	0.031*	−1.88e−5	9.49e−6	0.38

Note. $^{*}p < 0.05$

Med = 10, SD = 2.65) in the first word formation task (U = 2300, p = 0.111, Cohen's d = −0.26, BF_{10} = 0.632, BF_{01} = 1.581); between the L-cohort (M = 7.92, Med = 4, SD = 4.43) and the H-cohort (M = 7.82, Med = 4, SD = 4.40) in the second word formation task (U = 2953, p = 0.902, Cohen's d = 0.02, BF_{10} = 0.181, BF_{01} = 5.517); or between the L-cohort (M = 10.76, Med = 13, SD = 4.03) and the H-cohort (M = 11.82, Med = 14, SD = 3.42) in the third word formation task (U = 1989, p = 0.087, Cohen's d = −0.28, BF_{10} = 1.143, BF_{01} = 0.875).

Originality and Economy of Expression

Concerning Originality and economy of expression, the differences between the H-cohort and the L-cohort are statistically significant with the exception of the second task. The H-cohort formed words in a slightly less transparent way (except for during the second task).

More specifically, as depicted in Table 5.46 and Figure 5.14, there are statistically significant differences between the L-cohort (M = 3.36, Med = 4, SD = 0.90) and the H-cohort (M = 2.96, Med = 2.5, SD = 0.99) in economy of expression in general (U = 2159, p = 0.011, Cohen's d = 0.43, BF_{10} = 3.847, BF_{01} = 0.260) and between the L-cohort (M = 3.51, Med = 4, SD = 0.86) and the H-cohort (M = 3.18, Med = 4, SD = 0.98) in the first word formation task (U = 2208, p = 0.030, Cohen's d = 0.37, BF_{10} = 2.395, BF_{01} = 0.418).

In contrast, there are no statistically significant differences between the L-cohort (M = 3.30, Med = 4, SD = 0.88) and the H-cohort (M = 3.42, Med = 4, SD = 0.94) in economy of expression in the second word formation task (U = 2332, p = 0.375, Cohen's d = −0.14, BF_{10} = 0.305, BF_{01} = 3.278). There is also a statistically significant difference between the L-cohort (M = 2.91, Med = 2.5, SD = 0.96) and the H-cohort (M = 2.56, Med = 2, SD = 0.84) in economy of expression in the third word formation task (U = 1904, p = 0.031, Cohen's d = 0.38, BF_{10} = 1.979, BF_{01} = 0.505).

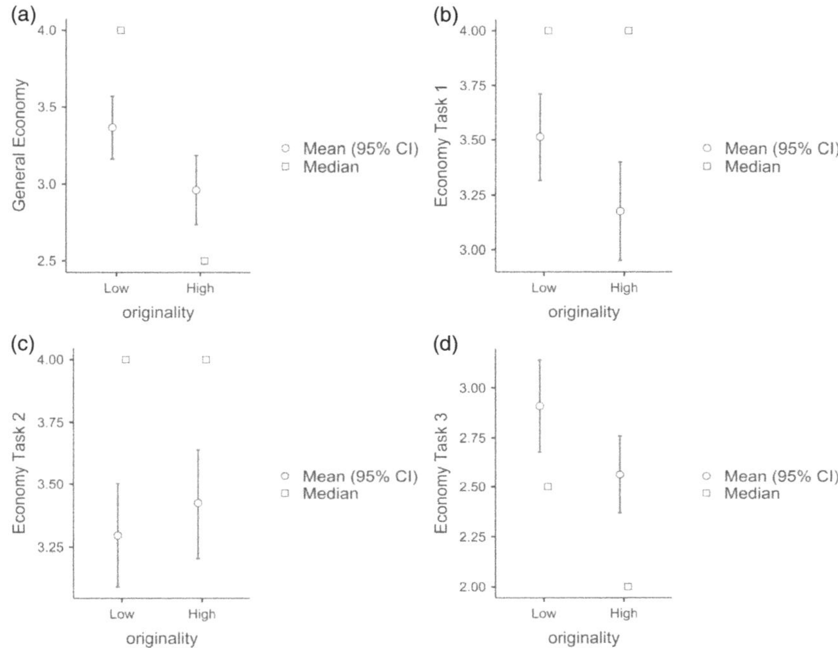

Figure 5.14 Descriptive plots for Originality and economy of expression

Elaboration and Semantic Transparency

Concerning Elaboration and semantic transparency, the differences between the H-cohort and the L-cohort are not statistically significant except for the differences in the third word formation task. The H-cohort formed words in a slightly more transparent way.

More specifically, as depicted in Table 5.47 and Figure 5.15, there are no statistically significant differences between the L-cohort (M = 9.95, Med = 10, SD = 3.40) and the H-cohort (M = 10.75, Med = 10, SD = 3.47) in semantic transparency in general (U = 2479, p = 0.120, Cohen's d = –0.23, BF_{10} = 0.418, BF_{01} = 2.391); between the L-cohort (M = 10.38, Med = 10, SD = 2.76) and the H-cohort (M = 11.14, Med = 10, SD = 2.41) in the first word formation task (U = 2472, p = 0.093, Cohen's d = –0.29, BF_{10} = 1.124, BF_{01} = 0.890); or between the L-cohort (M = 7.58, Med = 7, SD = 3.99) and the H-cohort (M = 7.56, Med = 4, SD = 4.31) in the second word formation task (U = 2755, p = 0.946, Cohen's d = 0.01, BF_{10} = 0.206, BF_{01} = 4.858).

In contrast, there are statistically significant differences between the L-cohort (M = 10.68, Med = 12, SD = 3.84) and the H-cohort (M = 11.96,

Table 5.47. *Mann–Whitney U test for Elaboration and semantic transparency*

				95% confidence interval		
	BF_{10}	U	p	Lower	Upper	Cohen's d
General transparency	0.42	2478.50	0.120	−2.00	1.30e−5	−0.23
Transparency Task 1	1.12	2471.50	0.093	−6.63e−5	2.65e−5	−0.29
Transparency Task 2	0.21	2755.00	0.946	−5.74e−5	4.74e−5	0.01
Transparency Task 3	3.18	2027.50	0.011*	−2.00	−6.82e−5	−0.34

Note. *p < 0.05

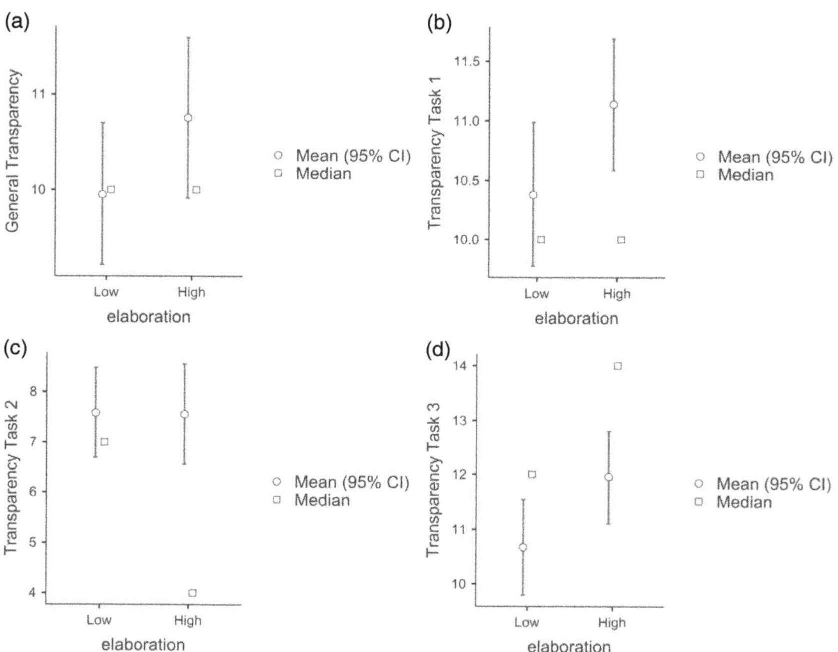

Figure 5.15 Descriptive plots for Elaboration and semantic transparency

Med = 14, SD = 3.61) in semantic transparency in the third word formation task (U = 2028, p = 0.011, Cohen's d = −0.34, BF_{10} = 3.177, BF_{01} = 0.315).

Elaboration and Economy of Expression

Concerning Elaboration and economy of expression, the differences between the H-cohort and the L-cohort are statistically significant in general and in the

Table 5.48. *Mann–Whitney U test for Elaboration and economy of expression*

	BF_{10}	U	P	95% confidence interval		Cohen's d
				Lower	Upper	
General economy	2.07	2360.00	0.025*	5.49e−5	4.19e−5	0.37
Economy Task 1	0.37	2621.00	0.246	−3.15e−5	2.15e−5	0.18
Economy Task 2	0.42	2520.00	0.258	−5.39e−5	5.22e−5	0.22
Economy Task 3	8.05	1968.00	0.005**	2.04e−5	7.07e−6	0.47

Note. *p < 0.05, **p < 0.01

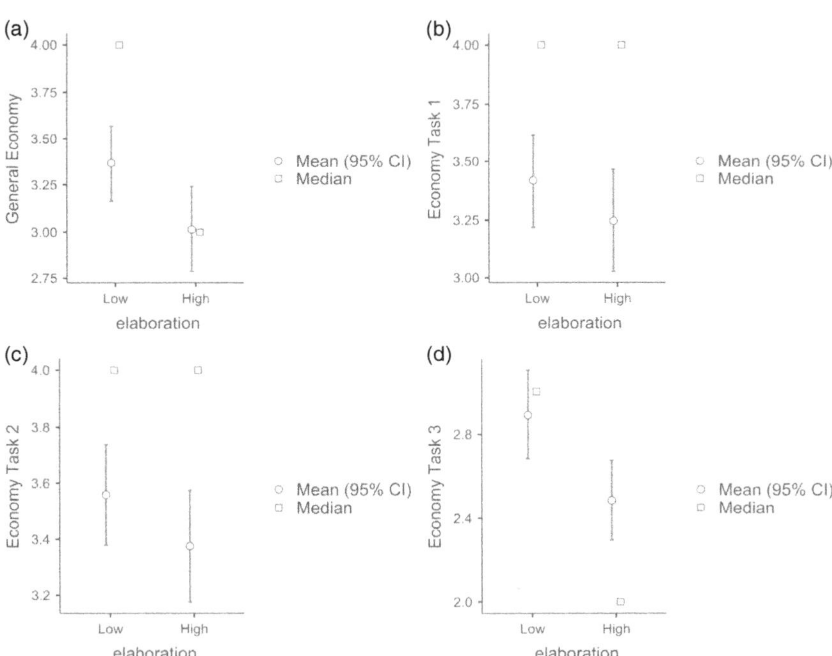

Figure 5.16 Descriptive plots for Elaboration and economy of expression

third word formation task. The H-cohort formed words in a less economical way.

More specifically, as depicted in Table 5.48 and Figure 5.16, there are statistically significant differences between the L-cohort (M = 3.37, Med = 4, SD = 4.00) and the H-cohort (M = 3.01, Med = 3, SD = 0.99) in economy of expression in general (U = 2360, p = 0.025, Cohen's d = 0.37, BF_{10} = 2.069, BF_{01} = 0.483).

Table 5.49. *Mann–Whitney U test for Flexibility and semantic transparency*

	BF_{10}	U	p	95% confidence interval Lower	Upper	Cohen's d
General transparency	0.20	2795.50	0.974	−3.32e−5	5.04e−5	0.01
Transparency Task 1	0.25	2672.50	0.693	−7.41e−6	3.57e−5	−0.06
Transparency Task 2	2.94	2103.50	0.018*	5.75e−5	3.00	0.40
Transparency Task 3	0.25	2288.50	0.560	−3.69e−5	2.05e−6	−0.09

Note. *$p < 0.05$

In comparison, there are no statistically significant differences between the L-cohort (M = 3.42, Med = 4, SD = 0.90) and the H-cohort (M = 3.25, Med = 4, SD = 0.95) in economy of expression in the first word formation task (U = 2621, p = 0.246, Cohen's d = 0.18, BF_{10} = 0.372, BF_{01} = 2.686) or between the L-cohort (M = 3.56, Med = 4, SD = 0.80) and the H-cohort (M = 3.38, Med = 4, SD = 0.80) in the second word formation task (U = 2520, p = 0.258, Cohen's d = 0.22, BF_{10} = 0.424, BF_{01} = 2.360).

There are, however, statistically significant differences between the L-cohort (M = 2.89, Med = 3, SD = 0.92) and the H-cohort (M = 2.49, Med = 2, SD = 0.81) in economy of expression in the third word formation task (U = 1968, p = 0.005, Cohen's d = 0.47, BF_{10} = 8.048, BF_{01} = 0.124).

Flexibility and Semantic Transparency

Concerning Flexibility and semantic transparency, the differences between the L-cohort and the H-cohort are not statistically significant except for the differences in the second task.

More specifically, as depicted in Table 5.49 and Figure 5.17, there are no statistically significant differences between the L-cohort (M = 10.34, Med = 10, SD = 3.38) and the H-cohort (M = 10.32, Med = 10, SD = 3.39) in semantic transparency in general (U = 2796, p = 0.974, Cohen's d = 0.01, BF_{10} = 0.197, BF_{01} = 5.083); between the L-cohort (M = 10.71, Med = 10, SD = 2.55) and the H-cohort (M = 10.87, Med = 10, SD = 2.39) in the first word formation task (U = 2673, p = 0.693, Cohen's d = −0.06, BF_{10} = 0.251, BF_{01} = 3.989); or between the L-cohort (M = 10.96, Med = 14, SD = 4) and the H-cohort (M = 11.29, Med = 14, SD = 3.91) in the third word formation task (U = 2289, p = 0.560, Cohen's d = −0.09, BF_{10} = 0.254, BF_{01} = 3.932).

In contrast, there is a statistically significant difference between the L-cohort (M = 8.89, Med = 9, SD = 4.43) and the H-cohort (M = 7.17, Med = 4, SD = 4.25) in semantic transparency in the second word formation task (U = 2104, p = 0.018, Cohen's d = 0.40, BF_{10} = 2.935, BF_{01} = 0.341).

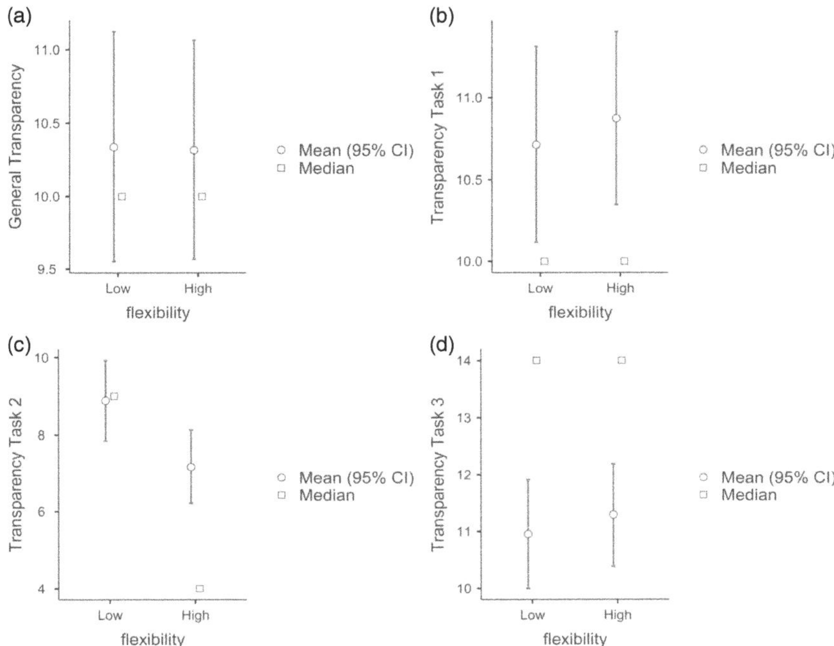

Figure 5.17 Descriptive plots for Flexibility and semantic transparency

Flexibility and Economy of Expression

Concerning Flexibility and economy of expression, the differences between the H-cohort and the L-cohort are not statistically significant.

More specifically, as depicted in Table 5.50 and Figure 5.18, there are no statistically significant differences between the L-cohort (M = 3.24, Med = 4, SD = 0.95) and the H-cohort (M = 3.29, Med = 4, SD = 0.92) in economy of expression in general (U = 2735, p = 0.762, Cohen's d = –0.06, BF_{10} = 0.244, BF_{01} = 4.103); between the L-cohort (M = 3.37, Med = 4, SD = 0.92) and the H-cohort (M = 3.38, Med = 4, SD = 0.91) in the first word formation task (U = 2759, p = 0.976, Cohen's d = –0.01, BF_{10} = 0.217, BF_{01} = 4.616); between the L-cohort (M = 3.19, Med = 4, SD = 0.92) and the H-cohort (M = 3.46, Med = 4, SD = 0.84) in the second word formation task (U = 2239, p = 0.057, Cohen's d = –0.031, BF_{10} = 1.079, BF_{01} = 0.927); or between the L-cohort (M = 2.85, Med = 2, SD = 0.97) and the H-cohort (M = 2.71, Med = 2, SD = 0.93) in the third word formation task (U = 2237, p = 0.397, Cohen's d = 0.15, BF_{10} = 0.381, BF_{01} = 2.623).

Table 5.50. *Mann–Whitney U test for Flexibility and economy of expression*

	BF_{10}	U	p	95% confidence interval Lower	Upper	Cohen's d
General economy	0.24	2734.50	0.762	−8.50e−5	5.87e−5	−0.06
Economy Task 1	0.22	2758.00	0.976	−4.27e−5	2.46e−5	−0.01
Economy Task 2	1.08	2238.50	0.057	−1.21e−5	5.86e−5	−0.31
Economy Task 3	0.38	2237.00	0.397	−1.19e−5	1.97e−5	0.15

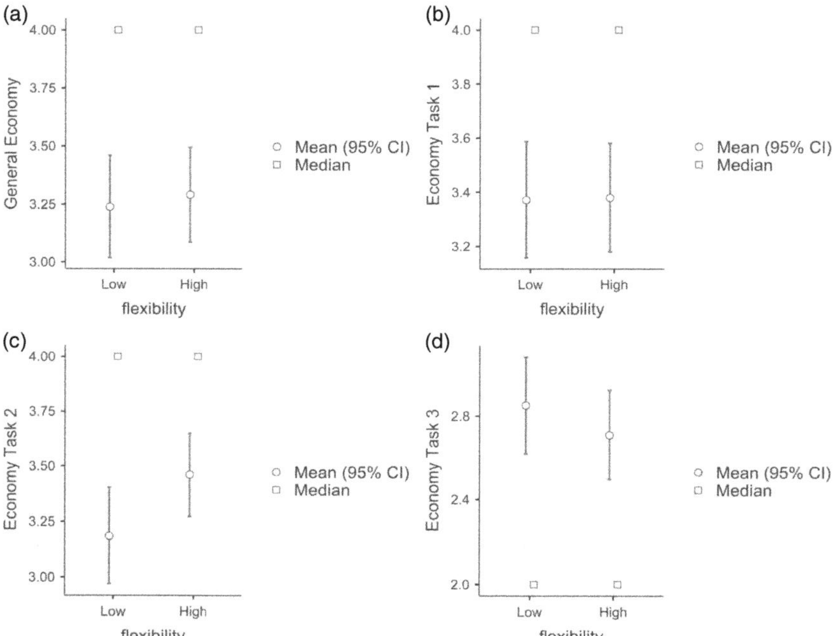

Figure 5.18 Descriptive plots for Flexibility and economy of expression

Fluency and Semantic Transparency

Concerning Fluency and semantic transparency, the differences between the H-cohort and the L-cohort are not statistically significant. The H-cohort formed words in a slightly less transparent way.

More specifically, as depicted in Table 5.51 and Figure 5.19, there are no statistically significant differences between the L-cohort (M = 10.75, Med = 10,

Table 5.51. *Mann–Whitney U test for Fluency and semantic transparency*

	BF_{10}	U	p	95% confidence interval Lower	Upper	Cohen's d
General transparency	0.20	2310.50	0.866	−3.55e−5	1.23e−5	0.02
Transparency Task 1	0.24	2215.00	0.649	−2.50e−5	5.02e−5	0.10
Transparency Task 2	1.00	1800.50	0.040*	−7.00e−5	4.00	0.39
Transparency Task 3	1.05	1762.00	0.094	−1.00	8.12e−6	−0.31

Note. *$p < 0.05$

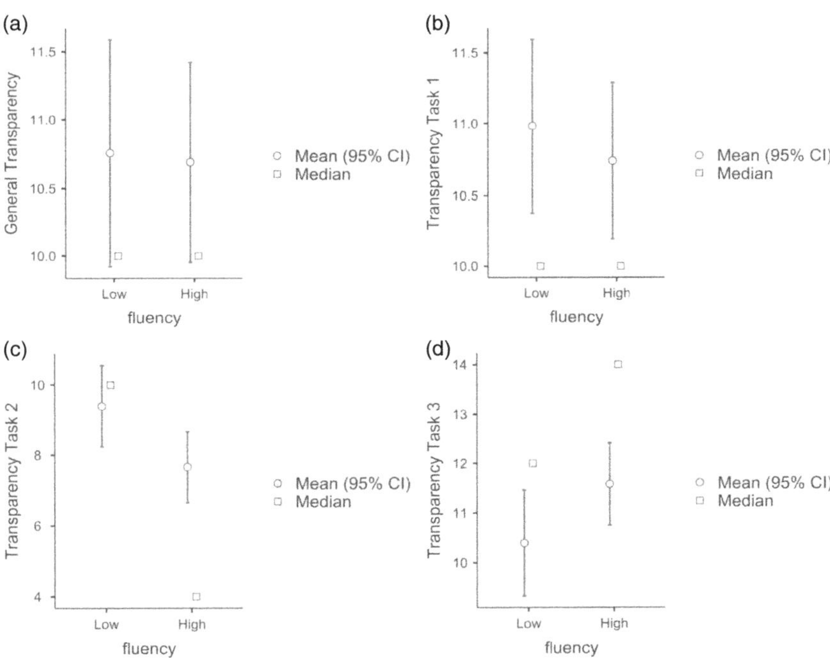

Figure 5.19 Descriptive plots for Fluency and semantic transparency

SD = 3.32) and the H-cohort (M = 10.69, Med = 10, SD = 3.29) in semantic transparency in general (U = 2311, p = 0.866, Cohen's d = 0.02, $BF_{10} = 0.200$, $BF_{01} = 4.992$) or between the L-cohort (M = 10.98, Med = 10, SD = 2.41) and the H-cohort (M = 10.74, Med = 10, SD = 2.47) in the first word formation task (U = 2216, p = 0.649, Cohen's d = 0.10, $BF_{10} = 0.238$, $BF_{01} = 4.210$).

Table 5.52. *Mann–Whitney U test for Fluency and economy of expression*

	BF_{10}	U	p	95% confidence interval Lower	Upper	Cohen's d
General economy	0.25	2264.50	0.685	−2.34e−5	6.47e−5	−0.07
Economy Task 1	0.29	2157.50	0.426	−7.49e−5	2.57e−5	−0.13
Economy Task 2	1.18	1821.00	0.043*	−5.28e−5	4.06e−5	−0.33
Economy Task 3	1.27	1716.00	0.050	−5.12e−5	9.20e−5	0.36

Note. *$p < 0.05$

On the other hand, there are statistically significant differences between the L-cohort (M = 9.39, Med = 10, SD = 4.62) and the H-cohort (M = 7.66, Med = 4, SD = 4.39) in semantic transparency in the second word formation task (U = 1801, p = 0.04, Cohen's d = 0.39, BF_{10} = 0.997, BF_{01} = 1.003).

There are no statistically significant differences between the L-cohort (M = 10.40, Med = 12, SD = 4.14) and the H-cohort (M = 11.58, Med = 14, SD = 3.58) in the third word formation task (U = 1762, p = 0.094, Cohen's d = −0.31, BF_{10} = 1.049, BF_{01} = 0.953).

Fluency and Economy of Expression

Concerning Fluency and economy of expression, the differences between the H-cohort and the L-cohort are statistically significant in the second task. The H-cohort formed words in a more economical way.

More specifically, as depicted in Table 5.52 and Figure 5.20, there are no statistically significant differences between the L-cohort (M = 3.11, Med = 4, SD = 0.97) and the H-cohort (M = 3.18, Med = 4, SD = 0.96) in economy of expression in general (U = 2265, p = 0.685, Cohen's d = −0.07, BF_{10} = 0.246, BF_{01} = 4.081) or between the L-cohort (M = 3.28, Med = 4, SD = 0.94) and the H-cohort (M = 3.40, Med = 4, SD = 0.91) in the first word formation task (U = 2158, p = 0.426, Cohen's d = −0.13, BF_{10} = 0.288, BF_{01} = 3.469).

However, there are statistically significant differences between the L-cohort (M = 3.05, Med = 3, SD = 1.01) and the H-cohort (M = 3.36, Med = 4, SD = 0.89) in economy of expression in the second word formation task (U = 121, p = 0.05, Cohen's d = 0.033, BF_{10} = 1.176, BF_{01} = 0.850).

There are no statistically significant differences between the L-cohort (M = 3.00, Med = 3, SD = 0.97) and the H-cohort (M = 2.67, Med = 2, SD = 0.89) in economy of expression in the third word formation task (U = 1716, p = 0.05, Cohen's d = 0.36, BF_{10} = 1.269, BF_{01} = 0.786).

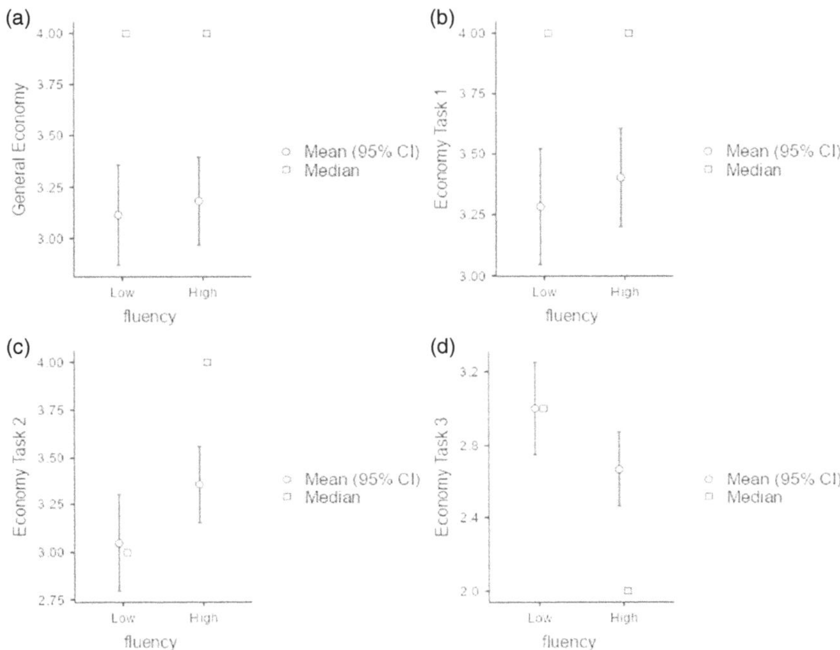

Figure 5.20 Descriptive plots for Fluency and economy of expression

Creative Strengths and Semantic Transparency

Concerning Creative Strengths and semantic transparency in the word formation test, the differences between the H-cohort and the L-cohort are not statistically significant except in the third word formation task. The H-cohort formed words in a slightly more transparent way (except in the second task).

More specifically, as depicted in Table 5.53 and Figure 5.21, there are no statistically significant differences between the L-cohort (M = 9.95, Med = 10, SD = 3.40) and the H-cohort (M = 10.82, Med = 11.50, SD = 3.53) in semantic transparency in general (U = 1750, p = 0.114, Cohen's d = −0.25, BF_{10} = 0.646, BF_{01} = 1.547); between the L-cohort (M = 10.29, Med = 10, SD = 2.68) and the H-cohort (M = 11.09, Med = 10, SD = 2.59) in the first word formation task (U = 1714, p = 0.092, Cohen's d = −0.25, BF_{10} = 0.827, BF_{01} = 1.210); or between the L-cohort (M = 7.96, Med = 7.5, SD = 4.16) and the H-cohort (M = 7.57, Med = 4, SD = 4.51) in the second word formation task (U = 1844, p = 0.594, Cohen's d = 0.09, BF_{10} = 0.239, BF_{01} = 4.176).

Table 5.53. *Mann–Whitney U test for Creative Strengths and semantic transparency*

	BF_{10}	U	p	95% confidence interval Lower	Upper	Cohen's d
General transparency	0.65	1750.00	0.114	−2.00	1.64e−5	−0.25
Transparency Task 1	0.83	1713.50	0.092	−3.59e−5	5.85e−5	−0.31
Transparency Task 2	0.24	1844.00	0.594	−3.10e−5	5.06e−5	0.09
Transparency Task 3	2.46	1362.50	0.013*	−2.00	−5.77e−5	−0.38

Note. *p < 0.05

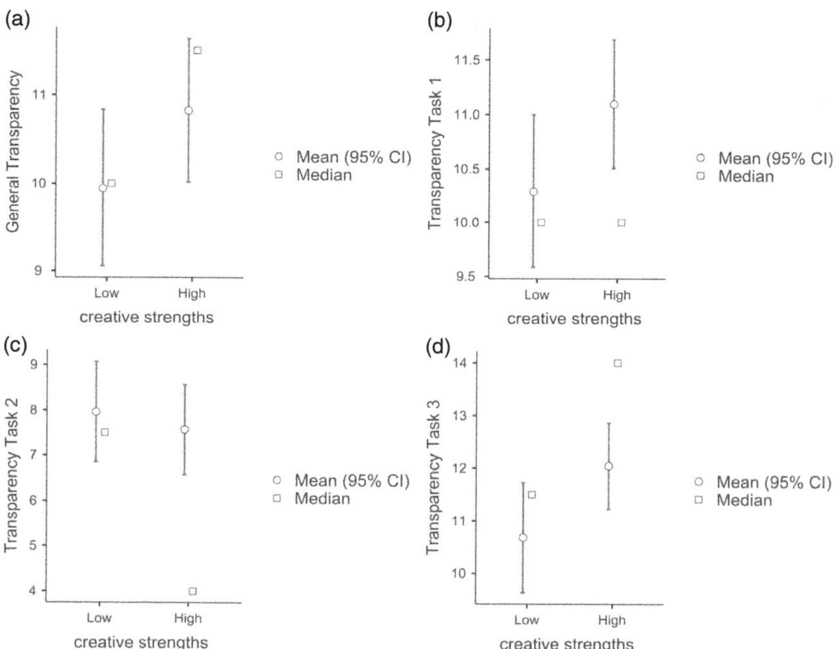

Figure 5.21 Descriptive plots for Creative Strengths and semantic transparency

However, there is a statistically significant difference between the L-cohort (M = 10.68, Med = 11.5, SD = 3.78) and the H-cohort (M = 12.04, Med = 14, SD = 3.51) in semantic transparency in the third word formation task (U = 1363, p = 0.013, Cohen's d = −0.38, BF_{10} = 2.459, BF_{01} = 0.407).

Table 5.54. *Mann–Whitney U test for Creative Strengths and economy of expression*

	BF_{10}	U	p	95% confidence interval Lower	Upper	Cohen's d
General economy	5.32	1596.00	0.010*	6.70e−5	3.05e−5	0.46
Economy Task 1	1.13	1742.00	0.091	−4.49e−5	1.00e−5	0.29
Economy Task 2	0.25	1854.00	0.605	−4.36e−5	4.91e−5	−0.05
Economy Task 3	8.03	1311.50	0.005**	4.92e−5	1.00	0.53

Note. $*p < 0.05$, $**p < 0.01$

Creative Strengths and Economy of Expression

Concerning Creative Strengths and economy of expression, the differences between the H-cohort and the L-cohort are statistically significant in general and in the third word formation task. The H-cohort formed words in a less economical way (except in the second task).

More specifically, as depicted in Table 5.54 and Figure 5.22, there is a statistically significant difference between the L-cohort (M = 3.34, Med = 4, SD = 0.91) and the H-cohort (M = 2.99, Med = 3, SD = 0.99) in economy of expression in general (U = 1596, p = 0.010, Cohen's d = 0.46, $BF_{10} = 5.323$, $BF_{01} = 0.188$).

There are no statistically significant differences between the L-cohort (M = 3.49, Med = 4, SD = 0.88) and the H-cohort (M = 3.22, Med = 4, SD = 0.97) in economy of expression in the first word formation task (U = 1742, p = 0.091, Cohen's d = 0.29, $BF_{10} = 1.125$, $BF_{01} = 0.889$) or between the L-cohort (M = 3.37, Med = 4, SD = 0.83) and the H-cohort (M = 3.42, Med = 4, SD = 0.87) in the second word formation task (U = 1854, p = 0.605, Cohen's d = −0.05, $BF_{10} = 0.250$, $BF_{01} = 3.997$).

There is a statistically significant difference between the L-cohort (M = 2.96, Med = 3, SD = 0.97) and the H-cohort (M = 2.49, Med = 2, SD = 0.83) in economy of expression in the third word formation task (U = 1312, p = 0.005, Cohen's d = 0.53, $BF_{10} = 8.026$, $BF_{01} = 0.125$).

Composite Score and Semantic Transparency

Concerning Composite Score and semantic transparency in the word formation test, the differences between the H-cohort and the L-cohort are statistically significant only in the third word formation task. The H-cohort formed words in a slightly more transparent way (except in the second task).

Table 5.55. *Mann–Whitney U test for Composite Score and semantic transparency*

	BF_{10}	U	p	95% confidence interval Lower	Upper	Cohen's d
General transparency	0.46	2110.00	0.137	−2.00	7.76e−6	−0.21
Transparency Task 1	0.44	2140.50	0.201	−7.61e−6	6.13e−5	−0.20
Transparency Task 2	0.30	2080.50	0.222	−6.02e−5	7.16e−6	0.23
Transparency Task 3	3.23	1641.50	0.018*	−2.39e−5	−1.10e−5	−0.43

Note. *p < 0.05

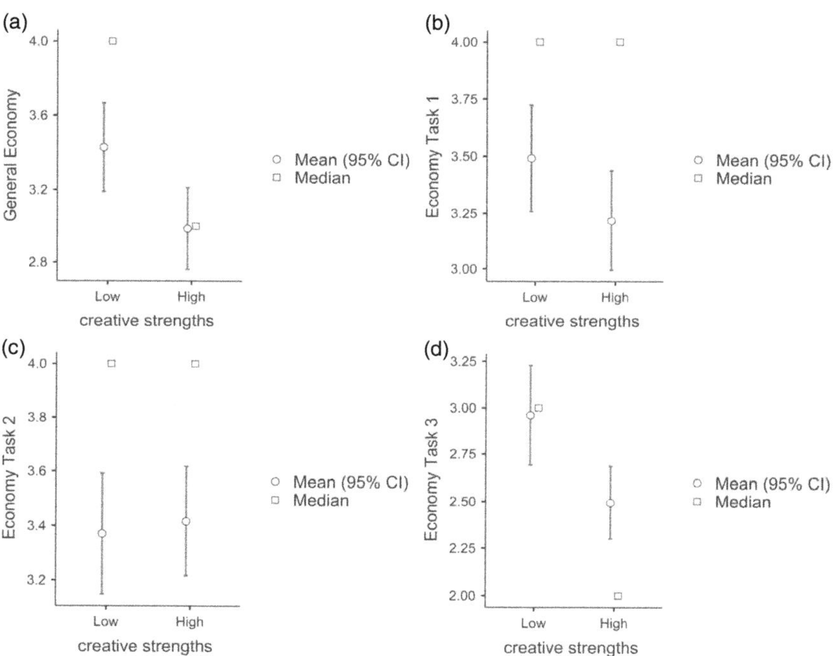

Figure 5.22 Descriptive plots for Creative Strengths and economy of expression

More specifically, as depicted in Table 5.55 and Figure 5.23, there are no statistically significant differences between the L-cohort (M = 10.53, Med = 10, SD = 3.19) and the H-cohort (M = 11.21, Med = 12.50, SD = 3.37) in semantic transparency in general (U = 2110, p = 0.137, Cohen's d = −0.21,

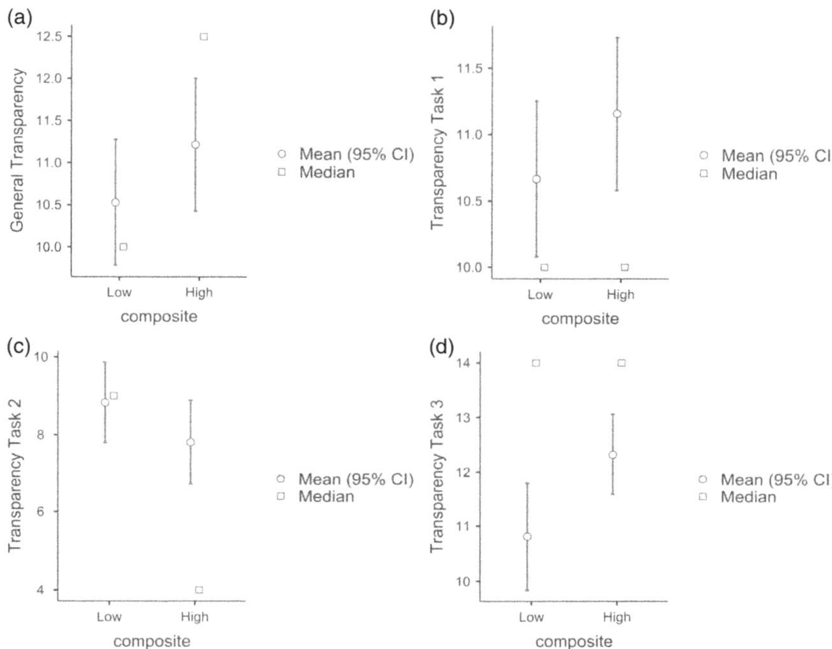

Figure 5.23 Descriptive plots for Composite Score and semantic transparency

BF_{10} = 0.458, BF_{01} = 2.182); between the L-cohort (M = 10.67, Med = 10, SD = 2.49) and the H-cohort (M = 11.16, Med = 10, SD = 2.47) in the first word formation task (U = 2141, p = 0.201, Cohen's d = −0.20, BF_{10} = 0.442, BF_{01} = 2.262); or between the L-cohort (M = 8.83, Med = 9, SD = 4.40) and the H-cohort (M = 7.81, Med = 4, SD = 4.52) in the second word formation task (U = 2081, p = 0.222, Cohen's d = 0.23, BF_{10} = 0.302, BF_{01} = 3.308).

However, there is a statistically significant difference between the L-cohort (M = 10.81, Med = 14, SD = 4) and the H-cohort (M = 12.32, Med = 14, SD = 3.05) in semantic transparency in the third word formation task (U = 1642, p = 0.018, Cohen's d = −0.43, BF_{10} = 3.234, BF_{01} = 0.309).

Composite Score and Economy of Expression

Concerning Composite Score and economy of expression, the differences between the H-cohort and the L-cohort are not statistically significant with the exception of the third task. The H-cohort formed words in a less economical way (except in the second task).

Table 5.56. *Mann–Whitney U test for Composite Score and economy of expression*

				95% confidence interval		
	BF_{10}	U	p	Lower	Upper	Cohen's d
General economy	0.96	2043.00	0.055	−4.30e−5	8.48e−6	0.33
Economy Task 1	0.37	2224.00	0.339	−8.14e−5	2.45e−5	0.16
Economy Task 2	0.22	2237.50	0.600	−3.04e−5	2.85e−5	−0.06
Economy Task 3	3.40	1616.00	0.011*	4.73e−5	2.85e−5	0.47

Note. *$p < 0.05$

More specifically, as depicted in Table 5.56 and Figure 5.24, there are no statistically significant differences between the L-cohort (M = 3.29, Med = 4, SD = 0.93) and the H-cohort (M = 2.97, Med = 3, SD = 0.98) in economy of expression in general (U = 2043, p = 0.055, Cohen's d = 0.33, $BF_{10} = 0.957$, $BF_{01} = 1.045$); between the L-cohort (M = 3.39, Med = 4, SD = 0.91) and the H-cohort (M = 3.24, Med = 4, SD = 0.95) in the first word formation task (U = 2224, p = 0.339, Cohen's d = 0.16, $BF_{10} = 0.367$, $BF_{01} = 2.727$); or between the L-cohort (M = 3.27, Med = 4, SD = 0.96) and the H-cohort (M = 3.33, Med = 4, SD = 0.91) in the second word formation task (U = 2238, p = 0.600, Cohen's d = −.06, $BF_{10} = 0.217$, $BF_{01} = 4.614$).

However, there is a statistically significant difference between the L-cohort (M = 2.89, Med = 2, SD = 0.96) and the H-cohort (M = 2.48, Med = 2, SD = 0.81) in economy of expression in the third word formation task (U = 1616, p = 0.011, Cohen's d = 0.47, $BF_{10} = 3.403$, $BF_{01} = 0.294$).

Further Issues

As with the secondary school respondents, we will mention two procedures controlling the false positives (a rejection of a true null hypothesis also known as type I error). When controlling the family-wise error rate with the more stringent Bonferroni (1936) correction, if all 48 comparisons are encompassed, only p values lower than 0.001 should be considered as statistically significant. When controlling the false discovery rate through Benjamini and Hochberg's (1995) procedure, only p values <0.005 could be considered statistically significant (one or two cases from all results are marked as statistically significant).

Furthermore, to provide information regarding the magnitude of the effect irrespective of the sample size, the effect size is reported. Considering the magnitude of the effect size according to the classical benchmarks of Cohen (1977, 1988), the results are as follows: (a) none of the results were large in magnitude; (b) a medium effect size was found for the differences between the

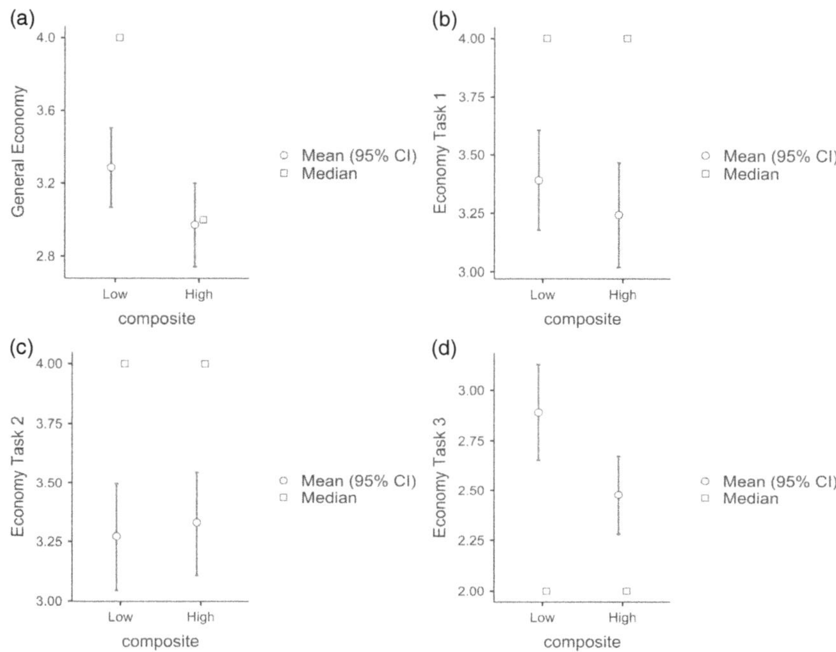

Figure 5.24 Descriptive plots for Composite Score and economy of expression

L-cohort and the H-cohort in Composite Score and economy of expression in the third word formation task, for Elaboration and transparency in the third word formation task, and for Creative Strengths and economy of expression in general and in the third word formation task; (c) a small effect size was found for the differences between the L-cohort and the H-cohort regarding Composite Score and semantic transparency in general and in the first and the second word formation tasks, for Composite Score and economy of expression in general and in the first word formation task, for Elaboration and semantic transparency in general and in the first and the third word formation tasks, for Elaboration and economy of expression in general and in the first and the second word formation tasks, for Fluency and semantic transparency in the first, second, and third word formation tasks, for Fluency and economy of expression in the first, second, and third word formation tasks, for Flexibility and semantic transparency in the second word formation task, for Flexibility and economy of expression in the second word formation task, for Originality and semantic transparency in general and in the first and second word formation tasks, for Originality and economy of expression in general and in the first and third word formation tasks, for Creative Strengths and semantic transparency in general and in the first and third word formation tasks, and for Creative Strengths and economy of expression in the first word formation task.

In addition, when pondering the strength of evidence for an alternative hypothesis from the Bayesian perspective (and the verbal interpretational scheme provided by Wagenmakers et al. 2017), the results are as follows: (a) anecdotal to moderate evidence for the alternative hypothesis relative to H0 was found for Composite Score and semantic transparency and economy of expression in the third word formation task, for Elaboration and semantic transparency and economy of expression in the third-word formation task, for Originality and general economy of expression, and for Creative Strengths and general economy of expression as well as in the third word formation task and (b) anecdotal evidence was found for Elaboration and semantic transparency in the first word formation task, for Elaboration and economy of expression in general, for Fluency and semantic transparency and economy of expression in the second and third word formation tasks, for Flexibility and semantic transparency as well as economy of expression in the second word formation task, for Originality and general transparency as well as semantic transparency and economy of expression in the third word formation task, and for Creative Strengths and semantic transparency in the third word formation task. This is in line with the proposal that some of these results could be false positives.

Considering the null results, there is (a) moderate evidence for the null hypothesis regarding Elaboration and transparency in the second word formation task, Fluency and general transparency and economy in the first and second word formation tasks and general economy in the first word formation task, Flexibility and general transparency in the first and third word formation tasks and general economy in the first and third word formation tasks, Originality and transparency and economy in the second word formation task, Creative Strengths and transparency and economy in the second word formation task, and Composite Score and transparency and economy in the second word formation task and (b) only anecdotal evidence for the null hypothesis regarding, for instance, Elaboration and general transparency and economy in the second task.

Summary of Inferential Statistics and Sensitivity Analysis

In a nutshell, when pondering the hypothesis in the sample of university students, the data here are more in line with the proposed hypothesis than in the case of the secondary school students, but the results are not conclusive across the individual TTCT scores and word formation tasks. More specifically, the results indicate that *there are differences in semantic transparency and economy of expression between the L-cohort and the H-cohort, especially in Composite Score, Creative Strengths, Originality, and Elaboration, but mainly in the third word formation task. In this task, the H-cohort formed words that are more semantically transparent and less economical in comparison to the L-cohort. Furthermore, the results indicate that there are differences in semantic transparency and economy of expression between the L-cohort and the H-cohort in Fluency and Flexibility, but, in contrast, mainly in the second word formation task and in the opposite direction: the H-cohort formed words that are less semantically transparent and more economical in comparison to the L-cohort.* There is, however, a noteworthy risk that some results are false positives due to multiple comparisons and due to the fact that, according to the Bayes factor, the evidence for the alternative hypothesis relative to H0 is anecdotal to moderate.

As in the case of the secondary school students, a sensitivity analysis was conducted where all variables were used in a non-dichotomized form (see also Körtvélyessy, Štekauer and Kačmár, 2021). For this purpose, Kendall's non-parametric τ correlation coefficient was used to corroborate if there is a relationship between the TTCT subscores and economy of expression, on the one hand, and semantic transparency, on the other, across the individual word formation tasks.

As can be seen in Table 5.57, significant correlations are found between the creativity subscores and economy of expression and semantic transparency, and these correlations are small in magnitude. Crucially, this pattern of results is in line with the main analysis because Flexibility and Fluency are negatively correlated with semantic transparency in the second word formation task. Incomparison, Composite Score, Originality, Elaboration, and Creative Strengths are found to be positively correlated to general transparency and negatively to economy of expression, mainly in the third word formation task and also for the general economy index.

To provide additional evidence, we computed the Bayes factor indicating the amount of evidence in support of the alternative hypothesis relative to H0 as well as the lower and upper 95% credible intervals (Table 5.58). There was strong to extreme evidence for the alternative hypothesis over the null hypothesis, especially in the third word formation task.

5.1.2.3 Summary II

(i) The data on university undergraduates give fairly strong support to Hypothesis 2 by demonstrating a much higher occurrence of failed answers in the L-cohort, especially in the second and third word formation tasks. This tendency is most evident in the creativity indicators/subscores *Creative Strengths*, *Composite Score*, and *Originality*, and slightly less evident in Elaboration.

Table 5.57. *Correlations among variables*

	Composite	Fluency	Flexibility	Originality	Elaboration	Creative Strengths
General transparency	0.06	−0.01	0.01	0.06	0.08	0.08
Transparency Task 1	0.06	−0.03	0.02	0.07	0.09	0.08
Transparency Task 2	−0.06	−0.10*	−0.09*	−0.04	0.00	−0.01
Transparency Task 3	0.13**	0.07	0.05	0.08	0.14**	0.13**
General economy	−0.09	0.02	0.01	−0.10*	−0.12*	−0.14**
Economy Task 1	−0.05	0.05	0.02	−0.10*	−0.06	−0.08
Economy Task 2	0.03	0.09	0.07	0.06	−0.07	0.01
Economy Task 3	−0.15**	−0.08	−0.07	−0.10*	−0.15**	−0.15**

Note. *$p < 0.05$, **$p < 0.01$

Table 5.58. *Strength of evidence for the alternative hypothesis relative to H0*

		Composite	Fluency	Flexibility	Elaboration	Originality	Creative Strengths
General transparency	Kendall's τ	0.06	−0.01	0.01	0.08	0.06	0.08
	BF_{10}	0.24	0.08	0.08	0.66	0.29	0.76
	Upper 95% CI	0.13	0.06	0.08	0.15	0.14	0.16
	Lower 95% CI	−0.02	−0.09	−0.07	0.00	−0.01	0.01
Transparency Task 1	Kendall's τ	0.06	−0.03	0.02	0.09	0.07	0.08
	BF_{10}	0.24	0.10	0.08	0.81	0.33	0.71
	Upper 95% CI	0.13	0.05	0.09	0.16	0.14	0.16
	Lower 95% CI	−0.02	−0.11	−0.06	0.01	−0.01	0.00
Transparency Task 2	Kendall's τ	−0.06	−0.10	−0.09	0.00	−0.04	−0.01
	BF_{10}	0.28	2.32	1.23	0.08	0.13	0.08
	Upper 95% CI	0.01	−0.03	−0.02	0.08	0.04	0.07
	Lower 95% CI	−0.14	−0.18	−0.17	−0.08	−0.12	−0.09
Transparency Task 3	Kendall's τ	0.13*	0.07	0.05	0.14*	0.08	0.13*
	BF_{10}	17.66	0.32	0.20	21.33	0.46	10.62
	Upper 95% CI	0.21	0.14	0.13	0.21	0.15	0.20
	Lower 95% CI	0.05	−0.01	−0.03	0.05	−0.00	0.05
General economy	Kendall's τ	−0.09	0.02	0.01	−0.12	−0.10	−0.14**
	BF_{10}	0.93	0.09	0.08	6.97	1.68	49.79
	Upper 95% CI	−0.01	0.10	0.09	−0.04	−0.02	−0.06
	Lower 95% CI	−0.16	−0.05	−0.06	−0.19	−0.17	−0.22
Economy Task 1	Kendall's τ	−0.05	0.05	0.02	−0.06	−0.10	−0.08
	BF_{10}	0.17	0.19	0.08	0.28	2.27	0.79
	Upper 95% CI	0.03	0.13	0.09	0.01	−0.03	−0.01
	Lower 95% CI	−0.13	−0.02	−0.06	−0.14	−0.18	−0.16
Economy Task 2	Kendall's τ	0.03	0.09	0.07	−0.07	0.06	0.01
	BF_{10}	0.10	1.11	0.41	0.39	0.27	0.08
	Upper 95% CI	0.11	0.17	0.15	0.01	0.14	0.09
	Lower 95% CI	−0.05	0.01	−0.01	−0.15	−0.02	−0.07
Economy Task 3	Kendall's τ	−0.15***	−0.08	−0.07	−0.15***	−0.10	−0.15**
	BF_{10}	101.55	0.65	0.30	102.25	1.59	91.41
	Upper 95% CI	−0.07	−0.00	0.01	−0.07	−0.02	−0.07
	Lower 95% CI	−0.23	−0.16	−0.15	−0.23	−0.18	−0.23

Note. $*BF_{10} > 10$, $**BF_{10} > 30$, $***BF_{10} > 100$

(ii) Although the number of comparisons between the H-cohort and the L-cohort is not statistically significant, there is a *general tendency towards forming new complex words of higher semantic transparency and lower economy in the H-cohort.* The creativity indicators/subscores that appear to be related to word formation creativity in the sense of this tendency include *Originality*, *Elaboration*, *Creative Strengths*, and *Composite Score*, primarily in the third word formation task as some of these are statistically significant. The indicators that appear to run counter to this tendency are Fluency and Flexibility in the second word formation task.

(iii) The choice of a naming strategy seems to be influenced by the nature of the naming task. This is evident from the different naming strategies that are employed predominantly in solving individual naming tasks. While in Task 1 in which the respondents could select a complex word from a set of options, the respondents of both cohorts according to all creativity indicators preferred OT1 (transparency degree 7 – maximum transparency), OT9 (transparency degree 3), and OT2 (transparency degree 5), the tasks that required the application of a more demanding analysis of the object to be named at the onomasiological level and its representation at the morphemic level show competition between the most transparent and least economical OT1, on the one hand, and the less transparent and more economical OT3, on the other. At the same time, there is a substantial difference between Tasks 2 and 3. While semantic transparency degree 2 is the central naming type in Task 2 (based on verbal descriptions), degree 7 is an unambiguously dominant naming option in Task 3 (based on drawings).

(iv) Considerable differences can also be found inside individual tasks, which suggest that the specific features of an object to be named may exert their influence upon the selection of a naming strategy. This is especially evident in the key role of transparency degree 3 in Task 1.1. In the other experimental tasks, its role approaches zero.

(v) The data show a minimum or peripheral role (in giving names to Agents/Patients) of three onomasiological types, which represent various degrees of economy of expression: OT4 (transparency degree 4) and OT6 (transparency degree 1) represent the highest economy of expression, and to them, one can add OT5 (transparency degree 6; medium economy).

5.1.3 *Comparison of the Results in word formation: Secondary School Students versus University Undergraduates*

Two hypotheses were formulated at the beginning of this research. Hypothesis 1 postulated higher semantic transparency of the older age group, that is, the

Table 5.59. *Comparison of OT1 percentages in the secondary school students (SS) and university undergraduates (UU) groups – L-cohorts*

	Task 1		Task 2		Task 3		Tasks 1–3	
	SS	UU	SS	UU	SS	UU	SS	UU
Originality	45	32	35	36	66	57	48	41
Elaboration	43	35	29	30	60	60	44	41
Flexibility	38	36	32	38	55	60	41	44
Fluency	43	38	31	45	59	53	44	45
Cr. Strengths	39	34	29	32	52	57	39	41
Comp. Score	42	32	30	35	57	58	43	41

Table 5.60. *Comparison of OT1 percentages in the SS and UU groups – H-cohorts*

	Task 1		Task 2		Task 3		Tasks 1–3	
	SS	UU	SS	UU	SS	UU	SS	UU
Originality	42	44	33	38	62	72	48	51
Elaboration	41	41	36	35	66	71	47	48
Flexibility	42	42	26	30	52	67	40	46
Fluency	40	38	33	36	62	70	45	47
Cr. Strengths	39	41	33	35	66	73	45	50
Comp. Score	42	41	33	35	64	72	46	49

university undergraduates, compared to the group of secondary school students. Hypothesis 2 expected higher word formation creativity in the H-cohort of both age groups. Let us evaluate these hypotheses with regard to the results obtained for both age groups.

Hypothesis 1

There are no substantial differences between the two groups of respondents even though certain tendencies can be identified, as illustrated in Tables 5.59 and 5.60, which compare the percentages of OT1 in the two groups in Tasks 1–3 in individual indicators/subscores according to the data of the L-cohort.

First of all, it can be seen that while the percentage of OT1 is higher in the secondary school students (SS) group than in the university undergraduates (UU) group in all creativity indicators in Task 1 (most strikingly in Originality with a 13% difference, Composite Score – 10%, and Elaboration – 8%), in contrast to this, Task 2 provides the opposite picture: all percentages of OT1 are higher in the UU group (most strikingly in *Fluency* – 14% difference, *Flexibility* – 6%, and *Composite Score* – 5%). The differences in the other creativity indicators in Task 2 are negligible. Task 3 is ambiguous in this respect. Hypothesis 1 is only supported in *Flexibility* and *Creative Strengths*. The cumulative data do not provide any evidence of the higher preference of the UU students for semantically more transparent coinages.

Table 5.60 compares the two groups from the point of view of the H-cohorts of the SS and UU groups.

The data in Table 5.60 provide a different picture for the H-cohorts than that obtained from Table 5.59 for the L-cohorts. While in the L-cohorts the use of OT1 is higher in the SS group in all indicators/subscores in Task 1, the figures for the H-cohort are very similar or even identical in both age groups. Hypothesis 1 has weak support from Task 2 – while the percentage of the use of OT1 in the UU group is higher than in the SS group in five out of the six indicators/subscores (the exception being Elaboration), the differences do not exceed 5%. Strong support for Hypothesis 1 comes from the drawing-based *Task 3* in all indicators/subscores. The differences are striking, especially in *Flexibility* (15% difference), but also in *Originality* (10%), *Composite Score*, *Fluency* (both 8%), and *Creative Strengths* (7%). Nevertheless, the cumulative data (due to Tasks 1 and 2) are not so conclusively in favour of Hypothesis 1, because the biggest differences between the two age groups are only 6% for Flexibility and 5% for Creative Strengths.

The data thus show that the situation in the H-cohort is completely different from that in the L-cohort for all three tasks and in the cumulative values:

(a) In *the L-cohort*, Hypothesis 1 has found
  - strong support in *Task 2* from *Fluency*;
  - weak support in *Task 2* from Flexibility and Composite Score; and
  - weak support in *Task 3* from Flexibility and Creative Strengths.

(b) In the *H-cohort*, Hypothesis 1 has found
  - weak support in *Task 2* from Originality and Flexibility;
  - strong support in Task 3 from Flexibility, Originality, Composite Score, Fluency, and Creative Strengths; and
  - weak support in Task 3 from Elaboration.

The assumption of a different impact of creative potential on the L-cohort and the H-cohort is corroborated by comparing the average values of the use of the prevailing onomasiological types in Tasks 3 and 1. The most striking difference between the two cohorts concerns Task 3. While the average OT1 proportion in the UU L-cohort is 57.5%, it is 71% in the H-cohort. In Task 1, the average value in the UU L-cohort is 34.5%, and it is 41% in the

Table 5.61. *Comparison of OT3 percentages in the SS and UU groups – L-cohorts*

	Task 1		Task 2		Task 3		Tasks 1–3	
	SS	UU	SS	UU	SS	UU	SS	UU
Originality	6	10	56	56	23	30	26	30
Elaboration	8	11	60	54	24	27	28	29
Flexibility	5	9	54	52	30	29	28	28
Fluency	4	8	56	46	25	33	27	27
Cr. Strengths	7	11	61	55	28	25	30	28
Comp. Score	7	10	58	50	27	30	29	28

Table 5.62. *Comparison of OT3 percentages in the SS and UU groups – H-cohorts*

	Task 1		Task 2		Task 3		Tasks 1–3	
	SS	UU	SS	UU	SS	UU	SS	UU
Originality	6	6	62	53	29	23	30	26
Elaboration	5	9	56	61	25	22	27	29
Flexibility	8	5	66	64	33	23	34	29
Fluency	6	7	60	58	26	21	28	27
Cr. Strengths	7	7	60	58	22	22	27	27
Comp. Score	6	9	59	58	26	21	29	28

H-cohort. The cumulative values are 42% versus 48.5%. Interestingly, Task 2 values in these cohorts are very similar, and so are the cumulative values for all three tasks in the L-cohorts of the SS group.

In Tables 5.61 and 5.62, we compare the SS and UU groups from the point of view of the most frequent economical onomasiological type – OT3 (transparency degree 2, mid-level economy).

The OT3 data give further evidence of the influence of the nature of the word formation tasks upon the results of the two groups of respondents. The UU respondents' use of a more economical OT3 in the L-cohort is higher than in the SS group in Task 1 and clearly lower in Task 2 (except for Originality). OT3 is more common in the UU group in four indicators/ subscores (the exceptions being Flexibility and Creative Strengths), and the data for the cumulative value are ambiguous as a result of the contradictory results in the individual tasks.

Table 5.63. *Prevalence of the use of OT1 and OT3 – L-cohorts*

	OT1	OT3
Task 1	SS – all indicators	UU – all indicators
Task 2	UU – all indicators	SS – five indicators (plus equal values for the sixth indicator)
Task 3	SS – Originality, Fluency UU – Flexibility, Creative Strengths, Composite Score	SS – Flexibility, Creative Strengths UU – Originality, Elaboration, Fluency, Composite Score

Table 5.64. *Prevalence of the use of OT1 and OT3 – H-cohorts*

	OT1	OT3
Task 1	SS – Fluency, Composite Score UU – Originality, Creative Strengths SS=UU – Elaboration, Flexibility	SS – Flexibility UU – Elaboration, Fluency, Composite Score SS=UU – Originality, Creative Strengths
Task 2	SS – Elaboration UU – Originality, Flexibility, Fluency. Creative Strengths, Composite Score	SS – Originality, Flexibility, Fluency. Creative Strengths, Composite Score UU – Elaboration
Task 3	UU – All indicators	SS – Originality, Elaboration, Flexibility, Fluency, Composite Score SS=UU – Creative Strengths

Unlike the L-cohorts, the data for Task 1 do not show any clear differences between the SS and UU respondents in the H-cohorts. If individual indicators/ subscores are taken into consideration, the maximum differences between these groups are found for Elaboration and Composite Score (4% and 3%, respectively, in favour of the UU group), which is a relatively high difference with regard to the low percentage of OT3 in Task 1. In Task 2, the results are similar to the L-cohort. With the exception of Elaboration, the percentage use of OT3 is lower in the UU group, even if the only bigger difference between the two groups occurs in Originality (9%). Unlike the L-cohort, the use of OT3 is much higher in the SS group, with the biggest difference (10%) found in Flexibility.

If these results are viewed in relation to the use of OT1, they give a logical, complementary picture. A higher percentage of one onomasiological type in a particular indicator is accompanied by a lower percentage of the other onomasiological type and vice versa, as is evident from Tables 5.63 and 5.64.

In addition to the previous observations, there seems to be a tendency for a similar share of OT1 in the total number of coinages in all indicators/ subscores. For instance, the cumulative data show that the percentages in the L-cohort of the UU group are within a small range from 41% to 45%, for Task 3 from 53% to 60%, for Task 2 from 30% to 38% (with the exception of Fluency – 45%), and for Task 1 from 32% to 38%. In the H-cohort of the UU group, it is between 46% and 51% for the cumulative data, between 67% and 73% for Task 3, between 35% and 38% (with one minor exception) for Task 2, and between 38% and 44% for Task 1. Similar observations also apply to the SS group. This finding gives additional support to the observation of the influential role of the individual tasks upon the results.

Finally, there is considerable agreement in the indicators/subscores that exert influence on the selection of word formation strategies in the SS and UU groups. While in the SS group, there is only *Creative Strengths* which gives important support to Hypothesis 1, *Composite Score*, *Elaboration*, and *Fluency* support its postulations, too. In the UU group, the number of indicators/subscores that play an important role in this respect is higher. They comprise *Originality*, *Elaboration*, *Creative Strengths*, and *Composite Score*.

Hypothesis 2

Hypothesis 2 postulates higher creativity (lower percentage of failed answers) in the H-cohort. While no universal evidence of the relevance of this hypothesis has been found – with unequal percentages of failed answers in the L-cohort and the H-cohort across all three tasks of the word formation experiment – the results of the UU group give strong support to Hypothesis 2 in Originality, Elaboration, Creative Strengths, Composite Score, and Fluency in Task 2 and the same indicators/subscores, with the exception of Fluency, in Task 3. The most evident support comes from *Creative Strengths*, *Originality*, and *Composite Score*. The hypothesis is primarily contradicted by Flexibility.

In the SS group, the hypothesis has found much less support. Hypothesis 2 has been violated in almost all creativity indicators/subscores in Task 2. Better results of the H-cohort have been found for *Flexibility* in Task 1, *Elaboration* in Task 2, and all indicators – mainly *Originality* – in Task 3, with the exception of Flexibility. The data thus show the role of the age factor in word formation creativity, even if this role varies by word formation task and by creativity indicator/subscore.

The data suggest that the H-cohort of the UU group, that is, the older group of respondents, manifests more substantial evidence of higher word formation creativity than the data of the secondary school respondents.

5.2 Creativity and Word Interpretation

5.2.1 Secondary School Students

The influence of creative potential, identified by means of the TTCT scores for individual creativity indicators/subscores, upon the way language speakers interpret potential words will be evaluated from the point of view of four criteria: (i) Predictability Rate (PR); (ii) Objectified Predictability Rate (OPR); (iii) average number of readings per cohort member; and (iv) hapax legomena.[2] The evaluation will be related to Hypotheses 3, 4, and 5, as specified in the Introduction.

5.2.1.1 Predictability Rate

While this parameter does not tell us much about interpretational creativity, it serves as an input for the computation of the OPR that, according to our hypothesis, is relevant to the assessment of creativity. Nevertheless, it is included in this analysis for three reasons: (i) the ranking of the individual readings can tell us whether or not there are any differences between the L-cohort and the H-cohort in their interpretational preferences; (ii) it can indicate the influence of a word formation process (compounding vs. conversion, in our case) upon the interpretation of novel words and the differences between the two cohorts; and (iii) it can give additional support to Štekauer's claim (2005a) according to which, for each novel complex word, there is one (rarely two) strong reading in terms of meaning predictability, irrespective of the creative potential of language speakers.

First, the data are provided in the form of tables; then, they are briefly commented on in terms of the three aforementioned criteria. The ranking of readings is shown in Table 5.65.

(i) *Most predictable readings*

The most predictable readings are identical for all indicators/subscores in both cohorts for *baby book*: 'a book for a baby'. For *flower hat*, the most predictable reading in all indicators/subscores and in both cohorts is 'a hat made of flowers', with the exception of the Flexibility indicator, where the H-cohort prefers the reading 'a hat with a flower in it'. The reading 'a hat made of flowers' ranks third in this cohort, but the differences in the respective PR values of the three highest-ranked readings of *flower hat* are very low. The converted word *to boy* is in all indicators and both cohorts clearly dominated

[2] Some preliminary results are also presented in Körtvélyessy, Štekauer and Kačmár (2020).

Table 5.65. *The ranking of readings by indicator/subscore, cohort, and PR value*

	Cohort	Baby book	Flower hat	To boy	To tulip
Originality	L	a book for a baby	a hat made of flowers	to behave like a boy	to grow tulips
		a book about the care of a baby	a hat with a flower in it	to date a boy	to look pretty
		a small book	a hat with a flower pattern	to give something (sth) to a boy	to like flowers
		a photo album	a hat with a flower shape	to undergo gender-changing surgery	to pick tulips
	H	a book for a baby	a hat made of flowers	to behave like a boy	to grow tulips
		a book about the care of a baby	a hat with a flower pattern	to date a boy	to pick tulips
		a photo album	a hat with a flower in it	to be immature	to look pretty
		a book of records of one's baby	a hat with a flower shape	to dress like a boy	to blossom
Elaboration	L	a book for a baby	a hat made of flowers	to behave like a boy	to grow tulips
		a book about the care of a baby	a hat with a flower pattern	to date a boy	to like flowers
		a story of a baby	a hat with a flower in it	to undergo gender-changing surgery	to look pretty
		a photo album	the top of a flower	to be immature	to pick tulips
	H	a book for a baby	a hat made of flowers	to behave like a boy	to grow tulips
		a book about the care of a baby	a hat with a flower pattern	to date a boy	to look pretty
		a photo album	a hat with a flower in it	to be immature	to like flowers
		a small book	a hat with a flower shape	to undergo gender-changing surgery	to give a tulip to somebody (sb)
Flexibility	L	a book for a baby	a hat made of flowers	to behave like a boy	to grow tulips
		a book about the care of a baby	a hat with a flower in it	to date a boy	to look pretty
		a photo album	a hat with a flower pattern	to undergo gender-changing surgery	to like flowers
		a small book	a hat with a flower shape	to dress like a boy	to pick tulips
	H	a book for a baby	a hat with a flower in it	to behave like a boy	to grow tulips
		a book about the care of a baby	a hat with a flower pattern	to date a boy	to look pretty

Table 5.65. *(cont.)*

	Cohort	Baby book	Flower hat	To boy	To tulip
		a story of a baby	a hat made of flowers	to undergo gender-changing surgery	to like flowers
		a photo album	a hat with a flower shape	to be immature	to pick tulips
Fluency	L	a book for a baby	a hat made of flowers	to behave like a boy	to grow tulips
		a book about the care of a baby	a hat with a flower in it	to date a boy	to look pretty
		a photo album	a hat with a flower pattern	to undergo gender-changing surgery	to like sb
		a small book	a hat with a flower shape	to become matured	to look like a tulip
	H	a book for a baby	a hat made of flowers	to behave like a boy	to grow tulips
		a book about the care of a baby	a hat with a flower in it	to undergo gender-changing surgery	to look pretty
		a photo album	a hat with a flower pattern	to date a boy	to pick tulips
		a story of a baby	a hat with a flower shape	to be immature	to be a narcissist
Creative Strengths	L	a book for a baby	a hat made of flowers	to behave like a boy	to grow tulips
		a book about the care of a baby	a hat with a flower in it	to date a boy	to look pretty
		a story of a baby	a hat with a flower pattern	to undergo gender-changing surgery	to pick tulips
		a photo album	a hat with a flower shape	to look like a boy	to look like a tulip
	H	a book for a baby	a hat made of flowers	to behave like a boy	to grow tulips
		a book about the care of a baby	a hat with a flower pattern	to date a boy	to look pretty
		a photo album	a hat with a flower in it	to undergo gender-changing surgery	to pick tulips
		a book of records of one's baby	a hat with a flower shape	to be immature	to be a narcissist
Composite Score	L	a book for a baby	a hat made of flowers	to behave like a boy	to grow tulips
		a book about the care of a baby	a hat with a flower in it	to date a boy	to look pretty
		a photo album	a hat with a flower pattern	to undergo gender-changing surgery	to like flowers
		a book of records of one's baby	a hat with a flower shape	to dress like a boy	to look like a tulip
	H	a book for a baby	a hat made of flowers	to behave like a boy	to grow tulips
		a book about the care of a baby	a hat with a flower pattern	to date a boy	to look pretty
		a photo album	a hat with a flower in it	to be immature	to be a narcissist
		a small book	a hat with a flower shape	to dress like a boy	to pick tulips

Table 5.66. *Predictability rates for the most predictable reading of* baby book

Cohort	Elaboration	Fluency	Flexibility	Originality	Creative Strengths	Composite Score
Low	**0.541**	0.494	0.542	0.538	**0.480**	**0.554**
High	**0.507**	**0.531**	**0.564**	**0.566**	**0.462**	**0.554**

Table 5.67. *Predictability rates for the most predictable reading of* flower hat

Cohort	Elaboration	Fluency	Flexibility	Originality	Creative Strengths	Composite Score
Low	0.400	**0.355**	**0.383**	**0.301**	**0.291**	**0.500**
High	**0.549**	**0.332**	**0.181**	**0.262**	**0.261**	**0.338**

Table 5.68. *Predictability rates for the most predictable reading of* to boy

Cohort	Elaboration	Fluency	Flexibility	Originality	Creative Strengths	Composite Score
Low	0.187	0.215	**0.242**	0.186	0.200	0.191
High	**0.382**	**0.252**	**0.241**	**0.290**	**0.350**	**0.319**

Table 5.69. *Predictability rates for the most predictable reading of* to tulip

Cohort	Elaboration	Fluency	Flexibility	Originality	Creative Strengths	Composite Score
Low	0.032	**0.080**	**0.070**	0.077	0.081	**0.099**
High	**0.065**	**0.060**	**0.062**	**0.084**	**0.101**	**0.086**

by the reading 'to behave like a boy'. The same is true of the reading 'to grow tulips' of the converted word *to tulip*.

What picture emerges from a comparison of the PR values of the topmost readings in both cohorts for individual indicators/subscores? The data are summarized in Tables 5.66–5.69 (the higher PR values are given in bold).

The answer to the previous question is that the picture is rather blurred and fuzzy, with no evident tendency for higher PR values in either of the cohorts. The topmost PR values for *baby book* are remarkably similar in both the L-cohort and the H-cohort, all of them around 0.5. The maximum difference between the H-cohort and the L-cohort is as low as 0.37 for the Fluency indicator. The values of the two cohorts are identical for the Composite Score.

With the exception of Elaboration, the topmost PRs for *flower hat* are higher in the L-cohort. The differences are bigger than those for *baby book* in Elaboration (0.149), Flexibility (0.202), and Composite Score (0.162). In addition, the PR values of the most predictable reading for *flower hat* are much lower than those for *baby book* with a single exception: the H-cohort's Elaboration.

The PR values of the most predictable readings of *to boy* are lower than the PR values of the two compounds in all indicators/subscores of the L-cohort but higher than the values of *flower hat* in three indicators of the H-cohort.

The PR values of the topmost readings of *to tulip* are extremely low compared to all three other words.

In sum, the data suggest that PR values are predetermined by the acceptability of potential readings of a novel complex word. The acceptability of the meanings of the two potential converted words used in our experiment is clearly much lower than the acceptability of the meanings of the potential compounds. There are also relatively high PR differences between the two compounds as well as the two converted words. The values of the best predictable readings drop from *baby book*, through *flower hat* and *to boy* down to *to tulip*. The PR values for the topmost readings of these words map the results for these words in the experiment with 40 respondents (Štekauer 2005a), as presented in (19):

(19)	*baby book*	0.727
	flower hat	0.404
	to boy	0.358
	to tulip	0.290

A comparison of the data thus suggests that the most influential factor that determines the PR value of potential words is the acceptability of individual potential readings. This establishes the fundamental limits within which we can examine the influence of individual creativity indicators and subscores upon the interpretation of complex words.

Furthermore, there is no systematic dominance of either the L-cohort or the H-cohort in the PR values. Table 5.70 shows which of the cohorts dominates in individual creativity indicators/subscores for the four experimental words.

It follows from Table 5.70 that there is no creativity indicator/subscore that is dominated in all four experimental words by a single cohort. The H-cohort

Table 5.70. *Comparison of PR values of creativity indicators/subscores by most predictable readings across cohorts*

	Elaboration	Fluency	Flexibility	Originality	Creative Strengths	Composite Score
baby book	L	H	H	H	L	L/H
flower hat	H	L	L	L	L	L
to boy	H	H	L	H	H	H
to tulip	H	L	L	H	H	L

tends to feature higher PR values in Elaboration and Originality while the L-cohort prevails in Flexibility. All in all, there are no systematic differences between the L-cohort and the H-cohort, which means that *creative potential does not seem to affect the Predictability Rate if the topmost readings are taken into consideration.*

(ii) *Ranking: comparison of the L-cohort and the H-cohort*

The predictability strength of the topmost readings expressed in the PR gap between the topmost reading and the next lowest reading evidently overpowers the differences in the creative potential of the respondents. We should, therefore, focus our attention on the lower-ranked readings that are not affected by the dominant reading with the highest predictability strength. From this perspective, the PR values of the second, third, and the fourth ranks for the H-cohort and the L-cohort are highly interesting.

Baby Book While for *baby book*, in each creativity indicator/subscore and in both cohorts, the second rank is assumed by the reading 'a book about the care of a baby', the PR differences between the two topmost readings are considerable in general. What is important, with the exception of the third rank reading of the Composite Score ('photo album'), is that there is no agreement between the two cohorts in any of the creativity indicators/subscores at the third or fourth ranks.

Flower Hat This observation is confirmed by the data for the *flower hat* compound. The reading 'a hat made of flowers' evidently dominates over the other readings, whose PRs are much lower. The differences between the H-cohort and the L-cohort are evident in swapping the ranks of the readings 'a hat with a flower in it' and 'a hat with a flower pattern'. While the former ranks second in all L-cohort indicators/subscores with the exception of Elaboration, the latter ranks second in all H-cohort indicators/subscores with the exception of Fluency.

To Boy In the case of the converted word *to boy*, the agreement is almost complete in the two topmost ranks, with the exception of the second rank reading of the Composite Score. The dominance of the reading 'to behave like a boy' is overwhelming, and the second rank of the reading 'to date a boy' is also unambiguous. The differences, once again, occur in the next two ranks, where there is very little agreement. The H-cohort fairly frequently proposes the reading 'to be immature' that occurs only once in the L-cohort (Elaboration). On the other hand, the opposite reading 'to grow mature', which ranks fourth in the L-cohort in the Fluency indicator, does not find its place among the first four readings in any indicator/subscore of the H-cohort. The same is true of the readings 'to look like a boy' and 'to give sth to a boy' that occur among the topmost readings only in the L-cohort (Originality and Creative Strengths, respectively).

To Tulip Finally, the converted word *to tulip* is also characterized by one dominant reading, 'to grow tulips', in both cohorts. The second most predictable reading is 'to look pretty' in all but one creativity indicator in both cohorts, namely Elaboration in the L-cohort and Originality in the H-cohort. There is very little agreement in the third and fourth ranks. What makes the two cohorts strikingly different is primarily the reading 'to be a narcissist', which only ranks among the four highest-rank readings in the H-cohort (Fluency and Creative Strengths). The same is true of the readings 'to give a tulip to sb' (Elaboration) and 'to blossom' (Originality). Contrary to this, the reading 'to look like a tulip' ranks high only in the L-cohort (Fluency).

To sum up, the data show the strong influence of readings which language users find most easily accessible and therefore assign a high predictability value. *The strength of the top readings therefore does not seem to be affected by the creative potential in any of the creativity indicators/subscores. The situation at lower ranks is different and shows the tendency for the L-cohort and the H-cohort to behave differently in interpreting novel complex words.*

5.2.1.2 Objectified Predictability Rate

This parameter identifies the degree of acceptability of a reading with the highest PR value. The specific meaning of the next lower readings is insignificant. What matters, however, is their PR values and, especially and crucially, the difference in PRs of these readings, on the one hand, and the most predictable reading, on the other. It is this factor, labelled as the *Predictability Rate Gap* (PRG) by Štekauer (2005a), that determines the chances that the reading with the highest PR is selected by language users in preference to any other possible readings. This parameter can tell us a lot about the relation between the psychological phenomenon of creativity and a creative approach to the interpretation of new/potential words. Namely, it is postulated that the OPR values in the individual creativity indicators/subscores in the

Table 5.71. *Comparison of OPR values in the L-cohort and the H-cohort – Originality*

	baby book	*flower hat*	*to boy*	*to tulip*
L-cohort	0.663	0.484	0.838	**0.620**
H-cohort	**0.609**	**0.378**	**0.773**	0.651

Table 5.72. *Comparison of OPR values in the L-cohort and the H-cohort – Elaboration*

	baby book	*flower hat*	*to boy*	*to tulip*
L-cohort	0.674	**0.461**	0.853	**0.485**
H-cohort	**0.615**	0.529	**0.852**	0.565

Table 5.73. *Comparison of OPR values in the L-cohort and the H-cohort – Flexibility*

	baby book	*flower hat*	*to boy*	*to tulip*
L-cohort	0.580	0.476	0.840	0.745
H-cohort	**0.535**	**0.327**	**0.751**	**0.660**

L-cohort, which is characterized by low creativity values obtained by means of the TTCT, should be higher than those in the H-cohort. This hypothesis is based on the idea that less creative language users prefer more common and easily accessible interpretations while higher values of the individual creativity indicators/subscores are also projected onto the ability of language speakers to propose more peripheral, that is, less predictable, and therefore 'creative' interpretations. This should be reflected in tougher competition between the readings proposed by the H-cohort in general. As a result, the PRG between the most predictable reading and the other readings should be higher in the L-cohort. As in Section 5.2.1.1, we first introduce the data in the form of tables mapping the results for individual creativity indicators/subscores (with the lower OPR values in bold), and then the data are briefly commented on. Tables 5.71–5.76 compare the OPR values for the L-cohort and the H-cohort for each of the indicators/subscores.

Table 5.74. *Comparison of OPR values in the L-cohort and the H-cohort – Fluency*

	baby book	*flower hat*	*to boy*	*to tulip*
L-cohort	**0.553**	**0.487**	0.846	0.661
H-cohort	0.637	0.542	**0.790**	**0.606**

Table 5.75. *Comparison of OPR values in the L-cohort and the H-cohort – Creative Strengths*

	baby book	*flower hat*	*to boy*	*to tulip*
L-cohort	0.647	0.537	0.877	0.659
H-cohort	**0.552**	**0.405**	**0.806**	**0.631**

Table 5.76. *Comparison of OPR values in the L-cohort and the H-cohort – Composite Score*

	baby book	*flower hat*	*to boy*	*to tulip*
L-cohort	0.657	0.604	0.849	0.780
H-cohort	**0.641**	**0.464**	**0.824**	**0.656**

Hypothesis 3, specified in the Introduction, has been fully confirmed for the Flexibility indicator and both subscores, that is, Creative Strengths and Composite Score, because the OPR values of the H-cohort are lower for each of the experimental words. For Originality, the OPR values of the H-cohort are lower for three words. The exception is the converted word *to tulip* for which the OPR value in the L-cohort is slightly lower. For the two remaining indicators, Elaboration and Fluency, the results are ambiguous. In each case, the H-cohort's OPR values are lower in two words and higher in the two other words. The words that show a lower OPR value for the L-cohort in these two indicators are the compound *flower hat* and the converted word *to tulip*. It is difficult to say why the results for these words deviate (both in two indicators) from the general tendency because their interpretational demands do not seem to differ from the other compound and conversion, respectively. An explanation for this observation will require more extensive research focused on individual word formation processes and their influence upon interpretational creativity.

Table 5.77. *Comparison of the average number of proposed readings per respondent in the L-cohort and the H-cohort – Originality*

	baby book	*flower hat*	*to boy*	*to tulip*
L-cohort	2.52	2.47	1.36	1.43
H-cohort	**3.03**	**2.70**	**1.91**	**1.95**

Table 5.78. *Comparison of the average number of proposed readings per respondent in the L-cohort and the H-cohort – Elaboration*

	baby book	*flower hat*	*to boy*	*to tulip*
L-cohort	2.46	2.20	1.33	1.40
H-cohort	**2.97**	**3.08**	**1.83**	**1.70**

If we compare the total number of instances in which one of the cohorts shows lower OPR values, the ratio is 19:5 in favour of the H-cohort. From this, it follows that we can speak of a fairly *strong tendency for creativity indicators/subscores to boost the interpretation creativity of secondary school students.* However, not all creativity indicators enhance the creative approach to the interpretation of new complex words to the same degree. The indicator/ subscores which, based on our experimental data, enhance interpretational creativity beyond any doubt comprise *Flexibility*, *Creative Strengths*, and *Composite Score*; the Originality indicator also appears to have a partial boosting effect on interpretational creativity. The other two indicators, Elaboration and Fluency, behave ambiguously in this respect.

5.2.1.3 Average Number of Proposed Readings Per Cohort Member

According to Hypothesis 4, a language speaker with a higher TTCT score proposes a higher number of readings for individual experimental words. This parameter, therefore, should be highly indicative of the influence of the individual creativity indicators/subscores upon interpretational creativity. The data are first provided in the form of tables comparing the L-cohort and the H-cohort in terms of the average number of readings proposed by a cohort member (Tables 5.77–5.82). The higher values are given in bold. The data are then commented on.

The data give support to Hypothesis 4B because they convincingly show an unambiguous influence of both subscores, that is, *Creative Strengths* and *Composite Score*, as well as two out of the four indicators, *Originality*

Table 5.79. *Comparison of the average number of proposed readings per respondent in the L-cohort and the H-cohort – Flexibility*

	baby book	*flower hat*	*to boy*	*to tulip*
L-cohort	2.84	**2.67**	1.51	1.34
H-cohort	**2.86**	2.56	**1.76**	**1.63**

Table 5.80. *Comparison of the average number of proposed readings per respondent in the L-cohort and the H-cohort – Fluency*

	baby book	*flower hat*	*to boy*	*to tulip*
L-cohort	**2.84**	**2.67**	1.47	1.33
H-cohort	2.65	2.43	**1.65**	**1.59**

Table 5.81. *Comparison of the average number of proposed readings per respondent in the L-cohort and the H-cohort – Creative Strengths*

	baby book	*flower hat*	*to boy*	*to tulip*
L-cohort	2.41	2.25	1.22	1.45
H-cohort	**2.83**	**2.73**	**2.06**	**2.01**

Table 5.82. *Comparison of the average number of proposed readings per respondent in the L-cohort and the H-cohort – Composite Score*

	baby book	*flower hat*	*to boy*	*to tulip*
L-cohort	2.58	2.44	1.36	1.36
H-cohort	**2.86**	**2.80**	**1.89**	**1.85**

and *Elaboration*, upon interpretational creativity, because for each of them the average number of readings is higher in the H-cohort than in the L-cohort for each of the four experimental words. To these, we may add the *Flexibility* indicator, which features a higher average value for three experimental words, with the exception of *flower hat.* The same word, together with the other compound word, *baby book*, violates the general trend in the Fluency

Table 5.83. *Average differences between the H-cohort and the L-cohort in the average number of readings proposed by a cohort member*

Indicator/subscore	Average difference
Originality	0.45
Elaboration	0.55
Flexibility	0.25
Fluency	0.22
Creative Strengths	0.58
Composite Score	0.42

Table 5.84. *Average differences between the H-cohort and the L-cohort in terms of the average number of proposed readings*

	baby book	*flower hat*	*to boy*	*to tulip*
Average difference	0.36	0.49	0.48	0.40

indicator. This means that Hypothesis 4A is confirmed for *Elaboration* but not for Fluency.

While the data confirm the influence of the TTCT-based creativity scores beyond any doubt, it may be interesting to find out which of the hypothesis-confirming indicators shows the biggest difference between the H-cohort and the L-cohort values. The data are given in Table 5.83 for the individual indicators/subscores. Only those cases in which the H-cohort's value is higher than that of the L-cohort are represented.

The most conclusive dominance is found for *Creative Strengths*, *Elaboration*, *Originality*, and *Composite Score*. This criterion also shows that Fluency and Flexibility manifest much smaller differences in the average number of proposed readings by the two cohorts. This is especially surprising with regard to Fluency owing to the nature of this creativity indicator: It reflects the number of relevant answers in the TTCT, and this fact is expected to be reflected in a substantial difference between the two cohorts in terms of the average number of proposed readings.

In an effort to identify the reasons for the contradictory results in the compound *flower hat*, we calculated the average gaps between the H-cohort and the L-cohort in all the cases in which the H-cohort's value is higher. The results are summarized in Table 5.84.

The average difference data do not provide us with the answer to our question because, in all four indicators/subscores in which the average number

Table 5.85. *Mann–Whitney U test for Elaboration*

	BF_{10}	U	p	95% confidence interval Lower	Upper	Cohen's d
baby book	5.04	2500.50	0.010*	−1.00	−1.90e−5	−0.39
flower hat	99.88	2118.50	<0.001***	−1.00	−4.35e−5	−0.65
to boy	7.49	2411.00	0.004**	−1.00	−3.88e−5	−0.46
to tulip	0.70	2783.00	0.115	−1.00	1.71e−5	−0.28

Note. $^*p < 0.05$, $^{**}p < 0.01$, $^{***}p < 0.001$

of proposed readings per cohort member is higher in the H-cohort than in the L-cohort, the average gap is the highest precisely for the compound *flower hat*. Moreover, the differences in the values for the individual words are very small. An extension of this analysis in the next section provides a statistical evaluation of the average number of readings in the L-cohort and the H-cohort.

Statistical Evaluation

In this section, we will provide a statistical evaluation of the differences between the two cohorts in terms of the average number of readings per cohort member. For this purpose, the non-parametric Mann–Whitney U test will be employed. Furthermore, as in the previous case, beyond the null hypothesis significance testing, the effect size, confidence intervals, and Bayes factor are reported and interpreted. In addition, a sensitivity analysis is provided in order to corroborate the robustness of the results.

Elaboration Concerning Elaboration, the differences in the average number of readings between the two cohorts are statistically significant for three experimental words: *baby book*, *flower hat*, and *to boy*. The H-cohort provided more readings on average.

As depicted in Table 5.85 and Figure 5.25, there are statistically significant differences between the L-cohort (M = 2.50, Med = 2.00, SD = 1.27) and the H-cohort (M = 2.97, Med = 3.0, SD = 1.18) for *baby book* (U = 2500.50, p = 0.010, Cohen's d = −0.39, BF_{10} = 5.04); between the L-cohort (M = 2.25, Med = 2.0, SD = 1.25) and the H-cohort (M = 3.08, Med = 3.0, SD = 1.29) for *flower hat* (U = 2118.50, p = 0.001, Cohen's d = −0.65, BF_{10} = 99.88); and between the L-cohort (M = 1.33, Med = 1, SD = 1.05) and the H-cohort (M = 1.84, Med = 2, SD = 1.18) for *to boy* (U = 2411.00, p = 0.004, Cohen's d = −0.46, BF_{10}= 7.49).

However, the difference between the L-cohort (M = 1.29, Med = 1.0, SD = 1.08) and the H-cohort (M = 1.61, Med = 1.0, SD = 1.27) for *to tulip* is not

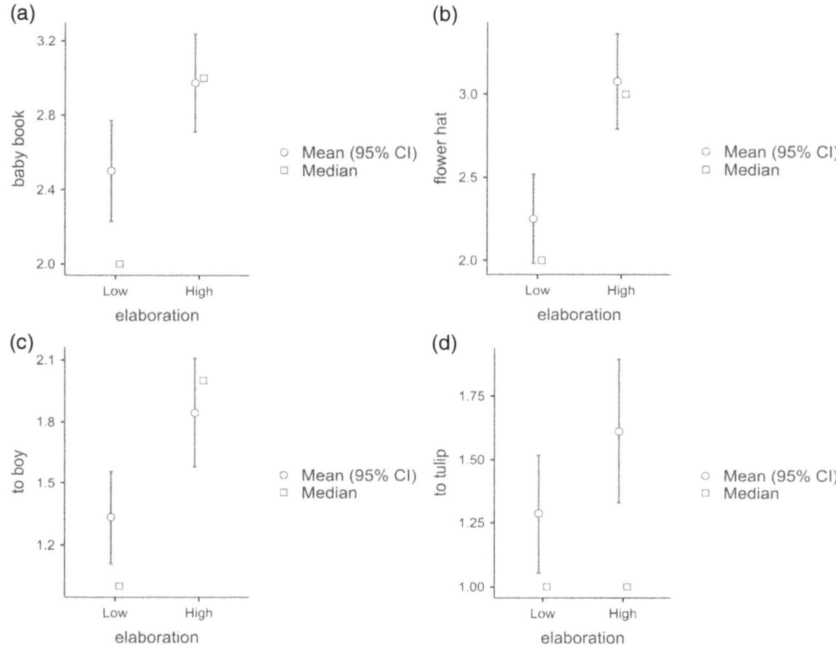

Figure 5.25 Descriptive plots for Elaboration

statistically significant (U = 2783, p = 0.115, Cohen's d = –0.28, BF_{10} = 0.70, BF_{01} = 1.43).

Fluency Concerning Fluency, the H-cohort provided slightly more readings on average for the experimental words *baby book* and *flower hat*; nevertheless, the differences between the two cohorts in the average number of readings are not statistically significant.

As depicted in Table 5.86 and Figure 5.26, there are no statistically significant differences between the L-cohort (M = 2.84, Med = 3, SD = 1.18) and the H-cohort (M = 2.65, Med = 3, SD = 1.35) for *baby book* (U = 3003, p = 0.339, Cohen's d = 0.15, BF_{10} = 0.28, BF_{01} = 3.61); between the L-cohort (M = 2.68, Med = 3, SD = 1.24) and the H-cohort (M = 2.45, Med = 2, SD = 1.39) for *flower hat* (U = 2929, p = 0.228, Cohen's d = 0.18, BF_{10} = 0.39, BF_{10} = 3.58); between the L-cohort (M = 1.46, Med = 1, SD = 1.10) and the H-cohort (M = 1.65, Med = 2, SD = 1.21) for *to boy* (U = 2982, p = 0.305, Cohen's d = –0.17, BF_{10} = 0.28, BF_{01} = 3.60); or between the L-cohort (M = 1.37, Med = 1, SD = 1.19) and the H-cohort (M = 1.59, Med = 1, SD = 1.42) for *to tulip* (U = 3071, p = 0.474, Cohen's d = –0.16, BF_{10} = 0.22, BF_{01} = 4.62).

Table 5.86. *Mann–Whitney U test for Fluency*

	BF_{10}	U	p	95% confidence interval Lower	Upper	Cohen's d
baby book	0.28	3003.00	0.339	−3.99e−5	1.00	0.15
flower hat	0.39	2929.00	0.228	−1.93e−5	1.00	0.18
to boy	0.28	2981.50	0.305	−1.00	4.35e−5	−0.17
to tulip	0.22	3071.00	0.474	−1.00	3.64e−6	−0.16

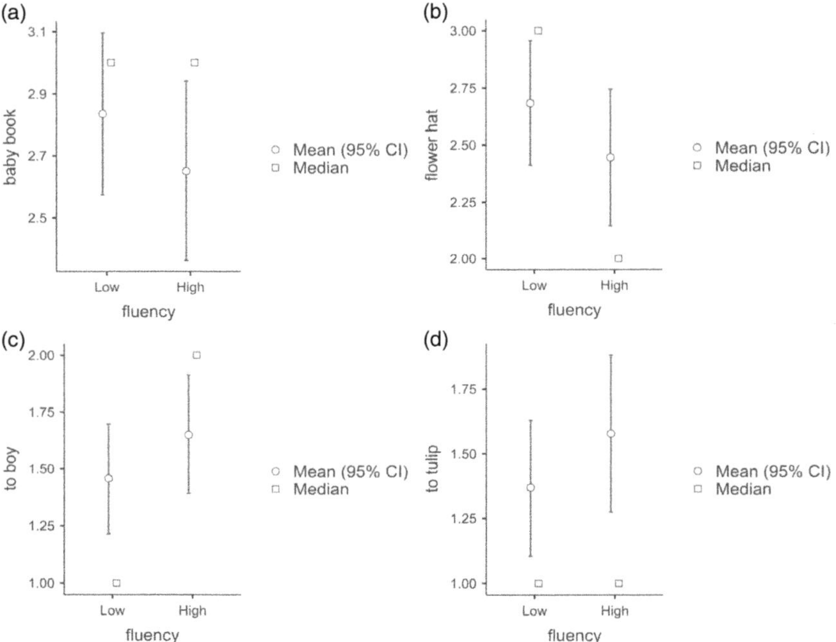

Figure 5.26 Descriptive plots for Fluency

Originality Concerning Originality, the H-cohort provided more readings on average. The differences in the average number of readings between the two cohorts are statistically significant for the experimental words *baby book*, *to boy*, and *to tulip*.

More specifically, as depicted in Table 5.87 and Figure 5.27, there are statistically significant differences between the L-cohort (M = 2.49, Med = 3,

Table 5.87. *Mann–Whitney U test for Originality*

	BF_{10}	U	p	95% confidence interval Lower	95% confidence interval Upper	Cohen's d
baby book	5.03	2288.00	0.008*	−1.00	−3.81e−5	−0.43
flower hat	0.29	2724.00	0.308	−1.00	9.74e−6	−0.18
to boy	9.47	2186.50	0.003**	−1.00	−2.17e−5	−0.51
to tulip	1.65	2420.50	0.033*	−1.00	−7.22e−6	−0.39

Note. *p < 0.05, **p < 0.01

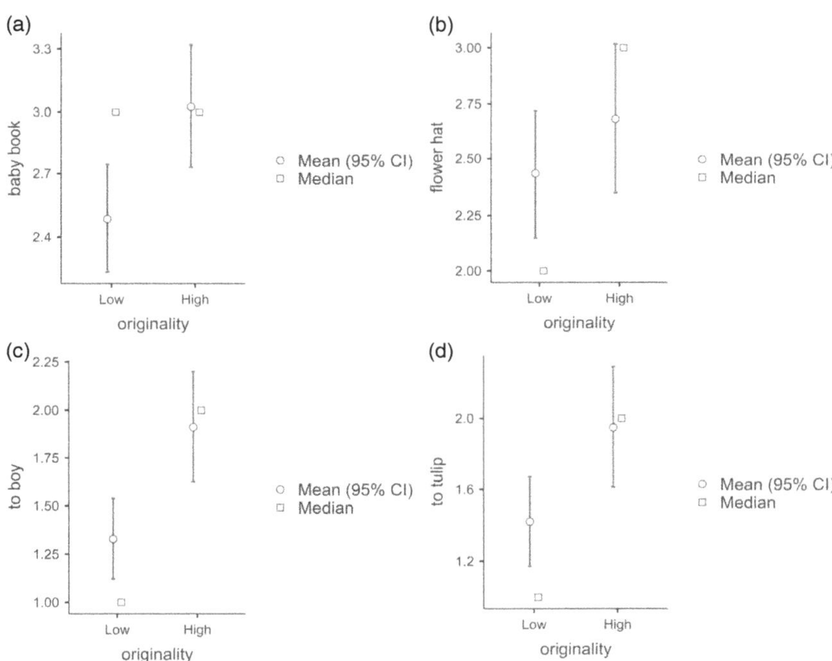

Figure 5.27 Descriptive plots for Originality

SD = 1.14) and the H-cohort (M = 3.03, Med = 3, SD = 1.34) for *baby book* (U = 2288, p = 0.008, Cohen's d = −0.43, BF_{10} = 5.03); between the L-cohort (M = 1.33, Med = 1, SD = 0.93) and the H-cohort (M = 1.91, Med = 2, SD = 1.30) for *to boy* (U = 2187, p = 0.003, Cohen's d = −0.51, BF_{10} = 9.47); and between the L-cohort (M = 1.42, Med = 1, SD = 1.11) and the H-cohort (M = 1.95, Med = 2, SD = 1.54) for *to tulip* (U = 2421, p = 0.033, Cohen's d = −0.39, BF_{10} = 1.65).

Table 5.88. *Mann–Whitney U test for Flexibility*

	BF_{10}	U	p	95% confidence interval Lower	Upper	Cohen's d
baby book	0.17	2594.50	0.893	−4.51e−5	2.44e−5	−0.01
flower hat	0.20	2547.00	0.743	−4.47e−5	1.00	0.09
to boy	0.31	2303.00	0.187	−1.00	5.73e−5	−0.23
to tulip	0.65	2268.00	0.144	−1.00	4.08e−5	−0.29

However, there are no statistically significant differences between the L-cohort (M = 2.43, Med = 2, SD = 1.27) and the H-cohort (M = 2.68, Med = 3, SD = 1.52) for *flower hat* (U = 2724, p = 0.308, Cohen's d = −0.18, BF_{10} = 0.29, BF_{01} = 3.40).

Flexibility Concerning Flexibility, for the experimental words *baby book, to boy*, and *to tulip*, the H-cohort provided slightly more readings on average; nevertheless, these differences are not statistically significant.

As depicted in Table 5.88 and Figure 5.28, there are no statistically significant differences between the L-cohort (M = 2.84, Med = 3, SD = 1.05) and the H-cohort (M = 2.85, Med = 3, SD = 1.47) for *baby book* (U = 2595, p = 0.893, Cohen's d = −0.01, BF_{10} = 0.17, BF_{01} = 5.84); between the L-cohort (M = 2.67, Med = 3, SD = 1.13) and the H-cohort (M = 2.56, Med = 3, SD = 1.55) for *flower hat* (U = 2547, p = 0.743, Cohen's d = 0.09, BF10 = 0.20, BF_{01}= 4.93); between the L-cohort (M = 1.49, Med = 1, SD = 1.18) and the H-cohort (M = 1.78, Med = 2, SD = 1.35) for *to boy* (U = 2303, p = 0.187, Cohen's d = −0.23, BF_{10} = 0.31, BF_{01} = 3.20); or between the L-cohort (M = 1.34, Med = 1, SD = 1.20) and the H-cohort (M = 1.74, Med = 2, SD = 1.50) for *to tulip* (U = 2268, p = 0.144, Cohen's d = −0.29, BF_{10} = 0.65, BF_{01} = 1.55).

Creative Strengths Concerning Creative Strengths, the differences between the two cohorts in the average number of readings are statistically significant for all experimental words. The H-cohort provided more readings on average for all four words.

More specifically, as depicted in Table 5.89 and Figure 5.29, there are statistically significant differences between the L-cohort (M = 2.34, Med = 3, SD = 1.10) and the H-cohort (M = 2.86, Med = 3, SD = 1.22) for *baby book* (U = 2254, p = 0.009, Cohen's d = −0.44, BF_{10} = 6.01); between the L-cohort (M = 2.21, Med = 2, SD = 1.15) and the H-cohort (M = 2.64, Med = 3, SD = 1.34) for *flower hat* (U = 2419, p = 0.050, Cohen's d = −0.34, BF_{10} = 1.42);

Table 5.89. *Mann–Whitney U test for Creative Strengths*

	BF_{10}	U	p	95% confidence interval		Cohen's d
				Lower	Upper	
baby book	6.01	2254.00	0.009**	−1.00	−8.98e−5	−0.44
flower hat	1.42	2418.50	0.050	−1.00	7.30e−5	−0.34
to boy	58.81	1872.50	<0.001***	−1.00	−6.07e−5	−0.70
to tulip	3.31	2314.00	0.020*	−1.00	−7.40e−6	−0.42

Note. *$p < 0.05$, **$p < 0.01$, ***$p < 0.001$

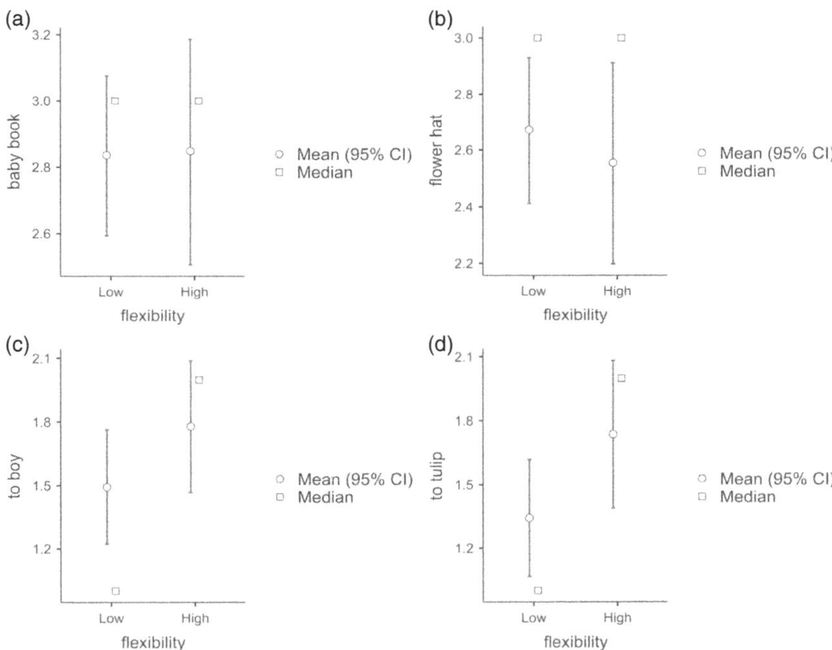

Figure 5.28 Descriptive plots for Flexibility

between the L-cohort (M = 1.26, Med = 1, SD = 0.9) and the H-cohort (M = 2.06, Med = 2, SD = 1.33) for *to boy* (U = 1873, p = 0.001, Cohen's d = −0.70, BF10 = 58.81); and between the L-cohort (M = 1.43, Med = 1, SD = 1.1) and the H-cohort (M = 1.99, Med = 2, SD = 1.48) for *to tulip* (U = 2314, p = 0.020, Cohen's d = −0.42, BF_{10} = 3.31).

Table 5.90. *Mann–Whitney U test for Composite Score*

	BF_{10}	U	p	95% confidence interval Lower	Upper	Cohen's d
baby book	1.34	2491.50	0.074	−1.00	3.06e−5	−0.34
flower hat	1.16	2449.50	0.055	−1.00	4.13e−5	−0.34
to boy	7.12	2136.50	0.002**	−1.00	−7.55e−5	−0.51
to tulip	3.79	2297.50	0.013*	−1.00	−1.38e−5	−0.46

Note. *p < 0.05, **p < 0.01, ***p < 0.001

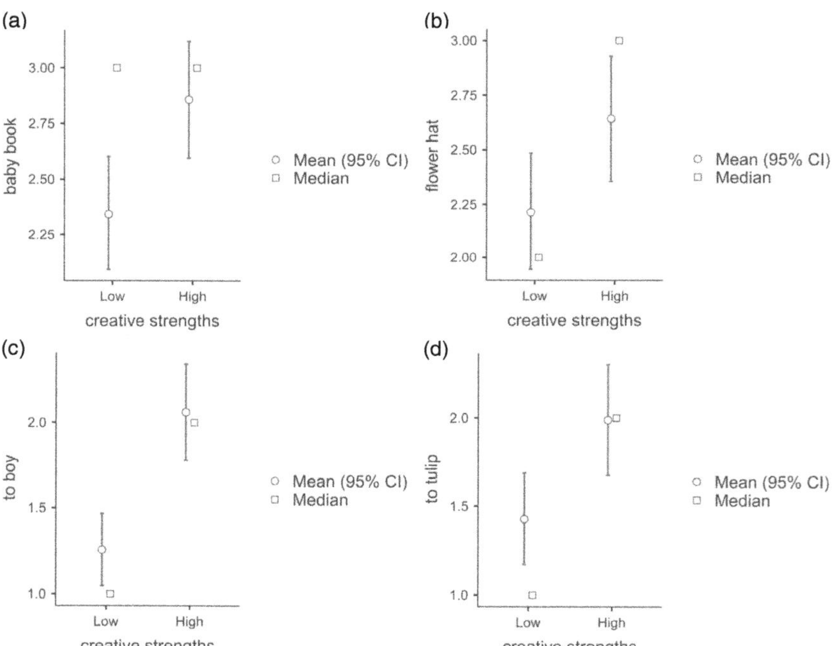

Figure 5.29 Descriptive plots for Creative Strengths

Composite Score Concerning Composite Score, the H-cohort provided more readings on average for all four experimental words. The differences between the two cohorts in the average number of readings are statistically significant for the experimental words *to boy* and *to tulip*.

More specifically, as depicted in Table 5.90 and Figure 5.30, there are statistically significant differences between the L-cohort (M = 1.36, Med = 1,

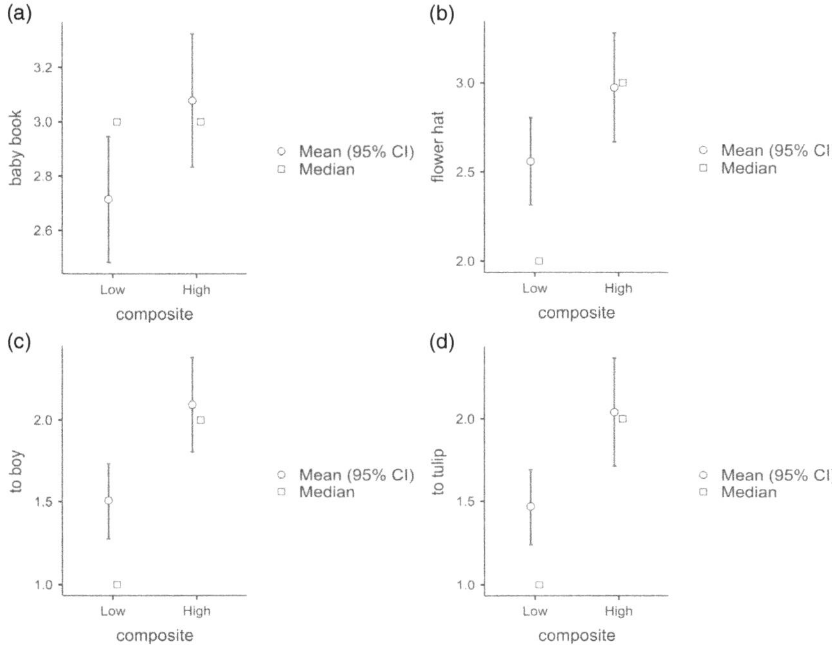

Figure 5.30 Descriptive plots for Composite Score

SD = 1.01) and the H-cohort (M = 1.89, Med = 2, SD = 1.27) for *to boy* (U = 2137, p = 0.002, Cohen's d = –0.51, BF10 = 7.02) and between the L-cohort (M = 1.36, Med = 1, SD = 1.11) and the H-cohort (M = 1.85, Med = 2, SD = 1.45) for *to tulip* (U = 2297, p = 0.036, Cohen's d = –0.46, BF10 = 3.79).

On the other hand, there are no statistically significant differences between the L-cohort (M = 2.58, Med = 3, SD = 1.05) and the H-cohort (M = 2.88, Med = 3, SD = 1.28) for *baby book* (U = 2492, p = 0.074, Cohen's d = –0.34, BF10 = –0.61, BF01 = 1.34) or between the L-cohort (M = 2.46, Med = 2, SD = 1.16) and the H-cohort (M = 2.8, Med = 3, SD = 1.44) for *flower hat* (U = 2449, p = 0.055, Cohen's d = –0.34, BF10 = 0.58, BF01 = 1.16).

Further Issues and Summary As the type I error (rejection of a true null hypothesis) increases due to multiple comparisons, we will, at least, briefly mention two procedures controlling the false positives as in the previous cases. When controlling the family-wise error rate with the more stringent Bonferroni (1936) correction, if all 24 comparisons are encompassed, only p values lower than 0.002 should be considered as statistically significant. However, in this case, the type II error (non-rejection of a false null hypothesis) could be exaggerated due to the diminished statistical power, masking potential discoveries. Therefore, we prefer to control the false discovery rate through Benjamini and Hochberg's (1995) procedure. Accordingly, out of all the significant findings, three could be considered as false discoveries. Stated differently, from the 11 statistically significant p values, 8 remained statistically significant even after adjustment (p values for FDR < 0.01).

In addition, the effect size was reported, providing the magnitude of the effect. Considering the magnitude of the effect size according to the classical benchmarks of Cohen (1977, 1988), (a) a medium to large effect size was found for the differences between the L-cohort and the H-cohort regarding *flower hat* in Elaboration and *to boy* in Creative Strengths and Originality, and a medium to large effect size was found for the differences regarding *to boy* in Elaboration and Composite Score; (b) a small to medium effect size was found for the differences between the L-cohort and the H-cohort regarding *baby book* in Elaboration, for *baby book* and *to tulip* in Creative Strengths, and for *baby book* and *to tulip* in Originality; a slightly smaller effect was found for the differences regarding *to tulip* in Elaboration, for *to boy* and *to tulip* in Flexibility, and for *baby book* and *flower hat* in Composite Score; and (c) a small effect size was found for the differences between the L-cohort and the H-cohort regarding all four words in Fluency, for *baby book* and *flower hat* in Flexibility, and for *flower hat* in Originality.

Moreover, from the Bayesian perspective (and the verbal interpretational scheme provided by Wagenmakers et al. 2017), there is (a) almost *extreme evidence* for the alternative hypothesis relative to H0 (predicting the differences between the L-cohort and the H-cohort) regarding *flower hat* in Elaboration; (b) *very strong evidence* regarding *to boy* in Creative Strengths; (c) moderate evidence regarding *to boy* and *baby book* in Elaboration, regarding *baby book* and *to boy* in Originality, regarding *baby book* and *to tulip* in Creative Strengths, and regarding *to boy* and *to tulip* in Composite Score; and (d) only anecdotal evidence for *to tulip* in Originality, for *flower hat* in Creative Strengths, and for *baby book* and *flower hat* in Composite Score.

When considering the null results, there is (a) *moderate evidence* for the null hypothesis regarding *baby book, to boy*, and *to tulip* in Fluency; *baby book, flower hat*, and *to boy* in Flexibility; and *flower hat* in Originality and (b) only *anecdotal evidence* for the null hypothesis regarding *to tulip* in Elaboration; *flower hat* in Fluency; *to tulip* in Flexibility; and *to boy* and *flower hat* in Composite Score.

Summary of Inferential Statistics and Sensitivity Analysis

In a nutshell, when pondering Hypothesis 4 in the sample of secondary school students, the results are partially in line with this hypothesis. The hypothesis predicted that the number of readings proposed by the H-cohort members is

Table 5.91. *Correlation matrix among variables*

	Composite Score	Fluency	Flexibility	Originality	Elaboration	Creative Strengths
baby book	0.10*	−0.05	−0.01	0.09*	0.16***	0.13***
flower hat	0.07	−0.06	−0.03	0.05	0.18***	0.11**
to boy	0.15***	0.01	0.04	0.13***	0.14***	0.17***
to tulip	0.10*	0.00	0.03	0.08*	0.11**	0.12**

Note. $^{*}p < 0.05$, $^{**}p < 0.01$, $^{***}p < 0.001$

higher than that proposed by the L-cohort members owing to their higher creativity potential identified by the TTCT. This was supported for some but not all TTCT scores and for some words more than for others.

More specifically, the H-cohort provided a higher number of readings when considering Composite Score, Elaboration, Creative Strengths, and Originality. Concerning the effect size, according to Cohen's benchmarks (1977, 1988), the majority of results are medium to large in magnitude. From the perspective of the Bayes factor, there is anecdotal to very strong evidence in favour of the alternative hypothesis relative to H0 for the majority of cases. However, Fluency and Flexibility do not seem to be relevant in the present context because the results are rather ambiguous, and the differences between the H-cohort and the L-cohort in the average number of proposed readings are not statistically significant. For example, according to the Bayes factor, the evidence in favour of the alternative hypothesis is anecdotal at best, and the effect size is rather small in magnitude. When considering the role of specific words, differences are mostly found for the converted word *to boy* (although some differences are also found for *baby book*, *flower hat*, and *to tulip*; however, these differences are much less consistent).

As one can argue that dichotomizing the data into L- and H-cohorts with a quartile split procedure could lead to the loss of statistical power, we aimed to corroborate the robustness of the previous analysis with a sensitivity analysis, as in previous cases. For this purpose, Kendall's non-parametric τ correlation coefficient is used.

As can be seen from Table 5.91, which depicts a correlation matrix among the variables, small to medium correlations are found between the creativity indicators/subscores and the average number of proposed readings per cohort member. The pattern of results is in line with the previous analysis. As in the main analysis, the correlations with the number of readings are found mainly for Elaboration, Creative Strengths, Composite Score, and Originality, but not for Fluency and Flexibility. High TTCT scores in Elaboration, Originality,

Creative Strengths, and Composite Score appear to boost the number of readings proposed by the respondents.

To provide further support, additional statistics are calculated, namely the Bayes factor, which indicates the amount of evidence in support of the alternative hypothesis relative to H0 as well as the lower and upper 95% credible intervals that can be interpreted in such a way that, given the observed data, the effect has a 95% probability of falling within the range. For the majority of statistically significant results, there is strong to extreme evidence for the alternative hypothesis (Table 5.92).

To sum up, the data thus give support to Hypothesis 4A only with regard to the *Elaboration* indicator. This hypothesis has not been supported for Fluency. Hypothesis 4B has found partial corroboration through the results of *Creative Strengths*, *Originality*, and *Composite Score.*

5.2.1.4 Hapax Legomena

This section aims to evaluate the criterion of hapax legomena in terms of Hypotheses 5A and 5B. Hypothesis 5A postulates that a reading proposed by a single member of the L-cohort is proposed by more members of the H-cohort, thanks to the higher creative potential of the latter. Hypothesis 5B expects the H-cohort to propose more hapax legomena that correspond to zero occurrences of such readings in the L-cohort for the same reason. Since it is the creativity indicator Originality that is characterized by the uniqueness of answers, both Hypotheses 5A and 5B will also be evaluated with a special focus on this indicator.

In Table 5.93, we relate the data for single-occurrence readings in the L-cohort and the H-cohort to individual creativity indicators/subscores followed by comments thereupon. The figures under the individual experimental words indicate the number of hapax legomena proposed by the two cohorts. The figures under the individual creativity indicators identify the number of cohort members who proposed that particular reading. HL stands for hapax legomenon.

Baby Book

Hypothesis 5A is confirmed for this compound with regard to the reading ‘registry office records’. Its single occurrence in the Originality indicator and in the Composite Score of the L-cohort corresponds with, respectively, six and three occurrences of that reading in the H-cohort. The same holds for the reading ‘a book with a list of names for babies’. Its single occurrence in the Originality and the Creative Strengths of the L-cohort corresponds with, respectively, five and four occurrences in the H-cohort.

The fact that the H-cohort’s single occurrence reading ‘a book having the shape of a baby’ has three occurrences in the Creative Strengths subscore of the L-cohort runs directly against the previous hypothesis.

Table 5.92. *Calculations based on the Bayes factor*

		Composite Score	Fluency	Flexibility	Originality	Elaboration	Creative Strengths
baby book	Kendall's τ	0.10	−0.05	−0.01	0.09	0.16***	0.13***
	BF_{10}	2.00	0.17	0.07	1.76	2348.94	136.08
	Upper 95% CI	0.17	0.02	0.06	0.15	0.22	0.20
	Lower 95% CI	0.02	−0.11	−0.08	0.02	0.09	0.06
flower hat	Kendall's τ	0.07	−0.06	−0.03	0.05	0.18***	0.11*
	BF_{10}	0.41	0.28	0.09	0.20	77,119.76	14.33
	Upper 95% CI	0.14	0.01	0.04	0.12	0.24	0.18
	Lower 95% CI	−0.00	−0.12	−0.09	−0.02	0.11	0.04
to boy	Kendall's τ	0.15***	0.01	0.04	0.13**	0.14***	0.17***
	BF_{10}	316.33	0.07	0.16	98.06	270.71	27,840.87
	Upper 95% CI	0.22	0.07	0.11	0.19	0.20	0.24
	Lower 95% CI	0.08	−0.06	−0.02	0.06	0.07	0.10
to tulip	Kendall's τ	0.10	0.00	0.03	0.08	0.11	0.12**
	BF_{10}	3.21	0.07	0.10	1.18	8.04	47.21
	Upper 95% CI	0.17	0.07	0.10	0.15	0.17	0.19
	Lower 95% CI	0.03	−0.06	−0.04	0.01	0.04	0.06

Note. $^{*}BF_{10} > 10$, $^{**}BF_{10} > 30$, $^{***}BF_{10} > 100$

Table 5.93. *Hapax legomena versus zero/multiple occurrences*

	Reading	Cohort	Elaboration	Fluency	Flexibility	Originality	Creative Strengths	Composite Score
baby book	'official document of a baby'	**L**	HL	HL	HL		HL	HL
L = 4		**H**	0	0	0		0	0
H = 2	'records of a pregnant woman'	**L**	0			HL		
		H	HL			0		
	'registry office records'	**L**				HL		HL
		H				6		3
	'a book with a list of names for babies'	**L**				HL	HL	
		H				5	4	
	'a book having the shape of a baby'	**L**					3	
		H					HL	
flower hat	'haircut'	**L**	HL		HL	HL	HL	HL
L = 5		**H**	HL		2	HL	HL	2
H = 6	'a person wearing a flower hat'	L	0	HL	0		0	
		H	HL	0	HL		HL	
	'a hat protecting one against flowers'	**L**	0	HL				
		H	HL	HL				
	'pretty hat'	**L**				HL	HL	
		H				HL	3	
	'romantic girl'	**L**					0	0
		H					HL	HL
	'flower meadow'	**L**				HL	2	
		H				2	HL	
to boy	'to bring up a boy'	**L**	HL	HL		HL	HL	HL
L = 6		**H**	HL	0		0	0	0
H = 5	'to play with a boy'	**L**	0	HL				
		H	HL	0				

	'to treat like a kid'	**L**		HL	HL	HL	HL	HL
		H		HL	HL	0	HL	0
	'to give birth to a boy'	L		HL				HL
		H		HL				3
	'to be a homosexual'	**L**			HL			
		H			4			
	'to voice-mutate'	**L**				0	0	0
		H				HL	HL	HL
	'to smell like a boy'	**L**					HL	HL
		H					0	0
	'to talk about a boy'	**L**					HL	
		H					0	
to tulip	'to compliment'	**L**	3	2	2			
L = 16		**H**	HL	HL	HL			
H = 10	'to live in the Netherlands'	**L**	HL	HL	HL	0	HL	HL
		H	HL	0	HL	HL	HL	HL
	'to feel happy'	**L**	HL					
		H	0					
	'to decorate with tulips'	**L**	HL					
		H	5					
	'to make a bouquet'	L	HL	2	HL	HL	HL	HL
		H	2	HL	HL	4	4	HL
	'to talk about tulips'	**L**	HL		HL	HL	HL	HL
		H	2		HL	0	2	4
	'to use drugs'	**L**		2	HL	HL	HL	HL
		H		HL	3	3	3	3
	'to grow tall'	**L**		0	0			0
		H		HL	HL			HL

Table 5.93. *(cont.)*

Reading	Cohort	Elaboration	Fluency	Flexibility	Originality	Creative Strengths	Composite Score
'to wear a dress with a tulip pattern'							
	L			HL			
	H			2			
'to be colourful'	**L**			HL			
	H			7			
'to be fragile'	**L**			HL	0		
	H			0	HL		
'to buy/sell tulips'	**L**			HL			HL
	H			2			2
'to smell like tulips'	**L**			3	HL	3	
	H			HL	2	HL	
'to make things from tulips'	**L**			2		HL	
	H			HL			
'to mature'	**L**				HL	HL	
	H				2	HL	
'to give a tulip to s.o.'	**L**				HL	HL	
	H				2	2	
'to be a narcissist'	**L**						HL
	H						14
'to draw tulips'	**L**						HL
	H						0

On the other hand, the single occurrence of the reading 'an official document of a baby' in all but one (Originality) indicator/subscore of the L-cohort has no counterparts in the H-cohort. The reading 'records of a pregnant woman' occurs only in the L-cohort's Originality indicator/subscore without any counterparts in the H-cohort. This finding contradicts Hypothesis 5B.

Flower Hat

While Hypothesis 5A is supported for the reading 'a haircut' in Flexibility and Composite Scores, the reading 'a pretty hat' in Creative Strengths, and the reading 'a flower meadow' in Originality, the latter also provides a counterexample in Creative Strengths. This last case clearly shows that a language speaker may be in the H-cohort with regard to one creative indicator/subscore and in the L-cohort with regard to a different one.

Hypothesis 5B is supported for the reading 'a person wearing a flower hat' for Elaboration, Flexibility, and Creative Strengths, and contradicted for Fluency. In the reading 'a hat protecting one against flowers', this hypothesis is confirmed for Elaboration. The reading 'romantic girl' supports Hypothesis 5B for Creative Strengths and Composite Score.

To Boy

There are two cases that favour Hypothesis 5A. The reading 'to be a homosexual' has a single occurrence in the Flexibility indicator of the L-cohort; the same reading in the same creativity indicator of the H-cohort was proposed by four respondents. The single occurrence of the reading 'to give birth to a boy' in the L-cohort corresponds to three occurrences in the H-cohort. There are no instances of the opposite nature.

Hypothesis 5B finds support in the readings 'to play with a boy' for Elaboration and 'to voice-mutate' for Originality, Creative Strengths, and Composite Score, but is contradicted by many more counterexamples: 'to bring up a boy' for Fluency, Originality, Creative Strengths, and Composite Score; 'to play with a boy' for Fluency; 'to treat like a kid' for Originality and Composite Score; 'to smell like a boy' for Creative Strengths and Composite Score; and 'to talk about a boy' for Creative Strengths.

To Tulip

The number of hapax legomena among the readings of this converted word is much higher compared to the other three experimental words. Their number in the L-cohort is considerably higher (16) than in the H-cohort (10). The most striking case for Hypothesis 5A is provided by the readings 'to be colourful' and 'to be a narcissist', whose single occurrences in the L-cohort's Flexibility indicator and Composite Score, respectively, correspond to 7 and 14 occurrences in the H-cohort. The reading 'to make a bouquet' occurs only once for

Table 5.94. *Number of HL-to-many occurrences of the proposed readings – comparison of the cohorts*

	L-cohort	H-cohort	L-cohort	H-cohort
baby book	HL	4	1	HL
flower hat	HL	4	1	HL
to boy	HL	2	0	HL
to tulip	HL	24	7	HL

Originality and Creative Strengths in the L-cohort as opposed to four occurrences each in the H-cohort, and the hapax legomena of the reading 'to use drugs' in the L-cohort's Flexibility, Originality, Creative Strengths, and Composite Score occurs three times for each of them in the H-cohort.

Opposite cases do occur as well; for example, the hapax legomena in the H-cohort's Elaboration, Flexibility, and Fluency correspond respectively to 3, 2, and 2 occurrences in the L-cohort; the reading 'to smell like tulips' supports the hypothesis for Flexibility and Creative Strengths and contradicts it for Originality.

The reading 'to live in the Netherlands' supports Hypothesis 5B for Originality and contradicts it for Fluency. There are several cases that contradict the hypothesis, such as 'to feel happy' for Elaboration; 'to talk about tulips' for Originality; 'to be fragile' for Flexibility; and 'to draw tulips' for Composite Score. On the other hand, support to the hypothesis has been identified in the reading 'to grow tall' for Fluency, Flexibility, and Composite Score and 'to be fragile' for Originality

A summary of the data for all four experimental words is provided in Table 5.94.

It follows from Table 5.94 that for each of the experimental words there is a partial confirmation of the hypothesis, which means that if a particular reading is proposed by a single respondent of the L-cohort there is a tendency for the same reading to be proposed by a higher number of respondents of the H-cohort. It may therefore be surmised that with less predictable readings, there is a higher number of respondents of the H-cohort who approach the interpretation process in a creative way. This tendency is, in principle, in accordance with the results obtained for the Objectified Predictability Rate (OPR). The OPR values tend to be higher for the L-cohort, which means that more respondents propose the most acceptable reading and far fewer of them propose less predictable readings.

Nevertheless, the aforementioned hypothesis has not been confirmed for each L-cohort's hapax legomenon. There are a number of instances of the

Table 5.95. *Hapax legomena versus zero occurrences – comparison of the cohorts*

	L-cohort	H-cohort	L-cohort	H-cohort
		Zero occurrences	Zero occurrences	
baby book	HL	6	1	HL
flower hat	HL	0	6	HL
to boy	HL	9	4	HL
to tulip	HL	5	3	HL

Table 5.96. *Many occurrences versus hapax legomena*

	L-cohort Many-to-HL	H-cohort Many-to-HL
Elaboration	1	3
Fluency	3	0
Flexibility	2	6
Originality	0	7
Creative Strengths	3	6
Composite Score	0	7

L-cohort's hapax legomena readings that have no occurrences in the H-cohort. Taking into consideration all the outcomes, we can evaluate the proposed Hypothesis 5A as *a mere tendency in the interpretation behaviour of the L-cohort versus the H-cohort* rather than a general principle.

Rather surprising data come from an analysis of those cases in which a hapax legomenon of one cohort corresponds with zero occurrences in the other (Hypothesis 5B). Since this is also an indicator of creative interpretation, one would expect a prevalence of hapax legomenon instances in the H-cohort with zero occurrences of that reading in the L-cohort. As shown in Table 5.95, the actual situation is different.

Clearly and surprisingly, the number of instances in which a hapax legomenon of the L-cohort corresponds with zero occurrences of the same reading in the H-cohort exceeds the opposite cases. This is even more surprising if we realize that the average number of readings per respondent is much higher in the H-cohort than in the L-cohort. From this, it follows that Hypothesis 5B has not been corroborated in our research.

An interesting picture emerges if the data are viewed by individual creativity indicators/subscores (Tables 5.96 and 5.97).

Table 5.97. *Hapax legomena versus zero occurrences*

	L-cohort	H-cohort	L-cohort	H-cohort
		Zero occurrences	Zero occurrences	
Elaboration	HL	2	3	HL
Fluency	HL	5	1	HL
Flexibility	HL	2	2	HL
Originality	HL	4	3	HL
Creative Strengths	HL	4	3	HL
Composite Score	HL	5	3	HL

The strongest evidence in favour of Hypothesis 5A is provided by *Originality* and *Composite Score* and, to a lesser degree, by *Flexibility* and *Creative Strengths*. The Fluency indicator provides the opposite result, which can be related to its ambiguous behaviour in terms of the OPR criterion.

The results presented in Table 5.97 run counter to our intuition: Originality, Creative Strengths, Composite Score, and, especially, Fluency show a higher number of cases contradicting Hypothesis 5B. There is no indicator/subscore that gives support to the expectation that there would be more cases of the H-cohort's hapax legomena versus the L-cohort's zero occurrences than vice versa.

5.2.1.5 Summary III

Six indicators/subscores of the psychological concept of creativity were evaluated in order to determine their influence on the language speakers' creativity in interpreting potential words by secondary school students. This evaluation was based on four criteria: the Predictability Rate, the Objectified Predictability Rate, the number of proposed readings per cohort member, and hapax legomena. For this purpose, the respondents tested by the TTCT were divided into an H-cohort and an L-cohort for each of the six indicators/subscores.

Our findings concerning the group of secondary school students can be summarized as follows:

(i) The *Predictability Rate* of new/potential words is predetermined by the overall acceptability of their individual potential readings. This appears to be *much higher for compounds than for converted words*.

(ii) Within these meaning predictability limits imposed by the underlying word formation processes, *none of the creativity indicators/subscores manifests the unambiguous dominance of the H-cohort over the L-cohort.* While the H-cohort reaches higher PRs than the L-cohort in Elaboration and Originality, the L-cohort shows higher PR values in Flexibility.

(iii) The data do not show any substantial differences between the two cohorts as far as the most predictable readings are concerned. In fact, the most predictable readings are identical for all experimental words and for each creativity indicator/subscore with the exception of *flower hat* for Flexibility. This evidently follows from the fact emphasized in Štekauer (2005a) that each potential word is dominated by one (rarely two) reading that is much more acceptable to language users than any other potential reading for that word. In other words, *the predictability of the topmost readings is so strong that it overpowers the influence of the creative potential represented by the individual creativity indicators/subscores*. The differences therefore should be sought at lower levels of meaning predictability. Here, they are evident and show the different interpretation preferences of the two cohorts.

(iv) The hypothesis that the L-cohort speakers prefer the most predictable, that is, the most common and the most easily accessible readings to the detriment of less predictable readings, should be manifested in higher values of the OPR: the gap between the PR values of the topmost readings and the readings with lower PR values should be bigger in the L-cohort than in the H-cohort. Hypothesis 3 has been confirmed for *Flexibility*, *Creative Strengths*, and *Composite Score*, and partly for *Originality*.

(v) The criterion of the average number of readings proposed for the experimental words provides a strong piece of evidence for the unequal interpretational creativity of the two cohorts in question. Hypothesis 4A has been supported for *Elaboration*. Hypothesis 4B has been corroborated for *Originality*, *Creative Strengths*, and *Composite Score*, and partly for *Elaboration* and *Flexibility*. With three exceptions, the H-cohort's average values are higher than those of the L-cohort. The biggest average differences between the two cohorts have been found for *Creative Strengths* and *Elaboration*.

(vi) With regard to hapax legomena, we hypothesized two tendencies: (i) the L-cohort's hapax legomena, that is, readings proposed by merely one respondent of that cohort, should correspond to more than one occurrence of that reading in the H-cohort (Hypothesis 5A) and (ii) the H-cohort's hapax legomena should be mostly absent in the L-cohort (Hypothesis 5B). These hypotheses are based on the postulate that a 'creative' hapax legomenon reading is rather an exception in the L-cohort and, therefore, might be proposed by several language speakers of the H-cohort, and given the higher creativity of the H-cohort, its members are expected to come up with readings that are absent in the L-cohort. Hypothesis 5A has been partly confirmed if all four experimental words are taken into consideration. While there are 34 cases in which a hapax legomenon reading of the L-cohort corresponds to more than one

Table 5.98. *Indicators/subscores with significant (S) or partial (P) support for the hypotheses*

Parameter	Indicator/subscore
Objectified Predictability Rate	**S:** Flexibility, Creative Strengths, Composite Score
	P: Originality
Average number of readings	**S: (4A) Elaboration**
	S: (4B) Originality, Creative Strengths, Composite Score
	P: (4B) Flexibility
Hapax legomena	**S:** (5A) Originality, Composite Score
	P: (5A) Flexibility, Creative Strengths

Table 5.99. *Indicators/subscores contradicting the hypotheses*

Parameter	Indicator/subscore
Objectified Predictability Rate	Fluency, Elaboration
Average number of readings	(4A) Fluency
Hapax legomena	(5A) Fluency
	(5B) all indicators/subscores

occurrence of that reading in the H-cohort, there are only nine cases of the opposite nature. If this hypothesis is evaluated by the individual creativity indicators/subscores, its strongest support is provided by *Originality* and *Composite Score*, and partly by *Flexibility* and *Creative Strengths*. Hypothesis 5B has not been confirmed at all. There are four indicators favouring the L-cohort.

(vii) Our results thus demonstrate that *not all creativity indicators/subscores enhance a creative approach to the interpretation of new words in the same way*. If we take into consideration three parameters (removing the Predictability Rate, which can indicate differences between the two compared cohorts but cannot be evaluated in terms of its influence on interpretational creativity), we get Tables 5.98 and 5.99.

(viii) It follows from Tables 5.98 and 5.99 that *Composite Score* is the most influential psychological creativity factor that boosts interpretational creativity. *Originality* and *Creative Strengths* are the two other factors with a very strong effect. *Flexibility* appears to partly enhance the creative approach to the interpretation of potential/new words. The status of Elaboration is rather ambiguous. On the other hand, Fluency runs directly against all the hypotheses.

5.2.2 University Undergraduates

5.2.2.1 Predictability Rate

As in Section 5.1.1.1, the data on university undergraduates are first provided in the form of tables, and then there are comments with regard to the individual criteria. The ranking of readings is shown in Table 5.100.

(i) *Most predictable reading*

The most predictable readings are identical for all indicators/subscores in both cohorts for *baby book* ('a book for a baby') and for *to boy* ('to behave like a boy'). For *flower hat*, the most predictable reading in all indicators/subscores of the L-cohort and in four cases of the H-cohort is 'a hat made of flowers'. Two exceptions in the H-cohort concern Originality and Creative Strengths, where this reading is replaced with 'a hat with a flower pattern'. While the reading 'to grow tulips' of the converted word *to tulip* dominates the rankings, there are two exceptions, too. These occur in the Originality indicator and in the Creative Strengths subscore of the L-cohort in which cases it swapped its position with the reading 'to look pretty'.

A comparison of the PR values in Tables 5.101–5.104 shows a tendency towards a higher PR value of the most predictable reading (irrespective of what it is) in the H-cohort. This is evident especially for *flower hat* (all six indicators/subscores) and for *to tulip*, with one exception, and also for the other two experimental words, where there are two exceptions for each of them. The higher PR values are given in bold.

While the topmost reading is selected by the majority of respondents in both cohorts, it follows from the computation of its PR value that the H-cohort 'trusts' the most predictable reading more than the L-cohort, which is manifested in assigning this reading a higher score on the seven-degree scale. This is evident if we compare the topmost readings for the experimental words by individual creativity indicator/subscore (Table 5.105).

The H-cohort features higher PR values for all four words in Flexibility and Composite Score.

Elaboration, Originality, and Creative Strengths also demonstrate the *tendency for the H-cohort to assign higher scores to the most predictable readings.*

(ii) *Ranking: comparison of the L-cohort and the H-cohort*

Baby Book The second-highest PR reading differs in various indicators/ subscores. In the L-cohort, the second rank is taken by 'a book about the care of a baby' four times and by the reading 'a book with a story of a baby' twice. The opposite proportion has been found for the H-cohort. Two readings, 'a book of records of one's baby' and 'photo album', occur only in the H-cohort.

Table 5.100. *Ranking of readings by indicator/subscore, cohort, and PR value*

	Cohort	Baby book	Flower hat	To boy	To tulip
Originality	L	a book for a baby	a hat made of flowers	to behave like a boy	to look pretty
		a book about the care of a baby	a hat with a flower in it	to date a boy	to grow tulips
		a book with a story of a baby	a hat with a flower pattern	to look like a boy	to be a narcissist
		a small book	a hat with a flower shape	to dress like a boy	to blossom
		a book for a baby	a hat with a flower pattern	to behave like a boy	to grow tulips
		a book with a story of a baby	a hat made of flowers	to be immature	to blossom
		a photo album	a hat with a flower in it	to look like a boy	to look pretty
		a small book	a hat with a flower shape	to date a boy	to decorate sth with tulips
Elaboration	L	a book for a baby	a hat made of flowers	to behave like a boy	to grow tulips
		a book with a story of a baby	a hat with a flower in it	to date a boy	to look pretty
		a small book	a hat with a flower pattern	to be immature	to blossom
		a book about the care of a baby	a hat with a flower shape	to look like a boy	to pick tulips
	H	a book for a baby	a hat made of flowers	to behave like a boy	to grow tulips
		a book about the care of a baby	a hat with a flower pattern	to be immature	to decorate sth with tulips
		a book with a story of a baby	a hat with a flower in it	to dress like a boy	to blossom
		a small book	a hat with a flower shape	to date a boy	to like flowers
Flexibility	L	a book for a baby	a hat made of flowers	to behave like a boy	to grow tulips
		a book about the care of a baby	a hat with a flower in it	to date a boy	to blossom
		a book with a story of a baby	a hat with a flower pattern	to look like a boy	to pick tulips
		a small book	a hat with a flower shape	to be immature	to look pretty
	H	a book for a baby	a hat made of flowers	to behave like a boy	to grow tulips
		a book with a story of a baby	a hat with a flower pattern	to date a boy	to look pretty
		a book about the care of a baby	a hat with a flower in it	to be immature	to blossom
		a small book	a hat with a flower shape	to dress like a boy	to decorate sth with tulips

Fluency	L	a book for a baby	a hat made of flowers	to behave like a boy	to grow tulips
		a book about the care of a baby	a hat with a flower in it	to date a boy	to look pretty
		a small book	a hat with a flower pattern	to be immature	to blossom
		a book with a story of a baby	a hat with a flower shape	to look like a boy	to pick tulips
	H	a book for a baby	a hat made of flowers	to behave like a boy	to grow tulips
		A book with a story of a baby	a hat with a flower pattern	to date a boy	to look pretty
		a small book	a hat with a flower in it	to be immature	to blossom
		a book about the care of a baby	a hat with a flower shape	to grow mature	to decorate sth with tulips
Creative Strength	L	a book for a baby	a hat made of flowers	to behave like a boy	to look pretty
		a book with a story of a baby	a hat with a flower in it	to look like a boy	to grow tulips
		a small book	a hat with a flower pattern	to dress like a boy	to pick tulips
		a book about the care of a baby	a hat with a flower shape	to date a boy	to blossom
	H	a book for a baby	a hat with a flower pattern	to behave like a boy	to grow tulips
		a book about the care of a baby	a hat made of flowers	to date a boy	to blossom
		a book with a story of a baby	a hat with a flower in it	to be immature	to decorate sth with tulips
		a photo album	a hat with a flower shape	to dress like a boy	to smell like a tulip
Composite Score	L	a book for a baby	a hat made of flowers	to behave like a boy	to grow tulips
		a book about the care of a baby	a hat with a flower in it	to look like a boy	to look pretty
		a book with a story of a baby	a hat with a flower pattern	to date a boy	to pick tulips
		a small book	a hat with a flower shape	to be immature	to smell like a tulip
	H	a book for a baby	a hat made of flowers	to behave like a boy	to grow tulips
		a book with a story of a baby	a hat with a flower pattern	to be immature	to blossom
		a book about the care of a baby	a hat with a flower in it	to date a boy	to look pretty
		a book of records of one’s baby	a hat with a flower shape	to dress like a boy	to decorate sth with tulips

Table 5.101. *Predictability rates for the most predictable reading of* baby book

Cohort	Elaboration	Fluency	Flexibility	Originality	Creative Strengths	Composite Score
Low	**0.730**	0.612	0.673	0.639	**0.759**	0.574
High	**0.655**	**0.681**	**0.732**	**0.739**	**0.616**	**0.698**

Table 5.102. *Predictability rates for the most predictable reading of* flower hat

Cohort	Elaboration	Fluency	Flexibility	Originality	Creative Strengths	Composite Score
Low	0.223	0.246	0.288	0.212	0.187	0.252
High	**0.400**	**0.276**	**0.383**	**0.380**	**0.373**	**0.474**

Table 5.103. *Predictability rates for the most predictable reading of* to boy

Cohort	Elaboration	Fluency	Flexibility	Originality	Creative Strengths	Composite Score
Low	0.317	**0.468**	0.366	**0.412**	0.325	0.344
High	**0.531**	**0.416**	**0.400**	**0.369**	**0.448**	**0.515**

Table 5.104. *Predictability rates for the most predictable reading of* to tulip

Cohort	Elaboration	Fluency	Flexibility	Originality	Creative Strengths	Composite Score
Low	0.016	**0.058**	0.051	0.033	0.039	0.029
High	**0.070**	**0.055**	**0.058**	**0.046**	**0.048**	**0.060**

In none of the indicators/subscores is there an agreement between the two cohorts in the third and fourth ranks.

Flower Hat Apart from the aforementioned top position of the reading ‘a hat with a flower pattern’ in two indicators/subscores of the H-cohort, there is a major difference concerning the other ranks. While in the L-cohort the ranking

Table 5.105. *Comparison of PR values in two cohorts by creativity indicator/ subscore – most predictable readings*

	Elaboration	Fluency	Flexibility	Originality	Creative Strengths	Composite Score
baby book	L	H	H	H	L	H
flower hat	H	H	H	H	H	H
to boy	H	L	H	L	H	H
to tulip	H	L	H	H	H	H

is identical for all indicators/subscores – the reading 'a hat with a flower in it' is systematically ranked second and the reading 'a hat with a flower pattern' is systematically ranked third – in the H-cohort, the latter reading ranks second and, in the two aforementioned cases, first. The reading 'a hat with a flower in it' is ranked third in all indicators/subscores.

To Boy The readings that occur in the top four ranks are much more heterogeneous compared to the experimental compounds. There are two important findings. First, in spite of this diversity, the reading 'to behave like a boy' has the highest PR in all indicators/subscores in both cohorts. This is the only agreement between the two cohorts. Second, ranks two to four do not coincide for the two cohorts in any of the indicators/subscores.

To Tulip If we disregard the topmost reading, the individual indicators/subscores show no agreement in the ranking of the other three readings in either of the cohorts, which indicates their influence on the cohorts' interpretational preferences. When comparing the two cohorts, it is obvious that they tend to prefer different readings. For example, the reading 'to decorate sth with tulips' ranks among the top four readings for all indicators/subscores in the H-cohort, but it is absent in the L-cohort. The reading 'to be a narcissist' occurs only in the L-cohort.

In sum, the general trend is similar to that in the group of secondary school students, that is, there is a strong influence of the readings that language users find most easily accessible and therefore assign a high predictability value. *The strength of the top readings therefore does not seem to be affected by the creative potential in any of the creativity indicators/ subscores. The situation at lower ranks is different and shows the tendency for the L-cohort and the H-cohort to behave differently in interpreting novel complex words.*

Table 5.106. *Comparison of OPR values in the L-cohort and the H-cohort – Originality*

	baby book	*flower hat*	*to boy*	*to tulip*
L-cohort	**0.720**	0.476	0.912	**0.384**
H-cohort	0.738	**0.425**	**0.842**	0.447

Table 5.107. *Comparison of OPR values in the L-cohort and the H-cohort – Elaboration*

	baby book	*flower hat*	*to boy*	*to tulip*
L-cohort	0.748	0.484	0.885	**0.400**
H-cohort	**0.637**	**0.441**	**0.848**	0.504

Table 5.108. *Comparison of OPR values in the L-cohort and the H-cohort – Flexibility*

	baby book	*flower hat*	*to boy*	*to tulip*
L-cohort	0.750	**0.486**	0.884	**0.490**
H-cohort	**0.650**	0.521	**0.808**	0.492

Table 5.109. *Comparison of OPR values in the L-cohort and the H-cohort – Fluency*

	baby book	*flower hat*	*to boy*	*to tulip*
L-cohort	0.739	0.433	0.895	**0.433**
H-cohort	**0.647**	**0.384**	**0.693**	0.505

5.2.2.2 Objectified Predictability Rate

As in Section 5.1.1.2, we first summarize the data in the form of tables. Tables 5.106–5.111 compare the OPR values for the L-cohort and the H-cohort for each of the indicators/subscores. The lower OPR values are given in bold.

Table 5.110. *Comparison of OPR values in the L-cohort and the H-cohort – Creative Strengths*

	baby book	*flower hat*	*to boy*	*to tulip*
L-cohort	0.788	0.403	0.871	0.574
H-cohort	**0.684**	**0.393**	**0.852**	**0.429**

Table 5.111. *Comparison of OPR values in the L-cohort and the H-cohort – Composite Score*

	baby book	*flower hat*	*to boy*	*to tulip*
L-cohort	0.733	0.560	0.896	0.397
H-cohort	**0.628**	**0.458**	**0.829**	**0.385**

Hypothesis 3 has been fully confirmed for both subscores, that is, *Creative Strengths* and *Composite Score*, because the OPR values of the H-cohort are lower for each of the experimental words. For *Elaboration* and *Flexibility*, the OPR values of the H-cohort are lower in three of the experimental words. The exception in both of these indicators concerns the converted word *to tulip*. In the two remaining creativity indicators, Originality and Flexibility, the OPR values of the H-cohort are lower only for two words each: *baby book* and *to tulip*, and *flower hat* and *to tulip*, respectively. Since the results contradicting our hypothesis are for each indicator bound to the converted word *to tulip*, it may be assumed that the nature of a new/potential word has its say in the process of interpretation.

If we compare the total number of instances in which one of the cohorts shows lower OPR values, the proportion is 18:6 in favour of the H-cohort. From this, it follows that we can speak of a *fairly strong tendency for creativity indicators/subscores to boost interpretation creativity*. However, not all creativity indicators enhance the creative approach to the interpretation of new/potential complex words to the same degree. The subscores which, based on our experimental data, enhance interpretation creativity beyond any doubt are *Creative Strengths* and *Composite Score*. The creativity indicators Elaboration and Flexibility also give support to Hypothesis 3, albeit to a lesser degree.

5.2.2.3 Average Number of Proposed Readings Per Cohort Member

This section evaluates the data in terms of Hypothesis 4. The data are summarized in Tables 5.112–5.117, with the higher values given in bold.

Table 5.112. *Comparison of the average number of proposed readings per respondent in the L-cohort and the H-cohort – Originality*

	baby book	*flower hat*	*to boy*	*to tulip*
L-cohort	2.68	2.42	1.50	1.71
H-cohort	**3.14**	**3.13**	**1.83**	**1.84**

Table 5.113. *Comparison of the average number of proposed readings per respondent in the L-cohort and the H-cohort – Elaboration*

	baby book	*flower hat*	*to boy*	*to tulip*
L-cohort	2.57	2.30	1.33	1.29
H-cohort	**3.25**	**3.33**	**2.03**	**2.25**

Table 5.114. *Comparison of the average number of proposed readings per respondent in the L-cohort and the H-cohort – Flexibility*

	baby book	*flower hat*	*to boy*	*to tulip*
L-cohort	2.61	2.44	1.49	1.63
H-cohort	**3.22**	**2.91**	**1.97**	**1.95**

Table 5.115. *Comparison of the average number of proposed readings per respondent in the L-cohort and the H-cohort – Fluency*

	baby book	*flower hat*	*to boy*	*to tulip*
L-cohort	2.75	2.56	1.66	1.86
H-cohort	**3.12**	**2.88**	**1.89**	**1.89**

The data show that *the average number of readings per cohort member for each of the indicators/subscores is higher in the H-cohort than in the L-cohort without exception!* This is an important piece of evidence of the influence of the creative potential on the interpretation creativity of language speakers. This fact means the *corroboration of both Hypothesis 4A and Hypothesis 4B.*

Table 5.116. *Comparison of the average number of proposed readings per respondent in the L-cohort and the H-cohort – Creative Strengths*

	baby book	*flower hat*	*to boy*	*to tulip*
L-cohort	2.69	2.50	1.44	1.39
H-cohort	**3.07**	**3.31**	**1.92**	**2.04**

Table 5.117. *Comparison of the average number of proposed readings per respondent in the L-cohort and the H-cohort – Composite Score*

	baby book	*flower hat*	*to boy*	*to tulip*
L-cohort	2.45	2.22	1.39	1.45
H-cohort	**3.34**	**3.34**	**2.21**	**2.24**

Table 5.118. *Average difference between the H-cohort and the L-cohort in the average number of readings proposed by a cohort member – evaluation by indicators/subscores*

Indicator/subscore	Average difference
Originality	0.41
Elaboration	0.84
Flexibility	0.47
Fluency	0.24
Creative Strength	0.58
Composite Score	0.91

Like in Section 5.2.1.3, we shall present the differences between the H-cohort and the L-cohort values. The data are given in Table 5.118 for the individual indicators/subscores.

By far the biggest differences between the H-cohort and the L-cohort are found in *Composite Score* and *Elaboration*, which means that these two creativity factors have the strongest influence on interpretation creativity according to this criterion. The smallest difference is identified in Fluency. This is not surprising in view of the preceding results, but it is extremely surprising owing to the nature of the Fluency indicator as already pointed out in Section 5.2.1.3 where the same situation was noticed for the secondary school students: since this indicator reflects the number of relevant answers in

Table 5.119. *Average differences between the H-cohort and the L-cohort in terms of the average number of proposed readings*

	baby book	*flower hat*	*to boy*	*to tulip*
Average difference	0.53	0.74	0.51	0.47

the TTCT, this fact is expected to be reflected in significant differences between the H-cohort and the L-cohort in the proposed readings per cohort member.

The differences between the two cohorts by individual experimental words are summarized in Table 5.119.

While the differences between the H-cohort and the L-cohort are most striking for the compound *flower hat*, the differences between the two cohorts with regard to the three other words are almost identical and, therefore, do not indicate the influence of a word formation process (compounding vs. conversion) on this facet of interpretation creativity in the group of university undergraduates.

Statistical Evaluation

In this section, we provide a statistical evaluation of the differences between the two cohorts with regard to the average number of proposed readings. As in the previous case, null hypothesis significance testing and the non-parametric Mann–Whitney U test are employed and supplemented with the Bayes factor. Furthermore, the effect size and confidence intervals are reported. After the main part of the analysis, a sensitivity analysis is provided.

Originality Concerning Originality, the differences between the two cohorts in the average number of readings are statistically significant for two experimental words: *baby book* and *flower hat*. The H-cohort provided more readings on average.

More specifically, as depicted in Table 5.120 and Figure 5.31, there are statistically significant differences between the L-cohort ($M = 2.61$, $Med = 3$, $SD = 1.23$) and the H-cohort ($M = 2.97$, $Med = 3$, $SD = 1.19$) regarding *baby book* ($U = 2158$, $p = 0.021$, Cohen's $d = -0.30$, $BF_{10} = 1.05$) and between the L-cohort ($M = 2.38$, $Med = 2$, $SD = 1.22$) and the H-cohort ($M = 2.96$, $Med = 3$, $SD = 1.48$) regarding *flower hat* ($U = 2062$, $p = 0.008$, Cohen's $d = -0.43$, $BF_{10} = 3.02$).

There are no statistically significant differences between the L-cohort ($M = 1.46$, $Med = 1$, $SD = 1.13$) and the H-cohort ($M = 1.74$, $Med = 2$, $SD = 1.28$) regarding *to boy* ($U = 2385$, $p = 0.162$, Cohen's $d = -0.24$, $BF_{10} = 0.51$,

Table 5.120. *Mann–Whitney U test for Originality*

	BF 10	U	p	95% confidence interval Lower	Upper	Cohen's d
baby book	1.05	2158.00	0.021*	−1.00	−4.53e−5	−0.30
flower hat	3.02	2062.50	0.008**	−1.00	−8.10e−6	−0.43
to boy	0.51	2385.00	0.162	−1.00	1.90e−5	−0.24
to tulip	0.18	2654.00	0.742	−1.00	4.29e−5	−0.08

Note. *p < 0.05, **p < 0.01, ***p < 0.001

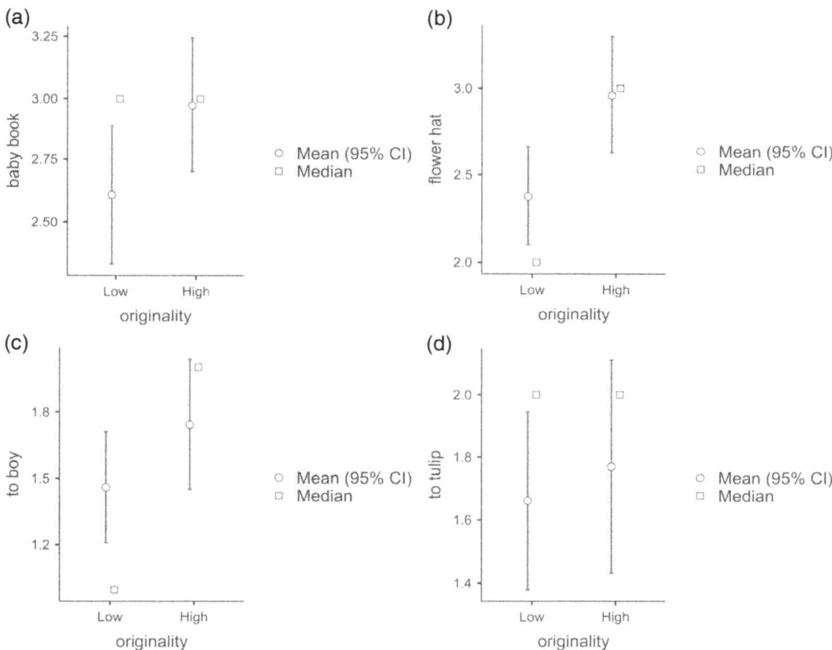

Figure 5.31 Descriptive plots for Originality

BF_{01} = 1.95) or between the L-cohort (M = 1.66, Med = 2, SD = 1.24) and the H-cohort (M = 1.77, Med = 2, SD = 1.49) regarding *to tulip* (U = 2654, p = 0.742, Cohen's d = −0.08, BF_{10} = 0.29, BF_{01} = 0.51, BF_{01} = 5.51).

Elaboration Concerning Elaboration, the differences between the two cohorts in the average number of readings are statistically significant for all

Table 5.121. *Mann–Whitney U test for Elaboration*

	BF $_{10}$	U	p	95% confidence interval Lower	Upper	Cohen's d
baby book	7.91	2065.00	0.002**	−1.00	−8.45e−5	−0.50
flower hat	129.42	1713.00	<0.001***	−1.00	−1.00	−0.70
to boy	370.49	1975.50	<0.001***	−1.00	−2.69e−5	−0.61
to tulip	22.86	1762.00	<0.001***	−1.00	−1.00	−0.74

Note. **$p < 0.01$, ***$p < 0.001$

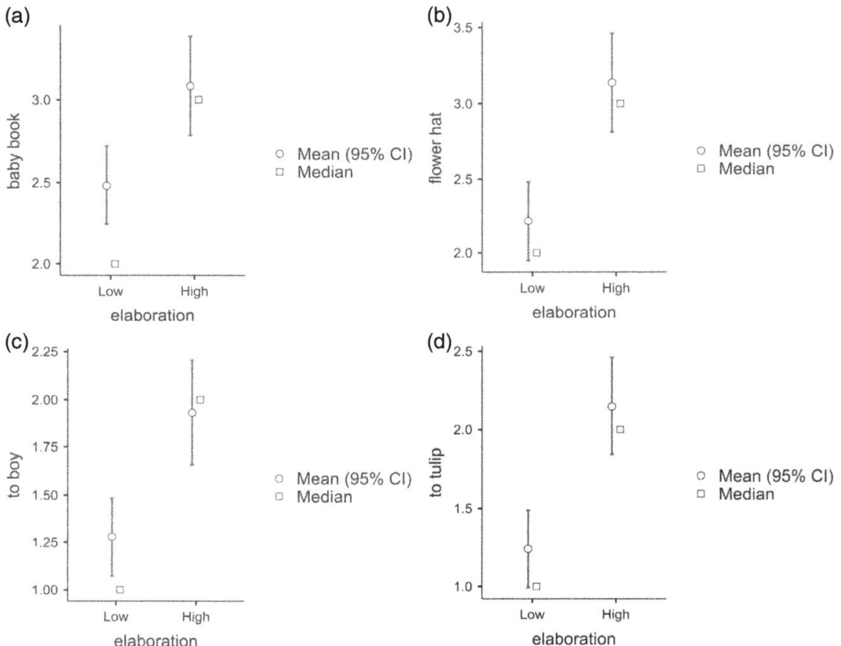

Figure 5.32 Descriptive plots for Elaboration

four experimental words. The H-cohort provided more readings on average for all four experimental words.

As depicted in Table 5.121 and Figure 5.32, there are statistically significant differences between the L-cohort (M = 2.48, Med = 2, SD = 1.08) and the H-cohort (M = 3.08, Med = 3, SD = 1.3) regarding *baby book* (U = 2065,

Table 5.122. *Mann–Whitney U test for Flexibility*

	BF_{10}	U	p	95% confidence interval Lower	Upper	Cohen's d
baby book	2.66	2130.00	0.009**	−1.00	−2.84e−6	−0.41
flower hat	0.39	2488.00	0.222	−1.00	5.64e−5	−0.21
to boy	2.35	2193.50	0.017*	−1.00	−6.76e−5	−0.40
to tulip	0.50	2416.50	0.132	−1.00	5.47e−5	−0.25

Note. *p < 0.05, **p < 0.01

p = 0.002, Cohen's d = −0.50, BF_{10} = 7.91); between the L-cohort (M = 2.22, Med = 2, SD = 1.21) and the H-cohort (M = 3.14, Med = 3, SD = 1.429) regarding *flower hat* (U = 1713, p < 0.001, Cohen's d = −0.70, BF_{10} = 129.42); between the L-cohort (M = 1.28, Med = 1, SD = 0.93) and the H-cohort (M = 1.93, Med = 2, SD = 1.19) regarding *to boy* (U = 1975, p < 0.1, Cohen's d = −0.61, BF_{10}= 22.86); and between the L-cohort (M = 1.24, Med = 1.0, SD = 1.12) and the H-cohort (M = 2.15, Med = 2.0, SD = 1.35) regarding *to tulip* (U = 1762, p < 0.001, Cohen's d = −0.28, BF_{10} = 370.49).

Flexibility Concerning Flexibility, the differences between the two cohorts in the average number of readings are statistically significant for the experimental words *baby book* and *to boy.* The H-cohort provided more readings on average.

As depicted in Table 5.122 and Figure 5.33, there are statistically significant differences between the L-cohort (M = 2.62, Med = 3, SD = 1.05) and the H-cohort (M = 3.11, Med = 3, SD = 1.34) regarding *baby book* (U = 2130, p = 0.009, Cohen's d = −0.41, BF_{10} = 2.66, BF_{01} = 0.38) and between the L-cohort (M = 1.46, Med = 1, SD = 1.01) and the H-cohort (M = 1.90, Med = 2, SD = 1.16) regarding *to boy* (U = 2194, p = 0.017, Cohen's d = −0.40, BF_{10} = 2.35, BF_{01} = 0.43).

There are no statistically significant differences between the L-cohort (M = 2.52, Med = 3, SD = 1.30) and the H-cohort (M = 2.80, Med = 3, SD = 1.38) regarding *flower hat* (U = 2488, p = 0.222, Cohen's d = −0.21, BF_{10} = 0.39, BF_{01}= 2.54) or between the L-cohort (M = 1.58, Med = 2, SD = 1.20) and the H-cohort (M = 1.89, Med = 2, SD = 1.25) regarding *to tulip* (U = 2417, p = 0.132, Cohen's d = −0.25, BF_{10} = 0.5, BF_{01} = 2.00).

Fluency Concerning Fluency, the differences between the two cohorts in the average number of readings are statistically significant only for the experimental word *baby book.* The H-cohort provided slightly more readings on average.

Table 5.123. *Mann–Whitney U test for Fluency*

	BF_{10}	U	p	95% confidence interval Lower	Upper	Cohen's d
baby book	1.01	1880.50	0.037*	−1.00	−1.04e−5	−0.32
flower hat	0.48	2039.50	0.174	−1.00	5.68e−5	−0.25
to boy	0.42	2052.50	0.189	−1.00	5.65e−6	−0.23
to tulip	0.19	2285.00	0.779	−2.20e−5	2.28e−5	−0.04

Note. * $p < 0.05$

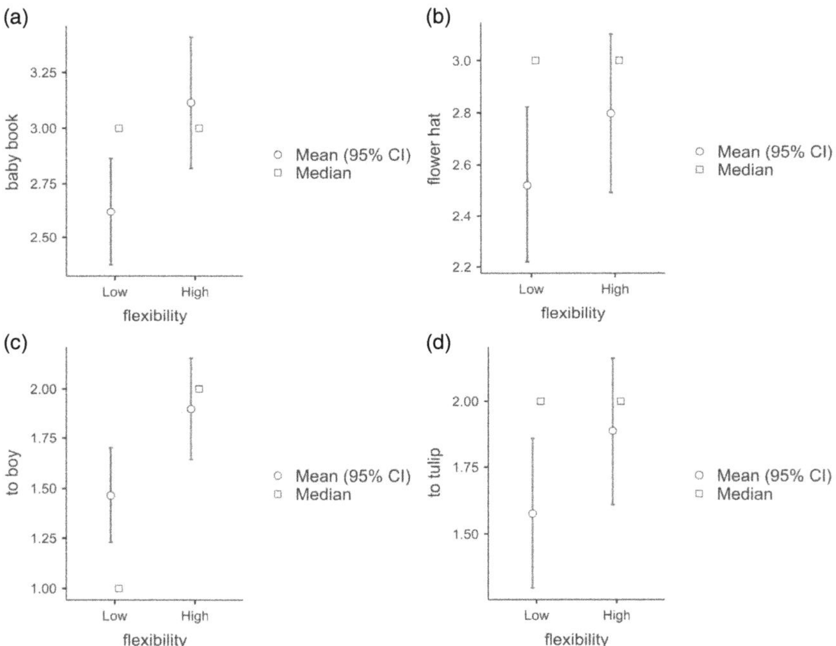

Figure 5.33 Descriptive plots for Flexibility

More specifically, as depicted in Table 5.123 and Figure 5.34, there is a statistically significant difference between the L-cohort (M = 2.66, Med = 3, SD = 1.15) and the H-cohort (M = 3.04, Med = 3, SD = 1.24) regarding *baby book* (U = 1881, p = 0.037, Cohen's d = −0.32, BF_{10} = 1.01, BF_{01} = 0.99), although this result might be false positive.

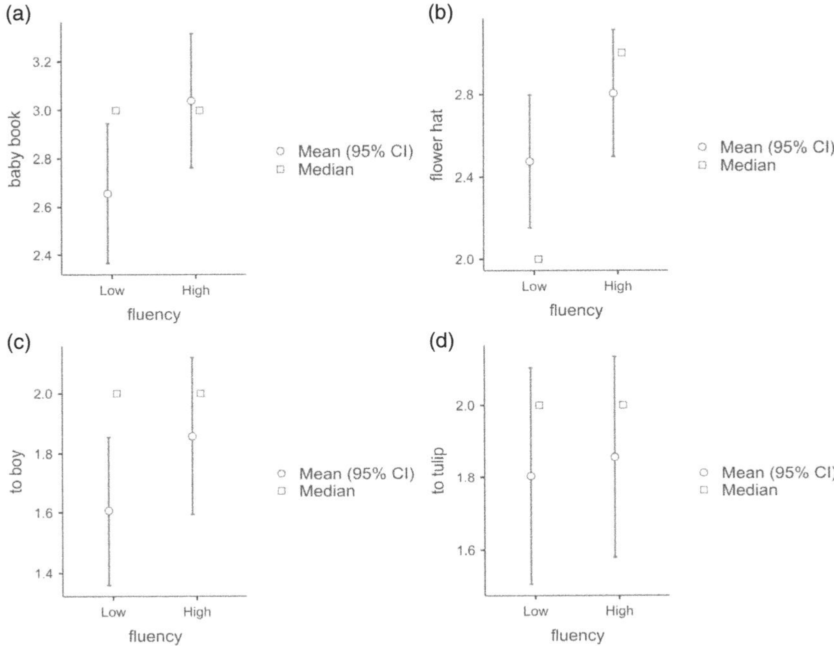

Figure 5.34 Descriptive plots for Fluency

There are no statistically significant differences between the L-cohort (M = 2.48, Med = 3, SD = 1.29) and the H-cohort (M = 2.81, Med = 3, SD = 1.38) regarding *flower hat* (U = 2040, p = 0.174, Cohen's d = –0.25, BF_{10} = 0.48, BF_{10} = 2.08); between the L-cohort (M = 1.61, Med = 2, SD = 0.99) and the H- cohort (M = 1.86, Med = 2, SD = 1.18) regarding *to boy* (U = 2053, p = 0.189, Cohen's d = –0.23, BF_{10} = 0.42, BF_{01} = 2.38); or between the L-cohort (M = 1.80, Med = 2, SD = 1.19) and the H-cohort (M = 1.86, Med = 2, SD = 1.24) regarding *to tulip* (U = 2285, p = 0.779, Cohen's d = –0.04, BF_{10} = 0.19, BF_{01} = 5.27).

Creative Strengths Concerning Creative Strengths, the differences between the two cohorts in the average number of readings are statistically significant for all four experimental words. The H-cohort provided more readings on average.

As depicted in Table 5.124 and Figure 5.35, there are statistically significant differences between the L-cohort (M = 2.59, Med = 2.50, SD = 1.36) and the H-cohort (M = 3.03, Med = 3, SD = 1.15) regarding *baby book* (U = 1561, p = 0.013, Cohen's d = –0.35, BF_{10} = 1.70); between the L-cohort (M = 2.41,

Table 5.124. *Mann–Whitney U test for Creative Strengths*

	BF $_{10}$	U	p	95% confidence interval Lower	Upper	Cohen's d
baby book	1.7	1561.00	0.013*	−1.00	−3.23e−5	−0.35
flower hat	45.87	1368.00	<0.001***	−1.00	−8.85e−5	−0.57
to boy	2.53	1554.00	0.012*	−1.00	−4.56e−5	−0.42
to tulip	5.54	1512.00	0.007**	−1.00	−8.05e−6	−0.51

Note. *p < 0.05, **p < 0.01, ***p < 0.001

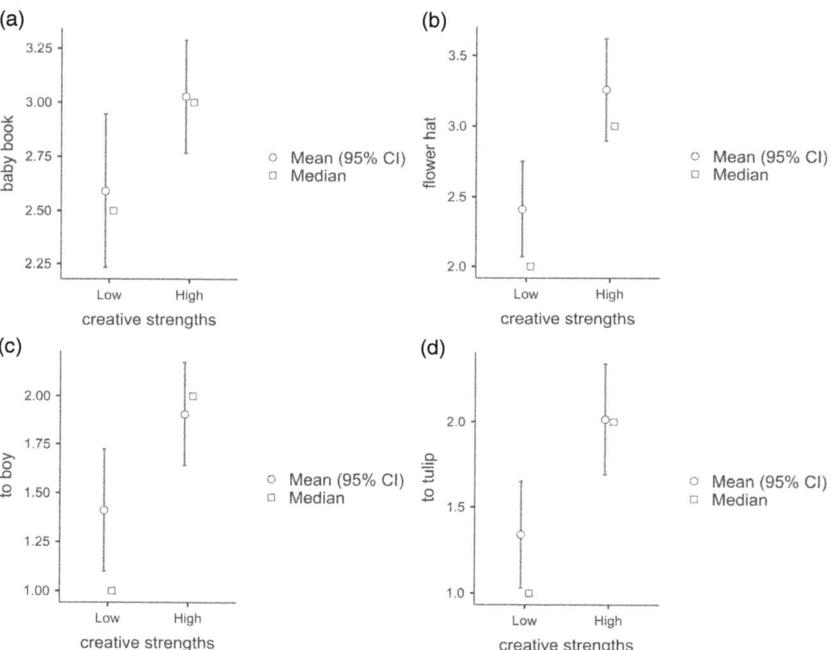

Figure 5.35 Descriptive plots for Creative Strengths

Med = 2, SD = 1.30) and the H-cohort (M = 3.26, Med = 3, SD = 1.59) regarding *flower hat* (U = 1368, $p < 0.001$, Cohen's d = −0.57, $BF_{10} = 45.89$); between the L-cohort (M = 1.41, Med = 1, SD = 1.19) and the H-cohort (M = 1.91, Med = 2, SD = 1.17) regarding *to boy* (U = 1554, p = 0.012, Cohen's d = −0.42, BF10 = 2.53); and between the L-cohort (M = 1.34,

Table 5.125. *Mann–Whitney U test for Composite Score*

	BF_{10}	Statistic	p	95% confidence interval Lower	Upper	Cohen's d
baby book	87.95	1610.00	<0.001***	−1.00	−2.55e−5	−0.66
flower hat	356.80	1518.50	<0.001***	−1.00	−1.00	−0.72
to boy	21.99	1630.50	<0.001***	−1.00	−1.16e−5	−0.66
to tulip	4.86	1860.00	0.008**	−1.00	−3.41e−6	−0.46

Note. **p < 0.01, ***p < 0.001

Med = 1, SD = 1.8) and the H-cohort (M = 2.01, Med = 2, SD = 1.43) regarding *to tulip* (U = 1512, p = 0.007, Cohen's d = −0.51, BF_{10} = 5.54).

Composite Score Concerning Composite Score, the differences between the two cohorts in the average number of readings are statistically significant for all four experimental words. The H-cohort provided more readings on average.

More specifically, as depicted in Table 5.125 and Figure 5.36, there are statistically significant differences between the L-cohort (M = 2.59, Med = 3, SD = 0.96) and the H-cohort (M = 3.30, Med = 3, SD = 1.19) regarding *baby book* (U = 1610, p < 0.001, Cohen's d = −0.66, BF_{10} = 87.95); between the L- cohort (M = 2.34, Med = 2, SD = 1.20) and the H-cohort (M = 3.30, Med = 3, SD = 1.43) regarding *flower hat* (U = 1519, p < 0.001, Cohen's d = −0.72, BF_{10} = 356.80); between the L-cohort (M = 1.37, Med = 1, SD = 0.95) and the H-cohort (M = 2.10, Med = 2, SD = 1.22) regarding *to boy* (U = 1630, p < 0.001, Cohen's d = −0.66, BF_{10} = 21.99); and between the L-cohort (M = 1.53, Med = 1, SD = 1.20) and the H-cohort (M = 2.11, Med = 2, SD = 1.34) regarding *to tulip* (U = 1860, p = 0.008, Cohen's d = −0.46, BF_{10} = 4.86).

Further Issues As for the group of secondary school respondents, we will briefly mention two procedures that are used to control the type I error (a rejection of a true null hypothesis also known as false positive findings). When controlling the family-wise error rate with the more stringent Bonferroni (1936) correction, if all 24 comparisons are encompassed, only p values lower than 0.002 should be considered as statistically significant (8 p values). As in the previous case, we prefer to control the false discovery rate through Benjamini and Hochberg's (1995) procedure. Accordingly, out of all the significant findings, one could be considered as a false discovery. Stated differently, from 17 statistically significant p values, 16 remained statistically significant even after the adjustment (p values for FDR < 0.021).

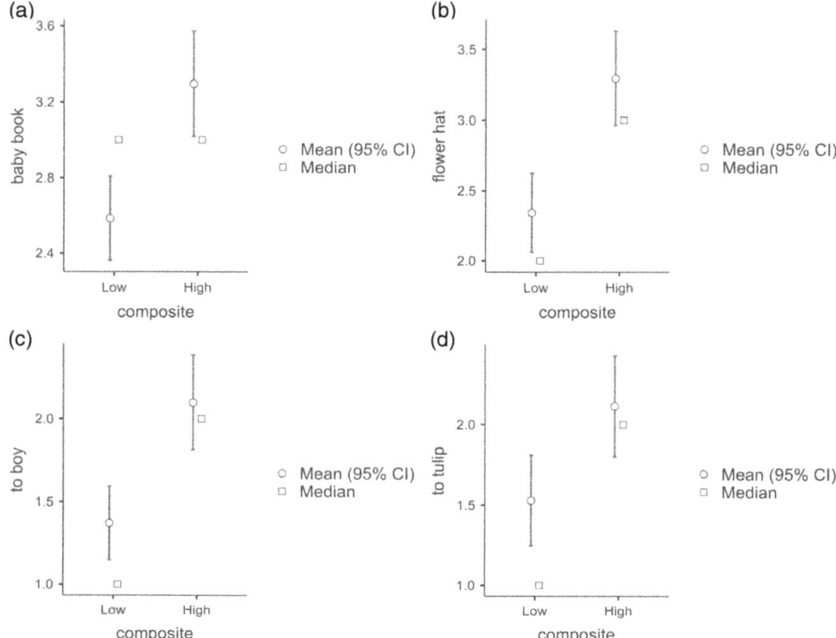

Figure 5.36 Descriptive plots for Composite Score

Considering the magnitude of the effect size according to the classical benchmarks of Cohen (1977, 1988), (a) an *almost large effect size* was found for the differences between the L-cohort and the H-cohort regarding *to tulip* and *flower hat* in Elaboration and *flower hat* in Composite Score; (b) a *medium effect size* was found for the differences between the L-cohort and the H-cohort regarding *baby book* and *to boy* in Elaboration, *flower hat* and *to tulip* in Creative Strengths, and *baby book* and *to boy* in Composite Score; and (c) a *small effect size* was found for the differences between the L-cohort and the H-cohort regarding the remaining words except for *to tulip* in Fluency and Originality, which were below the 0.2 threshold.

In addition, from the Bayesian perspective (and the verbal interpretational scheme provided by Wagenmakers et al. 2017), there is (a) *extreme or very strong evidence* for the alternative hypothesis (predicting the differences between the L-cohort and the H-cohort) relative to H0 regarding *flower hat* and *to boy* in Elaboration and Composite Score, *flower hat* in Creative Strengths, and *baby book* in Composite Score; (b) *strong evidence* regarding *to tulip* in Elaboration; (c) *moderate evidence* regarding *baby book* in Elaboration and *to tulip* in Creative Strengths and Composite Score; and (d) only *anecdotal evidence* for *baby book* in Fluency and *to tulip* in Creative Strengths.

Moreover, considering the null results, there is (a) moderate evidence for the null hypothesis regarding *to tulip* in Fluency and Originality, *flower hat* in Originality, *to boy* and *baby book* in Flexibility, and *to tulip, to boy,* and *baby book* in Fluency and (b) only anecdotal evidence for the null hypothesis regarding *to tulip* in Elaboration, *flower hat*, *to boy*, and *to tulip* in Flexibility, and *flower hat* in Fluency.

Summary of Inferential Statistics and Sensitivity Analysis

In a nutshell, when pondering Hypothesis 4 in the sample of university undergraduates, the results are mostly in line with this hypothesis, and even more convincingly than in the case of the group of secondary school students. The hypothesis predicted that the average number of readings proposed by the H-cohort members is higher than that proposed by the L-cohort members owing to the higher creativity potential identified by the TTCT. This hypothesis is, in fact, in accordance with the data but not necessarily for all TTCT scores and for some word conditions more than for others. The differences between the H-cohort and the L-cohort have been found to be statistically significant especially in relation to *Composite Score*, *Elaboration*, and *Creative Strengths*. Concerning the effect size, according to Cohen's benchmarks (1977, 1988), the majority of results are medium to large in magnitude. From the perspective of the Bayes factor, there is moderate to extreme evidence in favour of the alternative hypothesis relative to H0 for the majority of cases. The results related to Fluency and Flexibility are, however, much more ambiguous. The differences are statistically significant only in some instances; according to the Bayes factor, the evidence in favour of the alternative hypothesis is zero to anecdotal, and the effect size is smaller as well – a small to medium effect. In fact, there is anecdotal to moderate evidence for the null hypothesis for some comparisons. These results thus mean that, unlike Hypothesis 4B, Hypothesis 4A has only been confirmed partly, that is, for Elaboration but not for Fluency.

As in the previous case, to corroborate the robustness of the previous analysis due to potential limitations of the data's dichotomization into the L-cohort and the H-cohort by means of the quartile split procedure, a sensitivity analysis is conducted in which all variables are used in a non-dichotomized form. Next, Kendall's non-parametric τ correlation coefficient is used to corroborate the relationship between the average number of readings in four tasks and the TTCT indicators/subscores.

Table 5.126 represents a correlation matrix among the variables. As can be seen, correlations are found between the creativity indicators/subscores and the average number of proposed readings. These correlations are small to medium in magnitude. Such a pattern of results corresponds with the main analysis. As in the main analysis, the correlations with the average number of readings are present mainly for Elaboration, Creative Strengths, Composite Score, and

Table 5.126. *Correlation matrix among variables*

	Composite	Fluency	Flexibility	Originality	Elaboration	Creative Strengths
baby book	0.18***	0.10*	0.13**	0.11*	0.14**	0.15***
flower hat	0.19***	0.05	0.06	0.14***	0.20***	0.20***
to boy	0.16***	0.08	0.11*	0.10*	0.14**	0.14**
to tulip	0.13**	0.02	0.06	0.05	0.19***	0.14**

Note. *p < 0.05, **p < 0.01, ***p < 0.001

Originality, and this relationship is positive. This means that the average number of readings proposed by a cohort member is boosted by *Originality, Elaboration, Creative Strengths*, and *Composite Score*.

To provide further evidence, the Bayes factor is computed as it indicates the amount of evidence in support of the alternative hypothesis relative to H0 as well as the lower and upper 95% credible intervals. For the majority of statistically significant results, there is a strong to extreme evidence for the alternative hypothesis over the null hypothesis.

5.2.2.4 Hapax Legomena

This section aims to evaluate the criterion of hapax legomena in terms of Hypotheses 5A and 5B as specified in the Introduction. As in the group of secondary school students, we relate the data for single-occurrence readings in the L-cohort and the H-cohort to individual creativity indicators/subscores (Table 5.128). The figures under the individual experimental words indicate the number of hapax legomena proposed by the two cohorts. The figures under the individual creativity indicators identify the number of cohort members who proposed that particular reading. HL stands for hapax legomenon.

Baby Book

Hypothesis 5A holds for the reading 'an official document of a baby', where the single occurrences in Fluency, Creative Strengths, and Composite Score of the L-cohort correspond with two occurrences of that reading in each of these creativity indicators of the H-cohort. The same holds for the reading 'a registry office' in Elaboration and 'a book with names of babies' in Creative Strengths.

Furthermore, there are cases supporting Hypothesis 5B, viz. hapax legomena in the H-cohort have zero occurrences in the L-cohort, such as 'records of a pregnant woman' in Fluency and Originality and 'a book with names of babies' for Elaboration.

On the other hand, there are evident counterexamples to both parts of Hypothesis 5; for example, the H-cohort's hapax legomenon 'a book in the

Table 5.127. *Calculations based on the Bayes factor*

		Composite	Fluency	Flexibility	Originality	Elaboration	Creative Strengths
baby book	Kendall's τ	0.18***	0.10	0.13*	0.11	0.14**	0.15***
	BF_{10}	2684.17	1.62	17.28	2.96	30.58	149.34
	Upper 95% CI	0.25	0.17	0.20	0.18	0.21	0.22
	Lower 95% CI	0.10	0.02	0.05	0.03	0.06	0.07
flower hat	Kendall's τ	0.19***	0.05	0.06	0.14**	0.20***	0.20***
	BF_{10}	6673.82	0.15	0.25	70.34	46,497.15	63,618.39
	Upper 95% CI	0.26	0.12	0.13	0.22	0.27	0.28
	Lower 95% CI	0.11	−0.03	−0.02	0.07	0.12	0.12
to boy	Kendall's τ	0.16***	0.08	0.11	0.10	0.14**	0.14**
	BF_{10}	487.44	0.79	3.99	2.71	54.77	50.02
	Upper 95% CI	0.24	0.16	0.18	0.18	0.21	0.21
	Lower 95% CI	0.08	0.01	0.03	0.03	0.06	0.06
to tulip	Kendall's τ	0.13*	0.02	0.06	0.05	0.19***	0.14**
	BF_{10}	21.52	0.09	0.22	0.18	6509.25	71.54
	Upper 95% CI	0.20	0.10	0.13	0.13	0.26	0.22
	Lower 95% CI	0.05	−0.05	−0.02	−0.03	0.11	0.07

Note. $^{*}BF_{10} > 10$, $^{**}BF_{10} > 30$, $^{***}BF_{10} > 100$

Table 5.128. *Hapax legomena versus zero/multiple occurrences*

	Reading	Cohort	Elaboration	Fluency	Flexibility	Originality	Creative Strengths	Composite Score
baby	'records of a pregnant woman'	**L**		0		0		
book		**H**		HL		HL		
L = 5	'a book in the shape of a baby'	**L**	4					
H = 5		**H**	HL					
	'an official document of a baby'	**L**	HL	HL	HL		HL	HL
		H	0	2	0		2	2
	'sb who knows a lot about babies'	**L**		HL		HL	HL	HL
		H		0		0	0	0
	'registry office'	**L**	HL					
		H	3					
	'started book'	**L**	HL			0		
		H	0			HL		
	'a book with names of babies'	**L**	0				HL	
		H	HL				2	
flower hat	'a tulip bed'	**L**		HL	HL			
L = 5		**H**		4	4			
H = 4	'a bouquet'	**L**	HL	2		HL		0
		H	0	HL		0		HL
	'a haircut'	**L**			HL		HL	
		H			5		2	
	'a pretty hat'	**L**	HL		0			
		H	0		HL			
	'a romantic girl'	**L**	0			HL	0	0
		H	HL			HL	HL	HL
	'a flower meadow'	**L**	0			0		
		H	HL			HL		

to boy	‘to bring up a boy’	**L**		HL		HL	HL	HL
L = 6		**H**		5		7	8	6
H = 6	‘to play with a boy’	**L**					0	
		H					HL	
	‘to treat like a kid’	**L**		0				
		H		HL				
	‘to give birth to a boy’	**L**	HL	HL	HL	HL		HL
		H	6	4	4	5		10
	‘to be a homosexual’	**L**		HL				3
		H		2	HL			HL
	‘to voice-mutate’	**L**		HL	HL	HL		2
		H		HL	HL	0		HL
	‘to give sth to a boy’	**L**		HL	0	2		HL
		H		0	HL	HL		0
	‘to talk about boys’	**L**		0		HL	HL	HL
		H		HL		0	HL	0
to tulip	‘to paint tulips	**L**	HL	HL	0		HL	HL
L = 10		**H**	3	2	HL		3	3
H = 10	‘to live in the Netherlands’	**L**		3				
		H		HL				
	‘to be innocent’	**L**		0	0	0	0	0
		H		HL	HL	HL	HL	HL
	‘to decorate with tulips’	**L**					HL	HL
		H					11	13
	‘to feel happy’	**L**	HL	HL				
		H	0	0				
	‘to talk about tulips’	**L**	HL	HL	HL	HL	0	HL
		H	HL	HL	HL	HL	HL	HL
	‘to use drugs’	**L**	3	HL	HL		HL	HL
		H	HL	4	HL		HL	HL

Table 5.128. *(cont.)*

Reading	Cohort	Elaboration	Fluency	Flexibility	Originality	Creative Strengths	Composite Score
'to blush'	**L**		2				
	H		HL				
'to compliment'							
	L		0	0		HL	
	H		HL	HL		2	
'to make a bouquet'	**L**				2	HL	
	H				HL	HL	
'to be fragile'	**L**		2	2		HL	
	H		HL	HL		0	
'to make things from tulips'	**L**				HL		
	H				3		
'to grow tall'	**L**		HL				
	H		2				
'to be colourful'	**L**		3				
	H		HL				

shape of a baby' has four corresponding occurrences in Elaboration of the L-cohort, and the hapax legomenon 'sb who knows a lot about babies', which occurs in four indicators/subscores of the L-cohort, has no corresponding occurrence in the H-cohort.

Flower Hat

The hypothesis is strongly supported for the meanings 'a tulip bed' in Fluency and Flexibility (hapax legomena in the L-cohort vs. four occurrences in both of the indicators in the H-cohort) and 'a haircut' in Flexibility and Creative Strengths (respectively, five and two occurrences in the H-cohort). In addition, there are cases of the L-cohort's zero-correspondence with the H-cohort's hapax legomenon, including 'a romantic girl' in three indicators (Elaboration, Creative Strengths and Composite Score) and 'a flower meadow' (Elaboration and Originality).

Contrary to this, the H-cohort's single occurrence of 'a bouquet' in Fluency has two occurrences in the L-cohort, and the reading 'a pretty hat' in Elaboration of the L-cohort does not occur in the H-cohort. In the latter case, the Flexibility indicator illustrates the opposite situation.

To Boy

Very strong support for Hypothesis 5A comes from the readings 'to give birth to a boy', where a hapax legomenon in all indicators/subscores of the L-cohort, except for Creative Strengths, corresponds with a high number of occurrences in the H-cohort (from 6 to 10), and 'to bring up a boy': single occurrences of this reading in the L-cohort's Fluency, Originality, Creative Strengths, and Composite Score face numerous occurrences in the corresponding indicators/ subscores of the H-cohort (5, 7, 8, and 6, respectively). Furthermore, the H-cohort's single-occurrence readings 'to play with a boy' (Creative Strengths) and 'to treat like a kid' (Fluency) are not proposed by the L-cohort at all. There are minimum counterexamples among the readings for *to boy*.

To Tulip

The number of readings with hapax legomena is much higher for *to tulip* than for the other three experimental words and is equal in both cohorts (10). There is no clear tendency for the hapax legomenon versus multiple occurrences in relation between the L-cohort and the H-cohort, even if there are two evident instances of this sort. The most striking one concerns the meaning 'to decorate with tulips' for the subscores Creative Strengths and Composite Score with 11 and 13 occurrences (!), respectively, in the H-cohort. Another one concerns the reading 'to paint tulips'. However, counterexamples occur as well. The relation between zero occurrences in the L-cohort and hapax legomenon in the H-cohort is most evident for the reading 'to be innocent'. There are counterexamples also for this kind of relation.

Table 5.129. *Number of HL-to-many occurrences of the proposed readings – comparison of the cohorts*

	L-cohort	H-cohort	L-cohort	H-cohort
baby book	HL	5	1	HL
flower hat	HL	4	1	HL
to boy	HL	10	3	HL
to tulip	HL	10	6	HL

A summary of the data for all four experimental words is provided in Table 5.129.

It follows from Table 5.129 that for each of the experimental words there is a partial confirmation of Hypothesis 5A, which means that if a particular reading is proposed by a single respondent of the L-cohort, there is a tendency for the same reading to be proposed by a higher number of respondents of the H-cohort. It may be therefore surmised that for peripheral readings, there is a higher number of respondents of the H-cohort who approach the interpretation process in a more creative way. This tendency is, once again, in accordance with the results obtained for the Objectified Predictability Rate (OPR). The OPR values are higher for the L-cohort, which means that more respondents propose the most acceptable reading and fewer of them propose less acceptable readings.

Nevertheless, the aforementioned hypothesis has not been confirmed for each L-cohort's hapax legomena. There are a number of instances of the L-cohort's hapax legomena readings that have no occurrences in the H-cohort. Taking into consideration all the outcomes, we can evaluate *Hypothesis 5A as a tendency* in the interpretation behaviour of the L-cohort versus the H-cohort.

Ambiguity arises from the data that come from an analysis of those cases in which a hapax legomenon of one cohort corresponds with zero occurrences in the other cohort. Since this is also an indicator of creative interpretation, one would expect a prevalence of instances of a hapax legomenon reading in the H-cohort and zero occurrences of that reading in the L-cohort. As shown in Table 5.130, however, the situation is different.

The total number of instances in which the H-cohort's hapax legomenon corresponds with zero occurrences of that reading in the L-cohort is higher than the opposite case, but in no way it is an unambiguous proportion. This parameter appears to be influenced by individual words rather than underlying word formation processes. In any event, much more research is needed to conclude on the actual influence (if any) of this parameter upon interpretation creativity.

Table 5.130. *Hapax legomena versus zero occurrences – comparison of the cohorts*

	L-cohort	H-cohort	L-cohort	H-cohort
		Zero occurrences	Zero occurrences	
baby book	HL	7	4	HL
flower hat	HL	2	7	HL
to boy	HL	5	4	HL
to tulip	HL	3	9	HL

Table 5.131. *Many occurrences versus hapax legomena*

	L-cohort Many-to-HL	H-cohort Many-to-HL
Elaboration	2	3
Fluency	5	8
Flexibility	1	3
Originality	2	3
Creative Strengths	0	7
Composite Score	2	5

Table 5.132. *Hapax legomena versus zero occurrences*

	L-cohort	H-cohort	L-cohort	H-cohort
		Zero occurrences	Zero occurrences	
Elaboration	HL	5	3	HL
Fluency	HL	3	5	HL
Flexibility	HL	1	6	HL
Originality	HL	4	4	HL
Creative Strengths	HL	2	4	HL
Composite Score	HL	3	3	HL

If the same set of data is viewed by creativity indicators/subscores, the picture is as shown in Tables 5.131 and 5.132.

The strongest evidence in favour of our hypothesis is provided by *Creative Strengths* and, to a lesser degree, by *Composite Score*, *Fluency,* and *Flexibility*. The fact that many occurrences in the H-cohort correspond to a hapax legomenon in the L-cohort may be taken as an indicator of a *tendency*.

The strongest and, in fact, the only relevant evidence in favour of the higher interpretation creativity of the H-cohort (Hypothesis 5B) comes from *Flexibility* and, weakly, from *Creative Strengths* and *Fluency*. The data on the other indicators/subscores are rather ambiguous.

5.2.2.5 Summary IV

Our findings concerning the group of university undergraduates can be summarized as follows:

(i) The *Predictability Rate* (PR) of individual potential words is predetermined by the overall acceptability of the individual potential readings and appears to depend on the individual potential words. The highest PR value of the most predictable readings was identified for *baby book*, followed by *to boy, flower hat,* and, finally, *to tulip*, which featured a very low PR value for the most predictable reading.

(ii) The H-cohort manifests higher PR values of the most predictable readings for all four words in *Flexibility* and *Composite Score*. To them, we can add two indicators in which the PR value of the most predictable reading is higher in the H-cohort than in the L-cohort for three words, viz. *Elaboration*, *Originality*, and *Creative Strengths*.

(iii) The data do not show any substantial differences between the two cohorts as far as the most predictable readings are concerned. In fact, the most predictable readings are identical for all experimental words and for each creativity indicator/subscore with the exception of *flower hat* for Originality and Creative Strengths (H-cohort in both cases) and *to tulip* for Originality and Creative Strengths (L-cohort in both cases).

(iv) The hypothesis of smaller PR gaps between the topmost reading, on the one hand, and the lower-rank readings, on the other, projected onto smaller OPR values of the most predictable readings in the H-cohort has been fully confirmed for both subscores, that is, *Creative Strengths* and *Composite Score*, and partly for *Elaboration* and *Fluency*.

(v) The criterion of the average number of readings proposed for the experimental words provides an extremely strong piece of evidence for the unequal interpretation creativity of the two cohorts in question. The H-cohort proposed on average a higher number of readings per respondent than the L-cohort for *all indicators/subscores*. In the majority of cases, the differences are statistically significant, and the evidence is in favour of the alternative hypothesis over the null hypothesis. In particular, Hypothesis 4A has been supported for *Elaboration*, but not for Fluency. Hypothesis 4B found strong support in *Creative Strengths*, *Composite Score*, and *Originality*.

Table 5.133. *Indicators/subscores with significant (S)/partial (P) support for the hypotheses*

Parameter	Indicator/subscore
Objectified Predictability Rate	**S:** Creative Strengths, Composite Score
	P: Elaboration, Fluency
Average number of readings	**S: (4A) Elaboration**
	S: (4B) Creative Strengths, Composite Score, Originality
	P: (4B) Flexibility, Fluency
Hapax legomena	**S**: (5A) Creative Strengths
	P: (5A) Composite Score, Fluency, Flexibility
	S: (5B) Flexibility
	P: (5B) Creative Strengths, Fluency

Table 5.134. *Indicators/subscores contradicting the hypotheses*

Parameter	Indicator/subscore
Objectified Predictability Rate	Flexibility, Originality
Average number of readings	–
Hapax legomena	(5A) –
	(5B) Originality, Elaboration, Composite Score

(vi) Hypothesis 4A has been confirmed for *Elaboration*, but not for Fluency. Hypothesis 4B found strong support in *Creative Strengths*, *Composite Score*, and *Originality*.

(vii) Hypothesis 5A has not been confirmed conclusively. Rather than a general principle, we may speak about a tendency for the L-cohort's hapax legomenon to correspond to more than one occurrence of that reading in the H-cohort. This tendency is most evident for *Creative Strengths*. Hypothesis 5B has not been confirmed as a whole. In fact, the only indicator that corroborates it is *Flexibility*.

(viii) Our results demonstrate that the individual creativity indicators/-subscores have unequal impacts on the creative interpretation of new words. If we take into consideration three parameters (i.e. without PR, which can indicate differences between the two compared cohorts but cannot be evaluated in terms of affecting interpretation creativity), we get Tables 5.133 and 5.134.

(ix) It follows from Tables 5.133 and 5.134 that *Creative Strengths* and *Composite Score* are the most influential psychological creativity factors that boost interpretation creativity. The status of the other factors varies depending on the individual evaluation criteria. Originality shows the opposite effects in two criteria.

5.2.3 *Comparison of the Results of Secondary School Students versus University Undergraduates*

This section is devoted to a comparison of the results obtained from the two groups of respondents: a group of secondary school students (SS) and a group of university undergraduates (UU). This comparison pursues two objectives: (i) to find out whether the age difference (about 5 years) between teenagers and adolescents is reflected in their word interpretation achievements from the point of view of creativity. In other words, we want to find out whether the individual creativity parameters have equal/different effects upon the way young people from both age categories interpret new words. In the following sections, we compare all four parameters, that is, Predictability Rate, Objectified Predictability Rate, the average number of readings proposed by a cohort member, and hapax legomena.

5.2.3.1 Predictability Rate

We have pointed out that each potential complex word usually has one strong reading (rarely two readings) whose Predictability Rate (PR) significantly exceeds the PR of all the other readings of a given complex word. This has been confirmed in both groups of respondents in almost all cases. Thus, the reading 'a book for a baby' for the word *baby book* has clearly the highest PR in both groups of respondents (SS and UU), in both cohorts (L-cohort and H-cohort) and in all creativity indicators/subscores. The same is true of the reading 'to behave like a boy' for the word *to boy*.

The most predictable reading 'a hat made of flowers' for the word *flower hat* is replaced in three cases: SS H-cohort Flexibility ('a hat with a flower in it'), UU H-cohort Originality, and UU H-cohort Creative Strengths (in both cases, 'a hat with a flower pattern').

The topmost reading 'to grow tulips' for the word *to tulip* is replaced in two cases: UU L-cohort Originality and UU L-cohort Creative Strengths (in both cases, 'to look pretty'). Interestingly, in both experimental words, the exceptions bear on Originality and Creative Strengths.

This means that there is only a single exception in the SS group and that the six exceptions in the UU group are restricted to two creativity indicators/subscores.

If the lower ranks are taken into consideration, the scope of readings covered by the SS and UU groups is, with minor exceptions, the same, even if their respective rankings may differ. One such exception is the reading 'to undergo gender-changing surgery' for the word *to boy*, which only occurs in the SS group. Differences also concern the number of occurrences in the top four ranks and the cohort's preferences. So, for example, while the reading 'to be a narcissist' for the word *to tulip* occurs three times in the SS group (H-cohort Fluency, Creative Strengths, and Composite Score), it occurs only once in the UU group (L-cohort Originality). The reading 'to decorate sth with tulips' occurs among top four readings of the UU group's H-cohort in all six indicators/subscores, but it does not assume a position among the four most predictable readings of the SS group in any of the indicators/subscores.

It may be concluded that there are no substantial differences between the SS and the UU groups of respondents that might follow from the predictability strength not only of the most predictable reading but also the next lower readings. Since, however, the differences between the lower-ranked readings are usually smaller than the PR gap between the topmost reading and the next lowest reading, their ranking changes slightly across the two groups of respondents, two cohorts, and six indicators/subscores.

Tables 5.70 and 5.105 identify the cohorts with higher PR values for the most predictable reading for the individual indicators/subscores. The two groups have identical results for *baby book* but substantially differ in assigning PR values to *flower hat*: while in the SS group the PR values of the L-cohort are higher in five out of the six indicators/subscores, the situation in the UU group is the opposite, with all six indicators/subscores showing higher PR values in the H-cohort. Differences can also be identified for the converted words *to boy* and *to tulip*. In the former case, there are five indicators/subscores (with the exception of Flexibility) in the SS group that feature a higher PR value in the H-cohort; in the UU group, there are four indicators/subscores (the exceptions being Fluency and Originality). For the word *to tulip*, the H-cohort of the SS group dominates in only three indicators/subscores while the H-cohort of the UU group shows higher PR values in five indicators/ subscores.

The data do not allow us to draw any generalizations in terms of some principled differences in the influence of individual indicators/subscores upon the PR values of the most predictable readings. It may be concluded, however, that there is a slight tendency for the H-cohort of the UU group – in comparison to the SS group – to assign higher PR values to the most predictable readings than the L-cohort.

Finally, the PR values appear to be influenced by the concrete word as well as by the underlying word formation process. In both groups of respondents, the PR values of the most predictable reading are highest by far for *baby book* and lowest by far for *to tulip*. The PR values for *flower hat* are on average higher than the PR values for *to boy* in the SS group, while in the UU group their positions are swapped in both cohorts. These findings are not surprising in view of the semantic transparency versus economy of expression competition represented by the scales of transparency and economy in Figure 3.1. Both converted words of our experiment belong to OT8, which is, like OT4 and OT6, the most economically onomasiological type, more economical than OT3 that underlies the experimental compounds. On the other hand, it is slightly more transparent than OT6, thanks to the morphemic representation of the Actional constituent (determined onomasiological mark), which is absent in OT3. The higher PR values for *flower hat* in some cases as well as the universal dominance of the most predictable reading of *baby book* can be accounted for by the factor of the acceptability of their most predictable readings to language users in comparison to the most predictable readings of the converted words. From a different perspective, the interpretation of the converted words *to boy* and *to tulip* is necessarily and crucially bound to the prototypical features of 'boy' and 'tulip' as objects of extra-linguistic reality. It follows from our data that the features of 'tulip' seem to have posed a much bigger problem for language speakers than those of 'boy' in terms of the identification of the prototypical features that might serve as a motivation for the process of interpretation. It follows from this observation that the competition between semantic transparency and economy should be viewed against some other factors, especially the acceptability of the most predictable reading.

5.2.3.2 Objectified Predictability Rate

This criterion reveals an important role of both subscores in influencing interpretation creativity. Age does not seem to play a substantial role here, because in both the SS and the UU groups of respondents *the creativity subscores Creative Strengths and Composite Score manifest lower OPR values in the H-cohort for all four experimental words*. This observation is thus in accordance with Hypothesis 3. Four creativity indicators, Originality, Elaboration, Fluency, and Flexibility, behave differently. While *Flexibility* gives full support to the hypothesis in the SS group, its data in the UU group are ambiguous because the H-cohort's OPR is lower in only two words. The results of the two groups for *Originality* and *Elaboration* coincide in three words, and for Fluency only in one. None of these four indicators gives conclusive evidence of their influence upon interpretation creativity in both cohorts.

This observation confirms our former claim that not all creativity indicators/subscores behave in the same way with regard to interpretation creativity. The parameter of OPR thus does not indicate any principled age-based differences in interpretation creativity.

5.2.3.3 Average Number of Readings Proposed by a Cohort Member

This criterion provides us with the most important piece of evidence that the creativity of language users does influence, through its individual indicators/subscores, their interpretation creativity. This is most evident in the UU group, where *all indicators/subscores* show a higher average number of readings proposed by the H-cohort's respondents than by the L-cohort for all four words. The results of the SS group are analogical in four parameters, namely *Originality*, *Elaboration*, *Creative Strengths*, and *Composite Score*. For Flexibility, the value of the L-cohort is slightly higher than that of the H-cohort for *flower hat*. Fluency contradicts our expectations in both compounds. The lack of influence of the Fluency indicator upon interpretation creativity is further manifested if one takes into account the average differences between the H-cohort and the L-cohort in the average number of proposed readings. This value is smallest for Fluency for all indicators/subscores in both groups of respondents. This means that Hypothesis 4A has been confirmed for *Elaboration* but not for Fluency. This applies to both groups of respondents. Hypothesis 4B has been corroborated in a significant way for *Originality*, *Creative Strengths*, and *Composite Score* in both groups as well. The crucial role of the four aforementioned indicators/subscores is also reflected in the highest average differences. It should be pointed out that the older group of respondents, that is, the UU speakers, show substantially higher differences compared to the SS group in *Composite Score* and *Elaboration*. This suggests a boosting effect of age with regard to these two factors.

5.2.3.4 Hapax Legomena

Hypothesis 5A expects the H-cohort to propose more readings that correspond with the L-cohort's hapax legomena; according to Hypothesis 5B, the H-cohort is expected to propose more hapax legomena readings that correspond to zero occurrences of those readings in the L-cohort than vice versa. These expectations have only been partly confirmed for both age groups of respondents in relation to Hypothesis 5A, basically as a tendency that is most evident for *Creative Strengths* in the UU group and *Originality* and *Composite Score* in the SS group. Hypothesis 5B has only been confirmed for Flexibility in the UU group; it has not found any strong support in the SS group.

A comparison of the data by creativity indicator/subscore with regard to point (i) of the hypothesis shows similar results in both groups with the exception of Fluency, which contradicts our expectations in the L-cohort. If the data for both the SS and the UU groups are added up, we find that the strongest support for Hypothesis 5 comes from both subscores, *Creative Strengths* and *Composite Score*, as well as the *Originality* and *Flexibility* indicators.

5.2.3.5 Summary V

Our previous discussion and comparison of the data for the group of secondary students and the group of university undergraduates enable us to draw the following conclusions:

(i) There are no significant differences between the two age groups of respondents in any of the examined parameters, that is, Predictability Rate, Objectified Predictability Rate, average number of readings proposed by a cohort member, and hapax legomena, even though there appears to be a tendency for the older age group to propose more readings than the younger group, at least relative to some of the indicators/subscores. In principle, however, both groups confirm the same tendency. This conclusion does not exclude partial differences in individual indicators/subscores and cohorts.

(ii) The influence of the individual creativity indicators/subscores upon interpretation creativity is not identical. There are considerable differences between them. If the data for all three parameters are compared, it can be concluded that *Composite Score* and *Creative Strengths* have the strongest influence upon interpretation creativity. *Flexibility* and *Originality* are strong creativity-boosting factors in the SS group but not in the UU group, where Originality contradicts our hypotheses in two parameters. The indicator that runs counter to our expectations in the SS cohort in almost all cases is Fluency. Its results in the UU group are more positive, but it does not show major creativity-boosting effects in this group either.

(iii) The interpretation creativity of the H-cohort is in general higher than that of the L-cohort in both age groups of respondents.

(iv) The H-cohort of the UU group shows an unambiguous tendency to assign higher predictability values to the most predictable readings than the L-cohort: the proportion is 19:5 (comparing all 6 indicators/subscores × 4 words). The situation in the SS group is different: the proportion between the two cohorts is balanced, especially due to the compound *flower hat*, where the PR values of the L-cohort are higher in five indicators/subscores.

5.3 Creativity and Gender in Complex Word Formation and Complex Word Interpretation

5.3.1 Introduction

Runco et al. (2010: 354) maintain that, before 2010, "over 80 studies have been conducted to investigate basic differences between the genders in creative potential, and little support for any differences has been reported. In fact, one-half of these studies indicated no meaningful difference in creative potential among men and women, and one-third of the studies indicated that women and girls actually score slightly higher on creativity indices than do men and boys." Moreover, as noted by Abraham (2016: 614), "[a]ssessing gender differences in creativity is a controversial line of research to explore. And for good reason. It is naïve and wrong to suggest either that one gender is more creative than another, or that there are absolutely no differences between the sexes (Pinker 2009). The truth appears to be far more nuanced and complex." In other words, they are not generalizable across domains; they are far more subtle (Abraham 2016: 612).[3]

Very little in the former research was aimed at the examination of potential gender differences in word formation strategies, that is, whether males and females differ in the way they form new complex words, not to mention the exploration of creative aspects of word formation as discussed in this volume. Previous scarce research concerning gender differences in word formation dealt, in general, with the use of complex words and/or suffixes, that is, the products of word formation.[4] Similar conclusions can be drawn on research into gender differences in creative performance in interpreting novel/potential complex words.

The objective of the following sections is therefore to contribute to the effort aimed at the examination of potential gender differences in word formation and word interpretation creativity by combining selected psychological, psycholinguistic, and sociolinguistic factors. In particular, the purpose of this part of our research concentrates on interrelating how gender differences in the psychological test results project onto the word formation and word interpretation differences between male and female users of a language.

The gender-related data are evaluated in three different ways. The data are compared in each individual case by creativity parameters/subscores in terms of the comparison of the data for (i) male and female respondents within the

[3] For a representative overview of research into the relation between creativity and gender, cf. Baer and Kaufman (2008), Runco et al. (2010), Pagnani (2011) and Abraham (2016).

[4] See, for example, Rainer (1983) on the differences between Spanish female and male speakers in the use of diminutives, whose conclusions that women use more diminutives than men and that speakers use more diminutives when they talk to women than when they talk to men are in accordance with the more general observation of Newman et al. (2008: 232) that "women use more affect words." This is accounted for by Keune (2012) by the more 'informational' style of men versus the more 'involved' style of women, something that might be, in her view, biologically conditioned because women have, throughout history, been more intensively charged with the task of raising children. Similarly, Keune, van Hout, and Baayen (2006) found out that while in both the Netherlands and Flanders women use most affixes less productively than men, this does not hold for diminutive suffixes. Säily analyzed the British National Corpus to conclude that "*-ity* is used less productively by women, while with *-ness* there is no gender difference" (2011: 119), which she explains with both diachronic and synchronic reasons.

L-cohort and the H-cohort; (ii) male respondents between the L-cohort and the H-cohort and female respondents between the L-cohort and the H-cohort; and (iii) secondary school and university students.

5.3.2 Creativity, Gender, and word formation

This section examines the influence of the creative potential of language speakers upon word formation creativity against the background of the competition between the tendency to choose an economical solution and the tendency to choose a semantically transparent solution in coining new complex words. The data evaluation relies on the same seven-degree scale of semantic transparency and is also commented on from the perspective of a three-degree scale of naming economy. Another parameter that will be taken into consideration is the number of failed answers. We will compare the female and the male groups in the L-cohorts and the H-cohorts separately for each creativity indicator. We start with the group of secondary school students; this will be followed by an analysis of the data for university undergraduates. Finally, the results obtained for the two groups will be compared. This means that the final section will relate the two sociolinguistic criteria (gender and age) from the perspective of the psychological phenomenon of creative potential manifested in the field of complex word formation and complex word interpretation.

5.3.2.1 Secondary School Students

Semantic Transparency versus Economy of Expression

The data show that – like in the general analysis in Section 5.1 – the individual subtasks tend to manifest two strong onomasiological types, OT1 and OT3, which occur at the opposite ends of the transparency scale (transparency degree 7 and 2, respectively) and represent different degrees of economy of expression. This observation concerns both female and male groups and both the L-cohort and the H-cohort. The other onomasiological types and, therefore, the other transparency degrees are neglectable in the present experimental research focused on Agents and Patients. The only more relevant exceptions are OT2 (transparency degree 5) in the first two subtasks and OT9 (transparency degree 3) in subtask 1.1. OT1, OT4, and OT6 are used rarely, and the same is true of OT9, with the exception of the aforementioned subtask 1.1.

Therefore, in Tables 5.135 and 5.136, we examine the relative strength of the two most frequently used onomasiological types from the perspective of two different genders.

The data in Table 5.135 suggest that, taking into account the results for the L-cohort, there is a general tendency for female speakers to coin semantically more transparent complex words than male speakers who, on the other hand, prefer a more economical solution. This applies, with a few exceptions, to all

Table 5.135. *Comparison of the female and the male groups in terms of the strongest OTs – L-cohort (%)*

Task 1	OT1 (transparency degree 7)		OT3 (transparency degree 2)	
	Female	Male	Female	Male
Originality	47	40	3	7
Elaboration	44	40	4	10
Flexibility	37	37	2	8
Fluency	47	39	2	8
Creative Strengths	43	34	3	6
Composite Score	44	38	3	9
Task 2	OT1 (transparency degree 7)		OT3 (transparency degree 2)	
	Female	Male	Female	Male
Originality	40	25	52	60
Elaboration	31	28	61	57
Flexibility	32	30	50	60
Fluency	34	27	51	60
Creative Strengths	31	25	65	58
Composite Score	44	29	53	60
Task 3	OT1 (transparency degree 7)		OT3 (transparency degree 2)	
	Female	Male	Female	Male
Originality	66	57	23	32
Elaboration	64	55	21	27
Flexibility	57	58	29	31
Fluency	59	57	24	29
Creative Strengths	51	51	25	30
Composite Score	56	56	28	29
Tasks 1–3	OT1 (transparency degree 7)		OT3 (transparency degree 2)	
	Female	Male	Female	Male
Originality	50	39	24	32
Elaboration	46	42	27	29
Flexibility	42	41	25	32
Fluency	47	41	24	31
Creative Strengths	41	36	29	30
Composite Score	44	42	27	31

three tasks as well as to the cumulative data for all three tasks. Furthermore, this finding is true, again with a few exceptions, of all creativity indicators.

More specifically, in Task 1, the percentage of the use of the most transparent onomasiological type exceeds 40% for five out of six creativity

Table 5.136. *Comparison of the female and male groups in terms of the strongest OTs – H-cohort (%)*

Task 1	OT1 (transparency degree 7)		OT3 (transparency degree 2)	
	Female	Male	Female	Male
Originality	46	37	4	8
Elaboration	46	31	2	8
Flexibility	47	31	5	13
Fluency	44	35	3	8
Creative Strengths	44	30	3	12
Composite Score	47	31	5	9
Task 2	OT1 (transparency degree 7)		OT3 (transparency degree 2)	
	Female	Male	Female	Male
Originality	37	26	55	72
Elaboration	37	31	54	63
Flexibility	25	26	65	64
Fluency	34	30	59	58
Creative Strengths	37	26	54	67
Composite Score	35	31	55	65
Task 3	OT1 (transparency degree 7)		OT3 (transparency degree 2)	
	Female	Male	Female	Male
Originality	64	63	28	29
Elaboration	66	58	21	38
Flexibility	55	56	30	34
Fluency	61	60	25	29
Creative Strengths	68	59	20	32
Composite Score	61	53	28	38
Tasks 1–3	OT1 (transparency degree 7)		OT3 (transparency degree 2)	
	Female	Male	Female	Male
Originality	48	43	28	33
Elaboration	50	41	25	34
Flexibility	41	38	33	34
Fluency	46	42	27	28
Creative Strengths	49	37	24	35
Composite Score	48	38	28	35

indicators/subscores. Flexibility is the exception, and it is the only case where the use of OT1 in the female group is not higher than in the male group (the percentages are identical). On the other hand, the maximum percentage for the male group is 40%. The biggest difference between the two genders is found for *Composite Score* (16%). The use of the more economical and much less transparent OT3 is favoured more by the male speakers. This is confirmed for all six indicators/subscores.

In Task 2, female speakers employ a more transparent naming strategy according to all creativity indicators/subscores. The percentage differences are most striking for *Composite Score* and *Originality* (15%), while the smallest differences are for Flexibility (2%) and Elaboration (3%). However, the use of the less transparent OT3 is not higher than in the male group for all indicators/subscores. The exceptions are Elaboration and Creative Strengths.

In Task 3, we face minimum differences between female and male speakers. The percentages of OT1 are equal for Creative Strengths and Composite Score and almost identical for Fluency and Flexibility. The general trend indicated by the first two tasks has been confirmed for *Originality* and *Elaboration*. On the other hand, male speakers prefer OT3 from the point of view of all indicators/subscores. The biggest differences are found for *Originality* and *Elaboration*.

The cumulative results map the results obtained for the individual tasks. The frequency of the use of OT1 is higher in the female group than in the male group for all creativity indicators/subscores, the highest difference being 11% for *Originality* and the smallest for Flexibility. An analogy with the individual tasks has also been found for OT3: its percentages are higher in the male group for all indicators/subscores. The highest difference has been identified for *Fluency* (10%).

The H-group confirms the observations for the L-cohort, that is, while female speakers prefer semantic transparency, male speakers prefer more economical coinages.

In Task 1, this has been confirmed evidently for all creativity indicators/subscores: The average difference in the use of OT1 between the female and the male groups is 13% (!). The biggest difference is found for *Flexibility* and *Composite Score* (16%). Similarly, the use of the more economical OT3 is higher in the male group for all indicators/subscores. The biggest differences have been found for *Creative Strengths* (9%) and *Flexibility* (8%).

While Task 2 supports the general trend, an exception does occur: Flexibility shows almost identical percentages for both OT1 and OT3, and the same is true of Fluency with regard to economy. The strongest support for the general trend comes from *Originality* and *Creative Strengths*, both of which show an 11% difference between the female and the male groups in the use of OT1 and as high as a 17% difference for *Originality* and 13% for *Creative Strengths* in the use of OT3.

Task 3 provides ambiguous results for three creativity indicators: the values of the female and the male groups in using OT1 are almost identical for Originality, Flexibility, and Fluency and in using OT3 for Originality. The general trend is confirmed most strikingly for *Elaboration* (the difference in the use of OT3 is as high as 17%(!)) and for both subscores, that is, *Creative Strengths* and *Composite Score*.

Table 5.137. *Comparison of the female and the male groups for subtask 1.1 (%)*

L-cohort				
Subtask 1.1	OT2 (transparency degree 5)		OT9 (transparency degree 3)	
	Female	Male	Female	Male
Originality	32	52	66	36
Elaboration	43	32	52	52
Flexibility	31	40	64	36
Fluency	33	40	57	47
Creative Strengths	24	48	73	52
Composite Score	29	39	62	49

H-cohort				
Subtask 1.1	OT2 (transparency degree 5)		OT9 (transparency degree 3)	
	Female	Male	Female	Male
Originality	39	42	42	38
Elaboration	35	39	53	57
Flexibility	45	44	40	44
Fluency	45	38	43	33
Creative Strengths	45	43	49	38
Composite Score	38	44	46	40

The cumulative data give additional support to the observation that female speakers prefer semantic transparency more than male speakers while the latter prefer economy more than female speakers. The data are fairly conclusive and exceptionless in this respect, even if the Flexibility and Fluency indicators manifest small differences. The most conclusive results come from *Elaboration*, *Creative Strengths*, and *Composite Score*.

It should be noted, however, that the data in Task 1 are influenced by an extremely high percentage of OT9 (transparency degree 3) in subtask 1.1, where it is the most frequently used onomasiological type. This is due to the nature of this subtask as accounted for in Section 5.1.1.1, that is, the preference of many respondents to employ a metonymical representation of a person in a billboard by the person's body part, that is, the face. This strategy produced a fairly high number of exocentric compounds, that is, compounds whose onomasiological base is not morphemically represented. This subtask is one of two instances in which the competition does not involve OT1 and OT3. In this case, the competition is between OT9 (transparency degree 3) and OT2 (transparency degree 5), and therefore it is less dramatic in terms of semantic transparency and concerns a very similar level of economy of expression. The data for subtask 1.1 are summarized in Table 5.137.

Table 5.138. *Comparison of the female and the male groups for subtask 1.2 (%)*

L-cohort				
Subtask 1.2	OT1 (transparency degree 7)		OT2 (transparency degree 5)	
	Female	Male	Female	Male
Originality	58	41	42	56
Elaboration	49	42	49	55
Flexibility	45	35	52	61
Fluency	55	36	43	64
Creative Strengths	47	33	47	67
Composite Score	44	38	27	34
H-cohort				
Subtask 1.2	OT1 (transparency degree 7)		OT2 (transparency degree 5)	
	Female	Male	Female	Male
Originality	47	41	53	59
Elaboration	44	37	52	63
Flexibility	52	36	48	64
Fluency	47	40	53	53
Creative Strengths	45	35	55	59
Composite Score	52	40	48	55

In general, the differences between the female and male groups in the use of OT2 and OT9 are high in the L-cohort for all indicators/subscores with the exception of Elaboration. This is the only instance of a higher preference of the male group for more transparent coinages, and it is clearly affected by the nature of this specific naming task. At the same time, while the male group employs a more transparent OT2 much more frequently than the female group, the latter seems to be more creative because it is inclined to use a metonymical naming strategy much more frequently. The data for the H-cohort differ substantially. It is only Composite Score that supports the results obtained for the L-cohort.

The second instance of the deviation from the prevalent OT1 versus OT3 competition concerns subtask 1.2 in which the two strongest onomasiological types are OT1 and OT2, that is, two highly transparent onomasiological types. From the point of view of the use of these two types, and in accordance with the previously indicated tendency, the female group prefers OT1 and the male group prefers OT2, as represented in Table 5.138.

The tendency for the female speakers to prefer the most transparent OT1 and for the male group the less transparent but more economical OT2 is very striking and almost universal. The only exception is the H-cohort's Fluency

Table 5.139. *Inferential statistics regarding gender differences in word formation among secondary school students*

	BF_{10}	U	p	Cohen's d
General transparency	0.78	10,780.50	0.051	0.22
Transparency Task 1	55.08	9501.00	<0.001***	0.41
Transparency Task 2	0.84	10,135.00	0.047*	0.23
Transparency Task 3	0.26	9659.50	0.188	0.14
General economy	0.49	11,157.50	0.110	−0.19
Economy Task 1	11.79	10,059.50	0.003**	−0.36
Economy Task 2	0.79	10,327.00	0.069	−0.23
Economy Task 3	0.18	9940.00	0.366	−0.10

Note. *$p < 0.05$, **$p < 0.01$, ***$p < 0.001$

indicator in the use of OT2, which shows identical values. All the other results in both cohorts give very strong support to this tendency; the differences in the percentages between the female and male groups in all indicators are fairly high, amounting to as much as 24% for the L-cohort's Creative Strengths, 20% for the L-cohort's Flexibility, and 16% for the L-cohort's Originality in the use of OT1; 16% for the H-cohort's Flexibility in the use of OT1 (all in favour of female speakers); 21% for the L-cohort's Fluency and 20% for the L-cohort's Creative Strengths in the use of OT2; and 11% for the H-cohort's Elaboration in the use of OT2 (all in favour of male speakers).

All the other tasks of the word formation test, as discussed earlier, illustrate the main competition, that is, between the semantically transparent OT1 and the more economical and much more opaque OT3.

Assessment of General Gender Differences Using Inferential Statistics

Elaborating on Section 5.3.2.1, the main aim of this section is to corroborate the robustness of gender differences in word formation among secondary school students. Instead of dividing the sample into the H-cohort and the L-cohort by individual creativity scores, the focus of this section is shifted to a more general level of analysis aimed at assessing the general trend.

The results indicate that although secondary school females formed words more transparently and less economically in comparison to males in all three tasks, the differences between genders are conclusive and statistically significant only in the first word formation task. The results of the inferential statistics are shown in Table 5.139.

These descriptives are visually depicted in Figures 5.37 and 5.38 and summarized in Table 5.140.

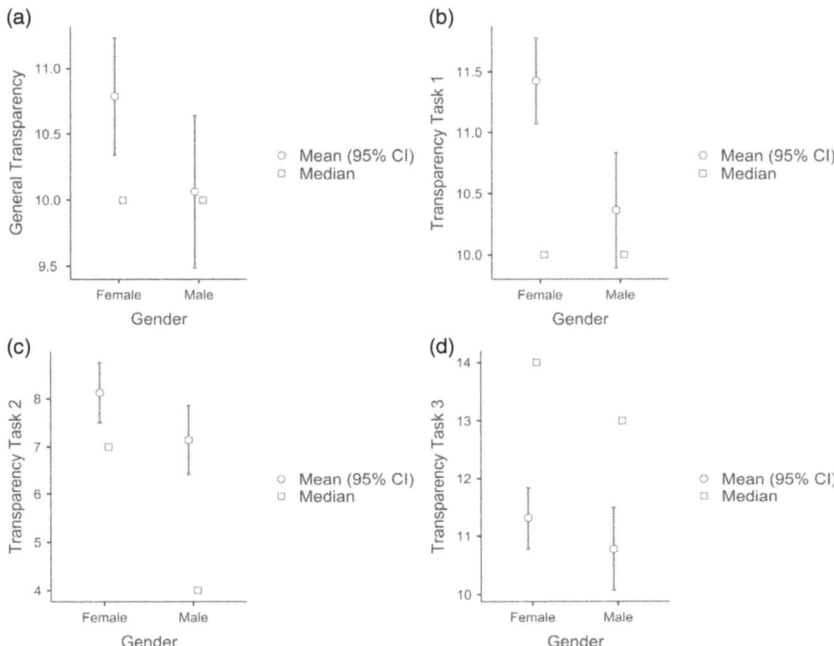

Figure 5.37 Differences between males and females regarding semantic transparency among secondary school students

Failed Answers Criterion

The data for the criterion of failed answers are summarized in Tables 5.141 and 5.142.

The proportion of failed answers is hypothesized to be indirectly proportional to word formation creativity. From the point of view of Task 1, the female group shows a higher degree of creativity in both cohorts, more conclusively in the H-cohort where the differences range from 7% for Flexibility to as much as 17% for *Composite Score*. The only exception to this general trend is the L-cohort's Elaboration.

Similar conclusions can be drawn for Task 2 (verbal description task) where, like in Task 1, it is especially the *H-cohort*'s results that suggest the much higher creativity of female speakers. The differences are fairly high in the H-cohort, ranging from 9% for Creative Strengths up to 22% for *Composite Score* and *Flexibility*, 23% for *Elaboration*, and as much as 25% for *Fluency*. In the *L-cohort*, the differences are smaller, the biggest one being 10% for *Fluency*. Moreover, Originality contradicts the general trend because the percentage of female's failed answers is higher by 5%.

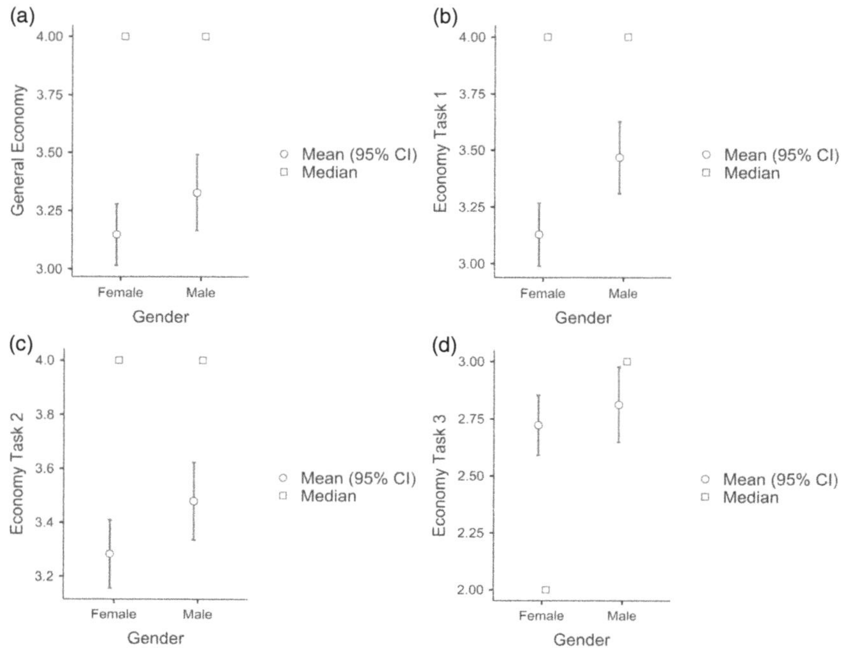

Figure 5.38 Differences between males and females regarding economy of expression among secondary school students

Task 3 provides a completely different picture. In the L-cohort, the percentage of failed answers is much higher in the female group for all creativity indicators. In the H-cohort, the results are ambiguous and seem to be strongly influenced by the TTCT scores for the individual creativity indicators/ subscores. While the data for Originality and Flexibility correspond with those of the L-cohort, which is especially relevant to Flexibility (12% difference), the other four indicators/subscores show the opposite result: the number of failed answers is higher in the male group, most conspicuously for *Creative Strengths* (10% difference). This result can be accounted for by two factors. First, it is the age factor that suggests that word formation creativity changes with increasing age with regard to certain creativity indicators. Second, word formation creativity is affected by the nature of the task in accordance with the theory of task specificity. In other words, the different results obtained for Tasks 1 and 2 versus Task 3 show that while the word formation creativity of female speakers is positively affected by the multiple selection and verbal description tasks, the drawing-based Task 3 favours the male group in some creativity indicators.

Table 5.140. *Descriptives concerning gender differences in word formation among secondary school students*

	Group	Mean	Median	SD	SE
General transparency	Female	10.79	10.00	3.19	0.23
	Male	10.06	10.00	3.29	0.29
Transparency Task 1	Female	11.43	10.00	2.51	0.18
	Male	10.36	10.00	2.67	0.24
Transparency Task 2	Female	8.13	7.00	4.40	0.32
	Male	7.14	4.00	4.04	0.37
Transparency Task 3	Female	11.31	14.00	3.60	0.27
	Male	10.78	13.00	3.88	0.36
General economy	Female	3.15	4.00	0.94	0.07
	Male	3.33	4.00	0.93	0.08
Economy Task 1	Female	3.13	4.00	0.99	0.07
	Male	3.47	4.00	0.90	0.08
Economy Task 2	Female	3.28	4.00	0.90	0.06
	Male	3.48	4.00	0.81	0.07
Economy Task 3	Female	2.72	2.00	0.90	0.07
	Male	2.81	3.00	0.91	0.08

Table 5.141. *Comparison of failed answers in the female and the male groups (%) – L-cohort*

	Task 1		Task 2		Task 3		Tasks 1–3	
	Female	Male	Female	Male	Female	Male	Female	Male
Originality	3	7	24	19	32	23	20	16
Elaboration	8	7	27	29	29	23	21	20
Flexibility	7	15	24	26	36	25	22	22
Fluency	7	15	19	29	33	25	17	23
Creative Strengths	1	9	21	23	33	27	18	20
Composite Score	5	10	19	25	32	23	19	19

5.3.2.2 Summary VI

The previous gender-based comparison of secondary school students in terms of semantically more transparent versus more economical onomasiological types reveals an unambiguous tendency for female speakers to prefer more transparent and for male speakers to prefer more economical naming strategies. This trend has been confirmed for both cohorts and for five out of six

Table 5.142. *Comparison of failed answers in the female and the male groups (%) – H-cohort*

	Task 1		Task 2		Task 3		Tasks 1–3	
	Female	Male	Female	Male	Female	Male	Female	Male
Originality	4	12	20	38	26	20	17	23
Elaboration	4	18	15	38	22	27	14	27
Flexibility	5	12	17	39	32	20	18	24
Fluency	7	21	25	50	29	32	20	34
Creative Strengths	3	14	26	35	23	33	14	27
Composite Score	1	18	20	42	20	26	12	29

creativity indicators/subscores. This means that there is no substantial difference between the speakers with a high score and a low score in the TTCT test: Both of these cohorts confirm the aforementioned general trend. Nevertheless, there are certain differences in individual tasks and individual creativity indicators/ subscores.

In Task 1, the trend of higher semantic transparency in the female group and higher economy in the male group is confirmed for all creativity indicators/ subscores in the H-cohort and for five creativity indicators/subscores in the L-cohort. The only exception is the Flexibility indicator.

In Task 2, this general trend is confirmed for *Originality*, *Fluency*, and *Composite Score* in the L-cohort, and *Originality*, *Elaboration*, *Creative Strengths*, and *Composite Score* in the H-cohort.

In Task 3, the trend is supported for *Originality*, *Elaboration*, and *Fluency* in the L-cohort and *Elaboration*, *Creative Strengths*, and *Composite Score* in the H-cohort.

The cumulative data suggest that the preference of the female speakers for semantically more transparent coinages is primarily bound to *Originality*, *Elaboration*, *Fluency*, and *Composite Score* in the L-cohort; and *Originality*, *Elaboration*, *Creative Strengths*, and *Composite Score* in the H-cohort.

The influence of the individual TTCT scores upon the preferences of the female and male groups is summarized in Tables 5.143 and 5.144.

Legend:

FS = full support for the tendency: significantly higher percentage in OT1 and lower percentage in OT3

PS = partial support for the tendency; small difference between the groups

C = contradicting the tendency: lower percentage in OT1 and higher percentage in OT3

Table 5.143. *Indicators/subscores relative to the tendency towards semantic transparency – L-cohort*

	Task 1			Task 2			Task 3			Tasks 1–3		
	FS	PS	C	FS	PS	C	FS	PS	C	FS	PS	C
Originality	✓			✓				✓		✓		
Elaboration	✓				✓		✓			✓		
Flexibility		✓		✓					✓		✓	
Fluency	✓			✓			✓			✓		
Cr. Strengths	✓				✓			✓			✓	
Comp. Score	✓			✓					✓	✓		

Table 5.144. *Indicators/subscores relative to the tendency towards semantic transparency – H-cohort*

	Task 1			Task 2			Task 3			Tasks 1–3		
	FS	PS	C	FS	PS	C	FS	PS	C	FS	PS	C
Originality	✓			✓				✓		✓		
Elaboration	✓			✓			✓			✓		
Flexibility	✓					✓		✓			✓	
Fluency	✓				✓			✓			✓	
Cr. Strengths	✓			✓			✓			✓		
Comp. Score	✓			✓			✓			✓		

The only creativity indicator that gives full support to the observed tendency in all three tasks as well as their cumulative evaluation is *Fluency*. The tendency is also strongly supported by *Originality* and *Elaboration*. Weaker support comes from Composite Score.

Elaboration, *Creative Strengths*, and *Composite Score* give support to the general trend in all three tasks as well as in the cumulative evaluation. Strong support also comes from *Originality*.

The situation according to the criterion of failed answers is given in Tables 5.145 and 5.146. Since we postulate that the proportion of failed answers is indirectly proportional to creativity, the tables indicate which of the two gender groups performs better in terms of creativity relative to the individual creativity indicators/subscores. Therefore, F in these tables means that the word formation creativity of the female group is higher, S indicates that the two groups achieved similar results, and M indicates better results in the male group.

Table 5.145. *Indicators/subscores relative to the tendency for failed answers – L-cohort*

	Task 1			Task 2			Task 3			Tasks 1–3		
	FS	S	C	FS	S	C	FS	S	C	FS	S	C
Originality	✓					✓			✓			✓
Elaboration		✓		✓					✓		✓	
Flexibility	✓			✓					✓		✓	
Fluency	✓			✓					✓	✓		
Cr. Strengths	✓			✓					✓	✓		
Comp. Score	✓			✓					✓		✓	

Table 5.146. *Indicators/subscores relative to the tendency for failed answers – H-cohort*

	Task 1			Task 2			Task 3			Tasks 1–3		
	F	S	M	F	S	M	F	S	M	F	S	M
Originality	✓			✓					✓	✓		
Elaboration	✓			✓			✓			✓		
Flexibility	✓			✓					✓	✓		
Fluency	✓			✓			✓			✓		
Cr. Strengths	✓			✓			✓			✓		
Comp. Score	✓			✓			✓			✓		

The failed answer criterion, unlike the criterion of competition between semantic transparency and economy of expression, compares the creativity of the group of females and the group of males. According to this criterion, in the L-cohort, the female group is more creative in terms of the first two tasks (with the exception of Elaboration in Task 1 and Originality in Task 2), while male speakers produced far fewer failed answers in the drawing-based Task 3. In this task, the differences in percentages of failed answers between the male and the female groups are fairly high, the highest being 11% for *Flexibility*. This suggests that while female speakers seem to perform better in verbal word formation tasks, male speakers seem to do so in drawing-based word formation tasks. Furthermore, the cumulative data show better creativity results for male speakers in four out of six indicators/subscores.

The data for the H-cohort favour the word formation creativity of the female group even more because the percentage of failed answers in the male group is higher for all indicators/subscores not only in the first two tasks and according to the cumulative data, but also for four indicators/subscores in Task 3. The only male speakers who perform better are those with higher TTCT scores in Originality and Flexibility.

H-Cohort versus L-Cohort

A comparison of the two cohorts with regard to the competition between semantic transparency and economy shows slightly different results for these cohorts. In both cohorts we observe the influence of Elaboration, Originality, and Composite Score; at the same time, there are indicators/subscores that exert unequal influence on the two cohorts, such as Creative Strengths and Fluency. A comparison of the two cohorts in terms of the failed answer criterion shows a substantial difference between the L-cohort and the H-cohort in the influence of the individual creativity indicators/subscores.

5.3.2.3 University Undergraduates

Semantic Transparency versus Economy of Expression

Analogically to the group of secondary school students, Table 5.147 summarizes the data for the two strongest onomasiological types, OT1 and OT3.

It follows from Table 5.147 that there is a general tendency for the L-cohort's female speakers to coin semantically more transparent complex words than the male speakers who, on the other hand, prefer more economical solutions. This applies, with a few exceptions, to all three tasks as well as to the cumulative data. Furthermore, this finding is true, again with a few exceptions, of all creativity indicators.

The gap in the proportion of the use of OT1 (transparency degree 7) between the female and the male groups is biggest in Task 1. The female group shows much higher percentages for *all creativity indicators/subscores*, exceeding a 40% share of all coinages with the exception of Creative Strengths. On the other hand, the male group's use of OT1 is mostly under 30%. The biggest difference has been found for *Originality* (20%). This tendency corresponds with a much higher percentage of the more economical OT3 (transparency degree 2) in the male group, which employs this OT in the range from 13% to 16%, compared to the female group, where the percentage is between 2% and 5%. The only exception is the Flexibility indicator, where the percentage of the female group is as high as 18%.

Task 2 confirms the general tendency observed in Task 1. The female respondents employ the more transparent naming strategy much more frequently according to *all creativity indicators/subscores*. The percentage difference ranges from 7% for Creative Strengths up to 18% for Elaboration. In this task, the male respondents use the more economical OT3 more frequently than the female speakers for all creativity indicators. The differences range from 5% for Originality up to 13% for Elaboration.

Table 5.147. *Comparison of the female and the male groups in terms of the strongest OTs – L-cohort (%)*

Task 1	OT1 (transparency degree 7)		OT3 (transparency degree 2)	
	Female	Male	Female	Male
Originality	43	23	5	15
Elaboration	47	29	3	15
Flexibility	45	28	18	13
Fluency	45	29	5	13
Creative Strengths	37	31	5	16
Composite Score	41	27	2	15
Task 2	OT1 (transparency degree 7)		OT3 (transparency degree 2)	
	Female	Male	Female	Male
Originality	42	32	53	58
Elaboration	43	25	45	58
Flexibility	46	30	49	55
Fluency	53	36	40	50
Creative Strengths	36	29	51	57
Composite Score	44	31	44	53
Task 3	OT1 (transparency degree 7)		OT3 (transparency degree 2)	
	Female	Male	Female	Male
Originality	58	54	32	30
Elaboration	65	55	28	32
Flexibility	68	55	26	29
Fluency	60	49	30	33
Creative Strengths	69	46	21	30
Composite Score	64	56	29	29
Tasks 1–3	OT1 (transparency degree 7)		OT3 (transparency degree 2)	
	Female	Male	Female	Male
Originality	47	35	27	32
Elaboration	52	35	23	32
Flexibility	54	37	24	30
Fluency	53	39	23	33
Creative Strengths	47	35	23	32
Composite Score	50	37	22	30

In Task 3 we find the highest percentage values of OT1. With the exception of Originality (58%), all of them are above 60% in the female group. They are higher than the values of the male group, the difference ranging from 4% for Originality up to 23% for *Creative Strengths*. It is interesting, however, that the

Table 5.148. *Comparison of the female and the male groups in terms of the strongest OTs – H-cohort (%)*

Task 1	OT1 (transparency degree 7)		OT3 (transparency degree 2)	
	Female	Male	Female	Male
Originality	44	40	7	4
Elaboration	42	34	9	10
Flexibility	42	31	3	14
Fluency	45	27	4	13
Creative Strengths	47	30	6	13
Composite Score	45	35	6	12
Task 2	OT1 (transparency degree 7)		OT3 (transparency degree 2)	
	Female	Male	Female	Male
Originality	37	39	54	50
Elaboration	33	38	62	59
Flexibility	32	24	61	74
Fluency	36	36	58	62
Creative Strengths	29	35	65	57
Composite Score	31	52	60	48
Task 3	OT1 (transparency degree 7)		OT3 (transparency degree 2)	
	Female	Male	Female	Male
Originality	74	63	19	34
Elaboration	72	72	21	22
Flexibility	68	65	22	24
Fluency	71	66	20	23
Creative Strengths	71	78	23	20
Composite Score	71	76	21	18
Tasks 1–3	OT1 (transparency degree 7)		OT3 (transparency degree 2)	
	Female	Male	Female	Male
Originality	52	47	26	27
Elaboration	49	47	34	30
Flexibility	47	39	27	33
Fluency	49	42	26	29
Creative Strengths	52	45	28	28
Composite Score	48	52	28	24

use of OT3 by the two gender groups is very similar in this task (with the exception of Creative Strengths, where the frequency of use of OT3 is higher in the male group by 9%).

The cumulative results map the results obtained for the individual tasks. The proportion of the use of OT1 is higher in the female group than in the male group for *all creativity indicators/subscores*, the highest difference being 17% for *Elaboration* and *Flexibility*. And the analogy with the individual tasks has also been found for OT3: its percentages are higher in the male group for all indicators. The highest difference has been identified for Fluency (10%).

Table 5.148 does not give unambiguous support to the findings for the L-cohort in terms of the overall trend of more semantically transparent coinages being preferred by female speakers and more economical coinages preferred by male speakers. The ambiguity stems from Tasks 2 and 3, that is, the tasks that impose higher demands on word formation creativity.

In Task 1, the share of OT1 in all coinages is higher in the female group according to *all creativity indicators/subscores*. The proportion of OT1 in the female group in this Task exceeds 40%; in the male group, it is well under 40% (except for Originality). The biggest differences have been found for *Fluency* (18%) and *Creative Strengths* (17%). The employment of the economical OT3 by the male group is generally higher, with the exception of Originality.

In Task 2, the use of OT1 is more frequent in the male group for four indicators (Originality, Elaboration, Creative Strengths, and Composite Score). The difference between the two groups is extremely high for Composite Score (31% vs. 52%). With Fluency showing identical percentages for both groups, only *Flexibility* manifests higher frequency of the use of OT1 in the female group. This picture is reflected in the use of OT3, which shows higher percentages in the female group for four indicators/subscores. The trend in the use of OT3, identified for the L-cohort, has only been confirmed for Flexibility and Fluency.

Task 3 provides a similar picture. With Elaboration showing identical percentages for both groups in the use of OT1, three indicators have a higher proportion in the female group (*Originality*, *Flexibility*, and *Fluency*). In contrast, the subscores Creative Strengths and Composite Score favour the male group. Creative Strengths and Composite Score reflect the results for OT1 by showing higher percentages of the use of OT3 in the female group. The higher proportion of OT1 in the female group for Originality, Flexibility, and Fluency is confirmed in the lower percentages of this group for these indicators in the use of OT3. The strongest evidence in favour of the preference of female speakers for transparent coinages comes here from *Originality*: the difference in the use of OT1 between the two groups in this indicator is 11% in favour of the female group; from the point of view of the use of OT3, it is as high as 15% in favour of the male group.

The cumulative results show a higher OT1 proportion in the female group for all indicators/subscores with the exception of Composite Score. The differences in general are not very high, with the highest differences found for Flexibility (8%) and Fluency (7%). The use of OT3 is higher in the male group only for Flexibility, Fluency, and, insignificantly (1%), Originality.

Table 5.149. *Comparison of the female and the male groups for subtask 1.1 (%)*

L-cohort				
Subtask 1.1	OT2 (transparency degree 5)		OT9 (transparency degree 3)	
	Female	Male	Female	Male
Originality	39	61	52	37
Elaboration	17	50	64	44
Flexibility	28	54	53	43
Fluency	31	60	56	40
Creative Strengths	27	55	59	42
Composite Score	27	62	59	38
H-cohort				
Subtask 1.1	OT2 (transparency degree 5)		OT9 (transparency degree 3)	
	Female	Male	Female	Male
Originality	34	47	52	41
Elaboration	40	56	46	32
Flexibility	37	48	55	44
Fluency	31	48	59	44
Creative Strengths	28	42	54	47
Composite Score	36	43	51	50

Composite Score clearly favours the preference of the male group for semantically transparent and more economical coinages.

As in the L-cohort, the data in Task 1 are influenced by extremely high percentages of OT9 (transparency degree 3) in subtask 1.1, where it is the most frequently used OT from among all OTs and competes with OT2 (transparency degree 5). The data for subtask 1.1 are summarized in Table 5.149.

While the data show a generally unexceptional preference of the male group for the more transparent OT2 in both cohorts and for all indicators/subscores, the female group is apparently inclined to OT9. This can be accounted for by the preference of the female group to propose more 'creative' coinages based on a metonymical representation of the object to be named, that is, an exocentric compound word that lacks a morphemic representation of the onomasiological base.

The second instance of deviation from the prevalent OT1 versus OT3 competition concerns subtask 1.2 in which the two strongest onomasiological types are OT1 and OT2, that is, two highly transparent OTs. From the point of view of the use of these two OTs, the female group prefers OT1 and the male group prefers OT2. The data are summarized in Table 5.150.

Table 5.150. *Comparison of the female and the male groups for subtask 1.2 (%)*

L-cohort				
Subtask 1.2	OT1 (transparency degree 7)		OT2 (transparency degree 5)	
	Female	Male	Female	Male
Originality	42	29	58	71
Elaboration	48	36	52	54
Flexibility	32	30	68	70
Fluency	41	37	59	63
Creative Strengths	32	44	64	56
Composite Score	27	36	73	64
H-cohort				
Subtask 1.2	OT1 (transparency degree 7)		OT2 (transparency degree 5)	
	Female	Male	Female	Male
Originality	55	25	43	69
Elaboration	54	32	46	62
Flexibility	43	33	53	63
Fluency	48	20	50	72
Creative Strengths	54	21	46	73
Composite Score	51	29	45	64

The tendency for the female speakers to prefer the most transparent OT1 and the male group the less transparent OT2 is almost universal. The only exceptions are the L-cohort's Creative Strengths and Composite Score. All the other results in both cohorts favour this tendency, which is especially evident in the H-cohort, where the differences in percentages between the female and male groups in all indicators are very high.

Assessment of General Gender Differences Using Inferential Statistics

As in the case of secondary school students, female university undergraduates formed words more transparently and less economically. However, these differences are statistically significant only for semantic transparency and economy of expression for Task 1 and for the general transparency and economy indices. The results of the inferential statistics are shown in Table 5.151.

The descriptive statistics regarding gender differences in word formation among university undergraduates are depicted in Figures 5.39 and 5.40 and summarized in Table 5.152.

Table 5.151. *Inferential statistics regarding gender differences in word formation among university students*

	BF_{10}	U	p	Cohen's d
General transparency	83.45	8662.50	<0.001***	0.43
Transparency Task 1	80.58	8885.50	<0.001***	0.43
Transparency Task 2	0.29	9783.00	0.201	0.15
Transparency Task 3	0.22	9213.50	0.234	0.13
General economy	100.46	9067.00	<0.001***	−0.44
Economy Task 1	48.56	9254.50	<0.001***	−0.41
Economy Task 2	1.82	9290.00	0.030*	−0.28
Economy Task 3	0.22	9280.00	0.272	−0.12

Note. *p < 0.05, ***p < 0.001

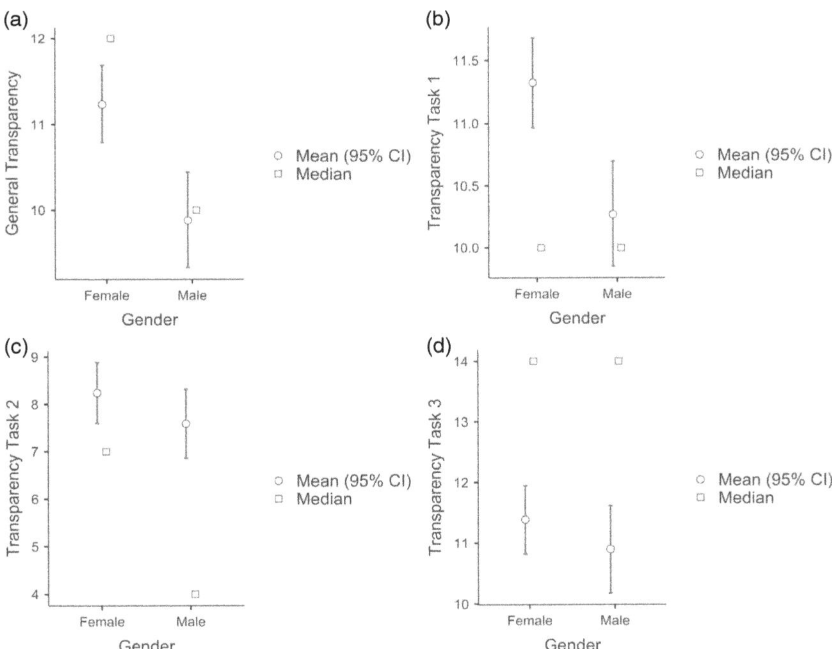

Figure 5.39 Differences between males and females regarding semantic transparency among university students

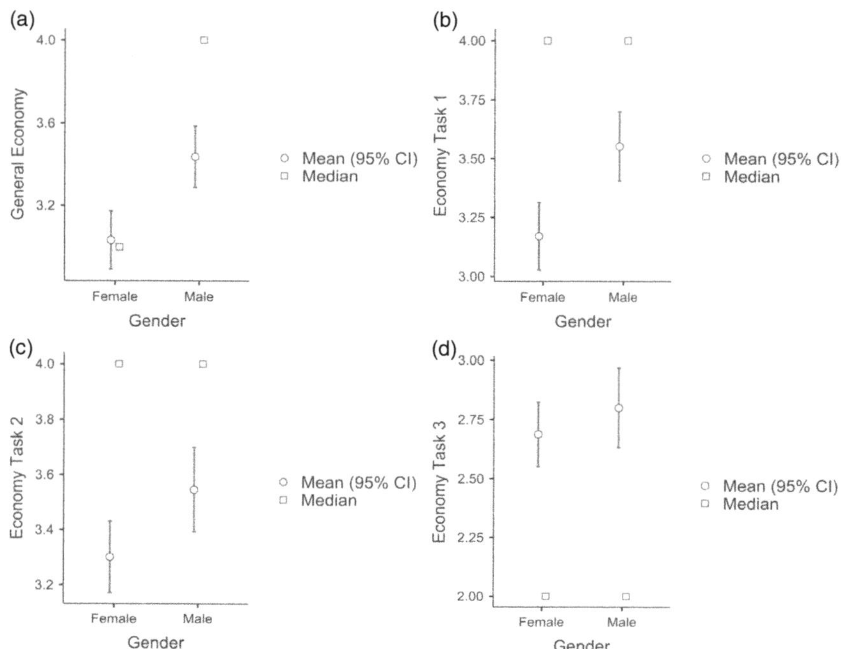

Figure 5.40 Differences between males and females regarding economy of expression among university students

Failed Answer Criterion

The data for the criterion of failed answers are summarized in Tables 5.153 and 5.154.

The data point out a very strong tendency for female speakers to be much more creative in solving word formation tasks because the number of failed answers in the female group is generally lower by, mostly, very high percentage values than in the male group. More specifically, in Task 1, there are no cases of a higher percentage of failed answers in the female group. The tightest result is found for the Creative Strengths subscore.

Creative Strengths shows similar results for both groups in Task 2 in the L-cohort. This appears to correlate with the special position of this subscore in the previously discussed analysis of the transparency versus economy competition. The data for Task 2 in the H-cohort are fully in line with the general tendency, which is very strong in this cohort. The differences between the female and the male groups in Task 2 are high for all indicators, the highest being 23% for *Flexibility* and *Fluency*. The data for the L-cohort are not equally conclusive: the differences are small, and, moreover, Originality and Composite Score feature a higher number of failed answers in the female

Table 5.152. *Descriptives concerning gender differences in word formation among university undergraduates*

	Group	Mean	Median	SD	SE
General transparency	Female	11.23	12.00	3.11	0.23
	Male	9.88	10.00	3.20	0.28
Transparency Task 1	Female	11.32	10.00	2.47	0.18
	Male	10.27	10.00	2.40	0.21
Transparency Task 2	Female	8.24	7.00	4.42	0.33
	Male	7.59	4.00	4.06	0.37
Transparency Task 3	Female	11.38	14.00	3.78	0.29
	Male	10.90	14.00	3.93	0.37
General economy	Female	3.03	3.00	0.97	0.07
	Male	3.44	4.00	0.85	0.08
Economy Task 1	Female	3.17	4.00	0.98	0.07
	Male	3.55	4.00	0.84	0.07
Economy Task 2	Female	3.30	4.00	0.89	0.07
	Male	3.55	4.00	0.85	0.08
Economy Task 3	Female	2.69	2.00	0.91	0.07
	Male	2.80	2.00	0.92	0.09

Table 5.153. *Comparison of failed answers in the female and the male groups (%) – L-cohort*

	Task 1		Task 2		Task 3		Tasks 1–3	
	Female	Male	Female	Male	Female	Male	Female	Male
Originality	0	5	33	31	26	33	20	23
Elaboration	1	4	26	29	13	32	14	22
Flexibility	1	5	26	31	16	32	14	23
Fluency	1	4	29	32	20	30	16	23
Creative Strengths	2	3	32	32	21	34	18	23
Composite Score	2	6	35	33	17	33	18	24

group. This seems to be the only exception to the aforementioned general trend because the data for Task 3 and the cumulative data give unambiguous support to the observation of the higher word formation creativity of female speakers according to this criterion.

5.3.2.4 Summary VII

The gender-based evaluation of the word formation data obtained from university respondents can be summarized as follows.

In Task 1, the trend of higher semantic transparency in the female group and higher economy in the male group in both the L-cohort and the H-cohort is

Table 5.154. *Comparison of failed answers in the female and the male groups (%) – H-cohort*

	Task 1		Task 2		Task 3		Tasks 1–3	
	Female	Male	Female	Male	Female	Male	Female	Male
Originality	3	6	16	29	16	25	12	20
Elaboration	3	13	18	28	18	28	13	23
Flexibility	3	5	18	41	21	29	14	25
Fluency	2	4	17	40	22	27	14	24
Creative Strengths	2	2	13	30	13	28	9	20
Composite Score	2	4	16	36	18	27	12	22

Table 5.155. *Indicators/subscores relative to the tendency in semantic transparency – L-cohort*

	Task 1			Task 2			Task 3			Tasks 1–3		
	FS	PS	C	FS	PS	C	FS	PS	C	FS	PS	C
Originality	✓			✓				✓		✓		
Elaboration	✓			✓			✓			✓		
Flexibility		✓		✓			✓			✓		
Fluency	✓			✓			✓			✓		
Cr. Strengths	✓			✓			✓			✓		
Comp. Score	✓			✓				✓		✓		

confirmed unambiguously for *Composite Score*, *Fluency*, *Elaboration*, and *Creative Strengths*. For *Originality*, the female group uses OT1 in both cohorts much more frequently, but the percentage of OT3 is a little bit higher in the H-cohort of the female group.

In Task 2, *Flexibility* is the only creativity indicator that gives support to this trend in both cohorts.

In Task 3, there are three creativity indicators supporting the trend in both cohorts: *Flexibility*, *Fluency*, and *Originality*, although the latter features a slightly higher proportion of OT3 in the L-cohort.

The cumulative data suggest that the preference of the female speakers for semantically more transparent coinages is primarily bound to those respondents who achieved high scores in the TTCT test for *Flexibility*, *Fluency*, and *Originality*, and partly for Creative Strengths and Elaboration. The data for Composite Score in the two cohorts contradict each other.

The influence of the individual TTCT scores upon the preferences of the female and male groups is summarized in Table 5.155 and 5.156.

Legend:

FS = full support for the tendency: significantly higher percentage in OT1 and lower percentage in OT3
PS = partial support for the tendency; small difference between the groups
C = contradicting the tendency: lower percentage in OT1 and higher percentage in OT3

Table 5.156. *Indicators/subscores relative to the tendency in semantic transparency – H-cohort*

	Task 1			Task 2			Task 3			Tasks 1–3		
	FS	PS	C	FS	PS	C	FS	PS	C	FS	PS	C
Originality		✓				✓	✓			✓		
Elaboration	✓					✓		✓			✓	
Flexibility	✓			✓			✓			✓		
Fluency	✓				✓		✓			✓		
Cr. Strengths	✓					✓			✓		✓	
Comp. Score	✓					✓			✓			✓

Table 5.157. *Indicators/subscores relative to the tendency for failed answers – L-cohort*

	Task 1			Task 2			Task 3			Tasks 1–3		
	F	S	M	F	S	M	F	S	M	F	S	M
Originality	✓					✓	✓			✓		
Elaboration	✓			✓			✓			✓		
Flexibility	✓			✓			✓			✓		
Fluency	✓			✓			✓			✓		
Cr. Strengths		✓			✓		✓			✓		
Comp. Score	✓					✓	✓			✓		

The creativity indicators/subscores that impose the strongest influence upon the preference of female speakers to form transparent words are Elaboration, Fluency, and Creative Strengths. Slightly lower support comes from Originality, Flexibility, and Composite Score.

The only indicator that gives full support to the tendency in question in the H-cohort is Flexibility.

The situation according to the criterion of failed answers is given in Tables 5.157 and 5.158.

Table 5.158. *Indicators/subscores relative to the tendency for failed answers – H-cohort*

	Task 1			Task 2			Task 3			Tasks 1–3		
	F	S	M	F	S	M	F	S	M	F	S	M
Originality	✓			✓			✓			✓		
Elaboration	✓			✓			✓			✓		
Flexibility	✓			✓			✓			✓		
Fluency	✓			✓			✓			✓		
Cr. Strengths		✓		✓			✓			✓		
Comp. Score	✓			✓			✓			✓		

It follows from this overview that the creativity indicators/subscores that impose the strongest influence upon creative performance in word formation are Elaboration, Flexibility, Fluency, and Composite Score. Partial support comes from Creative Strengths and Originality.

The creativity indicators/subscores that impose the strongest influence upon creative performance in word formation are Originality, Elaboration, Flexibility, Fluency, and Composite Score. Partial support comes from Creative Strengths.

H-Cohort versus L-Cohort

A comparison of the two cohorts with regard to the competition between semantic transparency and economy shows completely different results for these cohorts. This indicates that *the preferences of the H-cohort and the L-cohort with regard to this criterion depend on their respective creative potential.*

Contrary to this, a comparison of the two cohorts with regard to the criterion of failed answers shows very similar results for both cohorts in terms of the role of indicators/subscores in the female and the male groups. This suggests that *the influence of creative potential upon word formation creativity, as represented by the individual TTCT scores, appears to be subordinate to the gender factor.*

5.3.2.5 Gender-Based Comparison of the SS and UU Groups

(i) *Semantic transparency versus economy of expression*

A comparison of the SS and UU groups of the same gender using the most transparent onomasiological type is summarized in Tables 5.159 and 5.160.

Table 5.159. *Average values of OT1: comparison of the female and male groups of SS and UU respondents – L-cohorts*

	Females		Males	
	SS	UU	SS	UU
Task 1	43.7	43.0	38.0	27.8
Task 2	35.3	44.0	27.3	30.5
Task 3	58.8	64.0	55.7	52.5
Tasks 1–3	45.0	50.5	40.2	36.3

Table 5.160. *Average values of OT1: comparison of the female and male groups of SS and UU respondents – H-cohorts*

	Females		Males	
	SS	UU	SS	UU
Task 1	45.7	44.2	32.5	32.9
Task 2	34.2	33.0	28.3	37.3
Task 3	62.5	71.2	58.2	70.0
Tasks 1–3	47.0	49.5	39.8	45.3

The observations obtained from the data in Tables 5.159 and 5.160 can be summarized as follows:

A. Comparison of the same gender in the SS and UU groups:
   (a) The UU female students prefer the semantically most transparent OT1 in the drawing-based task in both the L-cohort and the H-cohort more than the SS female students. The results in Task 1 are very similar. A major difference concerns the different use of OT1 in Task 2. While in the H-cohort the percentages for the SS and UU groups are similar, the data for the L-cohorts show that the UU students use OT1 much more frequently.
   (b) The cumulative data as well as the data for Tasks 2 and 3 indicate that the preference for more transparent coinages increases with the growing age of female language users.
   (c) The data for the male group indicate the same trend in the H-cohort, that is, the use of OT1 by the UU group compared to the SS group is much more frequent. The difference between the UU and the SS groups is remarkable in Tasks 2 and 3 and from the point of view of the cumulative data.

(d) The data for the L-cohort run against the trend captured here in points (i) to (iii) owing to a slightly higher frequency of occurrence of OT1 in the SS group. The general trend identified in these points is also contradicted by the cumulative data, these being strongly influenced by a much higher frequency of OT1 in the SS group in the creatively simplest naming task based on multiple-choice.

(e) All in all, it can be observed that there is a tendency for older speakers to coin more transparent words more frequently than younger speakers. This general statement must, however, be taken with caution because the naming act is evidently affected by the nature of the naming task. The most conclusive evidence for the identified trend comes from the creatively more demanding verbal description-based and drawing-based tasks.

B. Comparison of the males and females in the SS and the UU groups:

The frequency of use of OT1 for the coining of new words by females is substantially higher than that by males in all three tasks as well as according to the cumulative data in

- L-cohort of the SS group
- L-cohort of the UU group
- H-cohort of the SS group

This general trend is violated by the data for Tasks 2 and 3 for the H-cohort of the UU group, where the percentages in Task 3 are fairly similar, and in Task 2 they even show a more frequent use of OT1 in the male group.

The previous observations thus suggest that it is possible to identify two general sociolinguistically determined trends:

(a) A trend according to which the employment of the semantically most transparent onomasiological type OT1, that is, the coining of the most transparent words, increases with age both in female and male speakers.

(b) A tendency according to which female speakers employ the semantically most transparent onomasiological type OT1, that is, the coining of the most transparent words, much more frequently than male speakers. This finding is further strengthened by the data on the use of OT3. This onomasiological type, more economical and much less transparent than OT1, is generally much more frequent in male speakers. This fact thus further adds to the observation that male speakers tend to prefer more economical naming solutions. This applies to both SS and UU language users.

(ii) *Average number of failed answers per cohort member*

In this section, we compare the female and male groups of SS and UU respondents in terms of their word formation creativity based on the percentages of

Table 5.161. *Average number of failed answers: comparison of the female and male groups of SS and UU respondents – L-cohorts (%)*

	Females		Males	
	SS	UU	SS	UU
Task 1	5.2	1.2	10.5	4.5
Task 2	22.3	30.2	25.2	31.3
Task 3	32.5	18.8	24.3	32.3
Tasks 1–3	19.5	16.7	20.0	23.0

Table 5.162. *Average number of failed answers: comparison of the female and male groups of SS and UU respondents – H-cohorts*

	Females		Males	
	SS	UU	SS	UU
Task 1	4.0	2.5	15.8	5.7
Task 2	20.5	16.3	40.4	34.0
Task 3	25.3	18.0	26.3	27.3
Tasks 1–3	15.8	12.3	27.3	25.7

failed answers. A comparison of the SS and the UU groups of the same gender is summarized in Tables 5.161 and 5.162.

As postulated in Hypothesis 2 and Section 5.1, the number of failed answers is indirectly proportional to the level of creativity. From this point of view, the word formation creativity of female UU speakers is higher than that of female SS speakers. This observation follows from the data on both the L-cohort and the H-cohort and for all three tasks as well as from the cumulative data. The only exception concerns the female L-cohorts' results in Task 2 in which the percentage of failed answers in the UU group is higher by almost 8% than that in the SS group. This contradicts the results in the H-cohort that confirm the general trend of higher word formation creativity of female speakers with increasing age. The observations of the female speakers' creativity in the formation of new words contradict the situation with male speakers. Their results are rather ambiguous. The situation identified for female speakers is supported in Task 1 in the L-cohort and Tasks 1 and 2 in the H-cohort. The percentages of failed answers in the other tasks indicate a higher word formation creativity of the SS male speakers or are roughly similar for both age groups.

The findings suggest that

(a) word formation creativity for female and male speakers follows a different development in the course of their maturation;
(b) word formation creativity is affected by the nature of the word formation task.

A comparison of the female and male groups leads us to the following conclusions:

(a) While the word formation creativity of female speakers in the L-cohort of the SS group is higher than that of their male counterparts in Tasks 1 and 2, Task 3 indicates that SS male speakers are more creative in the drawing-based naming tasks. As for the L-cohort of the UU group, the results are unambiguously in favour of higher word formation creativity in female speakers. This trend is confirmed by the data for all three tasks as well as by the cumulative data.
(b) In the H-cohort of the SS group, the previously indicated trend of higher word formation creativity of female speakers has been confirmed for all three tasks as well as for the cumulative data, even if the difference in percentages in Task 3 – unlike the other tasks – is as low as 1%. The data on the H-cohort of the UU group are unambiguous and conclusive: the differences in word formation creativity between the two genders are very high in favour of higher word formation creativity in female speakers.
(c) It may be therefore concluded that there is a general tendency for female speakers to achieve better results in the field of word formation creativity than their male counterparts, even though the differences between the two genders get obliterated to a considerable degree in the drawing-based task, an observation that gives further support to the theory of task specificity.

5.3.3 Creativity, Gender, and word interpretation

In evaluating the role of gender in the interpretation of novel/potential complex words, we take into consideration three basic criteria: the Objectified Predictability Rate, the average number of proposed readings per respondent in a given cohort, and hapax legomena. Furthermore, we examine the role of the number of readings proposed by a given cohort. As far as the criterion of hapax legomena, introduced in the general evaluation of the data by cohort, is concerned, it will not be examined by individual creativity indicator/subscore. The reason for this is that the data for individual gender-based cohorts indicate the dependence of the number of single occurrences, among other things, on the size of a cohort: small cohorts logically feature a higher number of hapax legomena. A small cohort therefore negates the very basic sense of the hapax legomenon as an indicator of interpretational creativity. For this reason, the criterion will be evaluated for the whole groups of male and female respondents. Finally, we do not take into account the parameter of the Predictability Rate because it does not reflect the creativity of language users either. Its value heavily depends on the acceptability of the most predictable reading that, in itself, depends on the nature of specific novel words rather than on the creativity of language users.

5.3.3.1 Secondary School Students

Comparison of Males and Females

Objectified Predictability Rate Tables 5.163–5.174 compare the Objectified Predictability Rates (OPRs) for male and female respondents separately for the L-cohorts and the H-cohorts by individual creativity indicator/subscore. Let us recall Hypothesis 3, which states that the lower the OPR, that is, the greater competition there is on the part of the second-, third-, and fourth-rank readings, the higher the level of interpretation creativity. We namely postulate that language users with low interpretation creativity rely on the most striking reading and find it difficult to come up with other interpretation options. In Tables 5.163–5.174, the lower OPR values, indicating higher interpretation creativity when comparing the male and the female groups of respondents, are given in bold.

Originality

Table 5.163. *Comparison of the male and the female groups: Objectified Predictability Rate, L-cohort – Originality*

L-cohort	*baby book*	*flower hat*	*to boy*	*to tulip*
Female	**0.636**	0.582	**0.751**	**0.693**
Male	**0.791**	**0.513**	**0.832**	**0.697**

Table 5.164. *Comparison of the male and the female groups: Objectified Predictability Rate, H-cohort – Originality*

H-cohort	*baby book*	*flower hat*	*to boy*	*to tulip*
Female	**0.626**	**0.370**	0.796	0.611
Male	0.665	0.381	**0.664**	**0.534**

Elaboration

Table 5.165. *Comparison of the male and the female groups: Objectified Predictability Rate, L-cohort – Elaboration*

L-cohort	*baby book*	*flower hat*	*to boy*	*to tulip*
Female	0.583	**0.366**	**0.792**	0.495
Male	**0.535**	**0.495**	**0.866**	**0.375**

Table 5.166. *Comparison of the male and the female groups: Objectified Predictability Rate, H-cohort – Elaboration*

H-cohort	*baby book*	*flower hat*	*to boy*	*to tulip*
Female	**0.503**	**0.473**	0.839	**0.560**
Male	**0.737**	**0.572**	**0.778**	**0.608**

Flexibility

Table 5.167. *Comparison of the male and the female groups: Objectified Predictability Rate, L-cohort – Flexibility*

	baby book	*flower hat*	*to boy*	*to tulip*
Female	**0.424**	**0.449**	**0.780**	0.693
Male	0.757	0.513	0.860	**0.600**

Table 5.168. *Comparison of the male and the female groups: Objectified Predictability Rate, H-cohort – Flexibility*

	baby book	*flower hat*	*to boy*	*to tulip*
Female	**0.646**	**0.354**	**0.723**	0.594
Male	0.650	0.494	0.762	**0.383**

Fluency

Table 5.169. *Comparison of the male and the female groups: Objectified Predictability Rate, L-cohort – Fluency*

	baby book	*flower hat*	*to boy*	*to tulip*
Female	**0.377**	**0.388**	0.841	0.663
Male	0.792	0.530	**0.775**	**0.574**

Table 5.170. *Comparison of the male and the female groups: Objectified Predictability Rate, H-cohort – Fluency*

	baby book	*flower hat*	*to boy*	*to tulip*
Female	**0.623**	**0.469**	**0.777**	**0.639**
Male	0.658	0.764	0.789	0.797

Creative Strengths

Table 5.171. *Comparison of the male and the female groups: Objectified Predictability Rate, L-cohort – Creative Strengths*

	baby book	*flower hat*	*to boy*	*to tulip*
Female	**0.493**	**0.525**	0.836	0.688
Male	0.752	0.551	**0.738**	**0.523**

Table 5.172. *Comparison of the male and the female groups: Objectified Predictability Rate, H-cohort – Creative Strengths*

	baby book	*flower hat*	*to boy*	*to tulip*
Female	**0.535**	**0.378**	**0.575**	0.659
Male	0.575	0.531	0.707	**0.580**

Composite Score

Table 5.173. *Comparison of the male and the female groups: Objectified Predictability Rate, L-cohort – Composite Score*

	baby book	*flower hat*	*to boy*	*to tulip*
Female	**0.462**	**0.463**	0.861	0.753
Male	0.795	0.563	**0.724**	**0.586**

Table 5.174. *Comparison of the male and the female groups: Objectified Predictability Rate, H-cohort – Composite Score*

	baby book	*flower hat*	*to boy*	*to tulip*
Female	0.639	**0.413**	0.797	0.667
Male	**0.628**	0.578	**0.754**	**0.617**

The results show that, given the same psychologically determined creativity level, female respondents manifest higher interpretation creativity than male respondents in three experimental words in the L-cohort and two words in the H-cohort for the Originality indicator. This means that the situation in the H-cohort does not favour either gender. It is interesting that female speakers of the H-cohort appear to be more creative in interpreting compound words while male speakers perform better with converted words. This is in contrast to the L-cohort, whose female speakers perform better with both converted words.

For Elaboration, female speakers do better in the H-cohort. There is no clear tendency in the L-cohort in terms of better performance either by gender or by experimental word.

Flexibility shows identical results for both cohorts because female speakers perform better in three words and male speakers' lower OPR is bound to the same word – *to tulip* – in both cohorts.

The H-cohort, when identified by means of the Fluency indicator, shows the most striking dominance of the female speakers from among all creativity indicator-based H-cohorts because females achieve lower OPR values for all four words. The situation in the L-cohort of Fluency is analogical to the results of the H-cohort identified by the Originality indicator, that is, male speakers perform better in interpreting converted words, and female speakers perform better in interpreting compound words.

Table 5.175. *Lower OPR values – male versus female, L-cohort*

	baby book	*flower hat*	*to boy*	*to tulip*
Female	5	5	3	1
Male	1	1	3	5

Table 5.176. *Lower OPR values – male versus female, H-cohort*

	baby book	*flower hat*	*to boy*	*to tulip*
Female	5	6	3	2
Male	1	0	3	4

The two subscores, Creative Strengths and Composite Score, provide us with identical results for the L-cohort, which are the same as in the L-cohort for Fluency. The same situation occurs with the H-cohort for Composite Score.

The data in Tables 5.163–5.174 enable us to draw two important conclusions:

(i) There is a tendency for secondary school female speakers to be more creative in their interpretation of novel/potential words. Four creativity indicators and one creativity subscore show the higher interpretation creativity of the H-cohort's females. The only exception to this tendency is Composite Score. The situation in the L-cohort favours female speakers as well, but by a narrow margin.

(ii) Female speakers perform better primarily in the creative interpretation of compound words while male speakers seem to do better when interpreting converted words. This suggests that the interpretation creativity of male and female speakers is also influenced by the word formation process that underlies the experimental words.

If we add up all the cases in which either of the gender-based groups shows better interpretation creativity results, we obtain the picture summarized in Tables 5.175 and 5.176.

It follows from Tables 5.175 and 5.176 that, generally, the *H-cohort's females* show the best interpretation results. They dominate in 16 out of 24 cases, most strikingly in the creativity indicator *Fluency*, but also in *Elaboration*, *Flexibility*, and *Creative Strengths*. The *females of the L-cohort* dominate in 14 cases, especially in the indicators *Originality* and *Flexibility*. From this, it follows that *Flexibility* is the creativity indicator that gives the strongest support to the observation of the higher interpretation creativity of female language users.

If we take the data by experimental word, we obtain another piece of evidence that a specific type of word formation process has its own effect upon creative interpretation. Female speakers show better interpretation results for Noun +Noun compounds whose interpretation options follow from numerous possible relations between the two members of the compound word structure. Where the speakers must rely on a single morphemically expressed constituent of the onomasiological structure – as in the case of conversion, that is, an extremely economical onomasiological type – it is male speakers who tend to be more creative in interpretation in both the L-cohorts and the H-cohorts.

Average Number of Readings Proposed by a Cohort Member

The data are first summarized in Tables 5.177–5.188. The higher average value when comparing female and male respondents is given in bold.

Originality

Table 5.177. *Comparison of the male and the female groups: Average number of proposed readings, L-cohort – Originality*

	baby book	*flower hat*	*to boy*	*to tulip*
Female	**2.86**	2.55	**1.47**	**1.63**
Male	2.55	**2.79**	1.33	1.27

Table 5.178. *Comparison of the male and the female groups: Average number of proposed readings, H-cohort – Originality*

	baby book	*flower hat*	*to boy*	*to tulip*
Female	**3.21**	**2.96**	1.98	**2.06**
Male	3.15	2.56	**2.07**	2.00

Elaboration

Table 5.179. *Comparison of the male and the female groups: Average number of proposed readings, L-cohort – Elaboration*

	baby book	*flower hat*	*to boy*	*to tulip*
Female	**2.81**	**2.47**	**1.49**	**1.49**
Male	2.41	2.22	1.30	1.16

Table 5.180. *Comparison of the male and the female groups: Average number of proposed readings, H-cohort – Elaboration*

	baby book	*flower hat*	*to boy*	*to tulip*
Female	**3.18**	**3.22**	1.86	**1.74**
Male	2.96	3.00	**1.95**	1.46

Flexibility

Table 5.181. *Comparison of the male and the female groups: Average number of proposed readings, L-cohort – Flexibility*

	baby book	*flower hat*	*to boy*	*to tulip*
Female	**3.02**	**2.72**	**1.79**	**1.74**
Male	2.65	2.65	1.13	0.81

Table 5.182. *Comparison of the male and the female groups: Average number of proposed readings, H-cohort – Flexibility*

	baby book	*flower hat*	*to boy*	*to tulip*
Female	3.04	**2.92**	1.88	**1.94**
Male	**3.23**	2.41	**1.94**	1.71

Fluency

Table 5.183. *Comparison of the male and the female groups: Average number of proposed readings, L-cohort – Fluency*

	baby book	*flower hat*	*to boy*	*to tulip*
Female	**3.12**	**2.77**	**1.64**	**1.57**
Male	2.68	**2.77**	1.26	1.03

Table 5.184. *Comparison of the male and the female groups: Average number of proposed readings, H-cohort – Fluency*

	baby book	*flower hat*	*to boy*	*to tulip*
Female	**2.70**	**2.80**	**1.77**	**1.77**
Male	2.45	2.05	1.73	1.50

Creative Strengths

Table 5.185. *Comparison of the male and the female groups: Average number of proposed readings, L-cohort – Creative Strengths*

	baby book	*flower hat*	*to boy*	*to tulip*
Female	**2.56**	2.41	**1.47**	**1.65**
Male	2.53	**2.43**	1.27	1.43

Table 5.186. *Comparison of the male and the female groups: Average number of proposed readings, H-cohort – Creative Strengths*

	baby book	*flower hat*	*to boy*	*to tulip*
Female	**3.07**	**2.88**	2.12	**2.14**
Male	2.86	2.59	**2.23**	2.00

Composite Score

Table 5.187. *Comparison of the male and the female groups: Average number of proposed readings, L-cohort – Composite Score*

	baby book	*flower hat*	*to boy*	*to tulip*
Female	**2.90**	2.43	**1.67**	**1.86**
Male	2.53	**2.50**	1.12	0.88

Table 5.188. *Comparison of the male and the female groups: Average number of proposed readings, H-cohort – Composite Score*

	baby book	*flower hat*	*to boy*	*to tulip*
Female	**3.02**	**3.18**	2.00	**2.02**
Male	2.81	2.38	**2.04**	1.81

The data show that secondary school female speakers unambiguously dominate in interpretation creativity. This applies to both the L-cohort and the H-cohort. The following indicators/subscores demonstrate the higher interpretation creativity of female speakers for all four words: Elaboration, Flexibility, and Fluency in the L-cohort and Fluency in the H-cohort.

Table 5.189. *Comparison of the male and the female groups: Average number of proposed readings, L-cohort*

	baby book	*flower hat*	*to boy*	*to tulip*
Female	**6**	**3**	**6**	**6**
Male	0	**3**	0	0

Table 5.190. *Comparison of the male and the female groups: Average number of proposed readings, H-cohort*

	baby book	*flower hat*	*to boy*	*to tulip*
Female	**5**	**6**	1	**6**
Male	1	0	**5**	0

Higher creativity in three words has been identified for the following indicators/subscores: Originality, Creative Strengths, and Composite Score in the L-cohort; and Originality, Elaboration, Creative Strengths, and Composite Score in the H-cohort.

This observation is further supported by Tables 5.189 and 5.190, which provide a summary of the female versus male comparisons in terms of the average number of readings proposed by a cohort member.

The higher creativity of the females in the L-cohort is even more striking here. Females feature a higher average number of proposed readings in 21 out of 24 cases. The higher creativity of the females in the H-cohort is also evident, even though the proportion is a little lower – 18:6. These findings in favour of the female respondents are violated by the data for *to boy*, which partly map the results for the converted words obtained with regard to the OPR, even if, in that case, it was primarily the experimental word *to tulip* in which the data favoured the group of male speakers. For the average number of proposed readings, the word *to tulip* favours the female respondents in all cases.

If the data are examined by indicators/subscores, we obtain the results provided in Table 5.191. The figures represent the number of cases in which either of the gender groups achieved a higher average number of proposed readings.

The only indicator that does not give support to the higher interpretation creativity of female speakers is Flexibility in the H-cohort. The strongest evidence for higher interpretation creativity is provided by the indicators *Elaboration, Flexibility*, and, partly, by *Fluency* in the L-cohort and *Fluency*

Table 5.191. *Average number of readings by individual indicators/subscores for all four experimental words*

		Originality	Elaboration	Flexibility	Fluency	Creative Strengths	Composite Score
L-cohort	**Female**	3	4	4	3*	3	3
	Male	1	0	0	0	1	1
H-cohort	**Female**	3	3	2	4	3	3
	Male	1	1	2	0	1	1

*The fourth result for both groups was identical.

Table 5.192. *Inferential results regarding gender differences in word interpretation among secondary school students*

	BF_{10}	U	p	Cohen's d
to tulip	2.29	10,562.50	0.023*	0.28
to boy	0.66	10,979.00	0.078	0.21
flower hat	1.13	10,474.50	0.016*	0.25
baby book	3.20	10,375.00	0.011*	0.30

Note. *$p < 0.05$

in the H-cohort. This means that female speakers feature higher interpretational creativity than men primarily in the creativity parameter *Fluency* without regard to their results in the TTCT. The data in Table 5.186 thus suggest that, *with regard to gender-related creative performance in complex word interpretation, creative potential does not seem to play any significant role.*

Assessment of General Gender Differences Using Inferential Statistics

Extending the previous discussion, this section focuses on general differences between males and females. The results indicate that females provided more readings than males. As depicted in Table 5.192, these differences are statistically significant for *baby book*, *to tulip*, and *flower hat*, although, according to the Bonferroni correction and Bayes factor, the two last-mentioned results could be false positives.

Descriptive statistics are shown in Figure 5.41 and Table 5.193.

Hapax Legomena

In order to compare the creativity of male and female respondents according to the criterion of hapax legomena, we decided to compare the whole sample of

Table 5.193. *Descriptives concerning gender differences in word interpretation among secondary school students*

	Group	Mean	Median	SD	SE
to tulip	Female	1.67	1.50	1.34	0.10
	Male	1.31	1.00	1.15	0.10
to boy	Female	1.74	2.00	1.21	0.09
	Male	1.49	1.00	1.10	0.10
flower hat	Female	2.66	3.00	1.29	0.09
	Male	2.34	2.00	1.30	0.12
baby book	Female	2.88	3.00	1.21	0.09
	Male	2.52	3.00	1.23	0.11

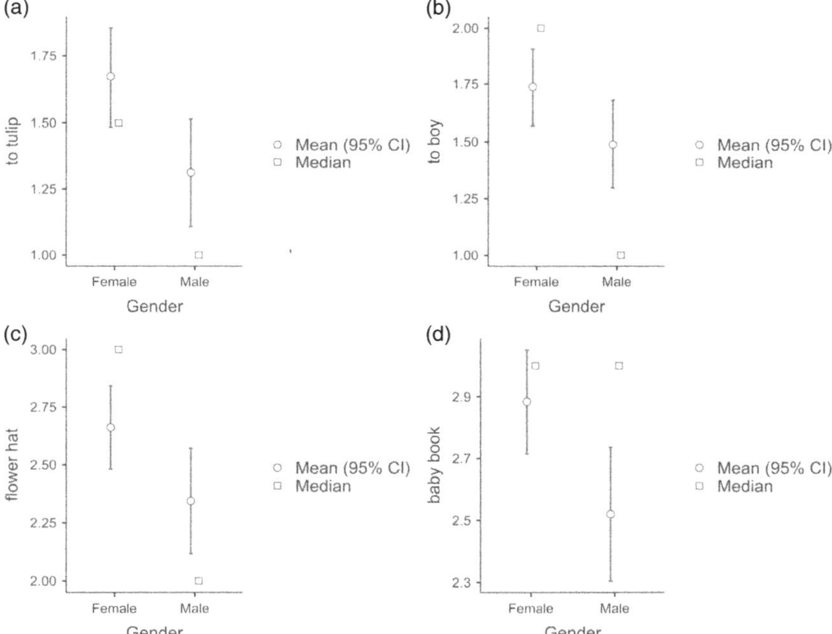

Figure 5.41 Differences between males and females regarding word interpretation among secondary school students

female versus male speakers because a low number of respondents in some of the gender-based cohorts with regard to individual creativity indicators/ subscores might seriously distort the results. This is obvious because a low number of respondents increases the chances of the occurrence of hapax

Table 5.194. *Hapax legomena versus zero/multiple occurrences:* baby book

Reading	Females	Males
'a document of a baby'	0	HL
'a started book'	0	HL
'a book with names of babies'	9	HL

Table 5.195. *Hapax legomena versus zero/multiple occurrences:* flower hat

Reading	Females	Males
'a hat against flowers'	HL	0
'a person wearing a flower hat'	HL	0
'a romantic girl'	HL	0
'a haircut'	4	HL

legomena. This criterion is therefore evaluated on the basis of a sample of 240 females and 151 males, which is, we believe, a sufficient number of respondents to preclude the occurrence of hapax legomena being due to a small research sample.

Since the creativity indicators/subscores are not taken into consideration, the results concern the differences between male and female speakers in their creative performance relative to the interpretation of novel/potential words, not the influence of creative potential (identified by the TTCT) upon interpretation. The data are considered by individual experimental word.

Baby Book

There is no hapax legomenon in the female group as opposed to three hapax legomenon readings in the male group: 'a document of a baby', 'a started book', and 'a book with names of babies'. While the first two hapax legomena have zero counterparts in the female group, the latter single-occurrence reading corresponds with nine occurrences in the female group. This situation is given in Table 5.194.

Flower Hat

Here, the situation is opposite to that for *baby book*. The female group produced three hapax legomena, namely the reading 'a hat against flowers' and two exocentric compounds: 'a romantic girl' and 'a person wearing a flower hat'. While the first reading corresponds to two occurrences in the male group, the other two readings have zero occurrences in the male group. Finally, there is a single hapax legomenon in the male group, 'a haircut', corresponding to four occurrences in the female group. The situation is captured in Table 5.195.

Table 5.196. *Hapax legomena versus zero/multiple occurrences:* to boy

Reading	Females	Males
'to bring up a boy'	HL	HL
'to play with a boy'	0	HL
'to talk to a boy'	2	HL
'to smell like a boy'	2	0
'to voice-mutate'	2	0
'to treat like a boy'	2	0

To Boy

There is one instance of a simultaneously occurring hapax legomenon in the female and the male groups. This concerns the reading 'to bring up a boy'. This is the only hapax legomenon in the female group. There are two more hapax legomena in the male group: 'to play with a boy' for which there is no counterpart in the female group and 'to talk about a boy', which has two occurrences in the female group. Furthermore, there are instances with zero occurrences in one group that correspond with more than one occurrence in the other group of respondents: while the readings 'to treat like a kid', 'to voice-mutate', and 'to smell like a boy' do not occur in the male group, they have two occurrences each in the female group. The situation is given in Table 5.196.

To Tulip

While there is no hapax legomenon in the male group, there are four in the female group: 'to feel happy', 'to be fragile', 'to grow tall', and 'to paint a tulip'. None of these readings occur in the male group. Moreover, zero occurrences of two readings in the male group, 'to talk about tulips' and 'to give a tulip to somebody', correspond to as many as five and nine occurrences, respectively, in the female group. There is a single case favouring the higher creativity of the male group, namely the reading 'to live in the Netherlands', because two occurrences of this reading in the male group stand against zero occurrences in the female group. The situation is captured in Table 5.197.

To sum up, the strongest evidence of the superiority of female speakers in terms of interpretation creativity is provided by the compound word *flower hat*, where there is no instance favouring the higher interpretation creativity of the male group. A similar situation can be observed for both converted words. In the cases of *to boy* and *to tulip*, there is merely one reading for each of them that contradicts this general picture. Given this situation, the data on the compound word *baby book* are rather surprising, albeit inconclusive, because there are only three instances that fall within the hapax legomenon criterion. Two of them favour the male group, while the third gives very strong support to the overall tendency.

Table 5.197. *Hapax legomena versus zero/multiple occurrences:* to tulip

Reading	Females	Males
'to feel happy'	HL	0
'to be fragile'	HL	0
'to grow tall'	HL	0
'to paint a tulip'	HL	0
'to give a tulip to somebody'	9	0
'to talk about tulips'	5	0
'to live in the Netherlands'	0	2

If all the instances falling within this criterion are added up, there are 15 readings in favour of the higher interpretation creativity of female speakers as opposed to 4 cases in favour of male speakers. All in all, the data on the hapax legomenon criterion enable us to draw a tentative generalization according to which there is a *strong tendency for female speakers to achieve better results in interpretation creativity.*

Comparison of the L-Cohort and the H-Cohort by Gender

This section focuses on the differences between the L-cohort and the H-cohort of the same gender in the individual creativity indicators/subscores. We start with an evaluation of the OPR. Then, we compare the data for the average number of readings proposed per cohort member.

Objectified Predictability Rate

Originality While the OPR values for all four words are lower in the H-cohort of the male group, the female group shows one exception to this trend, namely the word *to boy.*

Elaboration This indicator shows the opposite results compared to the Originality indicator. In the female group, the H-cohort's OPR values are higher for all experimental words except for *baby book*; in the male group, there are three words with higher OPR values in the H-cohort. The exception is represented by *to boy.*

Flexibility In the female group, the OPR values are lower in the H-cohort for three words, the exception being *baby book.* In the male group, all words in the H-cohort have lower values than the words in the L-cohort.

Fluency In the female group, the proportion is 2:2. A higher value in the H-cohort is found for both compounds (*baby book* and *flower hat*). In the male group, there are three words that have a higher value in the H-cohort. The exception is the word *baby book*.

Creative Strengths With the exception of *baby book*, the OPR values are lower in the females' H-cohort. The exception in the males' H-cohort is *to tulip*.

Composite Score The females' H-cohort features lower values in three cases. The exception is *baby book*. The males' H-cohort has a lower value only in the case of *baby book*.

If we sum up the comparison of the L-cohort and the H-cohort in the same gender group by individual creativity indicator/subscore, the results are ambiguous and inconclusive.

Our hypothesis has been confirmed (i.e. all four OPR values in the H-cohort are lower) in the following cases:

Male group
Originality
Flexibility
Female group
N/A

The hypothesis has been partly confirmed in the following cases:

Male group
Creative Strengths (exception: *to tulip*)
Female group
Originality (exception: *to boy*)
Flexibility (exception: *baby book*)
Creative Strengths (exception: *baby book*)
Composite Score (exception: *baby book*)

In sum, the results do not show the expected tendency for the less creative speakers to rely on the 'most easily interpreted' reading. This is especially true of the experimental word *baby book*, which mostly has a lower OPR value in the L-cohort. It may be hypothesized that this is caused by the availability of a relatively large number of readings that can be predicted fairly easily. In any case, the *OPR-based hypothesis has not been confirmed for the gender-based cohorts*.

Average Number of Readings Per Cohort Member

Originality Both the female and male groups of respondents are characterized by a higher average value in the H-cohort with a single exception – *flower hat* in the male group.

Elaboration The H-cohort shows higher values in both the male and female groups for all four words.

Flexibility While the average number value is substantially higher in the H-cohort of the male group than in the L-cohort and the differences in favour of the H-cohort are higher compared to the female group, it is the female group where the H-cohort's values are higher than those of the L-cohort in all four cases; the exception in the male cohort concerns the word *flower hat.*

Fluency The average number of readings is in one case (*baby book*) smaller in the female's H-cohort than that in the L-cohort. In the male group, *baby book* and *flower hat* have higher values in the L-cohort.

Creative Strengths Both the female and male H-cohorts show clearly higher values in all four words.

Composite Score The female H-cohort shows clearly higher values in all four words. In the case of the male group, the value for *flower hat* is higher in the L-cohort.

A comparison of the results of the L-cohort and the H-cohort of the same gender group is much more conclusive than in the OPR parameter and gives strong support to the hypothesis according to which the average number of proposed readings per cohort member should be higher in the H-cohort, that is, in the group of respondents who achieved higher scores in the TTCT. The most conclusive evidence has been provided by the creativity indicator *Elaboration* and the subscore *Creativity Strengths*. The exceptions mostly concern the word *flower hat.* Surprisingly, this observation does not fully apply to the creativity indicator Fluency that, in its TTCT score, reflects the number of answers per respondent. By implication, one would expect the biggest difference between the two cohorts in the interpretation creativity test to be for this indicator.

If the results for the OPR and the average number of readings are related, it can be seen that there is only one parameter that has strong effects on interpretation creativity in both of the evaluated criteria – the subscore *Creative Strengths*.

5.3.3.2 University Undergraduates

Comparison of Males and Females

Objectified Predictability Rate Like in Section 5.3.3.1, we start with a series of tables that summarize the data by individual creativity indicator/ subscore. They are followed by comments on the data. The lower OPR values in Tables 5.198–5.209 are marked in bold.

Originality

Table 5.198. *Objectified Predictability Rates in L-cohort – Originality*

	baby book	*flower hat*	*to boy*	*to tulip*
Female	**0.682**	0.435	**0.872**	**0.354**
Male	0.744	**0.385**	0.883	0.423

Table 5.199. *Objectified Predictability Rates in H-cohort – Originality*

	baby book	*flower hat*	*to boy*	*to tulip*
Female	**0.708**	**0.382**	0.843	**0.355**
Male	0.754	0.504	**0.680**	0.797

Elaboration

Table 5.200. *Objectified Predictability Rates in L-cohort – Elaboration*

	baby book	*flower hat*	*to boy*	*to tulip*
Female	**0.661**	**0.460**	0.904	**0.424**
Male	0.798	0.491	**0.851**	0.500

Table 5.201. *Objectified Predictability Rates in H-cohort – Elaboration*

	baby book	*flower hat*	*to boy*	*to tulip*
Female	**0.606**	**0.379**	0.841	**0.431**
Male	0.726	0.558	**0.760**	0.564

Flexibility

Table 5.202. *Objectified Predictability Rates in L-cohort – Flexibility*

	baby book	*flower hat*	*to boy*	*to tulip*
Female	0.761	**0.368**	0.874	0.564
Male	**0.748**	0.623	**0.816**	**0.450**

Table 5.203. *Objectified Predictability Rates in H-cohort – Flexibility*

	baby book	*flower hat*	*to boy*	*to tulip*
Female	**0.578**	**0.466**	**0.776**	**0.347**
Male	0.763	0.661	0.793	0.755

Fluency

Table 5.204. *Objectified Predictability Rates in L-cohort – Fluency*

	baby book	*flower hat*	*to boy*	*to tulip*
Female	**0.667**	**0.340**	0.911	0.419
Male	0.771	0.558	**0.809**	**0.326**

Table 5.205. *Objectified Predictability Rates in H-cohort – Fluency*

	baby book	*flower hat*	*to boy*	*to tulip*
Female	**0.549**	**0.365**	0.834	**0.368**
Male	0.813	0.534	**0.807**	0.670

Creative Strengths

Table 5.206. *Objectified Predictability Rates in L-cohort – Creative Strengths*

	baby book	*flower hat*	*to boy*	*to tulip*
Female	**0.658**	**0.340**	**0.738**	**0.406**
Male	0.867	0.399	0.929	0.660

Table 5.207. *Objectified Predictability Rates in H-cohort – Creative Strengths*

	baby book	*flower hat*	*to boy*	*to tulip*
Female	**0.652**	**0.382**	0.844	**0.364**
Male	0.755	0.416	**0.797**	0.479

Composite Score

Table 5.208. *Objectified Predictability Rates in L-cohort – Composite Score*

	baby book	*flower hat*	*to boy*	*to tulip*
Female	**0.726**	**0.428**	**0.834**	0.405
Male	0.732	0.634	0.846	**0.385**

Table 5.209. *Objectified Predictability Rates in H-cohort – Composite Score*

	baby book	*flower hat*	*to boy*	*to tulip*
Female	**0.575**	**0.427**	0.813	**0.382**
Male	0.739	0.548	**0.799**	0.678

The results show that for the creativity indicator Originality, female respondents manifest higher interpretation creativity than male respondents in three cases of the L-cohort and three cases of the H-cohort. The exceptions are *flower hat* in the L-cohort and *to boy* in the H-cohort, where males appear to be more creative according to the OPR parameter.

The same situation is obtained in the Elaboration indicator. The exception in both cohorts is *to boy*.

Flexibility provides a completely different picture in the L-cohort with lower OPR values in three words. On the other hand, the H-cohort gives full support to the general tendency in all four words.

The Fluency indicator shows the higher interpretation creativity of female speakers in the H-cohort, once again the exception being *to boy*. In the L-cohort, females are more creative for both compounds, while males are more creative for both conversions.

The subscore Creative Strengths gives strong support to the tendency of higher interpretation creativity in female speakers. Females dominate in all four words in the L-cohort and, with the exception of *to boy*, in all the other words in the H-cohort.

Composite Score also supports the conclusion of higher interpretation creativity in females. In both cohorts, females dominate in three out of four words. The exceptions represented by *to tulip* in the L-cohort and *to boy* in the H-cohort are characterized by very small OPR differences: 0.020 and 0.014, respectively.

The data in Tables 5.198–5.209 enable us to draw the following conclusions:

(i) All four psychological creativity parameters and two subscores indicate higher interpretation creativity in female speakers. In the *L-cohort*, females

Table 5.210. *Lower OPR values – male versus female: L-cohort*

	baby book	*flower hat*	*to boy*	*to tulip*
Female	5	5	3	3
Male	1	1	3	3

Table 5.211. *Lower OPR values – male versus female: H-cohort*

	baby book	*flower hat*	*to boy*	*to tulip*
Female	**6**	6	1	6
Male	0	0	5	0

manifest higher interpretation creativity primarily in *Creative Strengths* and also in *Originality*, *Elaboration*, and *Composite Score*. In the *H-cohort*, they seem to be more creative primarily in *Flexibility*, but also in all the other indicators/subscores. The only exception to this general tendency is the Flexibility indicator in the L-cohort, where the male speakers show higher interpretation creativity.

(ii) Taken by experimental words, the higher interpretation creativity of the female group is most conspicuously manifested in the interpretation of compounds in both the L- and the H-cohorts. Ambiguity is characteristic of the data on conversions. In the L-cohort, the male and female groups dominate in three creativity parameters each in both converted words. The results for the converted words in the H-cohort are even more confusing as they clearly show higher interpretation creativity in males for *to boy* and females for *to tulip*. In general, the differences in the OPR values between females and males are much higher if it is the female speakers who show higher interpretation creativity. If the male group dominates in this criterion, the differences between the OPR values achieved by the male and the female respondents tend to be rather small.

If we add up all the cases in which either of the gender-based groups shows better interpretation creativity results, we obtain the picture summarized in Tables 5.210 and 5.211.

It follows from Tables 5.210 and 5.211 that *the strongest support for the general tendency for higher interpretation creativity in female speakers comes from the H-cohort's females*. They dominate in 19 out of 24 cases. In the L-cohort, females dominate in 16 cases. Female speakers *primarily do better in the interpretation of compound words*. The converted words provide ambiguous results – there is no creative dominance of either gender in the

L-cohort, while in the H-cohort the results for the two converted words are the opposite.

Average Number of Readings Proposed by a Cohort Member

The data are first summarized in Tables 5.212–5.223 and then commented on. The higher average value when comparing female and male respondents is given in bold.

Originality

Table 5.212. *Comparison of the male and female groups: Average number of proposed readings, L-cohort – Originality*

	baby book	*flower hat*	*to boy*	*to tulip*
Female	**2.97**	**2.76**	**1.61**	**2.06**
Male	1.85	2.18	1.41	1.41

Table 5.213. *Comparison of the male and female groups: Average number of proposed readings, H-cohort – Originality*

	baby book	*flower hat*	*to boy*	*to tulip*
Female	**3.19**	**3.21**	**1.91**	**1.96**
Male	3.00	2.82	1.59	1.41

Elaboration

Table 5.214. *Comparison of the male and female groups: Average number of proposed readings, L-cohort – Elaboration*

	baby book	*flower hat*	*to boy*	*to tulip*
Female	**3.04**	**2.56**	**1.39**	**1.65**
Male	2.38	2.11	1.30	1.13

Table 5.215. *Comparison of the male and female groups: Average number of proposed readings, H-cohort – Elaboration*

	baby book	*flower hat*	*to boy*	*to tulip*
Female	**3.47**	**3.50**	**2.10**	**2.39**
Male	2.50	2.83	1.56	1.83

Flexibility

Table 5.216. *Comparison of the male and female groups: Average number of proposed readings, L-cohort – Flexibility*

	baby book	*flower hat*	*to boy*	*to tulip*
Female	**2.91**	**2.97**	**1.50**	**1.78**
Male	2.42	2.21	1.47	1.45

Table 5.217. *Comparison of the male and female groups: Average number of proposed readings, H-cohort – Flexibility*

	baby book	*flower hat*	*to boy*	*to tulip*
Female	**3.48**	**3.10**	**2.20**	**2.10**
Male	2.77	2.54	1.42	1.69

Fluency

Table 5.218. *Comparison of the male and female groups: Average number of proposed readings, L-cohort – Fluency*

	baby book	*flower hat*	*to boy*	*to tulip*
Female	**3.06**	**2.90**	**1.79**	**2.21**
Male	2.43	2.23	1.53	1.50

Table 5.219. *Comparison of the male and female groups: Average number of proposed readings, H-cohort – Fluency*

	baby book	*flower hat*	*to boy*	*to tulip*
Female	**3.43**	**3.18**	**2.16**	**2.04**
Male	2.53	1.88	1.42	1.58

Creative Strengths

Table 5.220. *Comparison of the male and female groups: Average number of proposed readings, L-cohort – Creative Strengths*

	baby book	*flower hat*	*to boy*	*to tulip*
Female	**3.41**	**3.05**	**1.91**	**1.77**
Male	2.16	2.13	1.16	1.16

Table 5.221. *Comparison of the male and female groups: Average number of proposed readings, H-cohort – Creative Strengths*

	baby book	*flower hat*	*to boy*	*to tulip*
Female	**3.32**	**3.64**	**2.16**	**2.44**
Male	2.89	3.00	1.63	1.27

Composite Score

Table 5.222. *Comparison of the male and female groups: Average number of proposed readings, L-cohort – Composite Score*

	baby book	*flower hat*	*to boy*	*to tulip*
Female	**2.91**	**2.59**	1.37	**1.82**
Male	2.29	2.10	**1.44**	1.33

Table 5.223. *Comparison of the male and female groups: Average number of proposed readings, H-cohort – Composite Score*

	baby book	*flower hat*	*to boy*	*to tulip*
Female	**3.38**	**3.45**	**2.27**	**2.16**
Male	2.93	2.93	1.86	2.07

Table 5.224. *Average number of readings by individual indicator/subscore with regard to four experimental words*

		Originality	Elaboration	Flexibility	Fluency	Creative Strengths	Composite Score
L-cohort	**Female**	3	3	1	2	4	3
	Male	1	1	3	2	0	1
H-cohort	**Female**	3	3	4	3	3	3
	Male	1	1	0	1	1	1

The data show that, according to the criterion of the average number of readings proposed by a cohort member, female speakers unambiguously dominate in interpretation creativity. This claim applies to almost all female–male comparisons, that is, for all creativity indicators/subscores, for both cohorts, and across all experimental words, including compounds and conversions, with a single exception – the converted word *to boy* in the L-cohort. In general, the differences between females and males in this parameter are the lowest for the word *to boy,* which suggests that it posed serious problems for interpretation creativity in both genders. On the other hand, the values achieved by the male respondents for *to boy* are comparable to those for the other converted word *to tulip*. This means that it is the female group of speakers who found the interpretation of this word rather demanding.

This observation is further supported by Tables 5.189 and 5.190, which provide a summary of female versus male comparisons in terms of the average number of readings proposed by a cohort member.

If the data are examined by indicator/subscore, we obtain the results provided in Table 5.224. The figures represent the number of cases in which either of the gender groups achieved a higher average number of proposed readings.

The strongest evidence for the higher interpretation creativity of female speakers is provided by *Creative Strengths in the L-cohort and Flexibility in the H-cohort.* The results for Flexibility are, however, controversial, because the L-cohort's Flexibility indicator is the only creativity indicator contradicting the general tendency of female creative superiority. With the exception of Fluency, this tendency is supported by all the other indicators/subscores. If we add up the results for both cohorts, the female group achieved better results in 35 cases out of the total 48 comparisons.

Assessment of General Gender Differences Using Inferential Statistics

If gender differences are examined among university students, we find out that females provided more readings in comparison to males, as in the case of the secondary school respondents. It follows from Tables 5.225 and 5.226 and

Table 5.225. *Inferential results regarding gender differences in word interpretation among university students*

	BF_{10}	U	p	Cohen's d
to tulip	224.89	8676.00	<0.001***	0.46
to boy	7.46	9533.50	0.007**	0.34
flower hat	804.36	8082.50	<0.001***	0.50
baby book	3263.39	7874.00	<0.001***	0.54

Note. **$p < 0.01$, ***$p < 0.001$

Table 5.226. *Descriptives concerning gender differences in word interpretation among university students*

	Group	Mean	Median	SD	SE
to tulip	Female	1.99	2.00	1.44	0.11
	Male	1.37	1.00	1.20	0.11
to boy	Female	1.79	2.00	1.27	0.09
	Male	1.40	1.00	0.99	0.09
flower hat	Female	2.91	3.00	1.45	0.11
	Male	2.22	2.00	1.26	0.11
baby book	Female	3.04	3.00	1.24	0.09
	Male	2.40	2.00	1.06	0.09

Figure 5.42 that these differences are statistically significant for all the four conditions (even if a more stringent Bonferroni correction for multiple comparisons is applied).

Hapax Legomena

The sample of university undergraduates includes 207 female and 150 male respondents. The analysis does not follow the classification into creativity indicators/subscores for the same reason as with the group of secondary school students. The data are therefore provided by individual experimental word.

Baby Book

In the male group, there are two hapax legomena that have zero counterparts on the female side: 'a started book' and 'a book of babies for adoption'. There are also two opposite cases; these concern the reading 'records of a pregnant woman' and the exocentric compound reading 'one who knows a lot of babies'. Two other hapax legomenon versus multiple-occurrence cases include the readings 'a document of a baby' and 'a book with names of babies'. They favour female speakers because hapax legomena of the male group correspond

Table 5.227. *Hapax legomena versus zero/multiple occurrences:* baby book

	Females	Males
'a book with records of a baby'	HL	0
'one who knows a lot of babies'	HL	0
'a started book'	0	HL
'a book of babies for adoption'	0	HL
'a document for a baby'	5	HL
'a book with names of babies'	3	HL

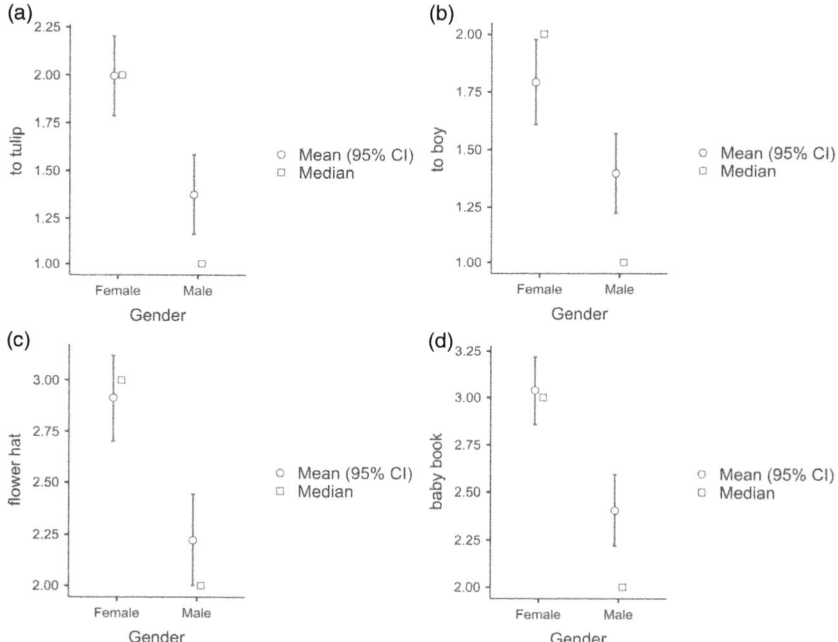

Figure 5.42 Differences between males and females regarding word interpretation among university students

with five and three readings, respectively, in the female group. The situation is captured in Table 5.227.

Flower Hat

Here, the data fully confirm the creative superiority of the female group. Two occurrences of 'a pretty hat' and 'a flower meadow' in the female group

Table 5.228. *Hapax legomena versus zero/multiple occurrences:* flower hat

Reading	Females	Males
'a pretty hat'	2	0
'a flower meadow'	2	0
'a romantic girl'	2	HL

Table 5.229. *Hapax legomena versus zero/multiple occurrences:* to boy

Reading	Females	Males
'to play with a boy'	0	HL
'to voice-mutate'	HL	3
'to be a homosexual'	HL	4
'to talk about boys'	HL	2
'to treat like a kid'	HL	0

correspond with zero occurrences in the male group. Moreover, the hapax legomenon 'a romantic girl' of the male group is surpassed by two occurrences in the female group. The situation is captured in Table 5.228.

To Boy

The data for the converted word *to boy* are in opposition to the results obtained from the compound words. Three hapax legomena ('to voice-mutate', 'to be a homosexual', and 'to talk about boys') of the female group correspond with three, four, and two occurrences, respectively, in the male group. Moreover, the hapax legomenon 'to play with boys' of the male group has zero occurrences in the female group. The only instance in favour of the female respondents concerns the reading 'to treat like a kid', which does not occur in the male group. The situation is given in Table 5.229.

To Tulip

This converted word supports the general tendency. The male group's hapax legomenon 'to mature' corresponds with ten occurrences in the female group; zero occurrences of 'to grow tall' and 'to feel happy' in the male group correspond with six and two occurrences in the female group, respectively. Two instances favour the higher creativity of the male group: 'to compliment' (hapax legomenon vs. two occurrences) and 'to talk about tulips' (zero vs. two occurrences). The situation is captured in Table 5.230.

Table 5.230. *Hapax legomena versus zero/multiple occurrences:* to tulip

Reading	Females	Males
'to feel happy'	2	0
'to grow tall'	6	0
'to mature'	10	HL
'to be innocent'	HL	0
'to compliment'	HL	2
'to talk about tulips'	0	2

If all the instances falling within this criterion are added up, there are twelve readings in favour of the higher interpretation creativity of female speakers as opposed to eight cases in favour of the higher interpretation creativity of male speakers. *This proportion provides us with a weak but in no way major confirmation of the higher interpretation creativity of female speakers* belonging to the group of university undergraduates.

Comparison of L-Cohort and H-Cohort Members by the Same Gender

The data introduced earlier enable us to evaluate possible differences in the individual creativity indicators/subscores between the L-cohort and the H-cohort of the same gender of university undergraduates in relation to individual creativity indicators/subscores. We start with the evaluation of the OPR. Then, we will compare the data for the average number of readings proposed per cohort member.

Objectified Predictability Rate

The comparison of the OPR values between the L-cohort and the H-cohort of the same gender is expected – in accordance with our hypothesis – to show lower OPR values in the H-cohort. In the female group of respondents, this expectation is confirmed for *Composite Score*, where the OPR values of the H-cohort are lower than those of the L-cohort for all four experimental words. For *Elaboration, Flexibility,* and *Fluency*, the results are 3:1 in favour of the H-cohort. The exceptions are *to tulip* for Elaboration and *flower hat* for Flexibility as well as Fluency. The data for Originality and Creative Strengths neither favour any of the cohorts nor show the influence of any of the experimental words on this result. All in all, *the basic tendency for OPR values in the female group is for there to be lower OPR values in the H-cohort than in the L-cohort* (proportion 17:7), *indicating higher interpretational creativity in the female H-cohort.*

The situation in the *male group is much more ambiguous, and, contrary to the female group and to our hypothesis, the data slightly favour the L-cohort* (13:11). This is especially true of Originality and Flexibility. In both of these indicators the OPR values are lower, with the exception of the converted word *to boy*. The opposite result, one favouring the H-cohort, has been found only for *Creative Strengths*. What is interesting is that the OPR value of the male H-cohort is lower in all comparisons of the converted word *to boy*.

If we sum up the data for the L-cohort and the H-cohort in the same gender group by individual creativity indicator/subscore, the results are ambiguous and inconclusive.

Our hypothesis has been confirmed absolutely (i.e. all four OPR values in the H-cohort are lower) in the following cases:

Male group
N/A
Female group
Composite Score

The hypothesis has been partly confirmed in the following cases:

Male group
Creative Strengths (exception: *flower hat*)
Female group
Elaboration (exception: *to tulip*)
Flexibility (exception: *flower hat*)
Fluency (exception: *flower hat*)

In sum, while the results show a tendency for the less creative speakers (L-cohort) to rely on the 'most predictable interpretation' in the female group of respondents, this hypothesis has not been confirmed for the male group.

Average Number of Readings Per Cohort Member

Originality Both female and male groups of respondents are characterized by a higher average value in the H-cohort, with a single exception that concerns the converted word *to tulip*. While in the female respondents the average value is slightly higher (by 0.1) in the L-cohort, in the male group both cohorts achieved an identical value (1.41).

Elaboration The H-cohort shows higher values in both the male and the female groups for all four words.

Flexibility While the average value in the H-cohort of the female group is higher than in the L-cohort for all four words, there is one exception in the male group: the average value for the converted word *to boy* is higher by a narrow margin (0.05) in the L-cohort.

Fluency This creativity indicator appears to be most ambiguous of all. There is one exception to the general tendency in the female group which, like in Originality, concerns the conversion *to tulip*. The average values in the male L-cohort are higher in two words: *to boy* and *flower hat*. The data for the L-cohort and the H-cohort in these indicators show very low differences in the average values for all four words.

Creative Strengths The males' H-cohort shows higher values than the L-cohort in all four words, and the only exception in the female group is the compound word *baby book*. The average number of proposed readings per respondent for compound words is fairly high in both cohorts, exceeding three readings per cohort member.

Composite Score The average values of the H-cohort are higher in both the female and the male groups for all four words.

A comparison of the results of the L-cohort and the H-cohort of the same gender group is fairly straightforward, with the exception of the Fluency indicator in the male group. This is most surprising with regard to Hypothesis 4B. In all the other indicators, the H-cohort achieves higher average scores absolutely or in the majority of cases, as is evident from the following summary:

Absolute dominance of the H-cohort (i.e. higher average number of proposed readings per cohort member in all four words):

Female group
- Elaboration
- Flexibility
- Composite Score

Male group
- Elaboration
- Creative Strength
- Composite Score
- Partial dominance (proportion 3:1)

Female group
- Originality
- Fluency
- Creative Strength

Male group
- Flexibility
- Fluency
- Originality*

(*The proportion in this case is 3:0, with the values for the converted word *to tulip* being identical.)

This parameter gives strong support to the hypothesis according to which the average number of proposed readings per respondent should be higher in the H-cohort, that is, in the group of respondents who achieved better results in the TTCT. If both male and female groups are taken into consideration, the most conclusive dominance of the H-cohort in this respect has been observed for the creativity indicator *Elaboration* and the *Composite Score*. In addition, strong support comes from *Flexibility*, *Creative Strengths*, and also from *Originality*. The results for the Fluency indicator are rather ambiguous.

If the results for the OPR and the average number of readings are related, it can be seen that there is no parameter that unambiguously supports interpretation creativity in both of the evaluated criteria and in both cohorts. *Composite Scores*, which plays a crucial role in the average number of readings, also boosts the interpretation creativity of female speakers in terms of the OPR for all four words; however, its role in the male group is ambiguous. *Elaboration* is also an indicator that supports the hypothesis to a considerable degree. It has absolute dominance in both male and female groups in terms of the average number of readings, and it shows lower OPR in the H-cohort than in the L-cohort for three out of four words (except for *to tulip*). Its role in boosting interpretation creativity in the male group is questionable. The influence of the other indicators/subscores varies with the specific indicator/subscore and gender group.

5.3.3.3 Comparison of the Secondary School Student and University Undergraduate Groups Based on the Gender Results

The findings concerning the differences in interpretation creativity between the male and female respondents can be summarized as follows:

(i) Objectified Predictability Rate:

Females show higher interpretation creativity, especially thanks to their results in interpreting the experimental compounds where they clearly dominate in both the H-cohort and the L-cohort in both secondary school and university undergraduate groups. The situation with converted words is different. For *to boy*, both males and females perform equally in the L-cohort and the H-cohort of the secondary school group and the L-cohort of the university undergraduate group. The male results are much better in the H-cohort of the university undergraduate group. The results for *to tulip* are contradictory: while in the secondary school group the male speakers perform in a more creative way in both cohorts, the female respondents are clearly dominant in interpretation creativity in the H-cohort. This result does not fit the overall picture. In any case, the results suggest that interpretation creativity is affected, inter alia, by the nature of the new/potential word or, better, by the underlying word formation process.

From the point of view of the creativity indicators, the dominance of the female speakers of the secondary school group is most striking in *Flexibility*, which is also a strong interpretation creativity booster of the H-cohort of female speakers in the university undergraduate group. Surprisingly, then, this indicator favours male speakers of the L-cohort in the university undergraduate group. In general, however, *all creativity indicators/subscores tend to boost the interpretation creativity of female speakers*, even if their boosting effect is not the same.

(ii) Average number of readings proposed per cohort member:

This criterion provides us with even more conclusive evidence of the higher interpretation creativity of female speakers. The results in the university undergraduate group give almost absolute support to the observation that female speakers are interpretationally more creative. On the other hand, in view of this parameter, the converted word *to boy* posed some problems for the female group as is evident from the mostly minimum differences between male and female results.

As for the influence of the creativity indicators/subscores, it may be concluded that all of them function as boosters of the interpretation creativity of female speakers.

(iii) Hapax legomena:

There is a strong tendency for female speakers to be more creative in their interpretation of new/potential words. This tendency is stronger in the secondary school group than in the university undergraduate group.

(iv) In sum, the results show higher interpretation creativity in females than males.

The gender-based comparison of the L-cohort and the H-cohort has brought the following results:

(i) Objectified Predictability Rate:

The secondary school group does not show any clear tendency if the H-cohort and the L-cohort are compared within the same gender. The general hypothesis has been fully confirmed in the *male* group for *Originality* and *Flexibility* and partly in *Creative Strengths*. No full confirmation has been found for the female group, though partial support comes from Originality, Flexibility, Creative Strengths, and Composite Score.

In the university undergraduate group, the results are opposite, that is, there is no full support from the male group; partial support has been identified in *Creative Strengths*. In the *female* group, full support comes from *Composite Score;* and partial support comes from Elaboration, Flexibility, and Fluency.

All in all, the results for the male group are, in principle, different from those of the *female* group, suggesting that the impact of individual creativity indicators in the two gender groups are not identical.

(ii) Average number of readings proposed per cohort member:

Like in the general part of the research, the gender-based analysis of the relation between the H-cohort and the L-cohort also gives much more conclusive results than the data based on the OPR. The strongest evidence in favour of the general hypothesis in the *secondary school group* in both the *male* and the *female* respondents is primarily provided by *Elaboration* and *Creative Strengths*. In addition, full support has also been identified in *Originality, Flexibility,* and *Composite Score* for the *female* group of respondents. This means that the tendency for higher interpretation creativity, judged on the basis of the average number of readings per cohort member, is stronger in the female group.

Among the *university undergraduate* respondents, the dominance of the H-cohort in interpretation creativity is even *bigger than in the SS speakers in both the male and the female groups in all indicators/subscores*, except for Fluency in the male group. An absolute superiority of the *female* group has been found in *Elaboration*, *Flexibility*, and *Composite Score*; and the male group has been found in *Elaboration*, *Creative Strengths*, and *Composite Score*.

A comparison of the secondary school students and university undergraduates thus means that the two groups of respondents give full support to the general hypothesis in the following indicators/subscores:

Male group
Elaboration and Creative Strengths
Female group
Elaboration and Composite Score

However, the results obtained for the other indicators/subscores are also very strong, with the exception of Fluency.

6 Conclusions

Creativity, Word Formation, and Word Interpretation

A point of departure for our research is the idea that creativity in the fields of complex word formation and complex word interpretation stems from an inherent human capacity captured in psychology by the term 'creative potential'. Creative potential is understood in terms of divergent thinking and characterized as a "measure of ideation that fuels creative thinking" (Runco & Acar 2019: 244). This creative potential is then realized in the formation and interpretation of new complex words as creative performance. From this, it follows that our understanding of word formation creativity and word interpretation creativity as a universal human ability is different from and, at the same time, much broader than the common approaches to creativity in linguistics, in general, and in morphology/lexicology, in particular. The latter ranges from identifying creativity with productivity, through restricting it to the formations that are unpredictable and/or deviate in some way from the established rules, up to an extremely restricted notion of creativity limited to a few examples of words that are created *ex nihilo*, that is, that are not based on existing morphemes. Contrary to these approaches, creativity in our conception bears on all new complex words.

Thus, creativity in the field of complex words is conceived as the cognitively founded creative performance of language speakers when forming and/or interpreting complex words that is variously predetermined by individual aspects of their creative potential (i.e., Originality, Fluency, Flexibility, Elaboration, Creative Strengths, and Composite Score) and that is characterized by originality, usefulness, appropriateness, relevance, and effectiveness.

Such a comprehension of creativity is new in the field of complex words and, by implication, requires a specific approach to its exploration. This is also due to the multiplicity and complexity of interrelated factors that affect the relation between the creative potential and the creative performance in the two microdomains studied in our research. This necessitated an interdisciplinary approach combining relevant theoretical and methodological principles of psychology, linguistics, psycholinguistics, and sociolinguistics.

Creative potential is represented by four creativity indicators and two subscores (Originality, Elaboration, Flexibility, Fluency, Creative Strengths, and Composite Score), each of them assessing a different aspect of the creative potential of the respondents by means of the Torrance Test of Creative Thinking (TTCT). The scores obtained in this way were related to the results obtained by means of a word formation test and word interpretation test. The influence of creative potential on creative performance in word formation and word interpretation has been examined from the perspective of two sociolinguistic parameters: the age and the gender of language speakers. These parameters were evaluated by comparing (i) the secondary and the university students and (ii) the groups of male and female respondents. The evaluation was primarily based on comparisons of the L-cohort and the H-cohort for each of the creativity indicators/subscores, separately for the secondary school students and for the university undergraduates, and separately for the male and the female groups. As a result, we worked with and evaluated a fairly high number of variables and relations that made it possible to assess the extent of the influence of creative potential upon creative performance from various points of view. Furthermore, in order to give support to the findings arrived at by evaluating the results obtained for the two groups with the high and low scores, we also performed statistical evaluations covering all respondents wherever the method of examining the creative performance enabled it (sensitivity analysis).

The research has proven that the employed onomasiological theory is a feasible theoretical framework for research into creativity because it has brought valuable insights into the field in question. This is because it makes it possible to relate the TTCT-based creativity indicators and subscores to various naming strategies represented by individual onomasiological types and to interpretation strategies that can be accounted for by, *inter alia*, the principles of the meaning predictability theory.

The research was based on several hypotheses that were formulated either on the basis of previous research or on the principles of the creative performance testing methods. The part of our research that was implemented without any tentative hypothesis, and was, therefore, exploratory in its nature, was that concerning potential gender differences. This was due to two reasons: first, there has not been any previous research in this field, and second, the numerous studies exploring potential differences in creativity between females and males have not brought any conclusive results.

In the following discussion, we evaluate the individual hypotheses specified in Section 4.5.

General Hypothesis

In general, owing to their higher creative potential in the TTCT test, the H-cohort will be able to comply with the word formation and word interpretation tasks better than the L-cohort. This should comply with the data obtained in the sensitivity/robustness analysis.

Hypothesis 1

Referring to Körtvélyessy (2010), it is hypothesized that while university undergraduates will prefer to form new complex words with higher semantic transparency, the tendency towards economy of expression will be stronger in the younger group of respondents. This hypothesis will be evaluated in relation to

(i) *the two age-based groups of respondents;*
(ii) *the H-cohort and L-cohort specified for each creativity indicator and subscore in both age groups;*
(iii) *male and female respondents.*

A general version of this hypothesis suggests that word formation strategies change with increasing age (see also, for example, Berko-Gleason 1958; Štekauer et al. 2005*).*

The results point out the role of age, the nature of the word formation task, and individual creativity indicators/subscores as important influential factors. While Hypothesis 1 has not found full support in all of its aspects, it is possible to identify a clear tendency complying with this hypothesis.

In the L-cohort, this hypothesis finds strong support in the results obtained in Task 2 (verbal instruction), primarily for Fluency, and weaker support for Flexibility and Composite Score. In Task 3, Hypothesis 1 finds weak support for Flexibility and Creative Strengths.

In the H-cohort, the most conclusive corroboration of Hypothesis 1 is provided by the results for Task 3, especially for Flexibility, Originality, Fluency, Composite Score, and Creative Strengths. Contrary to Task 3, support for the hypothesis from Task 2 is not as overwhelming: weak support comes from Originality and Flexibility.

Viewed from the perspective of gender differences, it can be concluded that the preference for more transparent coinages increases with age for both female and male speakers, especially with regard to Tasks 2 and 3.

Hypothesis 2

The percentage of failed/zero answers in the word formation test will be lower in the H-cohort than in the L-cohort owing to the much higher scores of the H-cohort in the TTCT test.

(*cont.*)

The results for the secondary school students and university undergraduates differ, which indicates age-based differences in word formation creativity. The creative potential of the secondary school respondents seems to affect their word formation creativity to a very restricted extent. This finding runs against Hypothesis 2. In general, the L-cohort performs better in Tasks 1 and 2, and the H-cohort performs better in Task 3. The results of the university students give conclusive support to Hypothesis 2 in Task 2 and partly in Task 3. The results are substantially affected by the specificity of the word formation task.

The creativity indicators that give support to Hypothesis 2 in the secondary school group vary in individual tasks. Thus, the most influential creativity indicator in Task 1 is Flexibility; in Task 2 it is Elaboration; and in Task 3 it is Originality.

In the university undergraduates group, the strongest support for Hypothesis 2 comes in Tasks 2 and 3 from Originality, Creative Strengths, and Composite Score. Since Fluency reflects the number of relevant answers, it was expected that Hypothesis 2 would be confirmed primarily for this creativity indicator. This expectation has been confirmed neither in the university undergraduate group nor in the secondary school group of respondents. This means that this factor does not have, surprisingly, the expected effect on word formation creativity.

Hypothesis 3

The values of the Objectified Predictability Rate in the individual creativity indicators/subscores in the L-cohort should be higher than those in the H-cohort. This hypothesis is based on the idea that language speakers with a lower creative potential (as determined by the TTCT) prefer more common interpretations (primarily, the most acceptable, most predictable reading) while the H-cohort members are also able to come up with (thanks to their higher creative potential) less predictable, more peripheral, and more 'creative' interpretations. This difference is projected onto tougher competition between the predictability rates of the readings proposed by the H-cohort which, consequently, is reflected in the lower OPR values of the H-cohort (Štekauer 2005a).

Hypothesis 3 has been fully confirmed for Flexibility, Creative Strengths, and Composite Score in the group of secondary school students and for Creative Strengths and Composite Score among university undergraduates. These results suggest that, for the criterion of the Objectified Predictability Rate, there are no substantial differences in interpretation creativity of the two age groups covered in our research.

Hypothesis 4

The average number of readings proposed by the H-cohort members is higher than that proposed by the L-cohort members owing to the higher creativity potential identified by the TTCT. This hypothesis has two parts:

Hypothesis 4A is primarily relevant to the creativity indicators Fluency and Elaboration, according to which the H-cohort, identified within the TTCT, is characterized, respectively, by a higher number of relevant answers (Fluency)/ higher number of details (Elaboration) than the L-cohort. A substantial difference in the TTCT scores between the two cohorts should be projected onto a substantial difference in the interpretation creativity test between the two cohorts.

Hypothesis 4B postulates that the H-cohort achieves better results in all the other creativity indicators/subscores in the interpretation test than the L-cohort, even if the differences between the two cohorts can vary owing to unequal creativity features represented by the individual creativity indicators.

In both the secondary school and university undergraduate groups of respondents, Hypothesis 4A has been conclusively confirmed for Elaboration, but not for Fluency. Hypothesis 4B has also been confirmed in both groups for Originality, Creative Strengths, and Composite Score.

Hypothesis 5

This hypothesis has two parts:

Hypothesis 5A postulates that a reading that is proposed by a single member of the L-cohort (hapax legomenon) is proposed by more than a single member of the H-cohort. This hypothesis is based on the postulate that a hapax legomenon of the L-cohort is proposed by more than one member of the H-cohort owing to their higher creative potential.

Hypothesis 5B postulates that the H-cohort proposes more hapax legomenon readings that correspond to zero occurrences of those readings in the L-cohort than vice versa. This hypothesis is based on the postulate that a cohort with higher creative potential is able to propose more 'peripheral' readings of low meaning predictability that will not appear in the L-cohort.

Both Hypotheses 5A and 5B are primarily relevant to the creativity indicator Originality, which concerns the uniqueness of answers. In other words, the less frequent answers are valued more in terms of the creativity indicator Originality. Since the H-cohort achieved much higher scores in this creativity indicator in the TTCT than the L-cohort, it is hypothesized that this result will be projected onto the hapax legomenon results in the interpretation creativity test.

(*cont.*)

This postulate is in accordance with the assumption that creativity is related to uniqueness or statistical rarity (Abraham 2016: 610).

In neither the secondary school group nor the group of university respondents has Hypothesis 5A been confirmed for each hapax legomenon, but the results of the L-cohorts and the H-cohorts may be evaluated as a tendency in the sense of this hypothesis. Its strongest support among the secondary school respondents comes from Originality and Composite Score, with weaker support from Flexibility and Creative Strengths; in the university undergraduate group, it is most evident for Creative Strengths.

However, the results concerning the hapax legomenon criterion mostly contradict our expectations formulated in Hypothesis 5B. The only indicator that corroborates it is Flexibility in the group of university undergraduate respondents.

Hypothesis 6

The results of the H-cohort and the L-cohort in word formation creativity will not coincide with their results in interpretation creativity. This hypothesis is based on the conception of microdomains and task specificity (Baer & Kaufman 2005; Baer 2020), the implications of which for our research mean that the tasks of the word formation test and the word interpretation test represent two different microdomains, two different specific tasks.

This hypothesis has been fully justified by the results, but its assessment must be viewed from a broader perspective. In fact, the differences between the results of the two cohorts in word formation creativity and word interpretation creativity naturally follow from what has been indicated in several places in this monograph: creative performance cannot be determined by a single general relationship because it varies in relation to the opposition between and/or the role of

(i) the secondary school versus university undergraduate groups, that is, different age groups;
(ii) word formation versus word interpretation;
(iii) the individual creativity indicators/subscores;
(iv) the individual word formation criteria (semantic transparency vs. economy of expression; failed answer criterion);
(v) the individual word interpretation criteria (Predictability Rate, Objectified Predictability Rate, average number of readings proposed by a cohort member, and hapax legomena);
(vi) the nature of the tasks included in the word formation test; and
(vii) the nature of word formation processes underlying the interpretation test.

(*cont.*)

By implication, there are a number of factors that, in their mutual interaction, affect the influence of creative potential through its individual creativity indicators/ subscores upon creative performance in forming and interpreting new/potential complex words. Therefore, the only way to determine this influence is to assess each aspect of word formation and word interpretation creativity independently of one another. This is, at the same time, an answer to our General Hypothesis from the Introduction.

This overview of the most important findings on the basis of the formulated hypotheses should certainly be completed with some basic observations of the influence of age and gender upon creative performance.

As for the role of age in word formation, the results depend on the nature of the word formation test task. Hypothesis 1 has been conclusively confirmed for Fluency, and slightly less for Flexibility and Composite Score in Task 2 and for Flexibility and Creative Strengths in Task 3 when comparing the L-cohorts. For the H-cohort, Hypothesis 1 gets strong support for all creativity indicators/ subscores in Task 3, the strongest being for Flexibility. The creativity indicator Flexibility thus seems to be the most influential factor in terms of Hypothesis 1, and this hypothesis finds much stronger support when comparing the H-cohorts.

Similar findings are obtained for Hypothesis 2, which is corroborated much better for the group of university undergraduate students who manifest its validity mainly for Creative Strengths, Originality, and Composite Score, and partly for Elaboration and Fluency. The support for Hypothesis 2 among the secondary school students is much weaker. This indicates the development of creative performance in word formation with increasing age (at least with regard to the compared age groups).

The comparison of the two age groups in terms of interpretation creativity shows the role of the individual comparative parameters. The parameter of the Objectified Predictability Rate does not indicate any principled age-based differences in interpretation creativity. Contrary to this, a tendency can be traced here for the older age group to propose more readings than the younger group for some of the indicators/subscores. The most evident support for the age factor according to this criterion has been identified for Composite Score and Elaboration. As for the hapax legomenon criterion, the results suggest the changing role of the influence of individual creativity indicators with increasing age. While Hypothesis 5A has been corroborated for *Originality* and *Composite Score* in the secondary school group, it is Creative Strengths that is a crucial creativity-boosting factor in the university undergraduate group. Hypothesis 5B has only been confirmed for Flexibility in the university undergraduate group and has not found any strong support in the secondary school group.

The results show that the influence of age upon interpretation creativity varies depending on the specific parameter and creativity indicator/subscore.

As far as the gender-related results are concerned, our findings suggest that there is a fairly strong tendency for female language speakers to both form and interpret new complex words in a more creative way than their male counterparts. This finding calls for further investigation of the mediating and moderating factors.

While the present research provides novel and encouraging findings, it cannot be more than an introductory probe into creativity in the field of complex words. The complexity of the previously outlined relations among numerous factors that affect creative performance in the examined areas suggests that our initial observations and findings will need further and extensive examination. Therefore, we hope that this monograph will encourage future research into potential mechanisms (mediators) and boundary conditions (moderators) of the relationship between creative potential, on the one hand, and word formation and word interpretation as acts of creativity by an individual language speaker, on the other, and that it can also instigate examinations of the role of other middle-level psychological variables, for example, personality, in coining and interpreting new complex words.

References

Abraham, Anna. 2013. "The Promises and Perils of the Neuroscience of Creativity." *Frontiers in Human Neuroscience* 7: 246.

2016. "Gender and Creativity: An Overview of Psychological and Neuroscientific Literature." *Brain Imaging and Behaviour* 10: 609–618.

2019a. "Creativity and the Social Brain." In *The Palgrave Handbook of Social Creativity Research*, edited by Izabela Lebuda and Vlad P. Glăveanu, 527–539. Palgrave Studies in Creativity and Culture. Cham: Springer International Publishing.

2019b. "The Neuropsychology of Creativity." *Current Opinion in Behavioral Sciences* 27: 71–76.

Albert, Robert S. 1990. "Identity, Experience, and Career Choice among the Exceptionally Gifted and Eminent." In *Theory of Creativity*, edited by Mark A. Runco and Robert S. Albert, 13–34. Newbury Park, CA: Sage.

Amabile, Teresa M. 1996. *Creativity in Context: Update to the Social Psychology of Creativity*. Boulder, CO: Westview.

Arnaud, Pierre J. L. 2003. *Les composés timbre-poste*. Lyon: Lyon University Press.

Arndt-Lappe, Sabine, Angelika Braun, Claudine Moulin, and Esme Winter-Froemel, eds. 2018. *Expanding the Lexicon: Linguistic Innovation, Morphological Productivity, and Ludicity*. Berlin/New York: Mouton de Gruyter.

Aronoff, Mark. 1976. *Word Formation in Generative Grammar*. Linguistic Inquiry Monograph 1. Cambridge, MA: MIT Press.

2013. "Competition and the Lexicon." To appear in *Proceedings of the Annual Meeting of La Società di Linguistica Italiana*. Prepublication paper.

2020. "-less and -free." In *Complex Words: Advances in Morphology*, edited by Lívia Körtvélyessy and Pavol Štekauer, 55–64. Cambridge: Cambridge University Press.

Baas, Matthijs. 2019. "In the Mood for Creativity." In *The Cambridge Handbook of Creativity*, edited by James C. Kaufman and Robert J. E. Sternberg, 257–272. Cambridge Handbooks in Psychology. Cambridge: Cambridge University Press.

Baas, Matthijs, Carsten K. W. de Dreu, and Bernard A. Nijstad. 2008. "A Meta-analysis of 25 Years of Mood-Creativity Research: Hedonic Tone, Activation, or Regulatory Focus?" *Psychological Bulletin* 134, no. 6: 779–806.

Baayen, R. Harald. 1992. "Quantitative Aspects of Morphological Productivity." In *Yearbook of Morphology 1991*, edited by Geert E. Booij and Jaap van Marle, 109–149. Dordrecht: Kluwer Academic Publishers.

1993. "On Frequency, Transparency, and Productivity." In *Yearbook of Morphology 1992*, edited by Geert E. Booij and Jaap van Marle, 181–208. Dordrecht: Kluwer Academic Publishers.

1994a. "Derivational Productivity and Text Typology." *Journal of Quantitative Linguistics* 1: 16–34.

1994b. "Productivity in Language Production." *Language and Cognitive Processes* 9: 447–469.

2001. *Word Frequency Distributions*. Dordrecht: Kluwer Academic Publishers.

Baayen, R. Harald and Rochelle Lieber. 1991. "Productivity and English Derivation: A Corpus-Based Study." *Linguistics* 29, no. 5: 801–844.

Baer, John. 2020. "Domains of Creativity." In *Encyclopedia of Creativity*, 3rd ed., edited by Steven Pritzker and Mark Runco, 377–382. Amsterdam: Elsevier.

Baer, John and James C. Kaufman. 2005. "Bridging Generality and Specificity: The Amusement Park Theoretical (APT) Model of Creativity." *Roeper Review* 27: 158–163.

2008. "Gender Differences in Creativity." *The Journal of Creative Behaviour* 42, no. 2: 75–105.

Bagasheva, Alexandra and Christo Stamenov. 2013. "The Ludic Aspect of Lexical Inventiveness." *Quaderns de Filologia: Estudis lingüístics* XVIII: 71–82.

Barbot, Baptiste and Henry Eff. 2019. "The Genetic Basis of Creativity: A Multivariate Approach." In *The Cambridge Handbook of Creativity*, edited by James C. Kaufman and Robert J. E. Sternberg, 132–147. Cambridge Handbooks in Psychology. Cambridge: Cambridge University Press.

Batey, Mark. 2012. "The Measurement of Creativity: From Definitional Consensus to the Introduction of a New Heuristic Framework." *Creativity Research Journal* 24, no. 1: 55–65.

Bauer, Laurie. 1983. *English word formation*. Cambridge: Cambridge University Press.

2001. *Morphological Productivity*. Cambridge: Cambridge University Press.

2009. "Competition in English word formation." In *The Handbook of the History of English*, edited by Anns van Kemenade and Bettelou Los, 177–198. Malden, MA: Blackwell.

Beaty, Roger E., Mathias Benedek, Paul J. Silvia, and Daniel L. Schacter. 2016. "Creative Cognition and Brain Network Dynamics." *Trends in Cognitive Sciences* 20, no. 2: 87–95.

Beghetto, Ronald A. 2019. "Creativity in Classrooms." In *The Cambridge Handbook of Creativity*, edited by James C. Kaufman and Robert J. E. Sternberg, 587–606. Cambridge Handbooks in Psychology. Cambridge: Cambridge University Press.

Bell, Melanie and Martin Schäfer. 2016. "Modelling Semantic Transparency." *Morphology* 26: 157–199.

Benczes, Reka. 2005. "Creative Noun-Noun Compounds." *Annual Review of Cognitive Linguistics* 3: 250–268.

Benczes, Reka. 2006. *Creative Compounding in English: The Semantics of Metaphorical and Metonymical Noun-Noun Combinations*. Amsterdam/ Philadelphia: John Benjamins.

Benedek, Mathias and Emanuel Jauk. 2019. "Creativity and Cognitive Control." In *The Cambridge Handbook of Creativity*, edited by James C. Kaufman and Robert J. E. Sternberg, 200–223. Cambridge Handbooks in Psychology. Cambridge: Cambridge University Press.

Benedek, Mathias, Emanuel Jauk, Markus Sommer, Martin Arendasy, and Aljoscha C. Neubauer. 2014. "Intelligence, Creativity and Cognitive Control: The Common and Differential Involvement of Executive Functions in Intelligence and Creativity." *Intelligence* 46: 73–83.

Benjamini, Yoav and Hochberg Yosef. 1995. "Controlling the False Discovery Rate: A Practical and Powerful Approach to Multiple Testing." *Journal of the Royal Statistical Society: Series B* 57(1): 289–300.

Bergs, Alexander. 2019. "What, If Anything, Is Linguistic Creativity?" *Gestalt Theory* 41, no. 2: 173–184.

Berko-Gleason, Jean. 1958. "The Child's Learning of English Morphology." *Word* 14: 50–170.

Beversdorf, David Q. 2019. "Neuropsychopharmacological Regulation of Performance on Creativity-Related Tasks." *Current Opinion in Behavioral Sciences* 27: 55–63.

Bonferroni, Carlo E. 1936. "Teoria statistica delle classi e calcolo delle probabilità." *Pubblicazioni del R Istituto Superiore di Scienze Economiche e Commerciali di Firenze* 8: 3–62.

Boot, Nathalie, Matthijs Baas, Simon van Gaal, Roshan Cools, and Carsten K. W. De Dreu. 2017. "Creative Cognition and Dopaminergic Modulation of Fronto-Striatal Networks: Integrative Review and Research Agenda." *Neuroscience & Biobehavioral Reviews* 78: 13–23.

Borgwaldt, Susanne and Dina Lüttenberg. 2010. "Semantic Transparency of Compound Nouns in Native and Non-native Speakers." Poster presentation at the 14th Morphological Meeting, Budapest, May 13–16, 2010.

Bourque, Yves S. 2014. "Toward a Typology of Semantic Transparency: The Case of French Compounds." PhD diss., University of Toronto.

Carroll, John M. and Michael K. Tanenhaus. 1975. "Prolegomena to a Functional Theory of word formation." In *Papers from the Parasession on Functionalism*, edited by Robin E. Grossman, Jim L. San, and Timothy J. Vance, 47–62. Chicago: Chicago Linguistic Society.

Carter, Ronald. 2015a. "Foreword." In *The Routledge Handbook of Language and Creativity*, edited by Rodney H. Jones. London/New York: Routledge.

2015b. *Language and Creativity: The Art of Common Talk*, 2nd ed. London/New York: Routledge.

Casey, B. J., Sarah Getz, and Adriana Galvan. 2008. "The Adolescent Brain." *Developmental Review* 28, no. 1: 62–77.

Chang, Yu-Lin, Hsueh-Chih Chen, I.-Chen Wu, Jen-Ho Chang, and Ching-Lin Wu. 2017. "Developmental Trends of Divergent Thinking and Feeling across Different Grades for Taiwanese Adolescence between 1990's and 2010's." *Thinking Skills and Creativity* 23: 112–128.

Chomsky, Noam. 1964. *Current Issues in Linguistic Theory*. The Hague: Mouton.

1965. *Aspects of Theory of Syntax*. Cambridge, MA: MIT Press.

1966. *Cartesian Linguistics*. New York: Harper & Row.

1974. "Human Nature: Justice versus Power (a dialogue with M. Foucault)." In *Reflexive Water*, edited by F. Elders. London: Souvenir Press.

1976. *Reflections on Language*. London: Temple Smith.

1980. *Rules and Representations*. New York: Columbia University Press.

Christensen, Alexander P., Katherine N. Cotter, and Paul J. Silvia. 2019. "Reopening Openness to Experience: A Network Analysis of Four Openness to Experience Inventories." *Journal of Personality Assessment* 101, no. 6: 574–588.

Cohen, Jacob. 1977. *Statistical Power Analysis for the Behavioral Sciences*. Lawrence Erlbaum Associates.
1988. *Statistical Power Analysis for the Behavioral Sciences*, 2nd ed. Lawrence Erlbaum Associates.
Cook, Guy. 2000. *Language Play, Language Learning*. Oxford: Oxford University Press.
Costello, Fintan J. and Mark T. Keane. 1996. *Constraints on Conceptual Combination: A Theory of Polysemy in Noun-Noun Combinations*. Departmental Technical Report. Trinity College Dublin.
Cotter, Katherine N., Alexander P. Christensen, and Paul J. Silvia. 2019. "Creativity's Role in Everyday Life." In *The Cambridge Handbook of Creativity*, edited by James C. Kaufman and Robert J. E. Sternberg, 640–652. Cambridge Handbooks in Psychology. Cambridge: Cambridge University Press.
Cramond, Bonnie, Juanita Matthews-Morgan, Deborah Bandalos, and Li Zuo. 2005. "A Report on the 40-Year Follow-Up of the Torrance Tests of Creative Thinking: Alive and Well in the New Millennium." *Gifted Child Quarterly* 49, no. 4: 283–291.
Cropley, Arthur J. 2000. "Defining and Measuring Creativity: Are Creativity Tests Worth Using?" *Roeper Review* 23, no. 2: 72–79.
Csikszentmihályi, Mihály. 1990. "The Domain of Creativity." In *Theories of Creativity*, edited by Marc A. Runco and Robert S. Albert, vol. 115, 190–212. Thousand Oaks, CA: Sage.
1999. "Implications of a Systems Perspective for the Study of Creativity." In *Handbook of Creativity*, edited by Robert J. Sternberg, 313–335. New York: Cambridge University Press.
D'Agostino, Fred. 1984. "Chomsky on Creativity." *Synthese* 58: 85–117.
Dal, Georgette and Fiometta Namer. 2018. "Playful Nonce-Formations in French: Creativity and Productivity." In *Expanding the Lexicon: Linguistic Innovation, Morphological Productivity and Ludicity*, edited by Sabine Arndt-Lappe, Angelika Braun, Claudine Moulin, and Esme Winter-Froemel, 203–228. Berlin/Boston: De Gruyter.
Darwin, Charles. 1859. *On the Origin of Species by Means of Natural Selection, or the Preservation of Favoured Races in the Struggle for Life*. London: John Murray.
Deshors, Sandra, Sandra Götz, and Samantha Laporte, eds. 2018. *Rethinking Linguistic Creativity in Non-Native Englishes*. Amsterdam/Philadelphia: John Benjamins.
Dienes, Zoltan and Neil McLatchie. 2018. "Four Reasons to Prefer Bayesian Analyses over Significance Testing." *Psychonomic Bulletin & Review* 25: 207–218.
Dokulil, Miloš. 1962. *Tvoření slov v češtině I. Teorie odvozování slov*. Praha: ČAV.
Downing, Pamela. 1977. "On the Creation and Use of English Compound Nouns." *Language* 53: 810–842.
Dressler, Wolfgang U. 2005. "word formation in Natural Morphology." In *Handbook of word formation*, edited by Pavol Štekauer and Rochelle Lieber, 267–284. New York: Springer.
Dressler, Wolfgang U. and Merlini Barbaresi, Lavinia. 1994. *Morphopragmatics*. Berlin: Mouton de Gruyter.
El-Bialy, Rowan, Christina L. Gagné, and Thomas L. Spalding. 2013. "Processing of English Compounds Is Sensitive to the Constituents' Semantic Transparency." *Mental Lexicon* 8, no. 1: 75–95.

Eysenck, Hans J. 1994. "The Measurement of Creativity." In *Dimensions of Creativity*, edited by Margaret A. Boden, 199–242. Cambridge, MA: MIT Press.

Fernandez-Dominguez, Jesus. 2009. *Productivity in English word formation: An Approach to N+N Compounding*. Pieterlen: Peter Lang.

Finin, Timothy W. 1980. *The Semantic Interpretation of Compound Nominals*. University of Illinois, Urbana, Coordinated Science Laboratory, Report T-96.

Fink, Andreas, Mathias Benedek, Human-F. Unterrainer, Ilona Papousek, and Elisabeth M. Weiss. 2014. "Creativity and Psychopathology: Are There Similar Mental Processes Involved in Creativity and in Psychosis-Proneness?" *Frontiers in Psychology* 5: 1211.

Fischer, E. 2000. *Linguistic Creativity. Exercises in 'Philosophical Therapy'*. Cham: Springer.

Florida, Richard L. 2006. *The Rise of the Creative Class: And How It's Transforming Work, Leisure, Community and Everyday Life*. New York: Basic Books.

Forbes, J. Benjamin and Donald R. Domm. 2004. "Creativity and Productivity: Resolving the Conflict." *SAM Advanced Management Journal* 69, no. 2: 4.

Forgeard, Marie. 2019. "Creativity and Healing." In *The Cambridge Handbook of Creativity*, edited by James C. Kaufman and Robert J. Sternberg, 319–332. Cambridge Handbooks in Psychology. Cambridge: Cambridge University Press.

Fox, Kieran C. R. and Roger E. Beaty. 2019. "Mind-Wandering as Creative Thinking: Neural, Psychological and Theoretical Considerations." *Current Opinion in Behavioral Sciences* 27: 123–130.

Frisson, Steven, Elizabeth Niswander-Klement, and Alexander Pollatsek. 2008. "The Role of Semantic Transparency in the Processing of English Compound Words." *British Journal of Psychology* 99, no. 1: 87–107.

Gabelentz, Georg von der. 1901. *Die Sprachwissenschaft, ihre Aufgaben, Methoden und bisherigen Ergebnisse*. Tübingen: Gunter Narr.

Gabora, Liane. 2019. "Creativity: Linchpin in the Quest for a Viable Theory of Cultural Evolution." *Current Opinion in Behavioral Sciences* 27: 77–83.

Gagné, Christina L. 2017. "Psycholinguistic Approaches to Morphology." In *Oxford Research Encyclopedia of Linguistics*, edited by Mark Aronoff. Oxford: Oxford Press.

Gagné, Christina L. and Edward J. Shoben. 1997. "Influence of Thematic Relations on the Comprehension of Modifier-Noun Combinations." *Journal of Experimental Psychology: Learning, Memory and Cognition* 1: 71–87.

Gagné, Christina L. and Thomas L. Spalding. 2009. "Constituent Integration during the Processing of Compound Words: Does It Involve the Use of Relational Structures?" *Journal of Memory and Language* 60: 20–35.

Gagné, Christina L. and Thomas L. Spalding. 2014. "Conceptual Composition: The Role of Relational Competition in the Comprehension of Modifier-Noun Phrases and Noun-Noun Compounds." *The Psychology of Learning and Motivation* 59: 97–130.

Gagne, Christina L., Thomas L. Spalding, and Kelly A. Nisbet. 2016. "Processing English Compounds: Investigating Semantic Transparency." *SKASE Journal of Theoretical Linguistics* 13, no. 2: 2–22.

Gajda, Aleksandra, Maciej Karwowski, and Ronald A. Beghetto. 2017. "Creativity and Academic Achievement: A Meta-analysis." *Journal of Educational Psychology* 109, no. 2: 269–299.

Galton, Francis. 1869. *Hereditary Genius: An Inquiry into Its Laws and Consequences*, vol. 27. London: Macmillan.
Gervás, Pablo. 2010. "Engineering Linguistic Creativity: Bird Flight and Jet Planes." In *Proceedings of the NAACL HLT 2010. Second Workshop on Computational Approaches to Linguistic Creativity*, 23–30. Los Angeles: Association for Computational Linguistics.
Glăveanu, Vlad Petre. 2010. "Paradigms in the Study of Creativity: Introducing the Perspective of Cultural Psychology." *New Ideas in Psychology* 28, no. 1: 79–93.
2013. "Rewriting the Language of Creativity: The Five A's Framework." *Review of General Psychology* 17, no. 1: 69–81.
Glăveanu, Vlad Petre and James C. Kaufman. 2019. "Creativity: A Historical Perspective." In *The Cambridge Handbook of Creativity*, edited by James C. Kaufman and Robert J. E. Sternberg, 9–26. Cambridge Handbooks in Psychology. Cambridge: Cambridge University Press.
Gleitman, Lila R. and Henry Gleitman. 1970. *Phrase and Paraphrase: Some Innovative Uses of Language*. New York: W. W. Norton and Co.
González Restrepo, Karen J., Cristian C. Arias-Castro, and Verónica López-Fernández. 2019. "A Theoretical Review of Creativity Based on Age." *Papeles del Psicólogo/ Psychologist Papers* 40, no. 2: 125–132.
Guilford, Joy P. 1950. "Creativity." *American Psychologist* 5, no. 9: 444–454.
1956. "Structure of Intellect." *Psychological Bulletin* 53: 267–293.
1986. *Creative Talents: Their Nature, Uses and Development*. Buffalo, NY: Bearly Ltd.
Hall, Geoff. 2015. "Literary Stylistics and Creativity." In *The Routledge Handbook of Language and Creativity*, edited by R. H. Jones, 206–217, Abingdon/New York: Routledge.
Hamawand, Zeki. 2011. *Morphology in English. Word Formation in Cognitive Grammar*. London/New York: Continuum.
Haspelmath, Martin. 2014. "On System Pressure Competing with Economic Motivation." In *Competing Motivations in Grammar and Usage*, edited by Brian MacWhinney, Andrej Malchukov, and Edith Moravcsik, 197–208. Oxford: Oxford University Press.
Hocevar, Dennis. 1981. "Measurement of Creativity: Review and Critique." *Journal of Personality Assessment* 45, no. 5: 450–464.
Hohenhaus, Peter. 2007. "How to Do (Even More) Things with Nonce Words (Other than Naming)." In *Lexical Creativity, Texts and Contexts*, edited by Judith Munat, 15–38. Amsterdam/Philadelphia: John Benjamins.
Horecký, Ján. 1983. *Vývin a teória jazyka* [*The Development and a Theory of Language*]. Bratislava: SPN.
Horecký, Ján, Klára Buzássyová, Ján Bosák. 1989. *Dynamika slovnej zásoby súčasnej slovenčiny [Dynamics of the Wordstock of the Present-Day Slovak]*. Bratislava: Veda.
Hrubovčák, Matúš. 2016. "A Sociolinguistic Research into word formation Strategies." *Language Use and Language Acquisition, B.A.S.* 22: 145–152.
Hunter, Samuel T., Katrina E. Bedell, and Michael D. Mumford. 2007. "Climate for Creativity: A Quantitative Review." *Creativity Research Journal* 19, no. 1: 69–90.
Ivancovsky, Tal, Oded Kleinmintz, Joo Lee, Jenny Kurman, and Simone G. Shamay-Tsoory. 2018. "The Neural Underpinnings of Cross-Cultural Differences in Creativity." *Human Brain Mapping* 39, no. 11: 4493–4508.

Janovcová, Lenka. 2015. "The Influence of Cognitive Abilities on Compound-Interpretation." PhD diss., P. J. Safarik University, Kosice.

Jauk, Emanuel. 2019. "A Bio-Psycho-Behavioral Model of Creativity." *Current Opinion in Behavioral Sciences* 27: 1–6.

Ji, Hongbo, Christina L. Gagné, and Thomas L. Spalding. 2011. "Benefits and Costs of Lexical Decomposition and Semantic Integration during the Processing of Transparent and Opaque English Compounds." *Journal of Memory and Language* 65: 406–430.

Jones, Rodney H. 2015a. "Creativity and Discourse Analysis." In *The Routledge Handbook of Language and Creativity*, edited by Rodney H. Jones, 61–77. Abingdon/New York: Routledge.

ed. 2015b. *The Routledge Handbook of Language and Creativity*. Abingdon/New York: Routledge

Juhasz, Barbara J. 2007. "The Influence of Semantic Transparency on Eye Movements during English Compound Word Recognition." In *Eye Movements: A Window on Mind and Brain*, edited by Roger P. G. van Gompel, 373–390. Amsterdam: Elsevier Science.

Jung, Rex E. and Muhammad O. Chohan. 2019. "Three Individual Difference Constructs, One Converging Concept: Adaptive Problem Solving in the Human Brain." *Current Opinion in Behavioral Sciences* 27: 163–168.

Jurčová, Marta and Eva Szobiová. 2008. *Torranceho figurálny test tvorivého myslenia. Príručka* [*Torrance Figural Test of Creative Thinking. A Manual*]. Bratislava: Psychodiagnostika.

Kampylis, Panagiotis G. and Juri Valtanen. 2010. "Redefining Creativity – Analyzing Definitions, Collocations and Consequences." *The Journal of Creative Behavior* 44, no. 3: 191–214.

Karwowski, Maciej, Jan Dul, Jacek Gralewski, Emanuel Jauk, Dorota M. Jankowska, Aleksandra Gajda, Michael H. Chruszczewski, and Mathias Benedek. 2016. "Is Creativity without Intelligence Possible? A Necessary Condition Analysis." *Intelligence* 57: 105–117.

Kaufman, James C. and Ronald A. Beghetto. 2009. "Beyond Big and Little: The Four C Model of Creativity." *Review of General Psychology* 13, no. 1: 1–12.

Kaufman, James C. and Robert J. Sternberg. 2019. "Preface." In *The Cambridge Handbook of Creativity*, edited by James C. Kaufman and Robert J. Sternberg. Cambridge Handbooks in Psychology. Cambridge: Cambridge University Press.

Kaufman, Scott Barry, Lena C. Quilty, Rachael G. Grazioplene, Jacob B. Hirsh, Jeremy R. Gray, Jordan B. Peterson, and Colin G. DeYoung. 2016. "Openness to Experience and Intellect Differentially Predict Creative Achievement in the Arts and Sciences." *Journal of Personality* 84, no. 2: 248–258.

Kecskes, Istvan. 2016. "Deliberate Creativity and Formulaic Language Use." In "Pragmemes and Theories of Language Use, Perspectives in Pragmatics," edited by K. Allan et al. Special issue of *Philosophy & Psychology* 9: 3–20.

Kecskes, Istvan. 2019. *English as a Lingua Franca: The Pragmatic Perspective*. Cambridge: Cambridge University Press.

Kenny, Dorothy. 2001. *Lexis and Creativity in Translation: A Corpus-Based Study*. St. Jerome.

Keune, Karen. 2012. "Explaining Register and Sociolinguistic Variation in the Lexicon: Corpus Studies on Dutch." PhD diss., LOT, Utrecht.

Keune, Karen, Roeland van Hout, and Harald R. Baayen. 2006. "Socio-Geographic Variation in Morphological Productivity in Spoken Dutch: A Comparison of Statistical Techniques." In *Actes des 8es journées internationales d'analyse statistique des données textuelles*, vol. 2, edited by J.-M. Viprey, 571–580. Besançon: Presses Universitaires de Franche-Comté.

Kim, Kyung Hee. 2005. "Can Only Intelligent People Be Creative? A Meta-analysis." *Journal of Secondary Gifted Education* 16, no. 2–3: 57–66.

2006. "Is Creativity Unidimensional or Multidimensional? Analyses of the Torrance Tests of Creative Thinking." *Creativity Research Journal* 18, no. 3: 251–259.

Kim, Kyung Hee. 2017. "The Torrance Tests of Creative Thinking – Figural or Verbal: Which One Should We Use?" *Creativity* 4, no. 2: 302–321.

Kim, Kyung Hee, Bonnie Cramond, and Joyce Vantassel-Baska. 2010. "The Relationship between Creativity and Intelligence." In *The Cambridge Handbook of Creativity*, edited by James C. Kaufman and Robert Sternberg, 395–412. Cambridge Handbooks in Psychology. Cambridge: Cambridge University Press.

Kleibeuker, Sietske W., Cédric M. P. Koolschijn, Dietsje Jolles, Carsten K. W. De Dreu, and Eveline A. Crone. 2013. "The Neural Coding of Creative Idea Generation across Adolescence and Early Adulthood." *Frontiers in Human Neuroscience* 7, no. 905: 1–12.

Kleibeuker, Sietske W., Carsten K. W. De Dreu, and Eveline A. Crone. 2016. "The Development of Creative Cognition across Adolescence: Distinct Trajectories for Insight and Divergent Thinking." *Developmental Science* 16, no. 1: 2–12.

Kleinmintz, Oded M., Tal Ivancovsky, and Simone G. Shamay-Tsoory. 2019. "The Two-Fold Model of Creativity: The Neural Underpinnings of the Generation and Evaluation of Creative Ideas." *Current Opinion in Behavioral Sciences* 27: 131–138.

Klembárová, Eva. 2012. "Contrastive Analysis of word formation in Children of Different Age." MA thesis, P. J. Šafárik University, Košice.

Körtvélyessy, Lívia. 2010. *Vplyv sociolingvistických faktorov na produktivitu v slovotvorbe* [*On the Influence of Sociolinguistic Factors upon Productivity in word formation*]. Prešov: Slovacontact.

Körtvélyessy, Lívia and Pavol Štekauer. 2014. "Derivation in a Social Context." In *The Oxford Handbook of Derivational Morphology*, edited by Rochelle Lieber and Pavol Štekauer, 407–423. Oxford: Oxford University Press.

Körtvélyessy, Lívia, Pavol Štekauer, and Július Zimmermann. 2015. "word formation Strategies: Semantic Transparency vs. Formal Economy." In *Semantics of Complex Words*, edited by Laurie Bauer, Lívia Körtvélyessy, and Pavol Štekauer, 85–114. Dordrecht: Springer.

Körtvélyessy, Lívia, Pavol Štekauer, and Pavol Kačmár. 2020. "On the Influence of Creativity upon the Interpretation of Complex Words." *The Mental Lexicon* 15(1): 142–160.

2021. "On the Role of Creativity in the Formation of New Complex Words." *Linguistics* 59(4): 1017–1055.

Kuznetsova, Polina, Jianfu Chen, and Yejin Choi. 2013. "Understanding and Quantifying Creativity in Lexical Composition." In *Proceedings of the 2013 Conference on Empirical Methods in Natural Language Processing*, 1246–1258. Seattle: Association for Computational Linguistics.

Ladányi, Mária. 2000. "Productivity, Creativity and Analogy in Word Formation (WF): Derivational Innovations in Hungarian Poetic Language." In *Approaches to Hungarian: Papers from the Pécs conference*, vol. 7, edited by Gábor Alberti and Istvaìn Kenesei, 73–90. Szeged: JATEPress. http://ladanyi.web.elte.hu/derivational_innovations.pdf.

Lamb, Sydney. 1999. *Pathways of the Brain. The Neurocognitive Basis of Language*. Amsterdam/Philadelphia: John Benjamins.

Langlotz, Andreas. 2015. "Language, Creativity and Cognition." In *The Routledge Handbook of Language and Creativity*, edited by Rodney Jones, 40–60. Abingdon: Routledge.

Lees, Robert B. 1960. *The Grammar of English Nominalizations*. Bloomington: Indiana University Press.

1970. "Problems in the Grammatical Analysis of English Nominal Compounds." In *Progress in Linguistics*, edited by Manfred Bierwisch and Karl E. Heidolph, 174–186. The Hague/Paris: Mouton de Gruyter.

Leopold, Werner. 1930. "Polarity in Language." In *Curme Volume of Linguistics Studies*, 102–109. Baltimore, MD: Waverly Press.

Levi, J. N. 1978. *The Syntax and Semantics of Complex Nominals*. New York: Academic Press.

Libben, Gary. 2015. "word formation in Psycholinguistics and Neurocognitive Research." In *word formation: An International Handbook of the Languages of Europe*, vol. 1, edited by Peter O. Müller, Peter Ohnheiser, Susan Olsen, and Franz Rainer, 203–217. Berlin: De Gruyter.

Libben, Gary, Martha Gibson, Yeo Bom Yoon, and Dominiek Sandra. 2003. "Compound Fracture: The Role of Semantic Transparency and Morphological Headedness." *Brain and Language* 84: 50–64.

Lieber, Rochelle. 1992. "Compounding in English." *Italian Journal of Linguistics* 4, no. 1: 79–96.

2010. *Introducing Morphology*. Cambridge: Cambridge University Press.

Lieber, Rochelle and Pavol Štekauer, eds. 2009. *Oxford Handbook of Compounding*. Oxford: Oxford University Press.

2014. *The Oxford Handbook of Derivational Morphology*. Oxford: Oxford University Press.

Lindsay, Mark. 2011. "Self-Organization in the Lexicon: Morphological Productivity as Competition." Talk presented at the LSA Summer Institute Workshop: Challenges of Complex Morphology to Morphological Theory, University of Colorado at Boulder, CO, July 27, 2011.

Lindsay, Mark and Mark Aronoff. 2013. "Natural Selection in Self-Organizing Morphological Systems." In *Morphology in Toulouse: Selected Proceedings of Décembrettes 7*, edited by Fabio Montermini, Gilles Boyé, and Jesse Tseng, 133–153. Munich: Lincom Europa.

Lubart, Todd, Vlad P. Glăveanu, Herie de Vries, Ana Camargo, and Martin Storme. 2019. "Cultural Perspectives on Creativity." In *The Cambridge Handbook of Creativity*, edited by James C. Kaufman and Robert J. Sternberg, 421–447. Cambridge Handbooks in Psychology. Cambridge: Cambridge University Press.

Luce, Robert Duncan. 1959. *Individual Choice Behaviour*. New York: Wiley.

Lyons, John. 1977. *Semantics*. Cambridge: Cambridge University Press.

MacWhinney, Brian. 2012. "The Logic of the Unified Model." In *The Routledge Handbook of Second Language Acquisition*, edited by Susan Gass and Alison Mackey, 211–227. New York: Routledge.
MacWhinney, Brian. 2014. "Conclusions: Competition across Time." In *Competing Motivations in Grammar and Usage*, edited by Brian MacWhinney, Andrej Malchukow, and Edith Moravcsik, 364–386. Oxford: Oxford University Press.
MacWhinney, Brian, Andrej Malchukov, and Edith Moravscik, eds. 2014. *Competing Motivations in Grammar and Usage*. Oxford: Oxford University Press.
Marchand, Hans. 1960. *The Categories and Types of Present-Day English word formation*. Wiesbaden: Otto Harrassowitz.
1965a. "The Analysis of Verbal Nexus Substantive." *Indogermanische Forschungen* 70: 51–71.
1965b. "On the Analysis of Substantive Compounds and Suffixal Derivatives Not Containing a Verbal Element." *Indogermanische Forschungen* 70: 117–145.
1974. *Studies in Syntax and word formation*. Edited by D. Kastovsky. Munich: Fink.
Marelli, Marco and Claudio Luzzatti. 2012. "Frequency Effects in the Processing of Italian Nominal Compounds: Modulation of Headedness and Semantic Transparency." *Journal of Memory and Language* 66, no. 4: 644–664.
Martinet, André. 1955. *Economie des changements phonétiques. Traité de phonologie diachronique*. Bern: Francke.
Marty, Anton. 1908. *Untersuchungen zur Grundlegung der allgemeinen Grammatik und Sprachphilosophie*. Halle: M. Niemeyer.
Mattiello, Elisa. 2013. *Extra-Grammatical Morphology in English. Abbreviations, Blends, Reduplicatives, and Related Phenomena*. Berlin: Mouton de Gruyter.
2018. "Paradigmatic Morphology Splinters, Combining Forms and Secreted Affixes." *SKASE Journal of Theoretical Linguistics* 15, no. 1: 2–22.
Maybin, Janet and Joan Swann. 2007. "Everyday Creativity in Language: Textuality, Contextuality and Critique." *Applied Linguistics* 28: 497–517.
Miall, David S. 2015. "Literariness." In *The Routledge Handbook of Language and Creativity*, edited by Rodney H. Jones, 191–205. Abingdon/New York: Routledge.
Moravcsik, Edith. 2014. "Introduction." In *Competing Motivations in Grammar and Usage*, edited by Brian MacWhinney, Andrej Malchukov, and Edith Moravcsik, 1–16. Oxford: Oxford University Press.
Motsch, W. 1970. "Analyse von Komposita mit zwei nominalen Elementen." In *Progress in Linguistics*, edited by Manfred Bierwisch and Karl E. Heidolph, 208–223. The Hague: Mouton.
Müller, Peter O., Ingeborg Ohnheiser, Susan Olsen, and Franz Rainer, eds. 2015/2016. *word formation: An International Handbook of the Languages of Europe*. Berlin: Mouton.
Munat, Judith. 2007. "Lexical Creativity as a Marker of Style in Science Fiction and Children's Literature." In *Lexical Creativity, Texts and Contexts*, edited by Judith Munat, 163–185. Amsterdam/Philadelphia: John Benjamins.
Murphy, Gregory L. 1988. "Comprehending Complex Concepts." *Cognitive Science* 12: 529–562.
Newman, Matthew L., Carla J. Groom, Lori D. Handelman, and James W. Pennebaker. 2008. "Gender Differences in Language Use: An Analysis of 14,000 Text Samples." *Discourse Processes* 45, no. 3: 211–236.

Onsman, Harry J. 1982. "Creativity and Linguistic Theory. A Study of the Creative Aspect of Language." MA thesis, University of Tasmania.

Pagnani, A. R. 2011. "Gender Differences." In *Encyclopedia of Creativity*, 2nd ed., edited by Mark A. Runko and Steven R. Pritzker, 551–557. San Diego: Academic.

Palmiero, Massimiliano, Chie Nakatani, Daniel Raver, Marta Olivetti Belardinelli, and Cees van Leeuwen. 2010. "Abilities within and across Visual and Verbal Domains: How Specific Is Their Influence on Creativity?" *Creativity Research Journal* 22, no. 4: 369–377.

Palmiero, Massimiliano, Dina Di Giacomo, and Domenico Passafiume. 2012. "Creativity and Dementia: A Review." *Cognitive Processing* 13, no. 3: 193–209.

Pepper, Steve and Pierre Arnaud. 2020. "Absolutely PHAB. Towards a General Model of Associative Relations." In "Semantics and Psychology of Complex Words," edited by Christina L. Gagné and Thomas L. Spalding. Special issue of *The Mental Lexicon* 15, no. 1: 100–120.

Pham, Hien and R. Harald Baayen. 2013. "Semantic Relations and Compound Transparency: A Regression Study in CARIN Theory." *Psihologija* 46, no. 4: 455–478.

Plag, Ingo. 1999. *Morphological Productivity. Structural Constraints in English Derivation*. Berlin/New York: Mouton de Gruyter.

2003. *word formation in English*. Cambridge: Cambridge University Press.

Pleskac, Timothy J. 2015. "Decision and Choice: Luce's Choice Axiom." In *International Encyclopedia of the Social & Behavioral Sciences*, edited by James D. Wright, 895–900. Amsterdam: Elsevier.

Plucker, Jonathan A. and Matthew C. Makel. 2010. "Assessment of Creativity." In *The Cambridge Handbook of Creativity*, edited by James C. Kaufman and Robert J. Sternberg, 48–73. Cambridge Handbooks in Psychology. Cambridge: Cambridge University Press.

Plucker, Jonathan A., Ronald A. Beghetto, and Gayle T. Dow. 2004. "Why Isn't Creativity More Important to Educational Psychologists? Potentials, Pitfalls and Future Directions in Creativity Research." *Educational Psychologist* 39, no. 2: 83–96.

Plucker, Jonathan A., Matthew C. Makel, and Meihua Qian. 2019. "Assessment of Creativity." In *The Cambridge Handbook of Creativity*, edited by James C. Kaufman and Robert J. E. Sternberg, 44–68. Cambridge Handbooks in Psychology. Cambridge: Cambridge University Press.

Pollatsek, Alexander and Jukka Hyönä. 2005. "The Role of Semantic Transparency in the Processing of Finnish Compound Words." *Language and Cognitive Processes* 20, no. 1: 261–290.

Prinzl, Marlies G. 2017. "Linguistic Creativity in (Re)translation: A Corpus-Based Study of Thjomas Mann's 'Der Tod in Venedig' and Its English versions." PhD diss., UCL.

Rainer, Franz. 1983. *Spanische Wordbildungslehre*. Tübingen: Max Niemeyer Verlag.

1988. "Towards a Theory of Blocking: The Case of Italian and German Quality Nouns." In *Yearbook of Morphology 1988*, edited by Geert Booij and Jaap van Marle, 155–185. Dordrecht: Foris.

Ratul, Tanvir. 2019. "Creativity: Concepts, Competition, Coexistence." In *Creativity in Language*, edited by Tanvir Ratul. Newcastle: Pre-Publication Preface.

Reddy, Siva, Diana McCarthy, and Suresh Manandhar. 2011. "An Empirical Study on Compositionality in Compound Nouns." In *Proceedings of the 5th International Conference on Natural Language Processing*, 210–218.

Reiter-Palmon, Roni, Kevin S. Mitchell, and Ryan Royston. 2019. "Improving Creativity in Organizational Settings: Applying Research on Creativity to Organizations." In *The Cambridge Handbook of Creativity*, edited by James C. Kaufman and Robert J. E. Sternberg, 515–545. Cambridge Handbooks in Psychology. Cambridge: Cambridge University Press.

Ren, Zhiting, Wenjing Yang, and Jiang Qiu. 2019. "Neural and Genetic Mechanisms of Creative Potential." *Current Opinion in Behavioral Sciences* 27: 40–46.

Rhodes, Mel. 1961. "An Analysis of Creativity." *The Phi Delta Kappan* 42, no. 7: 305–310.

Ritter, Simone M. and Nel Mostert. 2017. "Enhancement of Creative Thinking Skills Using a Cognitive-Based Creativity Training." *Journal of Cognitive Enhancement* 1, no. 3: 243–253.

Robinson, Douglas. 2015. "Creativity and Translation." In *The Routledge Handbook of Language and Creativity*, edited by Rodney H. Jones, 278–290. Abingdon/New York: Routledge.

Rohrer, C. 1966. "Review of Lees (1960)." *Indogermanische Forschungen* 71: 161–170.

Ronneberger-Sibold, Elke. 2008. "Word Creation: Definition, Function, Typology." In *Variation and Change in Morphology*, edited by Franz Rainer, Wolfgang U. Dressler, Dieter Kastovsky, and Hans Luschützky, 201–216. Amsterdam/Philadelphia: John Benjamins.

2012. "Blending between Grammar and Universal Cognitive Principles: Evidence from German, Farsi and Chinese." In *Cross-disciplinary Perspectives on Lexical Blending*, edited by Vincent Renner, François Mantiez, and Pierree Arnaud, 115–144. Berlin/Boston: Mouton de Gruyter.

Runco, Mark A. 1996. "Personal Creativity: Definition and Developmental Issues." *New Directions for Child Development* 72: 3–30.

2008. "Commentary: Divergent Thinking Is Not Synonymous with Creativity." *Psychology of Aesthetics, Creativity and the Arts* 2, no. 2: 93–96.

2014. "'Big C, Little c' Creativity as a False Dichotomy: Reality Is Not Categorical." *Creativity Research Journal* 26, no. 1: 131–132.

Runco, Mark A. and Selcuk Acar. 2012. "Divergent Thinking as an Indicator of Creative Potential." *Creativity Research Journal* 24, no. 1: 66–75.

2019. "Divergent Thinking." In *The Cambridge Handbook of Creativity*, edited by James C. Kaufman and Robert J. E. Sternberg, 224–254. Cambridge Handbooks in Psychology. Cambridge: Cambridge University Press.

Runco, Mark A. and Garrett J. Jaeger. 2012. "The Standard Definition of Creativity." *Creativity Research Journal* 24, no. 1: 92–96.

Runco, Mark A. and Daehyun Kim. 2013. "Four Ps of Creativity and Recent Updates." In *Encyclopedia of Creativity, Invention, Innovation and Entrepreneurship*, edited by Elias G. Carayannis, 755–759. New York: Springer.

Runco, Mark A., Bonnie Cramond, and Alexander R. Pagnani. 2010a. "Gender and Creativity." In *Handbook of Gender Research in Psychology. Volume 1: Gender Research in General and Experimental Psychology*, edited by Joan C. Chrisler and Donald R. McCreary, 343–357. New York/Dordrecht: Springer.

Runco, Mark A., Garnet Millar, Selcuk Acar, and Bonnie Cramond. 2010b. "Torrance Tests of Creative Thinking as Predictors of Personal and Public Achievement: A Fifty-Year Follow-Up." *Creativity Research Journal* 22, no. 4: 361–368.

Ruth, Jan-Erik and James E. Birren. 1985. "Creativity in Adulthood and Old Age: Relations to Intelligence, Sex and Mode of Testing." *International Journal of Behavioral Development* 8, no. 1: 99–109.

Säily, Tanja. 2011. "Variation in Morphological Productivity in the BNC: Sociolinguistic and Methodological Considerations." *Corpus Linguistics and Linguistic Theory* 7, no. 1: 119–141.

Sampson, Geoffrey. 2016. "Two Ideas of Creativity." In *Evidence, Experiment and Argument in Linguistics and Philosophy of Language*, edited by Martin Hinton, 15–26. Bern: Peter Lang.

Sandra, Dominiek. 1990. "On the Representation and Processing of Compound Words: Automatic Access to Constituent Morphemes Does Not Occur." *The Quarterly Journal of Experimental Psychology. Section A* 42, no. 3, 529–567.

Santana-Lario, Juan and Salvador Valera, eds. 2017. *Competing Patterns in English Affixation*. Bern: Peter Lang.

Scalise, Sergio. 1984. *Generative Morphology*. Dordrecht: Foris.

Schäfer, Martin. 2018. *The Semantic Transparency of English Compound Nouns*. Berlin: Language Science Press.

Schultink, Henk. 1961. "Produktiviteit als morfologisch fenomen." *Forum der letteren* 2: 110–125.

Semino, Elena. 2008. *Metaphor in Discourse*. Cambridge: Cambridge University Press.

Shoben, Edward J. 1991. "Predicating and Nonpredicating Combinations." In *The Psychology of Word Meanings*, edited by Paula J. Schwanenflugel, 117–135. Hillsdale, NJ: Erlbaum.

Silvia, Paul J. 2015. "Intelligence and Creativity Are Pretty Similar After All." *Educational Psychology Review* 27, no. 4: 599–606.

Simonton, Dean Keith. 2000. "Creativity: Cognitive, Personal, Developmental and Social Aspects." *American Psychologist* 55, no. 1: 151–158.

2012. "Creative Productivity and Aging." In *The Wiley-Blackwell Handbook of Adulthood and Aging*, edited by Susan Krauss Whitbourne and Martin J. Sliwinski, 477–496. Malden, MA: Wiley Blackwell.

2019a. "Creative Genius." In *The Cambridge Handbook of Creativity*, edited by James C. Kaufman and Robert J. Sternberg, 655–676. Cambridge Handbooks in Psychology. Cambridge: Cambridge University Press.

2019b. "Creativity and Psychopathology: The Tenacious Mad-Genius Controversy Updated." *Current Opinion in Behavioral Sciences* 27: 17–21.

2019c. "Creativity's Role in Society." In *The Cambridge Handbook of Creativity*, edited by James C. Kaufman and Robert J. E. Sternberg, 462–480. Cambridge Handbooks in Psychology. Cambridge: Cambridge University Press.

Smith, Gudmund J. W. and Ingegerd Carlsson. 1983. "Creativity in Early and Middle School Years." *International Journal of Behavioral Development* 6: 167–195.

Stein, Morris I. 1953. "Creativity and Culture." *The Journal of Psychology* 36, no. 2: 311–322.

Štekauer, Pavol. 1998. *An Onomasiological Theory of English word formation*. Amsterdam/Philadelphia: John Benjamins.

2005a. *Meaning Predictability in word formation*. Amsterdam/Philadelphia: John Benjamins.

2005b. "Onomasiological Approach to word formation." In *Handbook of word formation*, edited by Pavol Štekauer and Rochelle Lieber. Dordrecht: Springer.

2009. "Meaning Predictability of Novel, Context-Free Compounds." In *Handbook of Compounding*, edited by Pavol Štekauer and Rochelle Lieber, 272–297. Oxford: Oxford University Press.

2016. "Compounding from an Onomasiological Perspective." In *The Semantics of Compounding*, edited by Pius ten Hacken, 54–68. Cambridge: Cambridge University Press.

2017. "Competition in Natural Languages." In *Competing Patterns in English Affixation*, edited by Juan Santana-Lario and Salvador Valera, 15–32. Bern: Peter Lang.

Štekauer, Pavol and Rochelle Lieber, eds. 2005. *Handbook of word formation*. Dordrecht: Springer.

Štekauer, Pavol, Don Chapman, Slávka Tomaščíková, and Štefan Franko. 2005. "word formation As Creativity within Productivity Constraints. Sociolinguistic Evidence." *Onomasiology Online* 1–55.

Sternberg, Robert J. 2006. "The Nature of Creativity." *Creativity Research Journal* 18, no. 1: 87–98.

Sternberg, Robert J. and James C. Kaufman. 2010. "Constraints on Creativity: Obvious and Not So Obvious. In *Cambridge Handbook of Creativity*, edited by James C. Kaufman and Robert J. Sternberg, 467–482. Cambridge: Cambridge University Press.

Sternberg, Robert J., James C. Kaufman, and Anne M. Roberts. 2019. "The Relation of Creativity to Intelligence and Wisdom." In *The Cambridge Handbook of Creativity*, edited by James C. Kaufman and Robert J. Sternberg, 337–352. Cambridge Handbooks in Psychology. Cambridge: Cambridge University Press.

Swann, Joan, Robert Pope, and Ronald Carter. 2011. *Creativity in Language and Literature*. New York: Palgrave Macmillan.

Takeuchi, Hikaru and Ryuta Kawashima. 2019. "Implications of Large-Sample Neuroimaging Studies of Creativity Measured by Divergent Thinking." *Current Opinion in Behavioral Sciences* 27: 139–145.

Tin, Tan Bee. 2015. "Creativity in Second-Language Learning." In *The Routledge Handbook of Language and Creativity*, edited by Rodney H. Jones, 433–451. Abingdon/New York: Routledge.

Toolan, Michael. 2015. "Poetry and Poetics." In *The Routledge Handbook of Language and Creativity*, edited by Rodney H. Jones, 231–247. Abingdon/New York: Routledge.

Torrance, Ellis P. 1966. *The Torrance Tests of Creative Thinking—Norms, Technical Manual Research Edition—Verbal Tests, Forms A and B—Figural Tests, Forms A and B*. Princeton, NJ: Personnel Press.

1974. *The Torrance Tests of Creative Thinking—Norms, Technical Manual Research Edition—Verbal Tests, Forms A and B—Figural Tests, Forms A and B*. Princeton, NJ: Personnel Press.

1987. *Guidelines for Administration and Scoring/Comments on Using the Torrance Tests of Creative Thinking*. Bensenville, IL: Scholastic Testing Service, Inc.

1990. *The Torrance Tests of Creative Thinking—Norms, Technical Manual Figural (Streamlined) Forms A & B*. Bensenville, IL: Scholastic Testing Service, Inc.

1998. *The Torrance Tests of Creative Thinking—Norms, Technical Manual Figural (Streamlined) Forms A & B*. Bensenville, IL: Scholastic Testing Service, Inc.

Van Dijk, Marloes, Evelyn H. Kroebergen, Elma Blom, and Paul P. M. Leseman. 2018. "Bilingualism and Creativity: Towards a Situated Cognition Approach." *Journal of Creative Behavior* 53, no. 2: 178–188.

Van Lint, Trudeke. 1982. "The Interpretation of Compound Nouns." In *Linguistics in the Netherlands*, edited by Saskia Daalder and Marinel Gerritsen, 135–145. Amsterdam/Oxford: North-Holland.

Van Marle, Jaap. 1986. "The Domain Hypothesis: The Study of Rival Morphological Processes." *Linguistics* 24: 601–627.

Vásquez, Camilla. 2019. *Language, Creativity and Humour Online*. London: Routledge.

Vartanian, Oshin. 2019. "Neuroscience of Creativity." In *The Cambridge Handbook of Creativity*, edited by James C. Kaufman and Robert J. E. Sternberg, 148–172. Cambridge Handbooks in Psychology. Cambridge: Cambridge University Press.

Vicentini, Alessandra. 2003. "The Economy Principle in Language." *Mots Palabras Words* 3: 37–57.

Vizmuller-Zocco, Jana. 1985. "Linguistic Creativity and Word Formation." *Italica* 62, no. 4: 305–310.

1987. "Derivation, Creativity and Second Language Learning." *The Canadian Modern Language Review* 43, no. 4: 718–730.

Wagenmakers, Eric-Jan, Jonathan Love, Maarten Marsman et al. 2017. "Bayesian Inference for Psychology. Part II: Example Applications with JASP." *Psychonomic Bulletin & Review* 25(1):1–19.

Ward, Thomas B. and Evan S. Kennedy. 2017. "Creativity Research: More Studies, Greater Sophistication and the Importance of 'Big' Questions." *The Journal of Creative Behavior* 51, no. 4: 285–288.

Weiner, Robert. 2000. *Creativity and Beyond: Cultures, Values and Change*. Albany, NY: State University of New York Press.

Weisberg, Robert W. 1999. "Creativity and Knowledge: A Challenge to Theories." In *Handbook of Creativity*, edited by Robert J. Sternberg, 226–250. New York: Cambridge University Press.

Wong, Mungchen and Caren Rotello. 2010. "Conjunction Errors and Semantic Transparency." *Memory and Cognition* 38: 47–56.

Wu, Chi Hang, Yim Cheng, Hoi Man Ip, and Catherine McBride-Chang. 2005. "Age Differences in Creativity: Task Structure and Knowledge Base." *Creativity Research Journal* 17, no. 4: 321–326.

Wu, Xin, Wenjing Yang, Dandan Tong, Jiangzhou Sun, Qunlin Chen, Dongtao Wei, Qinglin Zhang, Meng Zhang, and Jiang Qiu. 2015. "A Meta-analysis of Neuroimaging Studies on Divergent Thinking Using Activation Likelihood Estimation." *Human Brain Mapping* 36, no. 7: 2703–2718.

Zawada, Britta Edelgard. 2005. "Linguistic Creativity and Mental Representation with Reference to Intercategorial Polysemy." PhD diss., University of South Africa.

Zhu, Xiaojin, Zhiting Xu, and Tushar Khot. 2009. "How Creative Is Your Writing? A Linguistic Creativity Measure from Computer Science and Cognitive Psychology Perspectives." In *CALC '09: Proceedings of the Workshop on*

Computational Approaches to Linguistic Creativity, 87–93. Stroudsburg: Association for Computational Linguistics.

Zimmer, Karl E. 1972. "Appropriateness Conditions for Nominal Compounds." *Working Papers on Language Universals (Stanford University)* 8: 3–20.

Zwitserlood, Pienie. 1994. "The Role of Semantic Transparency in the Processing and Representation of Dutch Compounds." *Language and Cognitive Processes* 9: 341–368.

Author Index

Subject Index

For EU product safety concerns, contact us at Calle de José Abascal, 56–1°, 28003 Madrid, Spain or eugpsr@cambridge.org.

www.ingramcontent.com/pod-product-compliance
Ingram Content Group UK Ltd.
Pitfield, Milton Keynes, MK11 3LW, UK
UKHW020340140625
459647UK00018B/2234

* 9 7 8 1 0 0 9 0 5 4 4 2 3 *